More Than
85 Broads

MORE THAN 85 BROADS

*Women Making Career Choices,
Taking Risks, and Defining Success
on Their Own Terms*

JANET HANSON

McGraw-Hill

Chicago   New York   San Francisco   Lisbon   London   Madrid   Mexico City
Milan   New Delhi   San Juan   Seoul   Singapore   Sydney   Toronto

1 2 3 4 5 6 7 8 9 0   DOC/DOC   0 9 8 7 6

ISBN 0-07-142368-0

This publication is designed to provide accurate and authoritative information in regard to the subject matter covered. It is sold with the understanding that the publisher is not engaged in rendering legal, accounting, or other professional service. If legal advice or other expert assistance is required, the services of a competent professional person should be sought.

> —*From a Declaration of Principles Jointly Adopted by a*
> *Committee of the American Bar Association and*
> *a Committee of Publishers and Associations*

The views expressed herein are the opinions and recollections of the contributors.

McGraw-Hill books are available at special discounts to use as premiums and sales promotions, or for use in corporate training programs. For more information, please write to the Director of Special Sales, Professional Publishing, McGraw-Hill, Two Penn Plaza, New York, NY 10121-2298. Or contact your local bookstore.

 This book is printed on recycled, acid-free paper containing a minimum of 50% recycled de-inked paper.

This book is dedicated with admiration and respect to:

Dort A. Cameron III

Joe Gregory

Sheila Wellington

The Hon. John C. Whitehead

and all the amazing women of the 85 Broads network.

"What community does is to help us believe in ourselves, to help one another succeed, and to say to ourselves that we can do great things. When one of us succeeds, we all do. Each of us is lifted up. And that's what community is at its best."

KATHLEEN KENNEDY TOWNSEND
From 85 Broads' Global Network Event,
"What's Your Destiny?"

ACKNOWLEDGMENTS

This book has been in the making for two years. It is a book that I am immensely proud of. I am most grateful to Mary Glenn, my editor at McGraw-Hill, for "seeing" the power of the 85 Broads story. No one could ever ask for a better editor than Mary.

The genius who guided this book to fruition and worked on the manuscript almost daily over the past 18 months is my own husband, Jeff Hanson. There is no better partner on earth than Jeff. In a word, he is an astonishing talent. This book would never have left the cutting room floor without Jeff's courage to see it through. He is my hero.

Working closely with Jeff on the interviews was my own sister, Mary Tiebout. A minister and artist by trade, she is also a brilliant storyteller in her own right.

I would also like to thank the 85 Broads team for their willingness to stay the course. I have had the extraordinary good fortune to work with women of exceptional talent. Analisa Balares, Melissa Hayes, Aneeqa Kayani, Jen Rusk, and Wendy Satin all contributed mightily to the task at hand. I would also like to thank Eric Holbrook, Carla Holtze, Aloysee Heredia, Julia McNamara, Selena Soo, Lynn Teo, Darren Brelesky, and Johanna Evans for their formidable efforts. My former sister-in-law, Barbara Johnson, has been the best listener and the best friend. To Phil Strassler, Jarett Wait, and John Gilliam, you are three of the best networkers I've ever met. And to Mark Schwartz and Pete Kiernan, you are both amazing true champions.

There are five people at Milestone Capital Management who have, since day one, been the most awesome team to work with—Barbara Hope, Marc Pfeffer, Janice Meehan, Colleen Yachimski, and Dana Melillo.

I am indebted to my parents, Patty and John Tiebout. I have always believed that I won the jackpot in the "parent lottery." My folks taught me the importance of positive thinking and to laugh out loud and make my own luck. And to my brother John, whom I adore, and who continues to laugh with me, and at me!

My inspiration every single day comes from my two beautiful children, Meredith and Christopher Hanson. They love their old mother and are two of the funniest kids on the planet. And they are my courage.

And to four of the finest doctors in New York City, whom I credit with saving my life: Drs. Susan Drossman, Laura Schiller, Alexandra Heerdt, and Diane Madfes. I am forever in your debt.

My love for a great story was burnished during my youth and throughout my adult life by my uncle, Phil Reisman, who was one of the funniest, warmest, and most brilliant storytellers I ever knew.

Lastly, I would like to thank Reed Abelson of *The New York Times*, who "broke" the 85 Broads story in October 1999. I asked Reed why she was willing to write the story in a way that showed the real power of the network. Her simple answer was that she wanted to be remembered as an "agent of change." And that is exactly what she has been. I am indebted to Reed for having enough faith that 85 Broads would become the network equivalent of what she herself wanted to be.

And to the thousands of women in the 85 Broads network, I hope you will continue to inspire women all over the world to *always* define success on their own terms.

CONTENTS

MORE THAN
85 BROADS

A VIEW FROM
A BROAD

In 1987, I resigned from a blockbuster 11-year career at the premier invest-ment banking firm of Goldman Sachs. I had gotten married in 1980 to a won-derful guy I worked with. We sat directly across from each other on the trading floor. We had been secretly dating for three years and so our engagement announcement was a tremendous shock to our colleagues in the Fixed Income Division. Unfortunately, we got divorced four years later when we figured out that while we loved being business colleagues, we were not in love. We con-tinued to sit across from each other on the sales desk as we truly enjoyed work-ing with each other. We even had "joint custody" of our teddy bear, Joe.

But then an interesting thing happened. My ex-husband immediately started dating lots of nice gals and I had no dates. I didn't even have a single prospect in sight. But having no dates allowed me to work longer hours. A year later, I became the co-manager of the Money Market Sales Group in New York, which was the first time in Goldman's history that a woman had been promoted to sales management. I was ecstatic. And since I didn't have a social life, I started working on the weekends as well. My "ex" thought I was crazy to take on more responsibility on top of a full client load, and he thought it was amusing that I was now his boss.

For the next year while he dated, I worked. He even got red roses from a gal on Valentine's Day. They were delivered right to his desk. About six months after we split up, we decided to go out to dinner for old time's sake.

We were drinking margaritas out of glasses the size of soup bowls and before long we were reasonably hammered. I looked at my "ex" and said, "Gee, we seem to be having so much fun, do you think we'll ever get back together?" I might as well have hit him in the face with a bucket of ice water; he looked at me and said, "No f'ing way!" Although hurt, I had the courage to ask him why; he looked at me and said, "Because you're too old." He told me that since he was no longer married to me, he was under no obligation to date someone "my age." At the time, I was 32 and he was 36. No one I've ever told this story to has understood why at that moment I thanked him. I thanked him because even though the message was brutal, it was the absolute truth. I started to think about the guys on the trading floor whom I worked with and realized that one of two things was true— they were either married and had kids or single and dating supermodels who were in their early 20s. At that moment I knew there was a very low probability that I would ever get remarried as long as I worked all day and entertained clients most nights.

In the three years that followed my divorce I had exactly two blind dates. They were guys that weren't "in the business," which meant that we had nothing in common. That was when I coined my favorite expression, "sometimes you just can't drink enough," to explain what a disaster the dating scene was for me. I was a Wall Street "big hitter" and wanted to date someone who was fun and sophisticated. I soon discovered that most of the cool guys wanted to date women who were beautiful and sexy, which was not an easy look to accomplish if you worked like a dog and looked like you had.

So in January 1987, when I was sailing in the Caribbean with my parents and siblings, I made the decision to resign from the firm. I was overweight, I drank too much, and I felt tired and old. I'd had an outrageous career at Goldman Sachs, worked with some of the best and smartest people on Wall Street, but I had no personal life. And worse than that, I had absolutely no prospects.

On April 15, the tax date, I left the firm. The "To All" memo said I was taking a leave of absence to open a marina with my father. To this day, I cringe when I think about that memo, as I needed appropriate "cover" for leaving. In reality, I was leaving because I was terrified that I'd never get remarried and have kids. I was turning 35 that year and the term *middle-aged* was starting to creep into my thought process. The day I walked out of Goldman Sachs was one of the most painful days of my life. I was leaving the best friends in the world, an ex-husband whom I still liked and admired, and a firm and a culture that for the most part, I loved and respected. I left my apartment in

New York City and moved to Princeton to live with my sister. I was so depressed that there were days when I couldn't even get out of bed. It took me almost two months to get on my bike and start the process of putting myself back together physically and mentally. And it took another three months before I started to feel like a human being.

One day during the summer I got a call from Peter Mathias, who was an internal consultant at Goldman Sachs. I liked Peter a lot and respected the work he had done for senior management. He had a doctorate in business from Harvard and was a brilliant strategic thinker. He wanted to know if I would like to work with him a few days a week on various projects, and I thought, what the heck, I can always quit if it doesn't work out.

And so in October of that year, I was back at 85 Broad Street. I'll never forget riding the elevator up to the 27th floor to visit all my friends. People I'd worked with for over a decade couldn't figure out why I'd come back. I remember one of my former colleagues shaking his head and saying, "I don't get it. You left the trading floor and a huge job just so you could come back here part-time to work in Personnel?!"

Actually, I didn't get it either. I had torpedoed my career at the firm just so I could work out for a summer and get back in shape. I was so embarrassed to be working in Personnel that I never went back to the trading floor.

Not long after I returned to GS, I reconnected with Jeff Hanson, a really nice young guy who had tried to interview me a few times as one of the firm's "culture carriers." I realized that I'd never made an attempt to get to know him, which was unfortunate as he had a brilliant analytical mind and was great fun to talk to. He was a little full of himself but not to the point of being obnoxious. After one date, we decided we were truly meant for each other. Three weeks later, we got engaged. That might have set the speed record for courtships, but it didn't feel that way. We got married on April 6, 1988, at City Hall. We would have gotten married sooner, but I wanted to wait until the sun was out which I thought would be a good omen. Amazingly, my brother and sister and I all got married within six months of each other. My brother, age 36, got married in November 1987, my sister, age 34, got married in January 1988, and I got married at age 35 in April 1988. It was pretty amazing given that all of us had been dating our future spouses for less than a year. My parents were understandably in seventh heaven.

On October 13, 1988, Meredith was born and two years later, on December 12, 1990, Christopher was born. During that time, Jeff left Goldman Sachs to launch a consulting business, which hadn't exactly been a barn-burning success. By the time Christopher was born, we were in dire financial straits. We were renting a house in Westchester and owned a house in Naples, Florida, which made no sense at all. I think I was about as depressed as I've ever been. In October 1990 I wrote the following entries in my diary:

October 9, 1990

Dear Diary,

I'm sitting here paying bills, doing absolutely ZERO that is fulfilling or satisfying and wishing that I could close my eyes and make it all go away. I want to start my own business but the only reason I'm doing it is because I'm embarrassed not to be doing SOMETHING. Then I think maybe I'll write a book, but after I come up with a title, I can't think of anything to say. I have NO ONE to talk to. No one who could say, hey, let's look at your options, let's figure out where it would be smartest for you to focus.

I'm thinking of starting a coaching business and yet *I'M* the one who needs coaching! If I could just believe in myself a little bit, if I could just get the right ball in play, if I could just get past my own depression and break free—I know there is a need for this type of service. I just need help putting it together and packaging it. Each day I get more and more despondent over my almost complete lack of faith in my ability. I have absolutely no support system.

October 10, 1990

Dear Diary,

I'm sitting here staring out my window wondering what I'm going to do with myself. If only we had enough money we could split but I figure we're stuck here for two more years. I'll probably start watching soap operas and drinking martinis at 2 o'clock in the afternoon. The boredom is excruciating. Maybe I should join some clubs. But I don't want to do that because I'm so afraid my personal time will be eaten up by dumb stuff.

I wish I could get into painting so I could spend Meredith's naptime more productively. All I do now is talk to my friends from work on the phone and refigure our finances for the thousandth time. Then I wait for Mer to wake up from her nap. Figuring out how to use up three hours after that is brutal.

I wish I had a best friend here. I wish I had a life here. This pretty much sucks....

On September 20, 1990, I had written a letter to Jon Corzine at Goldman Sachs telling him about the coaching business I hoped to start and why I thought it was so important for the women at Goldman Sachs:

Dear Jon,

I plan to start my own coaching business in the next few months and intend to target the women at Goldman as potential clients. Women need help in how to handle a dual-career marriage, maternity leave, time management, and getting and staying ahead in an increasingly competitive work environment. In the last three years, I have seen women opt to leave the firm rather than try to articulate their problems to management in a way that makes professional sense. Typically management doesn't even know there is a problem until the woman announces that she is leaving! Regrettably, this is because women find it extremely difficult to "connect" with their (male) managers. Women ask me for career advice because I was a manager, as they perceive that I have insight into how the firm is run/managed which they lack. In essence, they speak one "language," and I speak two. By "translating" what their (male) managers say I can provide them with greater insight, which helps build their confidence and self-esteem. As a rule, I look for what's positive in a work relationship to counter women's fears that the worst is happening.

If my business gets off the ground, maybe Goldman will want to hire me as a "field adviser."

Anyway, Jon, you've been a great friend. Without doubt, you have cared more about the people in the division—past and present—than all the other partners combined.

As always,

Janet

When Christopher was born two months later, all of my business plans went on indefinite hold. I used to say that when Meredith was born she looked at me and smiled and said, "Mom, let's go have coffee." When Christopher was born, he looked at me and started screaming. He was the most adorable baby but he was also the world's unhappiest. I am sure that my depression and plummeting self-esteem were contributing factors to how he viewed the world.

For the next 10 months I battled every single day to keep my head above water. I was mind-numbingly depressed and could barely get myself out of bed in the morning. I don't remember a single happy moment. Jeff and I fought almost constantly about money. I think it would be fair to say that I hated my life and felt like the walls were closing in on me. I realize now that I should have been on antidepressants but I was too afraid that I would gain even more weight. I was out of shape, had never lost the 50 pounds I'd gained from my pregnancy, and as a result, I had a totally shattered self-image.

February 19, 1991

Dear Diary,

It's been raining for a few days—it is so gray and disgusting outside. I am so bored. Jeff's job is going nowhere and Meredith is bored with being inside. I wake up feeling tired and depressed. Christopher has colic or something worse. He cries every night for about three hours. Mer tries very hard to be good—most of the time she is an angel.

I spend all my time thinking about Goldman Sachs and the fact that I have no future there. I wrote to Bob Rubin but he never wrote back.

April 20, 1991

Dear Diary,

Christopher is getting really cute but he cries a lot and has taken to waking up at 4 a.m. Last night I thought I was going to go crazy. He is so much more fussy than Meredith—maybe Mer was fussy too but she slept for 8 to 11 hours a night. Just what I need—f'ing sleep deprivation. Jeff and I have had four days of all out war. He isn't working with Peter anymore, which leaves us with zero income. He hasn't been paid since last December so we've already had five months of paying bills from our savings. We've notified the real estate company that we have to move by September 1. I don't know whether they'll give us back our security deposit or not.

I tried vainly to get a part-time job at Goldman. I feel so depressed. Things have been so utterly shitty for so long I can't imagine things getting any better. I can't believe how depressed I am.

July 9, 1991

Dear Diary,

Meredith and Christopher both have a stomach virus. Mer ran a temperature of 102 degrees on Sunday. Then yesterday she seemed better but then today after her nap she was lying on her changing table complaining that her stomach hurt and her head hurt. I took her into the living room to call the doctor and before I knew it she had thrown up all over me. She seemed to feel almost immediately better, but it suddenly occurred to me that that might be why Christopher had been throwing up all day. After he took his nap I took his temperature, which was 101 degrees so I gave him some Tylenol, which he proceeded to throw up. Meanwhile, Jeff is in Boston for two days doing some work for Fidelity.

I'm having lunch tomorrow with a guy I used to cover at Paine Webber who is now at Goldman Sachs. He's in the Asset Management Group and wants to talk to me about a job. After Christopher spent the morning crying and throwing up on me and Meredith was pulling leaves off the plants and jumping on the couch, I may seriously think about it.

July 18, 1991

Dear Diary,

I was interviewing—sort of—for a job in the GS Asset Mgmt. Group—five days a week and traveling one to two days a week. Forget it. I would rather have no money. Jeff is talking to people about consulting jobs; maybe something will come through.

We're taking C. to the doctor to see if he still has an ear infection. He is the unhappiest child I have ever seen. Meredith has become very difficult. She is constantly testing, which is so hard. Sometimes I just want to give up.

August 18, 1991

Dear Diary,

I'm sick of being depressed about everything—my weight, my life— maybe I need antidepressants.

I had two interviews on Friday. They both went pretty well although I guess there is some question about what I would actually be doing. I've got a few questions myself—such as how much I'm going to be paid, how much vacation I would get, and other small details. Corzine was thrilled to hear that I might be coming back to GS. This whole adjustment is going to be brutal. I know in my heart that I have no interest in working full time. I just hope it's worth going back.

Mer saved Christopher. He was crawling up the basement steps and M. called upstairs to let us know. We got to him about a second and a half before he fell back down the stairs. Mer is starting to have some fears. She is afraid of the stereo speakers and thinks they're people. Christopher is back on Tylenol with codeine for his teeth. His record is about an hour without going nuts.

October 16. 1991

Dear Diary,

So far I've been back at GS for two days. It wasn't terrible but it wasn't great either. I had today off. I think it will work out as long as I never have to be there more than two days in a row. Christopher is having ear surgery on Halloween. Bob Rubin wrote me a nice note saying he was glad that I was back. Meredith has been really tough. She is like Tarzan—swinging from couch to chair, running and leaping and yelling and is generally wired. I am trying very hard not to be bummed out.

October 3, 1992

Dear Diary,

My job is so frustrating. I just wish I had a million bucks in the bank! Then we could find a nice big house and the kids could have acres instead of a few feet to play on. Wouldn't that be great? I want to have horses and a huge farm. I also wish my job was a career and not a nightmare.

July 29, 1993

Dear Diary,

I've been on vacation all week although it sure hasn't felt like one. I've been obsessing about my job, which I hate. I just don't want to work there anymore, and I'm furious that we are in such a huge financial bind that I have to. We're putting the house on the market in a few weeks. Jeff had an article published this month in the Harvard Business Review and has gotten a request for a book outline from Oxford University Press. All of these things are nice, but they don't pay the bills this month or next month. What a dumb, stupid situation to be in.

September 13, 1993

Dear Diary,

Mer got stung by a bee at the park today. She was extremely brave. While she was trying to tell me what happened through her little gasps and sobs she said "Mom, I want it to be winter so it will snow on the bees and they will be covered up." Later she said, "We need to put a hat and some 'glubs' on so the bees won't get us."

Mer wanted to know what happened to the bee after it stung her. I told her the bee went to "bee heaven." She wanted to know if the bee was going to go up and sit on a cloud with Jesus. Christopher did his best to make her feel better. He wanted to fight the bee with his imaginary sword.

Not long after, I left Goldman Sachs for the last time. I had "outgrown" the firm and had never been able to resurrect my career. I had many wonderful friends there but I just couldn't make a go of it. Jeff and I decided we'd try our hand at consulting so we formed Hanson Consulting Group. Jeff did consulting work for Lehman Brothers and I worked for Citibank on a project in their Fixed Income Division. One day, I got a call from our accountant, Phil Strassler, who thought I should meet one of his clients in Greenwich, an interesting guy by the name of Dort Cameron. Jeff and I had been thinking about launching an asset management company called Learning Assets. Our plan was to launch a money market mutual fund and give part of the fees to educational causes. Dort liked the idea and being one of the legendary "deal guys," he agreed to help us get our fund off the ground.

It turned out that linking fees to charity wasn't going to fly so instead we named our new firm Milestone Capital Management. One of the dictionary definitions for milestone is "turning point." After six very tough years, it certainly was exactly that. As a business partner, Dort was tough, brilliant, and one of the most decent, generous, and honest people I'd ever met in all my years in the business.

Milestone grew steadily thanks to a strategic partnership we formed with Bear Stearns to market our fund. They were great partners and once again, it was thanks to a friend that we were lucky enough to forge that relationship. Phylis Esposito had left Goldman and ended up at Bear as a senior managing director. It was at her request that we went in to see the management team at Bear Stearns. Jeff and I gave a one-hour presentation and the strategic partnership was essentially forged by the end of the meeting. For the next few years, we had an amazing relationship with the folks at Bear—primarily through Mike Minikes, the firm's treasurer, who was just as tough, as brilliant, and as fair as Dort had been.

On November 17, 1997, I sent an invitation out to 30 of my closest former female Goldman colleagues to join me for dinner at the Water Club in New York City for the "first GS women's reunion." None of the invited women knew that 85 Broads was about to be unveiled. My sister, Mary, had designed the T-shirt, which showed a woman standing on a ladder, nailing up an "s" on a signpost that read "85 Broad." I had come up with the name for the network one afternoon when I was out walking our dogs. 85 Broads was now a reality, and Goldman's headquarters address, 85 Broad Street, would never again be thought of in quite the same way.

Thirty women came to the dinner, many of whom tell their unique stories in this book. A few weeks after we held our mini-reunion, I sent a thank-you note to all the attendees. I included an article written by Darla Moore, president of Rainwater Inc., which had just appeared in the December issue of *Worth* magazine. She was responding to criticism from women after being referred to as a "babe" in an article in *Fortune* magazine titled "The Toughest Babe in Business." In the *Worth* article she stated:

> You know what I think is one of the world's biggest wastes of time for a woman? Networking with other females. Where is that going to get you if men are the ones with all the power? Every single one of my mentors has been male. At no time have I ever encountered a woman who would have been a smart choice to help pull me up the ladder, to give me the tools and the power needed to make a difference.

I laughingly suggested to the new members of 85 Broads that we send a one-liner to Darla that said:

HEY BABE! GOOD LUCK FINDING ANOTHER BABE
TO HAVE LUNCH WITH!

A few weeks after our reunion at the Water Club, I realized that the network would never really take off unless we had a powerful way to stay connected. I happened to be talking to Anne Casscells, one of the smartest women I ever worked with at GS, and I mentioned that our gathering had all the makings of a "bad high school reunion," where you see everybody, exchange info and phone numbers, and then don't have any further interaction for five years. Anne thought about it for a second and then said, "Why don't you 'dot-com' the sucker?"

What Anne realized was that we could never become a true global powerhouse if we didn't exist in cyberspace where women could connect with each other 24/7. For the next two years, the Milestone Capital tech team (two brilliant young graduates from Oberlin College) spent some part of every day working on creating www.85Broads.com. In November 1999, Reed Abelson of *The New York Times* wrote an article on the front page of the Business Section titled "A Corporate Alumni Network Just for Women."

Reed had spent several days at our office in Yonkers interviewing the tech team, me, and other members of 85 Broads. The cool thing was that she mentioned that as an independent network, 85 Broads was *not* just for alumnae but for women who were currently at Goldman Sachs as well. The response to her article was awesome and in the days that followed, our membership skyrocketed to over 1,000 women. She got my "voice" just right, which was that I felt a keen sense of disconnection and isolation after leaving Goldman in 1987 and that I had created the 85 Broads network to help women stay connected to other smart women—not only during their careers but throughout their entire lives.

In the spring of 2000, I happened to be at Harvard Business School talking to students who belonged to the Women's Student Association. I was there to talk about the pros and cons of being an entrepreneur, and I somehow got off on a tangent about women in the 85 Broads network who had left GS to start their own businesses. Everyone present knew that 85 Broads was a network for current and former Goldman Sachs women and that I was the founder. Finally one gal raised her hand and said: "I think it's great that you launched the network, but I never worked at Goldman and don't see myself working for Goldman in the future, so you're talking about a network I can't join!"

The next day I sent an email out to the women at Harvard Business School announcing the launch of Broad2Broad—a unique "co-mentoring" initiative. In my email I stated that I thought that *mentor* implied "older" and "wiser" and that *mentee* implied "junior" and "less experienced." *Co-mentoring* was a term I made up to describe what I thought the relationship between these two groups should be, which was one of equals. I might be older and have worked longer but the gals at HBS, who I fondly referred to as "rockets," brought a unique set of skills to the table that I simply did not possess. These supersmart women spoke the "language" of technology and more importantly, understood its many applications. I could barely send an email and wouldn't have known what a hard drive was if it hit me in the face. For the first time, a women's network embraced its youngest members as professional equals and as true partners, which was a major paradigm shift.

What I passionately loved was being an "agent of change." Over the next few years, our Broad2Broad co-mentoring initiative would be rolled out on 30 graduate business school campuses, both in the United States and abroad.

In February 2001, my friend Michael Stoner asked me to join the board of the Johnnie Walker "Keep Walking" campaign. The purpose of the campaign was to award $500,000 in funding to individuals who had entered the "Keep Walking" business plan competition. That spring, we spent three days at Fisher Island in Florida with the PR and advertising people from Johnnie Walker to hone the message. Over the next few months, hundreds of business plans were submitted and culled for the best, most inspirational proposals, which even included a young cancer survivor who needed funding to climb Mt. Everest. On September 10, 2001, executives from Johnnie Walker joined us for a three-day media event at the Tribeca Grand Hotel which would include announcing the winners of the contest on the morning of September 11.

On the afternoon of September 10, I was at Citigroup for a meeting with Lisa Caputo, the president of Women & Co. I got caught in a hellatious downpour as I left 399 Park Avenue to drive down to the Tribeca Grand, which was just a few blocks north of the World Trade Center. The folks from Johnnie Walker had arranged for us to have dinner at City Hall, a great Manhattan restaurant. Before we left the hotel for the restaurant, we were in a private room near the lobby having a drink—all of us commented that the lightning and thunder looked and sounded fake—like the kind you'd see and hear in a 1950s horror movie.

The next morning was gorgeous—not a cloud in the sky and not even a wiff of humidity. We were to be downstairs by 8 a.m. to go to the Altman Building for the final candidate presentations and the announcement of the winners. The folks at Johnnie Walker had been working on the campaign for two years and were hoping that it would be one of the biggest media events in New York City that day. The event planners called my room several times to tell me to step on it as I was upstairs sending out last minute emails and had lost track of the time. I left the Tribeca Grand at 8:25 a.m. and thought what a fun day it would be.

One of the other board members was Josie Natori, who was a legend in the lingerie business. Josie and I were having breakfast together, and I remember we were talking about golf. Then the oddest thing happened. Two of the staffers from Johnnie Walker were huddled just a few feet from where Josie and I were sitting, and I heard one of them say "World Trade Center." I thought to myself— no one ever says "World Trade Center" unless something bad is happening.

We were asked to come into the main room where all of the cameras and TV equipment were set up to listen to the presentations of the final candidates who were still in the running for funding for their business idea. It was now 9:15 a.m. At about that time, my cell phone rang. I saw that it was Jeff calling me from our office and without listening, very tersely said, "I have to call you back," and hung up. Then other board members' cell phones started to ring and before we knew it, the show was over. The TVs were switched to CBS and CNN, and we all raced outside onto the street to see what was happening. I can remember being overwhelmed again by how blue the sky was and how it just didn't make any sense that the Trade Center was on fire. We were still operating under the "small Cessna crashing" scenario, so everybody was hopeful that the damage was minor.

But then the real and awful truth started to unfold on TV. Alan Chambers, who was one of the board members and whose wife Michelle was back at the Tribeca Grand, decided that he was going to walk back to the hotel to make sure she was all right. By now, the towers had fallen and while we were walking south, everyone else seemed to be walking north. Everybody it seemed needed to be outside. The police allowed us to cross the tape after we showed them our hotel keys. "Keep Walking" now took on a very sad and somber connotation.

Camilo Cruz, a board member from Miami, had what we figured was the honeymoon suite in the hotel. The Tribeca Grand only has eight floors and of all bizarre coincidences, Camilo's room had a staircase that led straight up to the roof. Alan, Michelle, Camilo, and I spent the next five hours on the roof of the hotel taking video footage and camera shots of what our eyes absolutely couldn't believe we were seeing. The emergency equipment being brought in made its way down Church Street as if in a funeral cortege. We watched as 7 World Trade fell down and not long after, the hotel turned off all the gas, fearing a gas main explosion in the area. That was when we decided to leave the roof and head down to the lobby and stay there.

At 4:30 on the morning of September 12, I packed up my laptop and all my luggage and headed north for Grand Central. None of the subway stations were operating until I got to 14th Street. I was exhausted and absolutely numb. I took the train to Yonkers and walked in with all my gear. Meredith and Christopher were thrilled to hear that I was out of the city, as were my parents.

On Thursday, September 13, I sent the following email out to every member of the 85 Broads network:

> Maggie Craddock, a true friend of 85 Broads, has offered to counsel any of our members who are struggling with stress-related issues in the aftermath of the World Trade Center tragedy on a strictly *pro bono* basis.

Maggie is a licensed therapist and currently provides executive coaching to many individuals in the Wall Street community, including members of 85 Broads. As many of you know, Maggie spoke at our first event last fall. Please don't hesitate to contact her.

Our thoughts and prayers are with all those who worked at the World Trade Center, including members of 85 Broads, as well as those who have lost friends and family in this unfathomable tragedy.

One of the first things I asked our team to do was to run a network search of all members who listed the World Trade Center as a work address. Seven of our members listed either Tower One or Tower Two in their profiles. We reached out to all of them immediately. A few hours later, we received an email from Christie Millard. The subject line in her email read "blessed to be alive."

Janet,

Thanks to God, survivor instinct and luck, I am alive and safe. It was an absolutely horrifying experience, beyond anyone's worst imagination, beyond what any special effects movie could ever re-create, but I made it down from the 78th floor of 2 WTC. Not everyone in my office did though, so this nightmare continues.

It's been a really tough few days. I've met with Maggie Craddock before, might have to call her up again. I know I need to see someone, but I'm finding it hard to accept help from anyone when I am so much better off than so many.

Please let me know the status of other 85 Broads members—I can only assume there were a number of them in the WTC complex. It is just sickening to think what the families of missing people are going through.

Christie

By the end of the week, we had heard from six of our seven members who had worked in one of the two towers. Then on Sunday I received this email from Rachel Simon, followed by other emails over the next days and weeks.

Sunday, September 16, 2001

Janet,

I wanted to let you know that I learned this evening that Cathy Chirls, a member of 85 Broads, was lost in the attack. Cathy contacted me over the summer and we met for lunch. We talked about what life was like after Goldman, discussing work, commuting, choosing our kids' schools, family, etc. Cathy was a lovely woman—we connected at lunch and I remember thinking that perhaps I had found a new friend.

Cathy was eager to help others. I shared my story with her about being laid off at Goldman a few months ago. After describing my work experience at Goldman, she immediately had two people she wanted me to meet. At the time, I told her that I was taking the summer off and she could give me their names in Sept/Oct when I started my job search.

I knew that Cathy worked at the WTC and emailed her this week asking if she was OK. Friday evening, her husband responded that she was missing. I forwarded your email to him.

Just wanted to let you know....

Rachel Simon

Wednesday, September 19, 2001

Janet,

It breaks my heart about Cathy Chirls. I was supposed to have lunch with her on Monday (because of our 85 Broads connection). We had to move it to Wednesday, never knowing that Tuesday would bring this horror. Thank you for getting the sad message out that she is among the missing. Please if you hear any more, let us know. I truly appreciate the extension of all the prayers and comfort.

Rosalie

Friday, September 28, 2001

Janet,

Thank you for the focus that you have given to Cathy Chirls. I knew Cathy when I worked at Goldman Sachs. After I was let go from the firm last March, she contacted me and we got to know each other better. She was incredibly resourceful in tracking me down and we started a friendship based on a common bond. We shared our thoughts about life on Wall Street for women, the challenges, the inequities, and how we could try to change certain things.

Although I only knew her for a short time, it was long enough to realize what a warm and understanding person she was. She was a woman just like all of us, who was juggling work and family. She was an experienced and bright Wall Street professional. She was a mother and wife. She was a friend.

Cathy knew the value of a network of professional women. She contacted me. She opened her heart to me and shared her candid and sincere perceptions.

I found myself drawn to Cathy very quickly. I know that we would have continued to grow close in a relationship based on honesty, respect, and support.

I was terrified for Cathy when the tragedy happened and when I saw the email from 85 Broads, my worst fears were confirmed. Cathy understood that women need to help each other. We were trying to help each other. Let's all keep helping each other.

With appreciation,

Ellen Luntz

After 9/11, wanting to be part of a "community" seemed to grow exponentially. Wall Street was undergoing a furious "headcount reduction" and many b-school grads weren't able to land a single job offer. The need to connect seemed more critical than ever. By 2002, our network had grown to over 5,000 members who lived in 150 different cities around the world.

Many milestones were reached that year. Alison Levine, 85 Broads member extraordinaire, was the captain of the first ever all-U.S. women's team to attempt to summit Mt. Everest. Although her team came within 280 vertical feet of the summit before being forced to turn back, it was an incredible accomplishment. Equally exciting was Alison's dedication of two new children's school sites in Nepal on behalf of 85 Broads and Room to Read, a wonderful nonprofit organization in San Francisco. The pictures of Alison in her orange 85 Broads cap with hundreds of school children was an absolute thrill. Not long after, 85 Broads member Kate Reid left her job at Goldman Sachs to teach at one of our two schools.

In September 2002, it was I who needed to reach out to the community of women in our network. I had just been diagnosed with breast cancer and was scheduled for surgery on October 21. I sent a letter to everyone in the network imploring them to get a mammogram and a sonogram if they were "at risk." It was the sonogram done by Dr. Susan Drossman that saved my life, as my mammogram hadn't detected a thing.

What astounded me was the number of emails I received from other members of the network who told me that they had had cancer too, not just breast cancer, but ovarian cancer, uterine cancer, and leukemia. Almost every one of them had been diagnosed in their late twenties or early thirties. Each and every one of them faced life-threatening challenges and every one of them shared their courageous stories with me.

Just as astoundingly, the day after I got home from the hospital the phone rang. It was Joe Gregory, who at the time was the co-chief operating officer of Lehman Brothers. Joe and I had had lunch in July, and he was calling to see how I was doing. I had only met him *once*. He wanted to give me some information that he thought would be helpful and just to say, "Hang in there." I remember staring at the phone after I hung up and thinking to myself, now there's a guy who understands the power of networking. In a word, I was completely blown away by his thoughtfulness.

For the next six months, I struggled with the fallout of my diagnosis. Only weeks after I was out of the hospital, I was back in again to have my ovaries removed as the type of breast cancer I'd had made me a likely candidate for ovarian cancer. A month after that, I had two skin cancer operations—one on my lip and one on my chest. The one on my face left a deep, one-inch scar from my nose to my lip. I had a three-inch vertical scar on my chest, which only added insult to injury. By the spring of 2003, my memory seemed to be leaking brake fluid due to the fact that I was now experiencing "traumatic menopause," a condition which occurs when your ovaries are removed and your body stops producing estrogen. I seemed to have virtually no short-term memory at all which made remembering who was in the network an almost unbearable challenge. And of course my own family got the brunt of my anger, depression, and frustration.

Throughout 2003, I met several times with Joe Gregory at Lehman Brothers because he wanted me to come work there. I told him I couldn't do that because I already had a "day job," which was to run Milestone Capital in addition to my growing network "empire." But by the end of 2003, he had talked me into coming back to the Street at the age of 51. In May 2004, I left my home in Bedford for 745 Seventh Avenue. It had been a decade since I'd worked in New York City and over 15 years since I'd been in a large office building. I had a new focus and a new mission. I was going to help Lehman Brothers become the preeminent "brand" with women on college and university campuses.

The experience of meeting new people and trying to remember their names, titles, and locations was utterly terrifying. When I ran into people on the elevator or in the building, I would act very friendly while at the same time try to rummage through my mental "attic" for a name or any reference as to how I might know the person I found myself talking to. It was not unusual for me to meet someone at a meeting and a week later run into them again and have no memory of the meeting or the person. It is a surreal moment which I have learned to move through as best I can. People will often look at me with astonishment as they think I'm either kidding or rude or both.

At the same time that I reported to work at Lehman Brothers, we launched Broad2Be, an exact replica of our Broad2Broad co-mentoring initiative, for women at some of the leading undergraduate schools. We piloted Broad2Be at Dartmouth and in May 2004 we held a wonderful event there for women undergrads and our Broad2Broad members at Tuck. It was a huge success and for the first time brought together undergraduate women with women in business school, as well as current and former women from Goldman Sachs.

Before long, we had over 50 Broad2Be schools in our network and in one year over 1,500 women joined the network, regardless of career focus. What I found to be absolutely stunning was the amazing cultural diversity on the campuses, and for the first time, I felt truly blessed to have launched the 85 Broads network. I was meeting women from all over the world and even though I couldn't remember their names or faces, I had an inner joy that lifted my spirits and helped me forget my own personal issues.

At Lehman Brothers, I had the opportunity to spend my summers meeting all of the female interns, both from undergraduate and graduate business school. I hosted two or three roundtable discussions a day, which I found to be both exhausting and exhilarating. We spent the hour and a half that we were together talking about what these amazing young women were passionate about. And we laughed about being a woman in a male-dominated business. In some of my 2005 summer roundtables I had women in the group who had been at Lehman Brothers the prior summer who hoped that I would immediately remember and recognize them. They would say, "It's great to see you again Janet," and I would thank them and say, "It's great to meet you!" Good thing these fabulous young women had a sense of humor.

Some days I would be almost manic and bursting with energy and sparkle. Some days no amount of coffee could keep me from feeling and sounding narcoleptic. Often I would receive an email or two following a roundtable discussion from the women who had attended.

Sent: Thursday, August 4, 2005 10:20 am
To: Hanson, Janet
Subject: My deepest gratitude

Good Morning Ms. Hanson,
    I was one of the young women at the roundtable yesterday and would like to express my deepest thanks. I went into the roundtable

ready to meet a managing director with an amazing background from whom I could learn many things. But little did I know I would meet an extraordinary woman whose words would stay with me for the rest of my life. Yesterday you told the group that we inspired you. Well I believe you inspired us much more than you could imagine. I walked out of that room stronger and more courageous than ever. I have not felt that secure in a long time. I would simply like to thank you for taking the time to reach out to us. I hope to stay in touch with you and share my career advancements with you for I am sure you can give me some amazing advice, although you have already given the group and me more advice than we could ever dream of. So once again, thank you for being an inspiration.

  My deepest thanks,

  Andrea

Over the past few years, people have often commented that I am a courageous soul. That is because I have the love and support of my wonderful family and the extraordinary friendship of a guy by the name of Rodney Eyles. I was first introduced to Rod in 1999, when he was in New York to play in a professional squash tournament. Rod was one of the greatest squash players to ever pick up a racquet. I loved his fierce determination, even though he was on the "back nine" of his career. He was 32 years old, which in squash is "geriatric" due to the pounding a player's body takes on the court. Rod was interested in teaching young up and comers in the United States how to play the game and so in 2000, he began coaching our son Christopher, who was 9 at the time. I had never known a professional athlete before, much less one from Australia! Rod's view of the sport and the world were unique and when he came to New York to teach Christopher, he always seemed to bring the brilliant Australian sunshine with him.

Before long, I became obsessed with getting myself into the best shape of my life. I started running and swimming and watching my diet. My weight dropped from 150 pounds to 110 pounds. I was in "the zone" and loving it. I found that my outlook on life was changing, that I was seeing everything from a more positive point of view and even though I was almost 50 years old, for the first time in my life I felt the incredible "high" of being an athlete.

As it turned out, I needed every ounce of strength and courage I could muster to get through the past few years. The women in the 85 Broads network will never know how much they've inspired me to keep charging ahead. Following my surgery for skin cancer in January 2003, I wrote in my diary:

Dear Diary,

I look terrible as my face is a wreck, as is my chest, but the real problem is my face. I have a one-inch incision from my left nostril through my lip and a three-incher down my chest. I am scaring people everywhere I go.

But I am trying. I am trying really, really hard. I don't know what else to do. Sometimes I get very, very angry because I'm under so much stress but I'm hoping that I will be able to continue to handle it somehow.... Talked to Rod a few times; he really cheered me up. I've tried to make sure that I'm exercising—that always hugely helps.

I try to listen to music and most of all I try to focus on the loves in my life that make each day so worth living, no matter how much pain I'm in, or how bad I look, or what the markets are doing to make me crazy. I can't duck and run just because I have a problem. I have to try harder, be stronger, think more clearly... I JUST HAVE TO KEEP GOING.

Mine is just one story. In the chapters that follow you will hear the stories of women who have had luck, success, failure, sadness, happiness, doubts, triumphs, depression, and everything else in between. They come from different cultures, different backgrounds, and different economic circumstances. What they all have in common is a keen desire to share their stories so that other women will "recognize" their voices. They are some of the smartest, hardest working women on the planet. They are a gutsy bunch. And most of all, they are unique.

2

TRAILBLAZERS

What's a trailblazer? What motivates someone to be one of the first ever to set out on a completely unknown and uncharted path? To lead the way for others when they themselves have no road map or prescribed formula, no real role models, and certainly no clear definitions of success? To focus on the positive and be driven by optimism and confidence, not by negativity or the status quo? To be leaders, not followers? Whether their careers spanned the seventies, the eighties, the nineties, or even just the last five years, all of the incredible women whose stories we'll hear in this chapter have chosen "the road less traveled," and often more than once throughout their careers and lives.

Each of these women has had to define and redefine success for herself, using her own internal compass to guide her career decisions and personal choices at critical moments when the "right" thing to do or the "best" way to go leads into totally unfamiliar territory. This is something we have seen throughout the 85 Broads network that still holds true today. Many of our Broad2Broad members in business schools and our Broad2Be members at undergraduate schools are creating opportunities for themselves that don't necessarily conform to mainstream career paths or traditional job descriptions. These incredibly talented women are increasingly "reading the ending first," as we like to say. They're redefining what it takes for companies to recruit and retain them. They are starting their careers with exit strategies already in mind. Or they are opting out of one-dimensional career tracks in favor of opportunities that can be truly integrated with how they want to live their lives and pursue their passions for the next four to five decades, not just the next four to five years.

Trailblazers, whatever their age or generation, are the ones who rewrite the rules of engagement. They set their own internal compasses and decide for themselves which direction is "north." We all hear a lot about a lack of role models and mentors for women in the workplace—which is one of the biggest reasons I started 85 Broads—but the truth is that trailblazers don't let a lack of role models or mentors stop them. They don't let a lack of *anything* stop them. If there aren't any women ahead of them, they look to the men ahead of them, or the women beside them, or their mothers and fathers and families, or whatever source of inspiration and self-determination they need to move ahead when others see no path there at all.

While there is no easy formula (by definition!) for being or becoming a trailblazer, the women in this chapter do have three things in common that I believe really distinguish them as trailblazers.

First, trailblazing alone is not enough. Simply being first or doing something different is not the true test of a trailblazer. Leaving a path that *others can follow*—finding ways to help them eventually go even further than you did or to discover their own unique directions—is the ultimate measure of trailblazing. And it's something that the women in this chapter have raised to an art form throughout their careers.

Second, trailblazers *build* something. They aren't afraid to push the envelope and take risks, but they're most passionate about investing their skills and incredible creative energy into building things that will have real and lasting value—businesses, families, causes, relationships, and reputations. Trailblazers aren't focused on the "barriers" of the past or the present—only on the possibilities of the future. Each of these women, in her own way, has not only followed her own dreams and instincts but has also been a positive agent of change in making these dreams a reality.

And finally, trailblazers never stop trailblazing in their work or in their lives. Many of these women have now left their original careers or positions, but they are all still blazing new trails, whether as executives, educators, philanthropists, or parents. They integrate trailblazing into every element of their lives, building strong relationships and partnerships with other trailblazers both professionally and personally.

In this chapter we'll meet women whose careers led the way for future generations of women. As we read these stories, we'll begin to see how each of these women has defined success on her own terms, how she created a new path, and how we can follow—not her footsteps, but her example—to ultimately blaze an awesome trail of our own.

ANNE BROWN FARRELL

Directly after earning a BA at Trinity, Anne went on to the Wharton School of Business receiving her MBA in 1973. That same year she joined Goldman Sachs and became the first woman to work in what was then known as the Fixed Income Trading Department.

"I actually got my start on Wall Street as a Girl Scout, and I never looked back."

Trust me, I was not your typical Girl Scout. Though I only realized this years later, my professional career was established at the tender age of 12, during a fund-raising fair that my troop had organized. The goal of the fair was to raise money for a trip by selling food. The girls behind the cash register had priced a lunch consisting of a hot dog, chips, and a pickle at only 25 cents. I quickly surmised that our costs were about 50 cents and that we were losing money with every meal we sold! We weren't even charging for our time! I was dumbstruck. How could they not realize this? How could they not take it seriously? Our enterprise was plummeting and my fellow Girl Scouts were too busy painting faces and making crafts to care. I knew that something had to be done. In an early display of leadership, I seized control of the cash register and raised the prices 200 percent. My career path was identified and I was on my way to Wall Street.

Another harbinger of my professional destiny came a few years later when my aunt gave me five shares of Syntex for Christmas. It was worth $25 a share at the time. I knew nothing about stocks but was excited to learn because stocks, to me, took on lives of their own. Within a short time, the stock split, then it split again. I watched with giddy anticipation as my five shares of stock quickly turned into almost $1,000. I was fascinated by the system and wanted to figure out how it worked. I began to call my father to check up on the stock from the pay phone in my high school's cafeteria. I followed this routine every day for three years. If only the Internet were available back then! As a child, my interpretation was simple—stockowners always made money. So, I wanted to be a stock owner. Easy as pie. Life was going to be great.

Now that I knew exactly what I wanted to do, I just had to figure out how to get there. The first step was to go to Trinity College where I majored in math. Don't forget, I graduated in 1971. Expectations for women's careers were low. People had the best intentions, but their frame of reference was limited by the secretarial duties to which most professional women tended. Most women with math degrees became teachers or housewives. I wanted more out of life. My career choice was so clear to me. I just had to be on Wall Street. I decided that business school was the best path to get there, so I applied to Harvard, Columbia, and Wharton and ended up choosing Wharton because of its curriculum.

I was thrilled that Goldman Sachs showed a strong interest in me due to my thesis on "using municipal bonds to finance a hospital." So, naturally, when I interviewed there, they wanted to stick me in that area of finance. But as I met more and more people who worked in that area, and as I saw their part of the floor, I decided it just wouldn't hold my interest for long. Writing a paper about it was one thing, creating an entire career around it was quite another, at least for me. I was seeking a certain type of personality. I found this personality while walking by the fixed income trading floor during one of my interviews. Though I was all the way across the room, the atmosphere and the energy completely and hopelessly mesmerized me. My career path was, finally, crystal clear. *That* was where I wanted to be! I wanted to be on the trading floor, not in investment banking or any other part of the business. Soon after, I became the first woman to join the Fixed Income Department of Goldman Sachs. That was 1973. GS wasn't a government dealer, which was a big obstacle because they couldn't buy and sell securities to the Federal Reserve. They became a dealer in corporate bonds, municipal bonds, and commercial paper around 1978 or 1979. There were no "screens" or computers. All inventory and prices of securities were on sheets of paper that were handed out in the morning and updated on an elaborate speaker-phone system throughout the day. The system connected to offices in Chicago, Boston, Philadelphia, San Francisco, Los Angeles, and Dallas. The average size of a trade was less than $1 million; by the time I left it was rarely less than $25 million. The trading floor was similar to what it is today—masses of people, no privacy, food all over the place, and at the time...*everyone smoked*!!!

I could not have gotten to where I did without the influence and help of many people. I have had a few mentors; I'm sure that they don't even know that they were my mentors. Malcolm Pryor, then a money market salesman in Goldman's Philadelphia office, taught me one of the most invaluable lessons that I have used throughout my life. *He explained to me the importance of providing measurable results.* This made sense to me and reminded me of my Girl Scout experience. Being measured is a big risk, as your results are open for public scrutiny. Many women back then were not comfortable with that; most were satisfied with career paths that were more secure. I am not a natural salesperson. I didn't like cold calling at all, but I did it because I had to. I found out many years later that one of my bosses had so little faith in me that he actually hired my replacement in anticipation of my failure. The supposed replacement ended up leaving seven years later—patient guy, no promotion—and I was still there!

The early days of my career at Goldman Sachs were strange, particularly as the only woman in the Trading Department. I remember that sometime in the fall of 1973 all the new associates were invited to the Yale Club for dinner with Gus Levy, who was the senior partner of the firm. Due to the importance of the event everyone arrived a little early, including me. And everyone went inside, except me. I was blocked at the door and told, "No women allowed—club policy." Of course, I was informed of this while my loyal male associates were trotting upstairs. No one even looked back. For over half an hour, I tried every way I could think of to slip in unnoticed. It was impossible. I didn't know what to do and I was beginning to panic. I had to be at that dinner! Finally, a sympathetic steward—sympathetic, perhaps, because I slipped him a $20 bill—snuck me up the service elevator. All eyes were on me when I finally entered the dining room. I was late, I was young, and I was in trouble. Gus announced to the group that I was a disgrace for showing up so late to the associates' dinner. Of course, he didn't know why I was late and he didn't give me the chance to explain. My boss glared at me too. Later, I seized an opportunity to explain to my boss what happened. He didn't really seem to care. Fortunately, Gus overheard the conversation. He was infuriated and demanded to know which idiot had chosen the Yale Club. That person turned out to be my boss, but not for long!

I've learned in my career that you will encounter roadblocks no matter who you are or who your mentors are. I have also learned that you can overcome them as long as you have credibility. To gain credibility, you need results, which you gain through clients and tenacity and hard work. If you have loyal clients, and you bring in revenue, your "value" to your firm is easy to measure. My ascent through the Goldman hierarchy took a lot longer than normal because no one expected me to stay and succeed. The fixed income business had been exclusively male up to that point. I hung in there even though some of my bosses were always ready, maybe even eager, to replace me. I focused on building successful client relationships and producing measurable results every single day.

Then another roadblock came along. Marriage. My boss once told me that he didn't want women working for him, especially married women. So, my fiancé's proposal was thrilling but terrifying, not because I was going to spend the rest of my life with this person, but because I would have to tell my boss! Well, I thought I had to tell my boss. When I did eventually get married, I did what every level-headed woman in my position at the time would do—I didn't tell my boss. He eventually found out, about six months later at the company Christmas Party. He, like many of the people in the office, assumed that I would immediately have a baby and never come back; and he, like those other doubters, was wrong.

Something terrible happened shortly after that, though it turned out to be fortuitous for my career advancement. When a colleague of mine died suddenly of a heart attack at 37 years old, management had no choice but to let me gradually take over our shared accounts. Eventually, 10 of the 15 largest clients on the desk were mine—names like Prudential, Bankers Trust, Chemical Bank. They were good clients but I made them *big* clients. No one could believe that I was making money the old-fashioned way—earning it. During my bonus discussion one year, there was particular scrutiny around one of my accounts where business had increased from $500,000 to $5M. "I want to know what you're doing to get these clients," someone said. "Are you having sex with them?" I was shocked but in a way found it funny. Can you imagine that happening today?

I spent nearly 22 years at Goldman Sachs. For eight of those years, I worked for a gentleman and a scholar, Jim Kautz, until he retired and then founded Sage Capital, a firm I would later join him at as a partner. He learned a lot from me about how to deal with women. When I would get frustrated with him, I would say, "I wish for you daughters that want big careers!" I can't help but chuckle now that his only daughter is a partner at a leading consulting firm. But in 1973, things were very different. Asking about maternity leaves and career paths, as women who interviewed with me years later would ask, just weren't topics you raised. One of the people who interviewed me at business school asked: "Why would we want you? You're going to get married and your husband won't want you to work." I gave him a puzzled look. "Why would I want to marry someone who doesn't want me to work?" He was dumbfounded. I got the job. And the really funny part is that when this same partner finally got married at age 42, I wished twin daughters for him and he ended up having *three* daughters! So he had his payback. In reality, a lot of "change" coming about for women on Wall Street today is because of the changing views that men have of women once their daughters are faced with the business realities that their fathers have had a hand in creating—and who can now have a hand in changing.

I think a lot of people set out to Wall Street hoping that it will instill some direction in their lives, but the truth is, people have to provide that direction for themselves. I tell my children that you should enjoy the people you work with first and foremost. You can do a lot of things coming out of college. Don't be afraid to shift your focus or change jobs if you want something more. When I changed jobs to go to Dallas for Goldman Sachs in the early 1980s, I didn't know if I could start something from scratch and build it into something. I could and I did. What I've never done is what a lot of other women do—point out how different or special they are to be a woman. Well, in my experience, this also points out your inadequacies. It takes away from your achievements. If a doctor is always pointing out that she's a "female" doctor, you get sick of it. You are more concerned with her competency than her gender.

I have to credit my accomplishments to my strong self-esteem, which stems from the love and support I have always received from my family. My mom, somewhat progressive for her generation, never encouraged me to get a teaching degree so that I'd have "something to fall back on," like so many other women did with their daughters. In fact, she wouldn't hear of my doing anything else or less than what I really wanted to do. She had faith in my abilities at a time when there were few role models to look to for guidance. Role models come in all shapes and sizes. I thank her to this day.

BETHANY MCLEAN

Bethany worked at Goldman Sachs before joining Fortune *magazine. Her trailblazing article, "Is Enron Overpriced?" was the first in a national publication to openly question the company's dealings. She and* Fortune *colleague Peter Elkind coauthored "The Smartest Guys in the Room: The Amazing Rise and Scandalous Fall of Enron."*

> "It's hard for someone who wants to be considered smart to say, 'Wait. I don't understand.' It's especially hard if everyone else around you says they do."

I came to *Fortune* magazine in 1995 after three years in investment banking at Goldman Sachs. I'd always dreamed of working as a journalist, and I decided that if there was ever going to be a time to try to make a living as a writer, this was it.

I got my job as a fact-checker (the most junior job on an editorial staff) because I was able to calculate compound annual growth rates and read balance sheets, thanks to my work at Goldman. But it was actually a great way to learn how to be a journalist. Being able to tell a story is important, but having your facts right is critical.

Because my storytelling skills were lacking (to say the least) when I first joined *Fortune*, I used my finance background as a way to distinguish myself. I focused on hard-hitting accounting stories, and as a result made some connections among short-sellers. That was why I learned about the trouble at Enron early on. Jim Chanos, the founder and president of Kynikos Associates, a private investment management group specializing in short-selling, asked me in early January 2001 if I could read Enron's 10-K and understand how this company was making any money. My tip-off from Jim was off the record, which meant that I couldn't attribute any comments to him. Instead, I had to gather my own data and be prepared to stand behind all of my own arguments.

Back in early 2001, Enron was a well-loved company. Most of the sell-side analysts had "Strong Buy" ratings on the stock and some had price targets of over $100 per share. *Fortune* had just named Enron the "Most Innovative Company" for the sixth year in a row. As it turned out, Enron was innovative; we just didn't know how innovative.

Once I started digging, I found a deep vein of skepticism running under the celebration of Enron. Phone calls to portfolio managers would yield the obligatory laudatory comments, but if I kept pushing, I'd hear things like, "Well, this is off the record, but the company is a black box. I don't understand anything about them." One manager said, "Well, I actually own a little bit of the stock but I'm really scared of it. They haven't actually made their numbers in any of the last quarters. They've always done it by pulling a trick. We all know that, but no one will call them on it."

Before my Enron story was published, I made the obligatory call to the company. I raised the issues I'd come across in their financial statements. Jeff Skilling, Enron's CEO, became very upset and accused me of being unethical for raising these questions without having done enough research to have a comprehensive understanding of the business. It is a frightening accusation, because it's always possible that you haven't done enough homework. And in some ways, Skilling was right. There was a lot I didn't know about Enron.

The following day, three Enron executives flew into New York from Texas to convince me that my analysis of Enron was faulty. Dealing with them was somewhat like entering a parallel universe. I'd say something that I thought was pretty obvious, like, "Well, your business is very complicated," and they'd counter by saying, "No, it's not. You just don't understand." But I had done my research and persisted. "You're a trading company. You make your money trading. So why do you deserve such a high multiple when Goldman Sachs, arguably the best trading company in the world, trades at 15 to 16x earnings? Why should you trade at 55x earnings?" They came back quickly saying, "We don't trade. We're a logistics company."

Under all the jargon, it was almost impossible to get a straight answer from the company about how they actually made money. They'd make analogies, such as, "Well, we're like Toyota," which made no sense. It became clear they weren't really going to answer my questions.

I was curious as to what effect the energy crisis in California was going to have on Enron's profits, so I asked, "If California goes away, can you continue to produce these numbers?" Their reply was that volatility had *no* effect on their profits. I asked more generally, "Let's say you traded exactly the same volume of electricity and natural gas in two given months. One month was very volatile. The next month, there's zero volatility. Are you going to produce the same amount of profit?" "Yes," said one executive. "No," said the other.

I also asked about the "related party transactions." It's interesting that despite all the later complaints about Enron's lack of disclosure, these transactions—and the fact that Andy Fastow ran a fund that did business with Enron—were actually in Enron's financial statements. You couldn't make any sense of the language, but it was there. Fastow was one of the executives who flew to New York to meet with me, and we actually had a fairly long discussion about what the related party transactions meant. It became clear to me during the meeting that it was an uncomfortable topic of conversation for him.

My experience at Goldman Sachs helped me in researching and writing this story. An analyst at GS knows better than to show up in a client meeting with incorrect numbers, and I took the same mentality when I approached Enron. I had already double-checked all of my figures, so I wasn't going to get caught with an obvious error. Goldman Sachs also taught me not to be intimidated, which was critical in a situation like this one.

The Enron case taught the business media that it is critical to understand the numbers. There's a tendency in business journalism to think that the story is the profile of the CEO or the description of the company's aspirations. That may be the case, but the story may also be the numbers, and you don't know if you don't look. Enron proved to business journalists that they have to speak the language of accounting, just as a political journalist would understand the language of Washington.

Frankly, I'm not sure that I would have been as critical of Enron if I had known its story first. I had the advantage of looking at the numbers before I heard the story. The 1990s were a decade when people cared about the story more than they did the fundamentals, and Enron had a really compelling story and a really charismatic management team to sell that story. Of course, it's much more fun to believe the happy, optimistic story about how a company is transforming the world than it is to crunch numbers. And in Enron's case, everyone did believe. Very few of our supposed watchdogs—the analysts, the bankers, the board, the rating agencies, the accountants—looked to see if the numbers supported the story.

One big lesson I take away from the Enron experience is the importance of admitting that you don't get it. It's hard for someone who wants to be considered smart to say, "Wait. I don't understand." It's especially hard if everyone else around you says they do understand. I've certainly been in situations where I've pretended to understand something I don't because I've been too embarrassed to admit otherwise. These days, whenever I'm tempted to do that, I try to remind myself of Enron.

When people say, "You broke the Enron story," I cringe and say, "I really didn't." After Enron's bankruptcy, the company was in the headlines for months, and there was so much wrongdoing that anyone who did something even slightly right got an undue amount of praise. It was an awkward period because I never felt that I deserved the attention I received. As a result, I wanted to do a really good job on the book. Thanks to my coauthor, Peter Elkind, and our editor, Joe Nocera, I'm proud of the *The Smartest Guys in the Room*. When people say, "I really love the book," I can honestly say, "Thank you." Now that the "Enron movie" [the documentary *Enron: The Smartest Guys in the Room*] based on the book has been released, the story has been brought to a wider audience. Critics say the Enron story has all the classic components of a Greek tragedy. Alex Gibney, the director of the film, gives a close-up on some of the financial details and a wider view of the business culture that allowed Enron's collapse to happen, and he tells the story in an exciting way. At least now, through exposure to the book and the documentary, more individual investors and more employees know that you can't always trust everyone. It has made people think.

PHYLIS ESPOSITO

Phylis began her Wall Street career at Citibank after receiving her MBA from Columbia. She later joined Goldman Sachs, where she became a vice president and trading desk manager. She then went on to hold senior management positions at Bear Stearns, Ameritrade Holding Corp., and other leading financial service firms.

> "The driving force of any business endeavor has to be the morals and ethics of doing what's right for everybody involved, for being totally credible, for being totally responsible, for being totally accountable."

Change was happening in all aspects of the business world in 1975 when I joined the training program for the capital markets area at Citibank. Though they were one of the leading commercial lending institutions at that time, and had always hired MBAs for various positions at the bank for domestic, international, retail, and commercial banking, I was in the first class of MBAs to train at Citibank for municipals, governments, and foreign exchange. In that training class there were five guys plus me. The industry was expanding, new technology was emerging, and educated, energetic women were making their way to Wall Street.

When Goldman Sachs hired me in 1980, I became the first woman to head a trading desk, and my job was to develop a totally new product—tax-exempt commercial paper. Even though Goldman was really on the cutting edge of the variable rates market in municipals, it's still tough to sell a new product. A lot of salespeople just don't want to bother with it because their careers weren't dependent on it and they didn't want their clients to be the "guinea pigs." But Janet [Hanson] really helped to set the example for others in selling the product. She had to show the clients where it filled a need and how to use it in their portfolios. She did what was good for the firm and good for the client, and because of that it was also good for her. After we established these new products, other firms successfully replicated them, resulting in what have become very large markets today. What we did was not only good for Goldman, who became a leader in that area, but it also led to diversity and growth across the entire marketplace.

Years later, I was interested in what Janet was going to do post-Goldman, and when we met for dinner, she described her idea about launching the first woman-owned investment advisory firm to manage institutional money market funds. I was a senior managing director in investment banking at Bear Stearns at the time, and I thought this could be an excellent vehicle for them. I arranged for Janet to present her idea to the firm, and I made the case regarding the benefits for Bear Stearns. Within a week, Bear said they wanted to do it. My job was to look out for the best interest of Bear Stearns, which didn't have its own money market fund at the time, and I saw what they could gain from it. When you create a new product, it's always great for clients—both for investing clients and issuing clients. It strengthens the marketplace, gives investors more options and diversifies the field. My endorsement wasn't about it being a woman-owned fund or because Janet was my friend. I firmly believed that the fund was an excellent fit for Bear Stearns. The fact that it was good for Janet was a bonus, but not the reason I supported it.

One of the things I find most interesting about 85 Broads is that it's not just about the networking—the advice, support, education, and insight part of it—but it's also about creating opportunities that have multiple benefits and beneficiaries. If something is just beneficial to me, that's great because I gain something: I get a new job out of it, let's say. But if my new job also diversifies the workforce and enhances the value proposition of an organization because it gives them expertise and skills that they're looking for, then it's a bonus for both sides. A network such as this not only provides contacts and a place to share ideas but also helps create opportunities that are mutually beneficial. That's a unique perspective—it is always about maximizing opportunities for all sides of the equation.

Sometimes in networks, like in the "old boy network," it's a zero-sum game, where people do favors for each other which are not based on merit. Here's an important distinction: the environment that was created in the "old days" of Goldman Sachs was about teamwork, maximizing opportunities, and accomplishing mutual goals. One of the most powerful things about those early days for all of us is that we didn't do it just for the business or the client or the relationship. We did it because it was the right thing to do. It was right for me to bring Janet's idea to Bear; it was right for Janet to sell my product.

The whole thing is built on integrity. And here I do give credit to Goldman for finding and hiring the most spectacular women, because the women at that time had to not only be just as good as the men, they had to be better. They were incredible in terms of their potential and skill set, but they were also incredible as people. Goldman had a culture of ethics and integrity that was about advancing the whole team. It wasn't about individual superstars or one department against another. We were all extremely helpful with one another in learning the business, giving advice, lending moral support— things you couldn't really go to the guys for because the guys were part of a separate exclusive network. I can't recall a single woman along the way in those early years who didn't want to help another woman.

The other aspect of this is that if you look at the early Goldman Sachs women, our reputations were impeccable. There was no compromising yourself or your relationships with your clients or co-workers to get ahead. It was reinforced in us. All of us were of the same ilk—we wanted to get ahead based on merit. I have to give credit to Goldman, because they had a high standard for getting through the door and frankly they were right.

What you find today is that women are fighting the battle to become a part of the majority, and that means it's no longer about the "gender" issue. We have to look at our commonality. There are more women coming out of business school now, we have much more strength in the discrimination laws, there are more employers who want women—in other words, many of the barriers are down. Yet because we have more women in senior management (I am one of an eight-member executive management team in a publicly traded company), the real issue now is for women to not think of themselves as women, for men not to think of themselves as men, but for all of us to think of ourselves as people.

I see 85 Broads continuing to extend the ideal by reaching out further, now including business school and undergraduate women. It's a living, breathing organization. We could have said, "Oh, we're Goldman women, we don't care about Lehman women or Merrill women or younger women." But 85 Broads is living up to what we were all about in the very beginning. 85 Broads doesn't separate us, it brings us all together.

The way I view the world is that it's in perfect balance: there's a beginning and an end; there's a positive and a negative. No matter what your age, it's the same skill set that you need—you need judgment, you need to understand yourself, you need to be honest, you need to treat everyone with the same respect, and you need to focus on the greater good.

JESSICA PALMER

Jessica moved from Kenya to the UK to attend the University of Bristol. Upon graduation, she joined Wells Fargo Bank in London, eventually transferring to the San Francisco office. She later went to work for Goldman Sachs and currently works at Citigroup as the head of risk management for the Global Corporate and Investment Bank. Jessica has been married for 25 years and is the proud mother of three children.

"Given my background, I have always been global, thought globally, and been able to operate successfully in a global milieu. One of the satisfactions of my career is seeing the financial industry change from the almost entirely domestic cottage industry it used to be into a truly global undertaking."

I am a farmer's daughter from Kenya. Taken another way, I am a remnant of the British Empire. My initial desire to move to America originated during a cross-country trek that I made on a Greyhound bus by myself while I was on summer break from University. There was something about this country...the size, scope, and freedom that simply awed me. I was bitten by the "American bug." This perspective led me to join Wells Fargo Bank in London after college.

When I look back upon my career and the breadth of all the jobs that I have landed, I realize that I haven't always necessarily been qualified on paper or had the relevant experience for each and every position. When I found myself landing in the deep end, I made up for my lack of experience and knowledge by being a good team player, sharing credit, and working damn hard.

I am very proud to have stayed standing on Wall Street all these years, long after most of the women I started with had left the business. Several of my client relationships have lasted the entire 25 years that I have been here.

One of my proudest accomplishments is my family. Having managed to stay married to the same man for 25 years, we have raised three well-adjusted, attractive, competent young adults from the three babies we started out with. My husband is an immigrant as well, and we are both devoted to our extended families. We spend our vacations visiting them as they are scattered across three different continents. I have proved that it is possible to have a family and demanding career. There just isn't much time for anything other than that!

My advice to the women out there is, above all, to have a sense of humor. Take risks and learn to wing it. Never give up. Don't build romantic castles of expectations about your career. Take the work world as it comes. Network and help other women, and men too. Figure out what makes men tick, and enjoy them as friends, colleagues, and clients. You won't be able to change them, so best to get along. Don't flirt, but stay feminine. And remember: Never wear linen. You will look like you are wearing sackcloth within 10 minutes of leaving your house.

KAREN COOK

Karen joined the Equities Division at Goldman Sachs in 1975, a year after she graduated from Wheaton College. She continued to work as an equity block trader at GS for 12 years until she left to stay at home with her two sons. Karen currently serves as chief investment officer for Steinhardt Management.

> "In hindsight, I would have done it all better. I would have done *everything* better!"

I look up as I cross the street on my lunch break from the New York Stock Exchange, where I'm a 23-year-old floor clerk. Fifty-five Broad Street looms in front of me, the headquarters of Goldman Sachs at the time. I don't know a soul at Goldman, but on an impulse, and to avoid the rain, I duck into the lobby in hopes of finding someone I can just leave my resume with. Having taken the GMATs (business school boards) on a whim just before graduating as a philosophy major from Wheaton College, and having deferred my entrance to Wharton to get a little experience on Wall Street, I am intrigued by the mystique of an investment bank like Goldman and the thought of possibly getting hired there. My brief experience on the NYSE has made me think about becoming an equity trader. A new era of competition began this spring on Wall Street; commission rates are no longer "fixed" and the institutional equity business is just beginning to take off. I head for the elevator and push the button for the floor that says "Equities." The doors open to a cramped reception area where a woman at the desk glances at me with something between disinterest and disdain.

I walk up to her with as much confidence as I can muster, introduce myself, and ask for the name of someone in the Trading Department to send my resume to. She, of course, refuses to give out any names and I, naturally, want to avoid sending my resume to Human Resources just to be filed away somewhere. So I persist. "There must be someone whose name you can give me." She's not budging and now neither am I. For several minutes we go round and round, until I notice someone pacing back and forth in the hallway just behind us. He finally stops, turns to me, and asks, "Who are you and what is it that you want?"

I blurt out, "I want to be an equity trader and I am just trying to get the name of someone to send my resume to."

Studying me with a kind of quizzical gaze, he asks, "Do you have time for an interview right now?" I stifle the urge to respond, "Are you kidding?" and follow Bob Rubin out to the trading floor for my first interview. Over the next week I have about 12 grueling interviews with some of the legends who built the Goldman culture. Eventually, after what seems an eternity to me but is actually about two weeks, I get a call from Bob Mnuchin, offering me a job on the trading desk, the caveat being that he wants me to start immediately. I jump at the chance to quit my job and cancel my holiday plans to travel down the Amazon River. A few days later I am the first woman to join the Equities Division, the first female trader in the firm's history, and one of only four women professionals at Goldman Sachs.

So began my 12-year career as an equity block trader at Goldman Sachs. Having postponed my entrance to Wharton twice, and knowing that there was no way I would ever leave my new job, I decided to get my MBA from NYU/Stern School at night. I also dragged along my co-worker, Richard Perry (now a noteworthy hedge fund manager), to classes most nights. My typical day consisted of waking up early, working on the trading desk at Goldman, rushing out to evening classes at NYU, and going out on a date after that, sometimes ending up in the wee hours at Studio 54. All I can say is that what I had going for me then was my age. I think I'd be dead if I tried to do that now even for just one day. Talk about life in the fast lane!

But fast-forward 12 years ahead to 1987. I've completed my MBA at night, I'm a senior block trader responsible for some high-profile industry groups, I provide trading coverage to a few select hedge fund clients and... I am happily married (having met my husband on a blind date and instantly fallen in love with his southern charm and grace) and have two young sons, ages two and four, along with the requisite nanny, two Labradors, and a cat. And I'm having a pretty difficult time balancing the demands of work with the demands of raising children. There were no role models for me, no sage sources of advice, no policies or procedures for part-time, no 85 Broads to turn to for mentoring. So I just did what my instincts told me, which was to say goodbye to my professional career and become a full-time mom. When I made this decision, it was a surprise to many people, including myself. I didn't exactly have a plan when I left Goldman Sachs, other than to be a full-time mom and that was sort of a scary thing. I had worked every single weekday since graduating from college. I wanted to have the time to do things I never did—take my boys to school, take a more active role in their growing up, focus on them rather than on all the stuff that needed to be done *around* them. I was 35 years old and about to embark on a new stage of my life.

In hindsight, I can say it's really good to have opportunities to reinvent yourself at different stages of life, to cast off old identities and create new ones, but it doesn't always feel that way at the time you're experiencing it. I sat on park benches for the next two years conversing with other women who had dropped out of the workforce—many of whom, like me, had left successful careers on Wall Street because they couldn't find a happy balance between work and family. They had opted out, and most of them couldn't figure out how or even whether to opt back in. Their dilemmas actually gave a friend and me the idea for Alternatrack, a new business venture that sought to identify creative ways to find flexible work arrangements for former Wall Streeters (essentially professional temps). We started with nothing more than a mission statement and then made the bold move to hold a press conference to announce the launch of our business. No one was more surprised than we were with the positive media coverage from publications such as *The Wall Street Journal, The New York Times, Fortune, Forbes,* and *Institutional Investor.* Maybe there was more of a need for this type of business than our own personal experiences had led us to believe. Goldman Sachs even hired me as a consultant to help the firm "better retain people like yourself." As the business evolved, it posed a new dilemma for me. Being an entrepreneur is a 24/7 occupation. At least trading hours were dictated by stock market hours. Besides, I loved trading and interacting with a room full of high-quality, ambitious, frenetic people. I also worried constantly about the success of this new endeavor, and I was taking time away from my kids. Good idea for a business, wrong time in my life.

So I sold my interest in the new business to my partner, and when I wasn't full-time mommying I focused some of my professional skills on philanthropic and educational organizations that I cared about. Inevitably I'd end up on the finance or investment committee, which was something that allowed me to stay engaged with investments but didn't compete with time spent with my sons. I also finally had time for obsessive/compulsive athletic pursuits, some days playing 27 holes of golf. All of this helped me avoid the pitfalls of jumping back "into the game" again too soon.

But as my sons grew older, being a full-time mom took on different dimensions, and I began to feel a gravitational pull back to the workplace. It was a bit tricky because I had lost my place in the pecking order at GS & Co. Almost everyone in my "career generation" was either running divisions, had become partners, or had moved on to running their own businesses. Rubin was in Washington, Mnuchin was retired. I couldn't just "go back" to trading (after all, it was a job for a younger woman), so it was time to reinvent myself again.

Actually, I've always thought less in terms of "plans" and more in terms of "purpose," much like I did when I first got off that elevator at 55 Broad Street. This has helped me to be open to opportunities as they arise and not miss a chance for renewal along the way, and it is, in fact, how I came to join Steinhardt Partners. Michael Steinhardt, then one of the most prominent hedge fund managers, needed someone to handle investor relations after a year of terrible performance in 1994. Having no experience doing anything like this before, I could have convinced myself that I was not qualified. Instead, trusting in my intuitive process and thinking about my GS & Co. trading background, my experience with some of the world's largest and most sophisticated institutional investors, my knowledge of hedge funds from both GS & Co., and working on philanthropic boards, not to mention the invaluable experience of full-time parenthood, I had enough confidence to say, "Sure, I can do this." When Michael later decided to retire from the business and return investors' capital, I "reinvented" myself again, staying on to manage the transition and eventually taking on the role of chief investment officer (CIO) for Steinhardt Management. Today, I oversee investments in a broad array of hedge funds and run a small fund of funds, with my work incorporating virtually every aspect of what I've learned as a trader, entrepreneur, board member/fiduciary, etc. Having elbowed my way back into the workforce, I guess I again define myself a lot by my work but that's OK. I still like the new me.

At every stage in my life I have had all kinds of role models who inspired me and even pushed me. Sometimes they just appeared; often I had to seek them out. I grew up in a traditional middle-class household where my mother, who was a schoolteacher, showed me firsthand how to develop both a family identity and a work identity. She taught fifth grade and was considered the most transformative and "best" teacher in the school. Later it was she, never me, who would walk her grandsons through the woods in the autumn, helping them identify maple, oak, and other trees and then painstakingly iron the leaves between pieces of wax paper, something I would never have the patience to do. I admire her for her strong work ethic and the fact that she was always there for me. Lance Armstrong, cancer survivor and seven-time winner of the Tour de France, and perhaps the most admired athlete in the world, is also an awesome inspiration for me. Just watching him makes me want to train harder and be a better athlete. Attitude is everything—I want to "live strong" too. A few years ago, when I turned fifty, I signed up for a two-week Navy SEAL's course. I was motivated because I had to prove to myself that I was strong enough to survive it. When this wacko drill instructor was barking orders at me and my much younger teammates, I knew that while I may not physically be up to every task, he would never break me mentally. One thing you have to develop in yourself is mental toughness and the will to go on. Traders need it. Mothers need it. Entrepreneurs need it. Athletes need it. Everybody needs it. Maybe I didn't run as fast or do pushups and squats as well as everybody else, but I just *wasn't going to be broken* by this guy. I guess I'm still pretty "OK" in terms of tough environments and taking risks. Maybe that's why I constantly want to find new ways to challenge myself.

Two favorite books that I've recently read are *Don't Let's Go to the Dogs Tonight* by Alexandra Fuller, about growing up in Zimbabwe, and *Swimming to Antarctica*, by long-distance swimmer Lynn Cox. I guess there's a certain theme running here: strong women are survivors! (I love going on safaris and I just swam the Hudson River.) I want to go to places I haven't seen and push myself to limits I haven't reached before. I recently returned from a trip to Azerbaijan with an organization that I am very committed to, The International Rescue Committee (IRC). I obviously like to be tested, but I also think I thrive in situations where I have the opportunity to learn, explore, and soak up the world with all of its luxuries and its sadness. I hope I'll have that attribute forever. One of the things that is so admirable about John Whitehead (former co-chairman of Goldman Sachs), for example, is that even in his early eighties he still works hard every day. He is someone who lives strong and knows how to give back philanthropically.

Every morning I wake up and make a list of what I need to accomplish that day. I've been doing this as far back as I can remember. I'm always trying to get through my list, because it's my way of setting daily goals. It's good to wake up every day with a purpose. I always say I'm a much more interesting person to have breakfast with than dinner. Janet has reminded us, through 85 Broads, just how important it is to "find your own voice." Janet and I and others had to find our own voices—we had no choice but to do so, both at Goldman Sachs and beyond. I've learned not to be threatened by change. I've also learned to be grateful for what I've got, for what I've achieved, and for every opportunity that I've earned along the way. In hindsight, I would have done it all better. I would have done *everything* better. I would have been a better trader, made more money, been more philanthropic. I would have had more children, been a better mother, a more devoted wife. I would have had a finer garden, been a marathon swimmer, had a lower handicap. I would have accomplished more things on my list. But you know what? I like my life so far and even though I've zigged and zagged through different stages, I've been able to sustain my ambition and still be happy too.

ANNE CASSCELLS

Anne graduated from Yale University in 1980 with a BA in British Studies and received her MBA at Stanford in 1985. After spending the next 10 years at Goldman Sachs in the Fixed Income Division, she went on to become the chief investment officer of Stanford's endowment and is now a principal at Aetos Capital.

> "Take tough classes, challenge yourself in new ways, make the most of your potential."

My mother graduated from law school in 1949, at a time when law schools had almost no women students. She was the only woman in her class to graduate. Regrettably, she never practiced law because she did not believe that anyone would give her the chance. This story haunts me. Like so many women of her generation, my mother's ability and passion were overlooked, even squandered. She got married and had four children. She later opened a decorating business and then worked in real estate, but she never got to fulfill her potential, and that was very hard for her.

My parents lived through the Depression, and my father was a battlefield surgeon in Italy during World War II. Years of deprivation had a profound impact on them. They were determined that their children should get a good education to protect them from life's vagaries. Their resolve had a motivating influence on us. My two brothers went to Yale, and I followed them there, while my sister went to the University of Virginia. There was an expectation that my brothers would become doctors, and that I would become a lawyer, like my mom had wanted to be. In college, preparing to go to law school, I studied liberal arts, with an interdisciplinary major in British history, literature, and art history. Although I was good at math and science, I largely ignored those subjects and am now not sure why I did that. I might have been a bit intimidated by a high school calculus teacher, but I also had the notion that science courses were only for those who were going to medical school, which I was not going to do since I thought I would follow my mom into law. I didn't realize that there were so many career paths out there, many of which depended on math and science. Now I have a passion for science and regret not taking it in college. Who knows? Maybe I would have ended up in biotechnology or in venture capital!

Graduating from college at a time when the economy was bad proved challenging, especially for liberal arts majors like me. It was the age of the second OPEC oil crisis, and jobs mostly went to petroleum engineers. I wanted to take a break before applying to law school but didn't know what career options were open to me, given my background. The banks and investment banks seemed more open to liberal arts majors, so I applied for training programs at banks. Through a combination of my good grades and good fortune, Morgan Stanley recruited me for their analyst program. Knowing absolutely *nothing* about the business—I didn't know the difference between a bank and an investment bank—I was perplexed that I was even offered an interview. I knew one other person who was also interviewing who was an athlete, as I was (I played varsity squash and was captain of the team). So I asked my interviewers, "Why did you call me? Are you calling all the jocks?" They thought this was pretty funny, so they let me into the next round of interviews and eventually I was offered a job. My question was not that far off. It turns out that Morgan Stanley placed a premium on leadership skills and the combination of athletic leadership and a good GPA landed me the job.

So I showed up on Wall Street, wide-eyed and innocent in my new blue suit with the funny bow ties women wore in the early 1980s. I had a lot to learn. Luckily, I spent the first two years doing internal consulting—analyzing new business opportunities for Morgan Stanley. This gave me a broad perspective on the company's investment strategy, marketing, and future plans. Early on, part of my job included reading a lot of legal documents. One late night, after the fourth time of reading a document, I realized that a life in the law would include writing lots and lots of legal documents and contracts. If I hated reading them, then the thought of writing them made the hairs on the back of my neck stand up. The next morning when I awoke, I decided that I would not be going to law school.

But now I had no career plan. I spent a lot of introspective time determining which elements of my job I really enjoyed. That was easy. I was attracted to sales and trading—the action, the openness, and the unpretentiousness of the trading people. But to work in that area, I knew that I needed additional training and specifically more quantitative skills, so I applied to business school. When Stanford accepted me, I was thrilled. And as luck often runs in twos or threes, the opportunity to spend one year overseas doing a

Rotary scholarship presented itself, so I deferred business school for one year. And I'm so glad that I did. My year abroad, studying in Wales, was one of the most important developmental experiences in my life. I arrived there during the late 1980s, and I was sent to a town in Wales whose local economy depended on coal mining. Coal mining had been enormously successful in Wales and other parts of Britain for over 100 years. Nearly every town had its own mine. The mines had employed thousands of people. As prosperity from the mines grew, their communities flourished; churches, hospitals, and schools were built. This way of life was now coming to an end. Communities were being irrevocably transformed as the government announced that the mines were no longer cost-effective and would be shut down. More than a century of mining in these towns was ending, and what had been a thriving, industrial community due to coal mining was becoming a center of unemployment and despair.

Members of the local Rotary clubs were trying to prevent this decline. These clubs are unique because they are made up of leading citizens who are deeply engaged in their communities. With the coal industry dying out and no other industry to replace it, people were thrown out of work. Many of the men were middle-age and had no other training, other than the mines. The towns turned from strong communities with happy family environments to almost unrecognizable places with high rates of crime, addiction, and spousal abuse. Many villages became like inner cities except that they were in semi-rural isolation. I met many of the local Rotary members who were trying to resurrect their towns and their way of life. I have never forgotten what a community goes through when the local economy dies and when individuals lose the ability to provide for their family. It really had a profound impact on my thinking later on.

After this year of unexpected personal growth, I went to Stanford Business School to study finance. It was an era of big expansion in financial markets. Fixed income markets, especially, were growing and innovating rapidly as documented in the book, *Liar's Poker* about the bank where I did my summer internship. I improved my quantitative skills a great deal while at Stanford and was attracted to work in fixed income sales and trading, where these skills would be especially useful. I was fortunate enough to graduate with honors, and I accepted a job in fixed income at Goldman Sachs upon graduation. That is where I met my mentor, Janet Hanson. Goldman assigns mentors to people. Janet was not my assigned mentor, but as soon as I met her, I assigned myself to her. Janet has been a true pioneer, and very brave and successful and generous. What providence to have someone like her helping me find my way through the firm and, at times, through life. Later, I was very lucky to work for Connie Duckworth, who became one of the first women partners at Goldman. She taught me many, many things, but especially some lessons in leadership—like giving all the credit to the people who work for you. As it turns out, if you do that, people will assume you must be a good manager, because your people keep doing great things.

In 1995, after 10 years at Goldman, I left. Once again, I was at a crossroads in my career. I felt that there was little room for me to grow in the sales and trading arena, and I wanted to find a new challenge. I had developed an interest in broader areas of investment than just fixed income, and I had started to explore asset allocation and investment planning topics on my own some years before. I wanted to move in that direction. I had also had a long-standing interest in the nonprofit sector as well as a strong affinity for my b-school alma mater. Amazingly, the ideal job found me—helping to invest Stanford's endowment fund, which was then about $4 billion.

For me, working at Stanford was a great way to demonstrate my love for the institution and to give back to it. It's great to be part of a university community. When you invest well and bring in higher than average gains for the endowment, the university has more money to spend on things like financial aid and cancer research. How inspiring is that? I worked on a number of things, including asset allocation, currency, and building up their hedge fund program. I was fortunate to learn a great deal in a relatively few years. It was like going back to school and getting another master's degree. In 1998, I was promoted to chief investment officer and oversaw the entire endowment for the next three years during the peak of the stock market and technology bubbles and in their aftermath. We worked hard to preserve the endowment's value as the market declined and we were pretty successful, which is very gratifying.

When the leadership of the university turned over, it was time for me to reevaluate. Should I stay on or seek a new challenge? I had a wonderful opportunity to start a new business with some great partners that would take the kind of investment program we had started at Stanford and make it available to other institutions through a fund of funds. This would add the challenge of being an entrepreneur and building something new to the challenge of investing (and investing well is always a challenge). I chose to embrace the new challenge, though I was sad to leave good friends behind.

My new venture, at Aetos Capital, is the perfect job for me at the perfect time. First, starting a business presents a whole new set of challenges. A start-up puts a huge premium on picking your people well. There is pressure to accomplish a lot of things at once, whether it is signing up clients or building the infrastructure to invest their assets or selecting a team of seasoned professionals and then getting them to work under tight deadlines. Here the great challenge is to manage people in a very intense environment and do great investing at the same time. It's a wonderful challenge to have, so I consider myself very fortunate. This job blends all of my skills. At Goldman Sachs, I learned a lot about trading and marketing. At Stanford, I worked a lot on the investing side. Here at Aetos Capital I work with both, and it gives me a lot of professional satisfaction.

At this point in my career, I have learned a few things that I'd like to share. First and foremost, learn everything you can—take hard courses, seek knowledge, broaden your horizons as much as possible. Working at Stanford, I had a huge learning curve to go through with so many different ways to invest—hedge funds, venture capital, leveraged buyouts, etc. It was like trying to drink from a fire hose. There were days when my head was packed full with information and I couldn't take in any more, but it was exhilarating while it built my skills.

Don't be afraid of trying something new. I have a real interest in science and technology now, and I'm sorry that I didn't study that in college. It's a fact that, in this day and age, science and technology are a part of your daily life whether you like it or not. Women in this country don't study enough math and science. We need to do that in order to be fully empowered.

The other advice I would give is to keep options open. Don't foreclose opportunities for the future. Also, cultivate people and relationships. The best way to do that is to generally not worry about what other people can do for *you*, but what you can do for *them*. There will be a surprising payback one day. Also, it is important to demonstrate your capabilities. In investment banking, when I started out, it was a struggle for women to attain a level of responsibility that would reveal their capabilities. It has gotten better but it's still not perfect. Look for positions that will be visible and will allow you to show what you can do. Be as close to the center of the action as you can. Opt for line responsibilities as opposed to support functions. Also, try to find ways to develop your skills at managing other people. If you advance in your career, you will surely need those skills.

And some life advice: I've learned that life is enriched by giving back to the community. My mother and father exemplified this way of living. Throughout his career, my father devoted part of his medical practice to treating poor people for free, and my mother was an active volunteer in many activities. Education is a real passion of mine; I have been a fund-raiser for my college, for my business school, and for a new library in San Francisco. I am also a Board member for KQED Public Broadcasting. When you discover what you're passionate about, volunteer, be a board member, send a check—do whatever you can to give back.

JACKI HOFFMAN-ZEHNER

After graduating from the University of British Columbia, Canada, Jacki joined Goldman Sachs in 1988 as an analyst in the Mortgage-Backed Securities Department. At the beginning of 1990 she began her trading career, and in 1996, at the age of 32, she was the youngest woman, and first female trader, to be invited into the partnership of the firm.

> "The list of people who positively influenced me at Goldman Sachs is a long one. It was the care and attention that they showed to my professional development that motivated me to do it for others."

The Goldman Sachs Fixed Income trading floor consisted of rows upon rows of long wooden desks, lined up to maximize the use of floor space and minimize the distance between the traders and salespeople it housed. If two people yawned at the same time, their arms could easily touch. It was a place were it was hard to keep secrets, and even harder to hide emotions. My one safe place was the last stall in the ladies' rest room, a place I affectionately called my office, where I would often go when the pressures of the trading floor threatened an explosion of tears. However, being one of the few women in a male-dominated workplace, it was an unwritten rule that we females had to learn to control such explosions.

Nevertheless, in my early years, I used my office a lot. Whether driven there by an obnoxious fellow trader, or an overdemanding salesperson, or simply because the weight of responsibility I felt committing the firm's capital merely grew too heavy on any particular day, my office became a safe haven. Despite popular opinion, I never thought of crying as a weakness; it was just my way of releasing the stress I felt from working in such an environment. Traders, however, were always looking for reasons to tease or torture one another, and had I allowed myself to cry at my desk, I would have made an easy target. In hindsight, I often took things too personally those first couple of years. Over time

I learned that some people are just plain nasty, while others use yelling and humiliation as their way of releasing stress. More importantly, I learned that there are times to fight back, and other times when you just have to let it go.

My first few years as a trader were both exciting and yet extremely challenging. The challenge was that no one could really teach you to be a good trader; you truly had to learn it. Learning meant making mistakes, recovering, and trying not to make those same mistakes again. The method of teaching was, and still is today, an apprenticeship system. You sit beside more experienced traders and try to absorb how they go about making decisions. To be a trader meant that you had to make decisions based on limited information that put the firm's capital at risk and that took some getting used to. My parents taught me that money had tremendous value and thus managing it was a big responsibility, especially when it was not your own. I was fortunate that the stress I felt was not often related to actually losing money, but rather the fear of losing it. Hard work, asking a lot of questions, and listening to the opinions of my customers all contributed to improving my judgment, which over time made me a more confident market maker.

Three years into my trading career, I began trading a particular sector of the mortgage market: 15-year pass-through securities. Trading a sector of the bond market was much like running your own small business, where you have a product that you buy and sell on behalf of your clients. The clients of Goldman Sachs were typically institutional—meaning pension funds, mutual funds, banks, insurance companies, government agencies, and hedge funds—not private individuals. Within the fixed income sphere, the mortgage market comprised an exceptionally large asset class, and therefore trades valued at a hundred million dollars or more were quite common and relatively easy to price. As a trader you would come to know which salespeople called on accounts that were capable of trading in large "size," and much effort was spent cultivating those relationships to ensure that you would be the one to get the call when a large trade was at hand.

One of Goldman's most prominent salespeople was a man affectionately known as "The Big Guy" due to the size of trades he did for his clients. He was a generation older then I was, but from day one he treated me like an equal. Although a gifted relationship manager with his clients, with the trading desk he was usually all business. He had a job to do, which was to get as much business in the Goldman door as possible, and he did that by delivering competent trade execution and outstanding advice. When he needed a mortgage trader to price a trade he would usually call over on an internal phone line because his desk was at the opposite end of the trading floor.

Everyone knew his deep, somewhat gravelly voice, so all he would have to say would be, "Jacki, pick-up" around the floor loudspeaker system, and I would jump to the line that connected the mortgage trading desk to his sales position. Although The Big Guy occasionally took a lap around the floor just to stretch his legs or chat about the prior night's Knicks game, for him to get up from his desk to walk over to the other side of the floor usually meant something special—a huge trade. Therefore, when the The Big Guy was on the move, all the traders would turn, hoping they were the stopping point.

One day, which started out feeling like any other day, The Big Guy's half-lap around the floor ended with him dropping down in the chair next to mine. Although I immediately turned to give him a welcoming nod, I pointed to my headset to let him know that I was on a call and would be off in a second. As I disconnected the call and removed my headset to give The Big Guy my full attention, he leaned forward with a slight smile on his face and quietly said, "Jacki, this is as big as it gets." I am sure he saw me jump slightly, but he did not break his gaze as he calmly explained what he wanted me to do. He asked me to sell to one client, looking to make a large asset allocation into my little piece of the mortgage universe, over a billion bonds in a variety of issues. I immediately turned my attention back to my computer so I could check on the availability of the bonds in question to see if such a large trade was even possible. Together we determined what particular bonds and in what size we could sell to the client. He needed to return to his desk to call the client back to let them know we would provide them with prices for the full size of the trade. The Big Guy was never one of the ones who yelled. Instead, with his quiet yet confident approach, one nod was all that was needed to convey his respect for my position despite my age and level of experience. "Call me when you have the prices, but don't take too long," he said, and with that he turned and walked back to his desk.

Although I kept my focus on working on the prices, I quickly realized that this trade represented an incredible long-term opportunity to define myself within the marketplace, not to mention an incredible opportunity to make, or lose, a significant amount of money for the firm. Almost immediately, my focus was interrupted by another trader who was just returning to his desk across the aisle. His job was to create structured bond offerings using mortgages as the underlying collateral for the offering and thus was always asking traders to provide information to him so he could work on the deals. This guy was a self-described Wall Street Hitter: big paycheck, fast cars, huge apartment, and an ego to match. He was extremely talented and very charismatic and loved to be at the center of attention.

On the trading desk, however, it is all about setting priorities, because you cannot be all things to all people every minute of the day, and at this particular moment I needed to focus on my career-making trade. Without acknowledging that I looked busy, this trader demanded my attention to help him to start working on a deal. I responded anxiously, saying that I was working on a trade and would get back to him, and then I turned back to my computer screen. Feeling that he was a better judge of my priorities than I, The Hitter decided to take his bad day out on me and picked up the phone which amplified his voice over the trading floor PA system and loudly said, "Excuse me, everyone, but our 15-year trader cannot do two things at once, so I cannot work on pricing a CMO deal for you currently. My opinion is that she might well be in the wrong profession." With a smug grin he spat at me with his eyes, and turned his back before I had a chance to respond. Smelling raw meat, the other lions in the den took their cue to start circling with their little add-ons, which I painfully tried to tune out. I just could not be called into battle at that moment, as my energy and attention was urgently needed somewhere else. I desperately wanted to run to my "office," but that had to wait.

Within 10 minutes I had come up with the prices, consulted with my desk, and called The Big Guy to relay them. I was confident that the client would be happy with the prices, and assuming that the trade would happen, my focus needed to shift to how to hedge the transaction. Hanging up the phone, I walked toward my attacker and responded to his far less than urgent request. He could tell I was upset by his teasing and chose to acknowledge it by laughing at me as if to say, "What's the matter girl, can't you take it?" I was not going to let him off the hook that easily, nor was I going to engage. "You respect me; I respect you; that is what we as professionals of this firm are called to do. Don't you ever treat me like that again." Burning with pent-up anger, as I turned to return to my seat, I heard the comforting voice of The Big Guy over the trading PA system saying, "Jacki, the trade is done." Turning back for a second to face the abuser, I said to myself, "Damn right I was done."

For the remaining hours in the trading day, I actively maneuvered to reduce the risk of the trade I had just completed. I traded up a storm. Never before had I done more transactions in a single day or traded so much volume. My adrenaline level was running incredibly high as I tried to capture some profitability of the trade by buying back what I could of what I had sold, without making it apparent to traders at other firms that such a large trade had happened. Though I ended the day with a huge amount of risk left to reduce, I felt very confident that this trade would end up being a good one for the client as well as for the firm. Never before had I felt so completely and professionally exhilarated. It was the trade of a lifetime, entrusted to me by one of the most talented and respected fixed income salespeople ever on The Street.

At the end of my trading frenzy, I retreated to my "office" and completely lost it. For a good 10 minutes I cried until the well had run dry. I had to release the stress of executing the largest trade of my career, while at the same moment experiencing undeserved humiliation. It wasn't until I patted my last tear dry that the smile crept onto my face. At that moment, sitting on a toilet seat in the last stall of the Goldman Sachs trading floor ladies' rest room, I knew I was a bond trader, a good one, and that I would make it on Wall Street. I flashed back to so many memories of everything it took to get me where I was: hard-working parents who were such role models, professors who cared that I learned, athletic pursuits that fed my competitive spirit, a deep-rooted feminist spirit that always whispered to me that I belonged anywhere a man did. All these factors that shaped my character and helped me to build the skills I needed in life to survive had been called into play those past five hours. It was a test, and I had passed.

Pulling myself out of my IMAX moment and back into reality, I finally felt OK enough to leave my office. A mortgage salesperson and friend was at the sink putting on her lipstick as I opened the stall door. "Rough day?" she asked. "You might say that," I responded, "But worth it."

Throughout my career at Goldman Sachs, individuals like The Big Guy, whose real name is Frank Coulson, were there to shape me professionally and enable me to develop the skills I needed to succeed as a Wall Street trader. Frank taught me that every person deserves to be treated with respect, regardless of age, experience, or "rank," and that investing time and energy in developing deep client relationships is the key to long-term success.

There were others who taught me, by way of their actions, what it means to be a good professional and a good person. My first manager, Tom Lasersohn, taught me that good leaders are good teachers. Tom was a brilliant tax attorney by training and yet was able to explain even the most complicated transactions in a way that a first-year analyst could understand. His patience was endless, as he knew that the better we analysts were at our jobs, the better we did as a department. More than that though, he truly cared about our professional development and making the work we did interesting to us. His sleeves were always rolled up ready to do the work and not just delegate it.

Michael Mortara, the head of the Mortgage Group when I first joined the firm and later head of the Fixed Income Division, paved the way for my success through his support and encouragement. Although he was my most senior manager, he got involved, and thus was able to give me counsel when I most needed it. Few traders make money all the time, and I distinctly remember that the first time I was having a really bad month Michael called me from Tokyo, where he was on business, to talk about it. Every trading position I had seemed to be losing money, but instead of calling me to brutally interrogate me as to why I could be so wrong, he gently questioned me about the conviction I had regarding my positions. He knew this was my first experience in having a truly bad month and that I was there late into the evening every night trying to figure out how to turn the ship around. At the end of a very long, empowering discussion, he just said, "I trust your judgment, Jacki, keep the trades on." Those are some of the most comforting words ever given to a young professional: "I trust you." Michael knew that no one could be harder on me than myself, so being heavy handed when I made mistakes was just not necessary.

Michael, a larger than life, legendary bond trader schooled in the eighties at Solomon Brothers, always acknowledged that it was likely not easy to be one of just a few women traders on Wall Street. I always felt he was rooting for me to succeed. Because I was not "one of the guys," he was a little different with me. He encouraged me to be true to myself and not worry too much about "being one of the guys." By regularly checking in with me to make sure I was okay, he opened the door to talk to him about situations that were challenging. First his advice and then his friendship, over my 14-year career at Goldman, were priceless.

Ann Kaplan, today a best friend, but in the early nineties one of only two women partners in the Fixed Income Division, showed me that it was my job as a woman to support other women. Because I was recognized early as a "high-potential" she made it her business to know me, even though I did not work for her. Ann was in my corner without my even knowing it. She felt as I do that Goldman had to ensure that doors were open to talented women and that their representation in the senior ranks of the firm were critical to the long-term success of the firm. She led the firm's early diversity initiatives, even though such efforts were not always career enhancing. Bottom line, she cared about people and making the firm a better place to work. At the end of the day, it is all about character, and that is Ann Kaplan.

The list of people who positively influenced me at Goldman Sachs is long indeed. It was the care and attention that they showed to my professional development as I moved up the ladder that motivated me to do it for others. A *trailblazer* describes someone who is a pioneer, who clears a new path, and although I did that in terms of being one of the first women trading desk heads, much of my trail was cleared by those who showed me such incredible support along the way. That is what made Goldman Sachs such an incredible place for so long. People cared about each other and worked together to bring out the best in one another.

3

ADVENTURERS

A woman who climbed the highest peaks on six continents and went on to lead the first-ever American Women's Everest Expedition, after surviving two major heart surgeries before the age of 31. Another woman who traveled with Bedouins in the desert, sold paintings door-to-door in Australia to raise enough money to complete her "solo" trip around the world, and qualified for the World Championships in Women's Rowing, all while completing her BA degree and two advanced law degrees before the age of 24. This same woman, 20 years later, would look back on a life filled with both professional successes and failures, personal triumph and unthinkable tragedy, and conclude: "I have an overwhelming capacity to move forward." Another woman who had never left Alabama until she was 21 and who today has earned an MBA, works for an investment bank, and has traveled to 42 countries. Another woman who was orphaned at age 7, later emigrated from East Germany to America, lived on welfare, took a job as a "temp" that would turn into a 30-year career in financial services, and who, as she prepared to turn 60, would run marathons and climb mountains with her daughter. And a young woman who recently left her analyst position with a premiere global investment bank to teach young children in Nepal at a school that was funded and built as part of the expedition led by the first woman described above.

What defines and drives women like these? What motivates them to envision and then conquer challenges way outside the "normal limits" of what others just unquestioningly accept and never try to push beyond, either in their careers or their lives? I believe it has a lot to do with the very concept of adventure, of having a *true spirit of adventure*. Adventure by its very nature involves risk. It's supposed to be hard. It's supposed to be uncertain. It's supposed to be daunting and sometimes overwhelming. But it's also supposed to be *exciting*. To be exhilarating. And ultimately to be self-defining.

In a recent landmark three-year study entitled *Women in Financial Services: The Word on the Street* (published by Catalyst, the leading nonprofit research organization for the advancement of women in business), 85 Broads was the only independent network recognized for its "best practices in creating internal and external networks of women and people of color." In this same study, Catalyst found that "large majorities of women cite several barriers to women's advancement in their firms"—including exclusion from informal networks of communication, lack of mentoring opportunities, and lack of role models—while most men "only cite women's commitment to family and lack of line or general management experience."

What was really fascinating about this was how different the reality described by Catalyst was from how it *felt* to be part of 85 Broads. We never focused on "barriers" because we never created any, at least not within the network itself. For us it wasn't so much about removing barriers as it was about creating positive change for women in every part of our lives and careers by connecting with each other. As our mission statement has said from the very start,

> "The value of 85 Broads is derived from a very simple but compelling principle. Our focus is extraordinarily positive and our mission is to create a global community of truly exceptional women who define success on their own terms, both personally and professionally."

I believe that these are two incredibly powerful elements of adventure that go hand in hand: a "no barriers" mindset and a completely positive, forward-looking community to embrace change.

One of the people I admire most is Kathleen Kennedy Townsend, former Lieutenant Governor of Maryland and eldest child of Bobby and Ethel Kennedy, who truly embodies these two "adventurer" qualities. Kathleen has spoken at a number of our 85 Broads events, but her speech at one of our first global events—"What's Your Destiny?"—really captured the essence of these qualities as she lives them in her own life:

> "I hope that what community does is to help you believe in yourselves, to help one another succeed, and to say to

yourselves that you can do great things. That you can be who you wanted to be when you dreamed of something fabulous when you were young. It's hard to dream. You're here because you're successful, but I would be surprised if not each and every one of you…in some sense has limits in your life or your career. Something is stopping you from being who you can be, from using the capacities you've been given and that you've developed. So I hope, and my experience has been, that when you find good friends who, like you, are searching for the good, you will do great things. And when you do, you will accomplish something so important, not only for yourselves, but for your sisters, and your sisters here at 85 Broads. Because when one of you succeeds, all of us do. Each of us is lifted up. And that's what community is at its best."

Following your own "destiny" is another attribute that is at the heart of adventure. One of the most powerful and courageous voices any of us can listen to is our own, but it is often the one that many women spend the least time cultivating and tuning into as we yield to the demands and perceived "boundaries" of our professional and personal lives. But this is not the case for adventurers. For them, pushing beyond those boundaries is what defines their destiny and creates their passion. At our "What's Your Destiny?" event it was also incredible (but not at all surprising really) to see how the 400-plus women of 85 Broads in attendance—successful professionals, entrepreneurs, and graduate business students—so closely related to the story of a very humble man whose life has been defined by destiny and adventure. Alan Chambers, another extraordinary individual I greatly admire, is a former British Royal Marine who led the first British team to successfully walk entirely unsupported and completely on their own to the North Pole (for which he was made a member of the Order of the British Empire, MBE). Here is an excerpt from his speech at our "What's Your Destiny?" event in May 2001:

> "The aim of my dream was to walk completely unsupported to the North Pole. Why? Why not! I used it as a challenge, and I used it as an opportunity. Everyone else who ever tried to do it had failed. But *why* had they failed? I researched the last 25 years of the history of

those expeditions to find out what the reasons were for their failures, and then I built an antidote into my plan for every single one. Because when I was ready to launch myself into what they called 'the hardest expedition'— the horizontal Everest—I wanted to make sure I had given myself and my team the best possible chance to succeed. And even though I spent five years preparing to meet this challenge, the critics, the old armchair explorers, and all the people who had tried before only gave me a ten percent chance of success."

The life-threatening obstacles which confronted Alan and his team during their 70-day historic trek to the geographic North Pole put the "career issues and challenges" that many of us tend to become preoccupied with into a much greater perspective. Overcoming these obstacles and managing the inherent risks of any adventure require extraordinary preparation, execution, and adaptability. These are also the hallmarks of adventurers. The higher-profile thrills, risks, and potential rewards of adventuring are matched with the far less glamorous qualities of patience, planning, persistence, and plain hard work—qualities we will see in our own adventurers' stories.

These thoughts were echoed by another world adventurer and former Royal Marine, Pete Goss, at our next global network event titled "What's Your Gift?"

"As adventurers, we are obviously attracted to high-risk challenges, but we want to embrace the risks on our own terms. We will undoubtedly make a few mistakes no matter how meticulous our plan, but we want to be able to manage the risks, learn from the mistakes, and move forward."

Looking ahead and moving forward by using the past to teach you and make you stronger—not constrain or weaken or limit you—is key to developing an adventurer's outlook. Or as Pete would say: "You always have two choices. You give up. Or you roll up your sleeves and get on with it."

This is a topic Pete Goss knows something about, having competed in four transatlantic and two round-the-world sailing races, including the prestigious and perilous Vendee Globe, a four-month, nonstop solo race through the treacherous waters and unpredictable climate of the Southern Ocean. It was in the 1996–97 Vendee Globe that Pete would abandon his quest to win the race and fight his way back over 160 nautical miles during one of the fiercest storms ever on record to dramatically rescue fellow competitor Raphael Dinelli, whose boat had capsized and was unreachable by any other means. (For this Pete was awarded the MBE and the French Legion D'Honneur.) In recalling those events for 85 Broads, Pete told us that "experts reckoned that Raphael had about 10 hours to live when I finally dragged him on board the Aqua Quorum....I will never forget his eyes at that moment. You have no idea the depth of emotion and gratitude you can see in a pair of eyes. You *can* literally see right into somebody's soul."

Pete Goss's message and manner of adventure, like that of Alan Chambers, captivated and inspired the members of 85 Broads as we spent the day finding our own unique answers to the question "What's Your Gift?" In describing his decision to turn back and risk his life to rescue a fellow competitor, as well as his team's quest to push the envelope and "challenge the norm," Pete touched on two more defining attributes of adventurers: *values* and *attitude*. About values, Pete had this to say:

> "When you do an ocean race, there is always one bad storm. You instinctively know it when it comes along... and this, without question, was going to be the big storm of the Vendee Globe. Within a three-hour period the winds went from a northerly 20-knot breeze around to the southwest, straight up to 40, 50, and then 60 knots of wind. I was hurdling through completely unpredictable seas at the slowest speed I could manage—28 to 30 knots! Imagine big breaking waves—just like you might see on a beach, except they are *six stories high*—picking your boat up and throwing it on its side, over and over again....
>
> Amidst all this I crawled down below to my email/ satellite system, which was beeping an alarm. I retrieved the message from the system and it was a mayday. Everybody asks me what I was thinking when I got that mayday. Well, I can tell you, I thought, 'damn ... just what I need.' Talk about timing! I found a chart. I wiped the water off it. I put a fix down on the position to find it was one of my fellow competitors, Raphael Dinelli. Unfortunately for him, he was 160 miles away and, even worse, he was dead upwind in now what were hurricane-force

conditions. And again, a lot of people ask me about the decision to turn around. I can tell you, it was very simple. In fact, I don't really think it was my decision. I think it was laid down many, many years ago by a tradition of the sea. If someone is in trouble, then you help them. That's it. It is black and white. And yet, I sat down and I thought about it for 30 seconds, perhaps a minute—I'm not sure, there was a lot going on—and I considered the consequences of the decision.

You think about your boat, you think about your family, you think about your life. I found that if you keep 'chipping away' at your life, then you come to a very clear and simple crossroads—you either stand by your morals and principles or you don't. It just popped up like a flag at that moment, and it is one of the most important lessons I have ever learned in life. *Your values are all you have.* You have nothing else. If you are stripped bare on a stage, it is your values that you are left with—as an individual, as a team, as a business, as a company, whatever it might be. You need to understand them, you need to know them, you need to live them, and you need to be able to look in that mirror in the morning. *Nothing is more important in leadership and in life.* Values are your final touchstone."

And Pete's description of *attitude* summed it up perfectly for the members of our network:

"The key to our team, just like 85 Broads, is *attitude.* Is the glass half full or is the glass half empty? 'Well,' we would say, 'drink the bastard anyway.' It is all about attitude, isn't it? And as you well know, when you challenge the norm with something big and something different, it will always be controversial. There will *always* be speculation and second-guessing. But we are prepared to put our neck on the block to try it. *We are prepared to take the risk.*"

The women whose stories we are about to hear are definitely "prepared to take the risk," and they all live and breathe the qualities we've just talked about—whether climbing mountains, running races, starting new businesses, raising children, or teaching in classrooms worlds away from their homes and families. They each share the adventurer's courageous spirit, sense of community, positive mindset, work ethic, dedication to values, and uncompromising attitude—all in pursuit of the destiny they have defined for themselves. And most of all they want to leave a legacy, something that outlasts the adventure itself. Something of greater value than simply reaching the goal, planting the flag, or leaving behind passing symbols of their accomplishments. They want to create something that helps and empowers others—something that passes the torch to the next generation of adventurers.

ALISON LEVINE

Alison worked in the Goldman Sachs Private Wealth Management Group for three years and was given a two-month leave of absence to lead the first American Women's Everest Expedition in the spring of 2002. Today she is a motivational speaker, consultant, and "adventure philanthropist."

"I climbed Everest to send a message about getting out there and going for it!"

It wasn't until after my second heart surgery that I became interested in climbing. I was 31 years old and I felt like I wanted to go out and do all kinds of things I would not have been able to do before because I was born with a rare heart disorder called Wolff-Parkinson-White Syndrome. After my surgery I challenged myself in ways I had never thought possible. I started climbing about 18 months after the second operation and within a few years I had climbed the highest mountains on six continents.

In February 2001, I was working for Goldman Sachs and was transferred to their San Francisco office. It was a tough time to be in the financial services industry. Morale was low and stress was high. I needed to focus 100 percent on my job, but in the back of my mind, I was really missing the mountains!

Funny how life works though. Six months later, I got an invitation to be part of a women's expedition to climb Mt. Everest. Wow! This was an opportunity I knew climbers would drool all over themselves for, but instead it just put a knot in my stomach, because I was 99 percent sure I couldn't come up with the two things I needed in order to make this really happen (1) the funding and (2) the time off from work. "People would kill for this job…people would kill for this job…" is what I kept telling myself. I thought about how hard it was for me to get the job—getting a good GMAT score, getting into a good MBA program, going through the interview process, working my tail off as a summer intern. I was afraid that if I even asked for the time off I'd sabotage my own career by giving management the impression that I was not very focused on the job and wasn't serious about my career. When people ask me what the scariest moment of my Everest trip was, I always tell them it was definitely standing in my boss's office asking for the time off.

Whoever said that people in investment banking aren't cool had never met my boss, Jim Milligan. He agreed to give me the leave of absence I would need to lead the expedition. Oh, but there was one more small detail—the funding. The American Women's Everest Expedition sort of needed a few hundred thousand dollars. We had to start fund-raising immediately. Without warning, the tragedy of September 11th occurred. At that point I thought our trip was not going to happen as the world was focused on war, terrorism, and global economic downturn. It just did not feel right to me to be fund-raising for an Everest climb when there were so many other things going on that needed America's attention.

Everyone involved thought it best to call off our climb. We didn't feel that it was appropriate to be asking for corporate sponsorship at that time. However, when the dust settled, I thought to myself: "Okay, now more than ever there needs to be a team of American women on Everest." I wanted to send a message to the world that we, as American women, were not going to let fear get the best of us. We were not going to stop living our lives and pursuing our dreams. No way! I knew it was still bad timing, but thought, "Hey, it's not a good time, but that's exactly why we should do it now." We thought it was a good message to send to America and to the rest of the world.

Although I had permission to take the time off and the other women on the team wanted to make the trip happen, it was still a complete long shot because we had a very short window of time to find the funding. Normally, people start planning an Everest expedition two or three years before the trip actually happens. We had less than seven months. To make matters more complicated and more stressful, I had decided to do the climb as a tribute to one of my all-time favorite sports figures, basketball coach Jim Valvano, also known as "Jimmy V," who died of cancer in 1993. So in addition to trying to get corporate sponsorship to cover the costs of our expedition, I was also fund-raising for a cancer research organization called the V Foundation that was founded by ESPN and Jimmy V before he died. I didn't want to just climb for the sake of climbing. I wanted to do it in a way that would have some impact, some kind of lasting effect. So, I was approaching corporations for sponsorship money for the team, and then I was approaching individuals to help me raise the money for the cancer research grant.

The pressure built as the clock ticked away toward our funding deadline. I was running on fumes. I'd go into the ladies' room and cry during the day just because I was so completely exhausted and was totally stressed that it was the 11th hour and we still did not have the funding for the team. And then came the magic phone call from Janet Hanson. She was the founder of 85 Broads, an organization I had heard of but knew nothing about. She basically said to me, "I understand you want to raise money to put a team of American women on Everest. You have three minutes to tell me your story. Go!" I don't even remember what I blurted out. All I remember is hearing her voice on the phone telling me that she was going to personally send me a check for $10K on behalf of the 85 Broads network to help me get started, and on top of that she was going to help me try to find additional sources of funding. Boom! That was it! That was all I needed to change my outlook on the situation. One little glimmer of hope that maybe I could pull this off. This woman had never heard of me, had never met me, had never previously talked to me, yet after three minutes she believed in me. At that point I started believing in me too! I just needed someone in my corner, working with me and supporting me instead of telling me it was a bad time, it was a bad idea, and that I should just hang up my ice ax for awhile and try again next year.

I soon turned into the consummate networker. If you didn't get a call from me asking for money it was only because I didn't have your phone number. I finally struck gold through Kevin Ropp, a friend from business school. Kevin worked for Ford Motor Company, and he agreed to funnel our idea up through the organization for me. In December 2001, Ford agreed to be our sponsor, and they wanted to sponsor the *entire climb*! All of those hours I put into the search for corporate funding had finally paid off. I went back to Janet and thanked her profusely and told her we didn't need her $10K anymore because I had secured 100 percent of our funding from Ford. She still wanted to find a way to help. We brainstormed on how the 85 Broads network could be involved with the climb. We decided to use her money to help girls in Nepal get an education since the illiteracy rate there is over 80 percent. Through 85 Broads' philanthropic organization, Miles to Go, we donated money to Room to Read and funded the construction of two new schools. The schools would be named "The 85 Broads Schools" and I would be part of the groundbreaking ceremony just as soon as I got back down the mountain. Things just kept getting better. Now that I knew I was for sure going to Everest, I could go all out in trying to help the V Foundation. More networking saved the day. Dukebasketballreport.com put a story about my fund-raising efforts on their Web site and I started to get donations from all over the country. Now I was well on my way to funding that research grant. I breathed a huge sigh of relief. I think I celebrated by treating myself to five hours of sleep that night. I considered that the ultimate in pampering.

In March 2002, we began our climb. Mt. Everest's summit is 29,035 feet above sea level, and the climb would take us approximately two months. Many of the major media outlets—CNN, CNBC, Fox, NBC, etc.—were tracking our every step and millions of people at home were cheering for us, watching our daily ascent. Discovery Channel was posting dispatches from the mountain on their Web site every few days. People from all over the world were sending us emails supporting us, which really helped keep our spirits high throughout the entire trip. I always knew climbing was the ultimate test of teamwork. The people on this trip were amazing. There was not one day when the women did not get along with each other, which is really amazing given the amount of time we spent together and the stressful conditions that Mt. Everest can throw at you.

After about seven weeks of eating bad food, living in a tent, dealing with altitude sickness, and using makeshift ice toilets, we were positioned to go for the summit. And, as with many an Everest expedition, ours was not without drama. After climbing throughout the entire night, a crazy storm blew in at 6:30 in the morning when the team was just 270 feet from the tippy top. That's less than a football field. But no one felt comfortable continuing in those conditions. Trust me, at that point it is harder to turn around than it is to keep going, especially given all of the work and sacrifice that went into putting the trip together. We knew people all over the world were following us, and we didn't want to disappoint anyone. But using good judgment never disappoints people. You always have to think about potential consequences, and for our team the risk was just not worth it. No way. It's the same as in the business world—good decision making is critical. You have to know when to walk away, even when you've come really far and you feel like you are oh-so-close to closing the deal.

I was back at my desk at 6 a.m. the morning after I returned from Nepal. As scary as it sounds, I missed the office and wanted to get back to work. I did not miss the actual job as much as I missed the people in my office and the "normal" human interaction. I realized immediately after my return that being at really high altitudes affects your brain. I was climbing above 28,000 feet without supplemental oxygen for about a half hour on summit day when there was a problem with my oxygen tank, and this took a toll on my gray matter. When I was driving to work I actually forgot how to get to my office. I had been driving there for two years, and now I couldn't remember what street to turn down to get to our building. When I finally got there, people were coming up to me and congratulating me, and I couldn't remember people's names. I forgot my work phone number. I also forgot which side of the car my gas tank was on, and I've had that car for 15 years. Spending a lot of time at high altitude takes a toll on your body and your mind, but luckily it is temporary. I think....

Shortly after my return from Everest my career took a really crazy detour. As soon as I got back I started getting phone calls from people who had seen us on TV or had read about the expedition. Over 450 media outlets covered the story of our climb, so we had more than our 15 minutes of fame if you add up all the minutes. The media exposure was something I often dreaded during the climb, as attempting to sound coherent during a live satellite video interview can distract you from your main goal—staying completely focused on not getting killed on a mountain. But apparently the hypoxia had a positive effect on me and somehow I must have said a few things that sounded enlightening or interesting, because corporations and other organizations began calling me and inviting me to come address their employees, executives, and clients. I started doing presentations for groups all over the country and talking to them about the parallels between climbing and the business world. The skills you need to be successful in the mountains are really no different from many of the skills you need to be successful in corporate America: leadership, building successful teams, dealing with a changing environment, decision making under pressure, and taking responsible risks.

In April 2003 I decided to leave Goldman Sachs so I could pursue a full-time career in public speaking and focus on combining two of my passions—adventure travel and philanthropy. I wanted to find a way to change the world through adventure, which eventually led to the founding of my nonprofit, the Climb High Foundation. Even though I was excited about this new path, I had a bit of a heavy heart when I left Goldman because I really loved the firm and the people; it was just the job itself I did not love. But the great thing about the transition was that Goldman became my first client. They hired me to speak at events for internal employees as well as at events for institutional and private clients. I even had the honor of speaking at a global investment banking conference where the other keynote speaker they hired was Bill Clinton. It's great to be able to tell people that the former President was once my opening act! Now I have a long list of corporate clients and am able to earn a living as a keynote speaker while I continue to build the Climb High Foundation.

In the spring of 2004 I trekked to the geographic North Pole. I went on this adventurous journey representing the 85 Broads Network. I went with a team of 13 Brits who were all successful businesspeople and who also happened to be amazingly strong athletes. The trip was about two weeks and the challenge this time was the cold and the fact that the polar ice cap we were traveling across was breaking up very quickly. We'd get to these big passages of open water and we'd either have to wait for them to freeze or start walking in the opposite direction hoping to find a spot that was narrow enough for us to cross. The most frustrating thing, by far, was the ocean current. We'd spend 13 hours traveling 4 miles in one direction, only to find out that we'd drifted 5 miles in the opposite direction overnight. Mentally, that kind of thing just wears you down. Again I got lucky with an amazing team and everyone pulled together and kept each other focused and we made it! I was pretty psyched to be waving that 85 Broads banner right in front of Santa's house. And the best part of the trip is that we raised enough money to build an orphanage for Ugandan children who have speech and hearing impairments. (Most orphanages will not take kids who have disabilities; these kids probably would have been left in the streets to fend for themselves.) Another successful "adventure with impact."

After this experience, I wanted to do something even bigger with the Climb High Foundation. I wanted to find a way to use mountains and adventure to help women in developing countries, and thought Africa would be a good place for my next project. So, in 2005 I traveled to the Rwenzori Mountains, which border Uganda and the Congo. My goal was to get local women there started in the trekking/mountaineering industry. This war-torn area had been shut down for years due to border conflicts, and although the mountains were now open again, a decent amount of rebel activity continued to plague the region. I was traveling with one other woman, Nicole Dreon, and we had no idea what we'd encounter once we got there. We didn't know if any women would even be interested in working as porters or if they would be permitted to climb. Many Ugandans believe it is taboo for women to go to the mountains as the Rwenzoris are considered to be the home of their gods. I arranged meetings with the Mountain Club of Uganda, the head of the local village, and the head of Rwenzori Mountaineering Services (which is responsible for tourism operations in the Rwenzoris). They all seemed a bit skeptical about women going up the mountain, but they agreed to support our efforts.

Once word of our objective spread through the village, seven local women came forward and expressed a desire to train to work in the mountains. We negotiated with the head of Rwenzori Mountaineering and got them paying jobs as porters on our climb of Mt. Stanley (16,763?). This was the first time any of them would be earning a paycheck. After nine days of mud, steep rock, snow, and ice, *all the women porters completed the entire trekking circuit. They made history!* Although we celebrated like crazy when we finished the trip, it was a bittersweet ending because two days after we finished the climb, nine UN peacekeepers in the Congo were killed. But the Climb High Foundation successfully completed its first mission in Africa, and I hope to continue similar efforts throughout other parts of the world.

SUSAN PAYNE

By the age of 24, Susan received three honors degrees, a BA in English Literature, and an MA and LLB in Law. After becoming Head of Emerging Market Sales in Europe for JP Morgan, she joined Goldman Sachs as head of Sales and Trading, Emerging Markets, Europe. In 1996, she founded Emergent Markets Consultants and, in 1997, Emergent Asset Management.

> "Bucking trends is important to me. Bucking trends is actually what defines me."

I am startled awake around 3:00 a.m. The cold blade of a very long knife is pressed under my chin and my head is being held down by a rough hand that I cannot see in the darkness. The owner of the hand and the knife is now speaking Arabic in my ear. Where am I? It's coming back to me now. I'm sleeping in a park in a market town outside of Tel Aviv because I had returned late from a backpacking trip with my friend Eliot—a trek that had unexpectedly resulted in us living with a Bedouin tribe for the past week.

I had been both thrilled and terrified when we hopped into the open-topped, beaten-up jeep at Neweba, near Sharm el Sheik, Egypt, with two Bedouins who took us on a two-hour journey to live with their tribe in the desert. I would never have suspected anyone could live there. The silence in the desert was deafening, and I felt like I was at the ends of the earth. I admit that both Eliot and I were often fearful for our lives over the course of our visit. There were stories of others before us having disappeared doing the same kind of thing, including a woman who had been drugged and sold into slavery. But they treated us well, and despite barely being able to communicate, their remote and primitive existence would leave a lasting impression on me.

And at this moment, as the shadowy figure of a man wearing a balaclava (black facemask) and speaking in strained Arabic hovered over me, I desperately wished we were back among the Bedouins and the endless beach of Neweba. I cautiously stretched over with my free arm and shook Eliot beside me. He awoke slowly, rubbing his eyes. I wiggled my toes to check that my passport and money were still in the bottom of my bag and then gently pushed the man's hand away from my throat while I asked him to take the knife away. Eliot and I both sat up, both resting on our knees, with me cautiously rolling up my bag while explaining to Eliot what was going on. Thankfully, Eliot spoke limited Arabic and explained that we had no money on us. Quite a long discussion ensued, during which time it was clear that the man had already stolen the backpacks that we had been using as pillows. Eliot spoke with him surprisingly kindly and at length, explaining that the man had already taken all of our belongings and we had nothing left to offer. I sat quietly, praying that he would disappear into the darkness and not slit our throats. After what seemed an eternity, he left and we went directly to the police station. At daybreak, we returned to our sleeping spot and discovered the contents of our bags scattered widely in among the bushes, every last item picked over, some taken. A fascinating experience for an 18-year-old— surreal, bizarre, and, luckily, as with the Bedouin tribe, one that I survived.

Years after this adventure, I completed two law degrees, worked for large law firms over three summers, and knew that a career in law was unsuitable for me—not the least because it would tie me down too much to a particular location. I wanted to travel and I wanted to have work that was immediately more global than a legal career would allow. So what could I do instead? I didn't really understand how financial markets worked but, based on my travels, I was fascinated by international markets. I decided that instead of pursuing an MBA, the conventional route that was hugely popular in the 1980s, I would try to join a bank that had a strong training program and was committed to creating a positive work environment for women. I was very sensitive to this, even at 24 years of age; I did a lot of legwork and research on which firms were the most female friendly so that my decision wouldn't be by chance. Trawling through various magazine articles on finance, I found compelling and positive articles about JP Morgan and its culture. I sought the advice of a few businesswomen who were far more experienced than I was, and they each confirmed Morgan as a good choice. Morgan at least had some women at senior levels, whereas the other banks where I interviewed had virtually none.

I interviewed in Morgan's New York office first, and within about 10 minutes I made it clear that I wanted to be in London, not New York. They were supportive of this, and thereafter I flew over to London to be interviewed just 48 hours before I was scheduled to leave for six months on my around-the-world trip. I told them soon after arriving at their Angel Court offices in London, "I've had other offers, but I really want this job. I'm prepared to stay for the whole day, but I'm going to India in less than 48 hours and I would like an answer from you by that time." They interviewed me virtually all day, moving me from person to person, and then called me the next morning and said, "You've got the job." So I boarded the plane knowing that I had the job I wanted. I remember this distinctively because JP Morgan really acted quickly when I walked in there that morning. They stepped up to the plate and treated me extremely well, which I never forgot.

It turned out that Morgan was a fortuitous choice for me. It provided a very eclectic group of people and backgrounds, rather than a homogeneous environment, and there were quite a few women. When I say that, there were about seven women out of 75 people in my global intake. So we're not talking heavy percentages here, but given finance at the time, it was pretty impressive. I rotated through equities, syndicate, and fixed income before I joined the newly formed emerging markets desk, as one of eight people. It was exactly where I wanted to be. I was in the right spot at the right time, given my personal history and previous exposure to emerging economies. It was very important for me to work in these economies because I was fascinated by them: analyzing them, visiting them, and building a business around them. Our team of eight (six in New York, two in London) ultimately built the business from the ground up; we evolved from two people in the London office, located in the corner of a room and out of the mainstream in every sense. In fact, the business was initially so embryonic that we did not even belong to a division in London. By the time I left, the global group had become a real profit center for the bank with over 250 dedicated emerging markets staff, and I was Head of Sales, Emerging Markets, Europe.

On my first day at Morgan I met David Murrin, and it was definitely "interest at first sight." He had just come back from the jungle, having been working in oil exploration in Papua, New Guinea, and he was quite outspoken and highly individualistic. We've now lived together for 18 years but have never been married. I am very happy not to be married, because it suits my character; I don't like doing things that people expect me to do, especially as I do not think it would make any difference to us as a couple. It's the commitment that makes the difference. My parents have been married for over 55 years, yet only one of my three siblings ever decided to formally marry. Perhaps my parents' union, married or not, has prepared me to take risks in my life; perhaps this is what allows me the freedom of not seeking the security of the legal bonds of marriage. One of the people who had a huge impact on me was my tutor in family law at Oxford, the insightful Dr. Ruth Deech. She and I went through case study after case study in family law focusing on marriages that had failed. The patterns consistently repeated themselves—women who had devoted themselves exclusively to their families found they were left with low self-esteem and little or no money when their marriages broke up. Perhaps this is a warning that, in most relationships, it is not the legal obligation that counts but the equality within the relationship, including some degree of financial self-sufficiency of both parties.

The patterns of my life are still the same 18 years later: you rely on yourself, you make your own choices, you are responsible for your own life. You can't blame anyone else if your marriage or anything else fails. I think the things one feels most passionate about are the big issues around which there are no real choices, where there is only one path at a certain time, like launching a company or starting a family. This is one method I use to gauge my level of commitment: When there is no real choice in my own mind—there may be in others' minds but not in my own mind—when I am dedicated to a process, I know that there is no alternative other than to move forward toward that goal. I always look forward.

After eight years at JP Morgan, I accepted an offer to join Goldman Sachs International as Executive Director and Head of Sales and Trading, where I would be responsible for developing the European emerging markets fixed income trading desk from scratch. Two years later, after a clear peak at the firm and during a tough market cycle, Goldman cut back in a number of areas, including emerging markets. As I was committed to this area and believed strongly in building businesses that would endure through all market cycles, I decided the time had come to pursue the path I had been considering for some time: to launch an emerging markets hedge fund.

At one of the 85 Broads events we had in New York, one of our members said, "Don't underestimate the power of working for a top organization." It became crystal clear to me how important my experience at Morgan and Goldman had been when I set out to start my investment fund. I knew that new companies gain strength through structure. I made sure the structure was very securely in place, that the budget worked, that our philosophy and process for investing were sound. Hard work with no certain outcome. I was enthusiastic because I was offered the chance to be seeded by an outside group. With the financing in place, I secured an office, and then spent eight months completing all the regulatory registrations. During that time, I set up a consultancy company called Emergent Markets Consultants and I worked with banks that wanted to set up trading desks in emerging markets, as well as consulting on broader issues in emerging economies.

When I launched Emergent Asset Management with David and a small team in April of 1997, our highest priority was to deliver returns in a creative, alternative environment. We started with only $5 million. We made strong returns through the Asia crisis and were ranked #1 globally by S&P/Micropal in our first year and a half before the Russian crisis in August 1998. During this time, we turned down two allocations of close to $250 million total in assets because the terms attached to those assets did not suit our philosophy of running the company—investors come first. If those sizable funds we had been offered were to leave abruptly, we would have cannibalized our remaining investors. Many people who are offered that sum to manage in their first year would bite the hands off those who offered it, but we did not accept large allocations early on. Instead, we established a solid and diversified base structure, and then promoted the fund once the structure was in place. We were able to secure the right staff and we put together various products that we thought would suit investors' differing appetites, depending on what risk they were prepared to take. We're at the point now where we have funds in place, and we can now continue to grow those funds. In order to diversify our revenue stream, we are also developing a joint venture and distribution arm to work on specialist funds, as well as a strategic consulting think tank providing advice to corporates and investors on both market and non-market trends.

As yachtsman and adventurer Pete Goss told us at an 85 Broads event, "The heart of entrepreneurship is realizing that you will face obstacles—obstacles are what you see when you take your eyes off the goal." This is very true. One of the critical parts of building our company was to create a multifaceted organization but, just as importantly, to be committed in difficult periods to learning the lessons of hard times. *Difficult periods are defining, and will continually need to be faced in building any business.* We have had many of them. It's a matter of understanding what has happened, how it has happened, and what we can learn from our experiences, always maintaining the highest level of integrity.

Difficult periods have taught their lessons and left their mark on my personal life as well. Following a straightforward pregnancy and birth in 2000, in 2002, I experienced the trauma of hemorrhaging and almost dying due to delayed surgery for correcting an ectopic pregnancy. Then, in 2004, I had to be intubated after another horrendous pregnancy and premature delivery. But the greatest tragedy and most formidable challenge of my life came with the death of my second son, Kai. At just two weeks old, having been progressing very well, Kai died of an extremely rare stomach infection. What I went through with Kai's death is defining because, quite simply, the ache in losing one's child is indescribable. The line can often be so paper thin between life and death, and endings are not always rosy. At its core, this type of event crystallizes what matters most: family, personal integrity, following one's heart, the kindness of strangers—to name only a few. The irrelevances and irritations of daily life fade in experiences this profound.

The impact of Kai's death created a series of epiphanies for me: what is truly important now does not marry exactly with what was before; the standards of conduct I am willing to accept have changed; how to behave in a crisis when something of this magnitude happens to others (never back off); that one must trust one's instincts and one's intuition in every aspect of one's life, not just business; and, finally, that the resilience of humankind is astonishing, whatever burdens are faced, many far worse than mine. Repeatedly, I recalled the quote: "Hard times don't build character, they reveal it." This would prove itself to be true many times over throughout those painful days and months, in both myself and in others.

I will never forget the minutiae of Kai's life nor his death, specifically the day of his death in our arms; nor do I wish ever to "get over it." A parent can never get over it. I actually want to positively hang on to his memory even though that still translates into quite palpable pain, because he was a part of me and will be for the rest of my life. Any parent who has lost a child will understand exactly this sentiment.

What happens to many people after an experience like this, and what I would actively resist in myself, is the tendency to become fearful and to back off from taking any risks. I have a tremendous capacity for risk. It is in my nature, and I hope it remains. Actually, losing Kai reinforced this trait. I am quite prepared to face risk because I've been to the dark side and not just once. Recently, however, almost two years after Kai's death, David and I had twins, a boy and a girl. They are a constant and very human reminder that one must never stop at an impasse, however gaping.

Facing risks and taking on challenges, both professionally and personally, are basic to a self-fulfilling life. The premise of making our own independent choices is that we have to accept the possibility of loss or failure. Failure is not comfortable, but it is not a final destination. Honestly, boredom frightens me far more than failure. Though I aim to excel at what I undertake, I am prepared to fail and, if I do, examine closely what has happened to learn from it and then move on. Equally, I would say one of my strongest characteristics is an overwhelming capacity to look forward and actively, positively seek challenges in order to feel completely alive.

WONITA WILLIAMS

Wonita was 21 before she ever left Alabama. She got a passport when she was 22 and has now been to 42 countries. She graduated from Kellogg in 2005 with an MBA in Finance and Management and joined the Industrial Natural Resources Group at Goldman Sachs in New York.

> "It took me a long time to get here, but I came from farther away."

The library in Camden, Alabama, is located on the top floor of the courthouse, a large, stark red brick building with big white pillars and white trim. I got out of school at 3 p.m., walked to the library to do the little things they needed help with, then read everything I could get my hands on until it was time to close. Sitting on the floor of the dark, cold library, interpreting the world through old and new books, a whole new amazing world opened up to me.

My parents chose not to have television or radio in the house. Being fairly religious and wanting to protect their six children from the influences of popular culture, they kept pretty tight control over our environment. My curiosity drove me to look things up in atlases and encyclopedias. When I was about 12, I started reading the newspapers—*The Progressive Era*, the local Wilcox County newspaper, *The Selma Times*, and *The Atlanta Journal Constitution*. My daily explorations at the library exposed me to a lot of serious issues in the world. From the perspective of a young child in the rural south, current events seemed like science fiction. By middle school I was reading *The Wall Street Journal* and *Financial Times*, and already getting hungry for this great big world that I was discovering on the printed page.

In my town, for African-American students like me, graduating from high school was not an expectation, but I was fortunate to grow up in a household where education was important. My parents expected me to go to college. Having gone to a segregated high school (segregated because the black students went there and the white students went to private schools), it was a bit of a surprise to my family that I decided to go to the University of Alabama, a mixed-race school. I had actually wanted to go out of state, but my scholarships had to be used in state. Even so, leaving my very small town (population 2,100) and going an hour and a half away to Tuscaloosa was as scary as going to another country, and I felt like such a foreigner in that environment that I found it easier to relate to the international students. But with my hunger for the world and all of its people, these new friends were just what I was looking for.

Every year I invited a huge group of my international friends to experience an American Thanksgiving at my parents' home. This was not only a great cultural experience for my friends, but it brought the world to my parents. Since I asked everyone to bring something from their home country as a gift to my parents, they brought the world in a literal way too. One year we all got to use chopsticks, thanks to my Japanese friend. My parents had never seen chopsticks before. Now their home has all sorts of artifacts from other parts of the world!

Though my parents are very happy with their life in Wilcox County, I was not destined to get a master's of education and go back to Camden to teach as my mother had, and as she wished for me. I was desperate for more and I set ridiculous goals for myself. Though people were really supportive of me, I kept my plans quiet because I didn't want anyone to tell me to lower my expectations or to tell me I couldn't do it. And there were plenty of reasons for people to think that someone with my background couldn't do it.

I got my Master's in Accounting and Taxation from the University of Alabama in 1998 and began working at Pricewaterhouse Cooper. I traveled all over the country and discovered that when I introduced myself, no one could understand me because my accent was so thick. I took voice and diction lessons so I could communicate with my clients. That was a barrier I could remove, so I did my best to remove it.

One of the greatest barriers anyone can have is the voice inside them that says they can't succeed or something that convinces them to be satisfied with their circumstances when they haven't yet tried to change them. In my town, where the expectations are low, only a small percentage of the students who graduate from high school continue on to college. One might think that the barrier is funding, but that is usually not the case. There is plenty of scholarship money available for students to attend schools in Alabama. The problem is that the money often goes unused because there aren't enough people who have qualified for the assistance. The challenge is to get students in the right mindset, to believe that graduation from high school and going to college is for them, not for some extraordinary kids. Graduation from high school *is* a great achievement, but one that they're all capable of. In the same way that my parents did for me, these kids need to be given the expectation of attending college.

My mother established the Community Center to provide an additional layer of support so students can get closer to achieving their goals. Whenever I am able to go back to Alabama, I talk to young people about things I didn't know as a kid. This doesn't just feel like an obligation; it would be a disservice to not say to each kid, "You are the person who should go to college; you should *want* to go to college. I grew up in Camden and I had the same career opportunities that you have. As long as you're determined, you can do anything you want." Sometimes they say, "You need to know someone to get those good jobs." And I tell them, "You know me."

It's a complicated problem. At times it seems like I'm throwing a cup of water on a five-alarm fire. But as I'm making my way to Wall Street, I can't forget about my community back home. In addition to helping the kids in Camden, I want to be a resource for African American women at the University of Alabama who might otherwise get left behind. I'd love to bring a group of them to New York to learn about careers on Wall Street and help them figure out a plan to get here, even if it's a plan that takes years. I didn't get here through traditional ways and though I wasn't one of the oldest people at Kellogg, I wasn't the youngest either. I've traveled all over the world and am now working at Goldman Sachs, one of the greatest firms in the country. It took me a long time to get here, but I came from farther away.

KATE REID

Kate joined Goldman Sachs after graduating from Hollins University in May 2000. She left her job at Goldman in Private Wealth Management to pursue an opportunity to teach in Dhading, Nepal, at one of the two schools constructed in partnership between 85 Broads and Room to Read.

> "Don't be afraid to be inspired, and don't be afraid to inspire others."

Upon my arrival in the village of Baireni where the Shree Bageshwori Secondary School was located, a sea of schoolchildren surrounded me as if I were a celebrity. Speaking only a few words of Nepali, I said "Hello" and "How are you?" They asked me several questions in Nepali that I did not understand, so I just smiled back.

With the herd of students in tow I made my way to my host father and brother who were waiting to take me to my new home. My host brother spoke only a limited amount of English and my host father hardly any at all. With my two backpacks, we set off up a steep hill. Twenty-five minutes later we arrived at a house surrounded by vegetable fields and animals. As I walked around, I began to question my decision to leave the United States to move in with a Nepali family.

It's difficult to explain to almost anyone from a developed nation, where the comforts of life and technology have changed our lifestyle to something so beyond where a developing nation is today, just how primitive life is in Nepal. Sometimes I wondered if Nepal was the land that time forgot.

85 Broads created a partnership with Room to Read, a nonprofit organization whose mission is to provide underprivileged children with the lifelong gift of education, sponsoring the rebuilding of two Nepali schools which will eventually educate over 2,000 students. While I was there, I taught at the Shree Bageshwori Secondary School and helped create a library for the school to have as a resource center.

Setting up the library was one of the more eye-opening experiences that I had while working in the schools. Nepal is a country with little structure or symmetry. The day is dictated by the rise and fall of the sun. Trying to create a highly structured environment in the library proved to be quite a challenge. We made posters with the library rules on them and charts with the different types of books and their corresponding colors. When I asked the teachers to use the tape to hang the posters up, there were signs that were plastered to the walls with over 20 pieces of tape instead of what I had envisioned: four evenly torn pieces on each corner. Tape was new to these teachers. I also enlisted the teachers' help in color-coding the books, putting a small torn piece of colored tape on the spine of the book one inch above the base of the book. By the end of the project I had tape all over the entire books, sometimes several pieces. Similarly, they put the book pockets that were to go in the back of the books in the front of the book, upside down, and some books had no pocket at all. I finally regrouped with them one more time to demonstrate the construction of the book. From then on things did run a little more smoothly, but I had to keep reminding myself that a library was something completely foreign to them and so familiar to me.

All of the work for the library had to be done quickly because before we were even finished, students were coming in to look at the books. The library created a quiet, peaceful environment for the students to use as a safe place to read or just think. It is hard for me to explain in words just how much of a difference the new school and library really makes to these villagers. It was exciting to be there as the final weeks of construction took place at the Shree Bageshwori Secondary School. The students could hardly wait for the staircase to be completed so they could take a look at the new classrooms on the second floor. Due to the current Maoist situation in Nepal, once the schools were completed, the school management committee felt that holding an inaugural ceremony would draw unwanted Maoist attention to the school, posing a threat to teachers and students.

With the library completed, I said good-bye to the school, the students, teachers, and my host family. It was sad to leave them as the work could go on for years. If anything, I hope to be remembered by the Nepalis as the friendly American who was able, if only for a short time, to share her language, stories, and pictures of a country thought of as Shangri La to the developing world.

After having the incredible fortune to take a year off from work to volunteer, travel around the world, and reflect on life, I decided to return to the States to pursue my MBA. Through all of these experiences, I have learned several lessons. The first is that it is OK to take a risk. I was asked countless times how I could leave a paying job at Goldman Sachs to volunteer in Nepal. From someone who had sat at a desk one day too long, I just knew that it was time to go. My two- to five-year plan wasn't a parallel image with where I was sitting, and I knew that it was time to take a risk and make a change.

The second lesson is not to take for granted just how incredibly fortunate we are to live in a free and democratic society. Even some of the most disadvantaged Americans are better off than most Nepalis, especially the women. We often take for granted the resources and freedoms we have here in the United States. Just the ability to vote is more than Nepalis have at the moment.

The most important lesson I learned is that one person alone can make such a huge difference in this world. About a month and a half into my volunteering experience, I met another volunteer and shared with her my classroom struggles and frustrations. She reminded me that, "It's about that one kid who gets it. That one quiet girl in the third row who, while the rest of the classroom is shouting 'green' when you are holding up an orange sign, she's learning it. To her, you are making all the difference in the world." There are hundreds of ways we can make the world a more peaceful, civil, and just community—and often opportunities await us that are within walking distance of our very own homes.

What really motivates me is the belief that there is always something better out there to strive for. I live by the phrase, "Don't be afraid to be inspired, and don't be afraid to inspire others." I want to change the living standard of people around the globe. If we have the ability to effect change, idleness is our only enemy. We can move forward and make a difference. I think my family all thought I was crazy when I quit my job at Goldman to go teach in Nepal and subsequently travel for a year, but they had faith. They knew I was going to make an impact and that I was following my passions and remaining true to myself. Over time, I have learned to accept who I am, including my strengths and flaws. Finally accepting this has allowed me to be a better sister, daughter, friend, and member of the global community. It's hard to love others if you don't love yourself.

HELGA SMITH

Helga grew up in East Germany and escaped to West Berlin at the end of her high school years. She moved to New York in 1965 and started a new life and family there. Helga received a degree in computer science from CUNY in 1977 and did computer-related work at CitiBank for 23 years. She then worked at Goldman Sachs for four years, giving business presentations in equities management.

"At 59, I ran my first marathon. At 62, I climbed Mt. Kilimanjaro. Better late than never."

I was born in East Germany, a country that does not exist anymore. Life was tough. My mother died when I was 7. I was in and out of orphanages, and my stepmother kicked me out when I was 17. Somewhere along the way, though, I must have caught the spirit of survival. While standing on my own two feet, I had to find my way in the world. If I made mistakes, I paid for them.

In 1961, the government constructed the Berlin Wall which fenced us in, making it impossible to leave the country. At the time, I had a close friend who happened to be engaged to a young man in West Germany. When she managed to escape successfully, I felt desperate. It did not take long for me to also find a way to escape, even though the penalty for such a deed was six years in prison. I left with nothing but the clothes on my back. Destiny was on my side and I managed to get to West Berlin. Starting from scratch was not easy and some people actually went back to the East because they could not handle living in a free society. But for me, I cherished this new-found freedom and the opportunities it offered. I could go where I wanted, do what I wanted. It did not take much persuasion to decide to go to the States when it became possible to do so.

I arrived in New York in January 1965 with one suitcase, $100 in the bank, fluent in German and with a bit of Russian but not one word of English. So, starting over in New York was much more difficult than it had been in West Berlin. Nevertheless, I worked where I could and studied English as quickly as possible. I must have been reasonably proficient when a year and a half later I married an American who did not speak any German. Five years later, we had three children and I was single again. My husband decided he did not want a family after all. So for the next 15 years, my priorities were set. Without any relatives, family support, or alimony, I had to go on welfare for awhile.

In the meantime, I was earning an associate degree at the local community college and eventually was looking for work. But without any experience this was difficult. So I took on temporary work, hoping to find a company that would hire me. Indeed, Citibank did just that. My starting salary was lower than my welfare payments, but I moved up and worked there for more than 20 years in a variety of positions. My most fulfilling job was generating business presentations for the traders on the trading floor. Even though time constraints were often severe, the team spirit was quite rewarding: the better I did my job, the better the traders were able to do theirs.

During the years at Citibank, my children grew up. My older son, Roger, attended Fordham University, became an artist, and married an Ecuadorian woman, who is also an artist. My daughter, Monica, decided at an early age that she would become a lawyer. She graduated first from the University of Pennsylvania and afterward from Harvard Law School. In between, she biked around the world and gained valuable experiences seeing firsthand how people live in other countries. She also realized "how fortunate she was to be born an American." If I was worried about her on this trip, I could not let her know. I had to support her and was happy when she arrived places safely. After her two-and-a-half-year stint at a major law firm in New York, she had paid off her student loans and was free to pursue her international passions.

She signed on with the U.S. Agency for International Development. She is now finishing her first four-year assignment in Egypt and looking forward to the next country she will be serving. I lost my younger son at age 20. This was the most painful experience in all my life.

In 1998 my daughter wanted to run in the New York Marathon. Even though I had never been athletic, I started running with her, at least short distances. I was 58 at the time. When a friend about my age announced that she was going to kill herself on her 60th birthday because she did not want to become old, I decided to do something more positive with my life: I was going to run a marathon! My goal was just to finish, which I did. Like many runners, I was hooked. So I trained properly and finished my second marathon fast enough to qualify for the Boston Marathon, which is the most prestigious in the country. My daughter had also qualified and was leaving for Egypt two days later, so we wanted to run Boston together. Graciously, she ran at my pace. Back at work, I started hanging my racing numbers in my cubicle. Some of the younger people came around asking about my running experiences. I am happy to say that I inspired some of them to become physically active.

All this running on hard surfaces was detrimental for my feet and I needed a new challenge. I had read that a person of average fitness should be able to climb Mt. Kilimanjaro, so I found a new goal. Luckily, my daughter was willing to accompany me on this adventure, and we both trained a new set of muscles to prepare for this trip.

At this time I was working for Goldman Sachs. I had left Citigroup when it merged with Travelers and our department was absorbed, leaving many Citibankers without work. Through the Women's Network of Goldman Sachs, I heard of Alison Levine who had not only climbed Mt. Kilimanjaro, but also six of the seven peaks of the world and was preparing to climb Mt. Everest with four other courageous American women. Listening to her talk, it occurred to me that my climb could be more meaningful if I turned it into a fund-raiser. So I picked an organization, FINCA, made up a flyer and started fund-raising. The Foundation for International Community Assistance gives small business loans primarily to female entrepreneurs around the world. Of course, FINCA was delighted to hear about my project. It was at this time that I contacted 85 Broads and asked for their help and involvement. Together, we raised almost $10,000 dollars which was distributed to e women of Tanzania, where Mt. Kilimanjaro is located. Even though it is p in the bucket of need, my contribution did help some people.

Climbing Mt. Kilimanjaro is not an afternoon stroll. Statistically, less than half the people who attempt to do so are successful. But my daughter and I had learned how to prepare for physical challenges. Besides, we had been in high altitudes in the Andes and the Himalayas, so we knew what to expect. Needless to say I was highly motivated; I really did not want to disappoint the 100+ contributors. We both managed to climb all the way to the top, each at our own pace. It was a wonderful feeling having climbed the roof of Africa. Successful climbers gain a great sense of accomplishment, whatever the reason they attempted this feat in the first place.

In the summer of 2004 I quit my job, on my own terms, because my work was not fun anymore and I wanted to do other things. I consider myself in transition. I do not know what I will be doing one year from now besides traveling. Currently I am training with blind people who want to run. Enabling someone else to enjoy something they would not be able to do by themselves is very rewarding.

There are many things I want to do, places to visit, subjects to learn, issues to get involved with. I am trying to live each day to its fullest, not just for myself, but hopefully for the benefit of others, too.

JACQUELINE TAN

Jacqui's first job was as an investment banking analyst at JPMorgan. Although she was promoted without an MBA, Jacqui chose to broaden her horizons and completed her MBA at the MIT Sloan School of Management in 2004. Jacqui has recently moved to Hong Kong to join McKinsey & Company.

> "My advice to other young women is to be open to new opportunities and to not shy away from the challenges."

If you drilled a hole from New York through the center of the earth, you would emerge in Perth, Australia. Perth is generally regarded as the most isolated capital city in the world. The city is closer to Singapore, which is across the sea, than it is to any other Australian capital city, as it lies across a vast desert. When I was four years old, in order to provide my brothers and me with opportunities for a better education, my parents decided to migrate to Perth from the even smaller city of Johor Bahru in Malaysia.

After completing my Bachelor of Commerce degree with first-class honors in finance at the University of Western Australia, I knew that the traditional path of graduates was to move to Sydney or Melbourne, or even to the regional financial hubs in Hong Kong or Singapore. Aiming high, I applied for a job directly on Wall Street. Given I had never lived nor studied in the United States, I consider myself fortunate to have received two offers from bulge-bracket firms.

When I first arrived in New York, I was excited by how fast everything moved—the pace of life and the pace of work. To state the obvious, New York is very different from Perth. Everyone is so transient and international and has such a diversity of life experiences. I met many unique people and acquired an even more international perspective.

When I joined JPMorgan's Emerging Markets Capital Markets (EMCM) group, it was at the height of the Russian ruble and Brazilian real devaluation—a very interesting time to be working on raising capital for sovereigns and corporates in Latin America and Asia. The volatile markets were exciting. We were designing, marketing, and executing innovative instruments that allowed our clients to tap the capital markets. During my first year and a half at JPMorgan, I got to work with and travel to countries that were literally on the other side of the world from my home town. I learned so much.

With the advent of the technology boom, I raised my hand to become part of it. Supported by mentors like Rachel Hines, the head of the EMCM group at the time, I was transferred to the Global Mergers and Acquisitions (M&A) group focusing on the telecom, media, and technology sector. I was certainly not disappointed working on several exciting and high-profile multibillion dollar deals. During the competitive and lean post-dot-com, post-JPMorgan–Chase merger years, I was promoted from an analyst to an associate, despite the fact that I did not have an MBA.

While I was extremely proud of my promotion, I was also keen to broaden my horizons and challenge myself further, so I pursued an MBA at the MIT Sloan School of Management. My years at Sloan provided some of the most valuable experiences I have had to date. Known for its innovation and intimate size, Sloan is a microcosm of the global community with amazing people from different cultural and professional backgrounds serving as an ideal testing ground for new ideas and different opinions. Sloan equipped me with a great set of tools to augment my finance skills and to help me become a good manager. In order to bridge an experience gap and to feed an interest in marketing, an area I had never worked in before, I spent a summer as a brand manager at Philips Norelco.

After graduation, I had an insatiable desire to move to Hong Kong, spurred by the Asian region's incredible growth potential over the next few decades. I expect China to become an absolute powerhouse. Prior to starting work, I spent an intensive six weeks studying Mandarin in the Beijing Language and Culture University. My brain was totally exhausted by the end of the intensive course, but this was an important step toward improving my ability to speak the language. Having recently joined McKinsey & Company's Hong Kong office, I look forward to learning from and contributing to its Corporate Finance and Strategy practice, as well as traveling throughout the Asia Pacific region.

I am absolutely passionate about seeking new experiences, and as my history demonstrates, I love traveling and am not at all averse to moving between continents. While it is potentially nerve-racking to move to new places where one has few or no friends, I find the experience ultimately quite rewarding. I have been personally enriched in having met so many people from different cultures and backgrounds; it makes me appreciate our world so much more.

Balancing family and life is of great importance to me. My family definitely was a consideration for my husband and me in our move to Hong Kong. While the flight time from Hong Kong to visit our parents in Perth is still about seven hours, it is certainly much less than the 24-hour flight time required from New York!

My most important role models to date have been a handful of women at JPMorgan with whom I had the good fortune to work. I was able to observe how they managed to balance the needs of their families with the demands of their successful careers. Their example makes me confident that I can do it too.

My advice to other young women is to be open to new opportunities and to not shy away from the challenges. When I made my big move to New York, the other side of the planet, over six years ago, I learned a lot about myself. International work and study experience is extremely relevant in a global economy, and the willingness and ability to adapt to new cultures is rewarding in many ways. Most importantly, I strongly believe that it is crucial to take time out to enjoy what you love—life is just too short not to!

4

ENTREPRENEURS

When I founded Milestone Capital Management in 1994, the discouraging and skeptical voices almost entirely drowned out the few encouraging and positive ones. "The market is too mature, the competition too strong and well entrenched, the opportunity too limited, the company too small and new, the risk of failure too high...." When we reached $200 million in assets under management in a little over six months, one of my friends and former colleagues from Goldman Sachs even called me to say, "Now you're not a joke anymore!" More than a decade later, Milestone Capital is responsible for managing over $2 billion in assets from leading corporations, banks, municipalities, and other institutional investors. And to the best of our knowledge Milestone is still the *only* woman-owned company of its kind in the entire $2.3-trillion U.S. money market fund sector to specialize exclusively in institutional money market fund management.

When I founded 85 Broads as an independent network in 1999, those same voices of skepticism seemed even louder and more discouraging. "Why would you want to create a network for *both* current and former Goldman Sachs women professionals? The 'formers' are all bitter and won't care about the 'currents,' and what benefit can there be for the currents anyway?" "You want to create a 'good old boy' network for women? Why do women need an exclusive network of their own? They're terrible at networking anyway." "High-powered women will never join. They don't join networks or 'support' groups, and they don't reach out to help other women."

But 85 Broads has, in fact, become a powerhouse network for over 10,000 of what I fondly refer to as the most incredible women on the planet. And it is now the success model for companies, alumnae associations, and other women's networks around the world. But what truly sets our global community apart goes beyond its uniqueness, its edginess, its recognition as a "best practices" network by Catalyst or the many other organizations now interested in replicating it. More than anything else, 85 Broads is the *ultimate entrepreneurial venture*. A pure act of faith in yourself and trust in the partnerships you can create. An unwillingness to compromise or be less than what you know in your heart you can create—regardless of conventional wisdom or the expectations of others. Tune out the other voices and tune in your *own* voice.

I truly believe that every woman, deep down, *is* an entrepreneur. If you are a stay-at-home parent, you are an entrepreneur. If you have left your home and country to pursue an education and a life different from anything you have ever known or are really prepared for, you are an entrepreneur. If you are navigating your career as a woman—most likely doing it with very few role models or mentors, more pressure, less upside reward, no good old boy network, more transitions and disruptions along the way, and no margin for error—you are an entrepreneur. If you are the CEO of your own life and career, you *are* an entrepreneur. Your name is on the door and your rear end is on the line every day.

The good news is that you're definitely not alone. The women we'll meet in this chapter have incredible stories to tell about their own unique brands of entrepreneurship. And even though their stories are as diverse as their backgrounds, they do share one common bond with each other and all the other women entrepreneurs of 85 Broads. They are, as I like to say, absolutely fearless. They are not afraid to fail. They are not afraid to succeed. They are not afraid to take risks. They are not afraid to ask for or to give help. They are not afraid to control their own destinies. They are not afraid to struggle. They are not afraid to change course. They are not afraid to start over. They are not even afraid to give up. They are only afraid of losing themselves if they don't pursue their own unique passions.

The women you'll meet in this chapter aren't listening to those other voices: the safe voices, the status quo voices, the negative voices. They are listening to their own voices. The voices that are saying: We are FEARLESS. We are PASSIONATE. We are ENTREPRENEURS.

Monique Maddy

Monique was born in Africa and completed most of her primary and secondary schooling abroad. She earned a BS from Georgetown University, an MA in developmental economics from Johns Hopkins University, and an MBA from Harvard Business School. Monique's book, Learning to Love Africa: My Journey from Africa to Harvard Business School and Back, *was published in 2004.*

> "I relied on the lesson my father gave me more than once, 'If you don't know where you are going, just remember where you came from.'"

Many people still look at the continent of Africa and see a massive social problem, rather than an attractive business opportunity. This false and exaggerated perception has been perpetuated in large part by the activities of major development aid agencies that, instead of eliminating or even reducing poverty, have turned it into a fine-tuned, highly lucrative, and growing industry. No country in the world has ever emerged from poverty and achieved economic growth via the soup kitchen. The path to economic growth is business, pure and simple. And business can only prosper in an environment that fosters political stability and respect for private property, promotes the health and education of its citizens, and allows them to pursue those opportunities that education provides.

It was extremely unconventional for me to be sent to boarding school in England when I was six years old, but in my parent's view, the pain of separation was the price that had to be paid for me to have the first-class education that would open doors to future academic and career opportunities. At age 11, I returned home to Liberia, becoming reacquainted with my family and the local culture. As the time for high school approached, my parents thought I should return to school in England. For my part, I saw this excursion as an opportunity to go to America, and they conceded to my wish. At St. John the Baptist School in Mendham, New Jersey, I concentrated on my studies and my hard work paid off with my acceptance to Georgetown University, my first choice, where I planned to study international relations.

Long before I arrived at Georgetown, I knew that I wanted to work for the UN, and therefore that it would be necessary to obtain my master's degree to get a good position there. As a result, I applied to the Johns Hopkins

University School of Advanced International Studies, from which I graduated in 1986, with a degree in development economics. I was elated when I was offered a job with the UN even before graduation. Not everyone in my milieu, including my father, who passed away shortly after I received this news, shared my optimism. Those who knew me well said that I would be stifled by the bureaucracy, and would probably move on to bigger and better things within five years. They turned out to be right.

In my first major assignment with the UN, I was assigned to an administrative post in Luanda, Angola. Although there may have been a few of the highly specialized divisions within the UN that were making a positive contribution to Angola and other countries, it was clear to me that most of what the UN was doing was exacerbating the situation by taking away the urgency of the governments to reform, and creating a codependency relationship that nobody wanted to end. I decided to direct my energy into something where I could make a lasting and tangible difference.

I was 27 and had nothing to lose by leaving my job. I decided to go to business school where I could get the skills I needed to do effective entrepreneurial work in Africa. Plan A was to apply to Harvard Business School. Then I chose to take a risk, to be in a place where my Harvard MBA could have an impact, and where few with my background and skills are actually willing to go. I chose to work in Africa.

One of the areas that I covered while at the UN was telecommunications. During that time I reached the conclusion that developing countries with limited telecommunications infrastructure could deploy state-of-the-art wireless technologies that had not yet even been applied to highly developed markets such as the United States—the leapfrog effect. To pursue my interest further, I conducted a field study during my second year at HBS, for which I raised $100,000 from various sponsors, including several major U.S. telecommunications companies. My supervising professor, Howard Stevenson, a brilliant man, and a noted authority on entrepreneurship, was alarmed. This amount of funding meant I had to deliver a viable product to my sponsors, beyond the realm of the academic, where mere grades were at stake. Howard's guidance and encouragement were indispensable to the success of the field study and the eventual transition to a new venture, and to this day he remains one of my closest advisers and friends.

Upon the completion of the field study, I recruited six first-year HBS students to work with me to test the concept and develop a pilot project for the business plan, which I would then take to the original corporate sponsors and/or venture capitalists. We chose Tanzania as our first country. It turns out that the five interns were more interested in African safaris than in African business plans. But this turned out to be a blessing in disguise, as it compelled me to launch an SOS to one of my HBS classmates who happened to be traveling in southern Africa at the time. Together, Côme and I completed the business plan, and by the end of the exercise, he had decided to abandon his lucrative job offer in the consulting world in favor of an opportunity to launch this new and exciting telecommunications venture. Our first investor was Waleed Iskandar, another HBS classmate. And thus, African Communications Group, later renamed Adesemi, after my paternal grandmother, was launched.

Our first service was the virtual phone service—a system consisting of wireless public pay phones, voicemail, and pagers. It provided customers that did not have access to telephone (over 99 percent of Tanzanians) with the opportunity to have a phone number and access to a network of pay phones from which to call family, friends, and acquaintances to either talk or leave messages. The Tanzanian government had initially doubted our ability to pull it off. After all, here we were, Côme and I, a couple of upstarts, with no money, no real technical knowledge, but wanting to start a telecommunications company! The government therefore gave us minimal hassle in the first stage and was more than happy to award us the necessary licenses to operate. What they had underestimated, however, was what we lacked in age and experience, we more than made up for in hubris. It was only after we had assembled a first-rate technical and management team that gave us the capabilities that we lacked, that the government realized that we constituted a formidable threat to its monopoly on telecommunications services, a monopoly that was not only encouraged, but financially supported by the World Bank! From then on, the gloves were off, and they were taking no prisoners. They were out to destroy Adesemi. Ultimately they would succeed, but, more importantly, the losers were the thousands of Tanzanian people who had come to rely on our services and the many who had been employed by the company in high-skilled jobs.

We were providing a good service and our customers loved us. Within three years of our arrival, we had built a seamlessly integrated wireless public pay phone network, launched a major marketing campaign, and dominated the public pay phone market, crushing the competition, including the underperforming and decrepit government network. Because of extensive international coverage of our Tanzanian operation, our approach attracted high-level attention, including a visit by the then First Lady Hillary Rodham Clinton. Soon we were being asked by developing countries all over the world to bring the Adesemi virtual phone system (public pay phones, voicemail, pagers) to their major cities and rural areas, where telephone pen-etration rates were low. Expanding to new countries with investor friendly governments and higher per capita incomes was very appealing to Adesemi and its investors, so we decided to take the plunge. We needed new capital to expand.

Our existing investors were of two kinds. The venture capitalists, the "do well" investors, shared this vision. The idea was to rapidly move into four or five new countries, establish operations there, and grow the business so that within four to five years Adesemi could be sold to a strategic investor or taken public on one or more of the major stock exchanges. By this time we had built up a whole organization; through a joint venture that we had estab-lished, we were already operating in a second country, Ghana, and had agree-ments to buy companies in Côte d'Ivoire and Sri Lanka.

The VCs committed $5 million of the $6 million required for the first phase of Adesemi's expansion beyond Tanzania. The commitment was condi-tional on the other investors, the "do gooders" (typically government-owned investment companies) providing their pro rata share. These investors had originally been brought into Adesemi as a precondition to the investment of the venture capital investors. The latter presumed, erroneously as it turned out in our case, that they had superior knowledge of doing business in Africa. The problem was that while they had better knowledge of Africa, they lacked cor-responding acumen in the business arena, particularly that of venture capital. They refused to put up their share, $1 million. Technically, we could have pro-ceeded with a scaled back version of our expansion plan with the $5 million committed capital. From a practical and legal point of view, however, if the VCs had invested the $5 million, the "do gooders" had the right, and proba-bly the intention, to seize that capital to pay off a loan that they had made to the Tanzanian subsidiary, making it unavailable to Adesemi for expansion. Adesemi would be limited to its Tanzanian operation, a one-trick pony, with dubious growth prospects and limited harvest opportunity for the VCs. As a result, the board voted to liquidate the company.

The "do gooders" seized the Tanzanian assets and through a combination of neglect and incompetence, ran the company into the ground. The service to the customers deteriorated and the employees lost their jobs. It was very unfortunate and, from our standpoint, rather anticlimactic. We had over-come far more formidable obstacles during the early years of Adesemi's exis-tence. Little did we suspect that the death knell would be an inside job.

It took a while for me to figure out what one might learn from this, my first major, and very public, defeat. I wasn't ready to go out and do something new right away. I wrote an article about the experience for the *Harvard Business Review*; after its publication I was given a contract by Harper Collins to write a book on the subject, but lengthened to include an account of my life prior to Adesemi. It was a good opportunity to put things into perspective and synthesize all that had occurred, in hopes that I could share the valuable lessons that I had learned on my entrepreneurial journey.

It was around that time that I decided to return to competitive running, given that I had continued to pursue the sport on a recreational basis throughout my entire life, and it was a good escape from the pages and pages that I would write each day. I also took advantage of the flexibility that I had during this period to go back to Africa (the Source). I went to Kenya where I could both complete my book and train with some of the best and most inspiring long-distance runners in the world. As a result, I found myself, at the age of 40, in the elite ranks of marathon running, due in particular to a personal best of 2:48 in the Boston Marathon in 2002. This whole experience further enriched my life, giving it a whole new dimension and the confidence, determination, and courage to move on in other areas of my life as well.

My book, *Learning to Love Africa: My Journey from Africa to Harvard Business School and Back*, was published in 2004. The title reflects the strong bond that I continue to have with Africa, despite the fact that I am now a U.S. citizen. It is truly a land of tremendous contrasts—hope and despair, tragedy and humor, savagery and compassion—and of immense physical beauty. All the elements that make for an enriched, varied, and meaningful life. Unfortunately, for far too long, the bad about Africa has outweighed the good, a phenomenon that is constantly and vigorously reinforced by the global media and by those international development aid agencies whose very lifeblood is the depiction of Africa as a continent in perpetual despair. Images of success do not fill their coffers.

Although for obvious reasons it is extremely difficult to get businesses to invest in a region where governments are unpredictable, the prospect of war is never far away, and per capita GNP is low, I believe more fervently than ever that if Africa is to permanently emerge from its current morass, it will do so on the labors of the titans of industry and not, as is currently the case, the titans of global poverty—or the self-proclaimed antipoverty gurus whose sole mantra of "more" appears to be inspired by another erstwhile ward of the state, Dickens' Oliver Twist. At least Oliver had the innate good sense and wherewithal to eventually take matters into his own hands to escape the life of welfare in favor of more entrepreneurial pursuits, albeit some questionable ones initially, that would lead to a happy ending. If only Africa's leaders could ensure their own people a happy ending by cutting or at least significantly reducing their dependence on the welfare cord. It has taken me a long time to come to the realization, but as a dear friend and mentor, Jorge Paulo Lemann, recently told me, "Be a success, build things, make a lot of money, help other people. That's what it's all about." He has it in the right order.

ANNE DIAS GRIFFIN

After receiving her BA at Georgetown in 1992, Anne worked in Goldman Sachs's Investment Banking Division in New York and London before receiving her MBA from Harvard Business School in 1997. She then moved on to become a portfolio manager and analyst at Soros Fund Management and then at Viking Global Investors. Anne founded and is now the managing partner of Aragon Global Investors, a long/short fund that focuses on global equities.

> "There will come a time in your career when you want to be your own boss."

Many people dream about starting their own business, but few put that desire into action. Being an entrepreneur means forging your own path, a path where your success depends directly on your business acumen and your perseverance. It is the riskier path. There is the risk of going into the unknown. There is the risk to your professional reputation. There is the risk of failure. If these risks challenge and excite you rather than scare you, you have the makings of an entrepreneur. For many entrepreneurs, the opportunity to prove oneself far outweighs the risk of failure.

Starting Aragon Global Management in 2001 was my first foray into the world of entrepreneurship. It has been an exciting four years, full of challenges, defeats, and successes. Aragon's team of five focuses on creating value through investing in public companies around the world.

I was not predestined to become a hedge fund entrepreneur. When I was younger, I was certain I wanted to be a foreign correspondent or a diplomat. I attended the School of Foreign Service at Georgetown University. During college, I had several internships with government organizations. I worked at the German Parliament on immigration issues and interned at a branch of the European Community. I mastered Spanish and German and worked to build the skills necessary to join the diplomatic community. During the school year, I wrote free-lance articles for *The Financial Times* and *The Detroit News*.

Toward the end of my college years, I interviewed with Goldman Sachs and was instantly impressed by the people I met and the enthusiasm they had for their careers. I ended up joining Goldman Sachs with great trepidation and excitement. With little background in finance, I believe that I was possibly one of the only analysts who didn't know the difference between debt and equity at the start of the training program! However, my work in journalism taught me one hugely important skill: the ability to quickly grasp the relationship and meaning of a disparate set of facts. This is an important skill in the world of investing where success or failure is often determined by one's ability to quickly make a decisive judgment based on an eclectic collection of data points, facts, and figures and less then perfect information.

My journalism skills, combined with the Goldman Sachs training program and the exposure to hundreds of different companies in different sectors, gave me the beginnings of an investment edge—analyzing the pieces and putting them together in an insightful way. Today, there is so much financial information and opinion readily available to investors that it's often like drinking from a fire hose. Information is not scarce, but quality independent judgment is.

There are three things that I've found in my career that have accelerated this learning process. The first accelerator is to find great mentors. The second is to set a stretch goal for yourself, a goal that you didn't think was possible to achieve. The third is to find a differentiating factor that will make you successful in a unique way relative to others.

When I graduated from Harvard Business School, I went to work at Soros Fund Management. At the time, Soros was, along with Tiger Management, the largest hedge fund in the world, topping $20 billion in assets. At Soros, I was mentored by a variety of senior portfolio managers, and learned by osmosis their understanding of how the markets worked. The stretch goal I set for myself was: "I want to become a portfolio manager within two years." To achieve this goal, I would have to quickly produce tangible results, namely, profits, for the fund. Working relentlessly, I created tangible results and demonstrated my passion to be an investor. In my second year at Soros, I had my chance. I was chosen to be the financial services sector portfolio manager.

After Soros, I joined Viking Global Investors, a start-up fund founded by a team of analysts from the hedge fund goliath Tiger Management. My stretch goal at Viking was to gain mastery of a new sector of the marketplace within a year. I negotiated to be responsible for covering the global media and Internet sectors. As it was a new fund, we only had a few months to start showing numbers. This is when I learned that mentors can also be your peers. There were several key analysts, both on the buy side and sell side, who had worked in media for years and who taught me the ropes of the business. They helped me get up to speed and sail ahead.

When I thought about starting my own fund, I questioned myself as to whether I was too young. Many people whom I asked for advice reminded me of my short history of investing. To put things in perspective, I was talking to people who had been investing for decades. Then, I went to see Julian Robertson, the founder and legendary manager of the Tiger Fund. My meeting with Julian had a profound impact on my life. Julian said to me, "I started with seven million dollars. If you can find seven million dollars, then you can get started!" Julian's words inspired me to go for it.

The amazing thing about starting a fund on your own is exactly that—getting started. You must convince prospective employees to join you before you have a business, before you have clients. You must convince investors to give you capital to manage before you have a track record, all of this under a fair amount of time pressure. Ultimately, it was Julian who became one of my anchor investors.

Aragon's global focus is both a reflection of my heritage and a significant competitive advantage. I was born in Strasbourg, France, to a Franco-German mother and a Franco-Argentinean father and heard three languages at home. Though markets outside the United States are less efficient, they're full of undiscovered and underanalyzed investment opportunities. Two of my mentors, Stanley Druckenmiller at Soros and Julian Robertson at Tiger, shared the belief that great opportunities are often found abroad. Their perspective helped to frame my strategy of investing on a global basis. Aragon's team reflects our global focus: between the five of us, we speak French, German, Spanish, Hindi, and Korean! This is extremely helpful when conducting interviews with foreign management teams and clearly represents an edge in our investment process.

When you realize what can be done on your own by finding your own path, you will be amazed. I spent the first 10 years being successful on someone else's terms. When you're on a steep learning curve, that's great. But when you reach a certain point, you will be driven by something other than money. To set out on your own, you have to let go of others' perceptions of you. You will always come across people who for one reason or another will think that you can't do it. By setting stretch goals, constantly refining your tool kit, and keeping your confidence, the challenges are a lot easier to overcome. You have to think big because no one else will do it for you.

R. MAY LEE

May ventured into the entrepreneurial world with the development of MarketBoy, an Internet auction company. Even though the timing of its launch coincided with the tragic events and economic downturn related to September 11, 2001, and led to MarketBoy's inability to gain traction, its technology and concept represent valuable innovations in the Internet marketplace. May is currently COO of RowenWarren, Inc., a full-service advertising firm based in New York.

"Failure is not trying."

I was born in Hong Kong and came to this country as an infant. My parents immigrated to the United States to give their children a better life. And they did give us a better life. I graduated from the University of Pennsylvania in 1985 and received my JD degree from NYU Law School in 1990. Subsequently, I worked at the Federal Reserve Bank of New York and eventually at Goldman Sachs, where I had the privilege to work with some of the brightest and most entrepreneurial people on Wall Street. Nonetheless, in the autumn of 2000 the Internet bug bit me. A colleague and friend from Goldman and I spent the next six months conducting due diligence and talking to prospective investors. In the final analysis, though, how does one decide to forgo a promising career at the best firm on Wall Street for an unknown risk? A successful entrepreneur in Silicon Valley told us simply that "failure is not trying." I was ready to go.

Casimir Wierzynski and I started a company called MarketBoy in July 2001. We took the familiar continuous double auction method (CDA) used in financial markets and applied it to the Internet and nonfinancial instruments, such as e-commerce in consumer electronics. The software mimicked securities trading where sellers post their prices and buyers post their bids on a screen in real time that can be seen by all participants. The CDA offered a variety of advantages over existing auction technology: By placing a bid, a buyer essentially entered a number of auctions simultaneously; sellers could see the "demand curve" by looking at all the bids and essentially lower the price by accepting a bid without anyone but the buyer knowing it; and finally, unlike other auction sites, all of the products were new.

Within one year, we raised capital to build a prototype, designed and built the website, and signed up 20 vendors who sold over 10,000 products. By August 2001, at soft-launch, our PR efforts and viral marketing efforts were starting to pay off for our September 2001 launch. We applied sound business principles that we had learned at Goldman, and we were prudent and cost-conscious. We had every expectation that we would launch successfully and attract the next round of money that would enable us to develop the technology further and market the site. Sadly, as we all know, the events of September 11, 2001, intervened and changed the course of all our lives.

Unable to raise funds or attract partners, we stretched our initial round of funds (with the support of some extraordinary investors formerly of Goldman Sachs) beyond the anticipated 12 months into 36 months. We altered our business model, pursued every partnership, and worked 24/7. Yet despite a wonderful idea, exceptional staff, and vibrant company culture, MarketBoy didn't work out in that iteration. Nonetheless, the technology of MarketBoy lives on and we continue to pursue the patent for our intellectual property. We hope to monetize that asset at some point in the future.

When I look back on that experience, I realize that I gained invaluable experience in a short amount of time. Although I was disappointed that MarketBoy didn't work out, starting my own company served as a bridge to a better, more exciting future. I love being an entrepreneur.

DEBORAH WARNER BROOKS

Deborah was a vice president of both the Asset Management and Fixed Income divisions at Goldman Sachs where she worked for nine years. She left to pursue a calling in the nonprofit sector, and since October of 2000, has served as president and CEO of The Michael J. Fox Foundation for Parkinson's Research.

> "The greatest irony of my career is that I got a chance to fully use my business skills and express my vision as an entrepreneur in the place people might least expect it— a nonprofit."

After working for Goldman Sachs for nine years, I found myself feeling very fortunate. In my corner of the financial world, the people were smart, the pace was fast, and I found meeting its challenges to be extremely satisfying. Still, there was something deep down that nagged at me.

In hindsight, I now realize that while I was happy and successful, I was searching for a higher meaning to my work. A shift to the nonprofit world seemed to hold the answer. By the fall of 2000, I finished a master's degree in marital and family therapy from Northwestern, adding social work training to my business skills. I then completed several assignments in nascent nonprofits, building skills along the way.

That's when I first heard that Michael J. Fox was starting a foundation, and that he thought someone with a business background would be a great fit. At the time, I had little understanding of Parkinson's disease, very little appreciation for the steep trajectory such a high-profile organization would take, or for the scale of a start-up of this magnitude. I heard about the job, met Michael, and we just clicked. Ten days later, I dove in.

Michael had this idea of creating an organization that was guerilla-like in its approach to cutting red tape and funding the best ideas. We didn't start with a vision about how to achieve that and, in retrospect, we were truly naïve about influencing the scientific enterprise. Yet sometimes a blank sheet of paper is very liberating. Plus, Michael and I shared a strong sense that the way to get started was just *to begin*.

If there is a lesson in my story it is this: Very often vision becomes apparent after the fact. What comes first is the ability to problem-solve in a practical way and the courage to boldly do what you think is right.

We started out with the idea that we should take a cue from the business world and hold ourselves accountable to the end goal of curing Parkinson's disease. We wanted to focus on outcomes as well as those discoveries that would have a tangible impact on patients' lives.

Much of science is hypothesis-driven and a quest for information in the purest sense. Our business approach applauds the analytical rigor of science, but demands more. We ask that our investments have the potential to be translated toward human health. What has made our efforts compelling is this attempt to marry the two skill sets. We embrace and respect contributions from these two approaches, but recognize that we operate on the fault line of natural tension between them. We believe that's where the magic and breakthroughs are. And this is how we've been able to do so much in such a short period of time.

Michael and I both believe that Parkinson's will be cured in our lifetime and I am confident that the work we're doing will make it happen all that much faster.

This has been such an amazing personal and professional journey and I've learned so much—from board members, from scientists, from patients in the

Parkinson's community, but most of all from Michael. His acute intelligence, his dispassionate approach to this disease, his sense of humor, and his sheer humanity are inspiring to me and everyone else involved. He makes us glad to put our heads down and charge ahead. It is special and rare to have that type of partnership with someone so remarkable and yes, so endearing.

When I sit back and reflect on how lucky I am in my newfound life, I wonder who could have envisioned such a path.

CLAUDIA WYSS

Claudia is from New Zealand and is currently in her second year at Harvard Business School. She received her MD from the University of Auckland and worked as a medical doctor and hospital administrator. Together with her father, Claudia has been an active investor in residential real estate in New Zealand. As part of her MBA studies she has been working on a new model of delivering health insurance to the uninsured in the United States and is likely to continue working on this venture after school.

> "Life is extremely valuable. If you're passionate about something, you should follow your passion now. Take the plunge. Dare to be different. You'd be surprised how much support you get from people who see that you're willing to be different. Maybe the people who support you are risk-takers themselves and see themselves in you and say, 'I was like that when I was younger. I now want to see other people doing that same thing.' I don't want to be that person who is afraid to take risks and I believe that the older you get, the harder it is to take the plunge."

During my postgraduate studies, I had the opportunity to work in the Rarotonga Hospital, a rural hospital in a developing Pacific island, and I was asked to identify strategies to improve efficiency in the Rarotongan hospital system. As a doctor, I was limited to helping one patient at a time; as a hospital manager with a background in medicine, I had the opportunity to help a greater number of people through better management. I therefore jumped head first into the business world.

Real estate is a great business; it allows you to maintain some independence and be fairly flexible with your time. What I find exciting is that the business is predominantly about structuring deals; the more creative ways that you can structure and negotiate a deal and find financing, the more likely you are to be successful. Because we structured our portfolio in a trust that earns a passive income, we can take greater risks in other business areas.

Although property managers now handle much of our real estate, I promote managing this business just like any other. It is important to consider tenants as customers and try to establish a long-term client relationship. We have found that by following this philosophy and looking after our tenants, they generally look after us in return. We have managed to mitigate the costs of high tenant turnaround by charging a fair and reasonable rent and by viewing the landlord-tenant relationship as a long-term partnership.

Inevitably, I have run into challenges in this business. One example relates to the lease negotiation of a food court that I was trying to develop. While I had managed to secure financing and find great tenants with whom we had a close relationship, the relationship with the landlords was not quite as amicable. In the process of negotiating the lease on a site, the owners attempted to add clauses and legal restrictions to the contract without informing me. These clauses would have forced me to assume the risk of the entire building structure of which I was only hoping to sublease a portion. The building was rather dilapidated and I was concerned that if core structural defects were identified during construction, we would be unable to afford the development and would risk losing the equity invested by the tenants and me. Given that I had 11 tenants who had put their life savings into this business and were extremely passionate about seeing it succeed, we had to decide whether we should continue with the development plans. I decided to sit down with the stakeholders so that we could identify a solution together. I gave my opinion that we should abandon the project as I had lost trust in the landlord and was concerned about the unreasonable financial risk. As I had anticipated, most of the business investors were upset, but the tenants all agreed that the circumstances were not good and we had to call the project off.

Of course it was a shame to see a deal fall through after having worked on it for such a long time. However, sometimes a project will come to that point when you have to accept that it's probably not worth finishing. Letting go can be a tough decision to make, but if you cannot trust your business associates or if the financial circumstances don't make sense, it's better to stop before you wind up in a great deal of trouble.

Given this experience, I became determined to gain a greater business education and network. As a result, I acquired a position as a hospital administrator so that I could better learn the workings of large organizations. In this job I learned that entrepreneurial opportunities need not apply only to start-ups, but can also reside in new business development or unusual projects within larger, seemingly sluggish organizations. Often these entrepreneurial projects carry a greater risk than working within a normal business function, but can be extremely exciting and can often lead to tremendous change within an organization. Being part of this change can often be as exciting as running your own business, but with the potential benefit of not risking your own equity within the business.

I was fortunate to negotiate the position of coordinating medical officer and became responsible for coordinating the medical expansion of a new surgical hospital. As in my past business experience, this largely revolved around developing a vision, building relationships, negotiating mutually beneficial deals with key stakeholders, surviving with limited resources, and staying strong in the face of adversity. It was fantastic to apply my business experience to the hospital business, and while I was rapidly promoted into a fairly senior role, I recognized that my business expertise was practical but rudimentary at best. If I was going to enter into an executive management position in the near future, bring some new ideas into the business, and be respected by the business community, a business education would be essential; hence I applied to Harvard Business School.

Looking back now on the lessons I have learned at business school, I am amazed at how I managed to survive in the business world with so little knowledge of theoretical business principles. Although we had invested in so many properties, I had never once attempted a net present value (NPV) calculation or other form of modeling. Perhaps the reasons why my lack of business expertise didn't create a disaster are that I was assisted by strong mentors with substantial business experience, I stuck to very simple but logical business principles I had learned from others, I relied on the input of an experienced legal and accounting team, and I thought outside the box.

One of my best and strongest mentors was my father. At a very early age he forced me to make decisions and to lead people who were often significantly senior to me. I was also responsible for negotiating most of the financing for the real estate properties and working with the legal and accounting team through the deals. There certainly was a tremendous learning curve, and I would not have been successful without my father's tremendous support, wisdom, and partnership. By watching my father interact with business associates, I gathered practical experience in negotiating and leading others. I also believe that having someone whom you trust implicitly, with whom you can discuss your ideas or concerns, is one of the most valuable aspects of a mentor.

Lastly, it appears that being "contrarian" in our investment decisions may have worked in our favor. During the 1990s tech bubble, while everyone was investing mostly in stocks, and real estate was considered unattractive, we invested largely in real estate. As a result, we bought properties when the market price was low, were forced to identify the best deals so we could convince bankers to support us, and later benefited from the rebounding markets. While we didn't exclude the stock market entirely, we focused on property investments that were undervalued, calculated simply according to cash flow returns and lack of popularity of certain markets. Perhaps this was motivated by Rockefeller's famous quote: "If your shoe shiner tells you to invest in the stock market, you had better get out."

REBECCA CARR EATON

Rebecca graduated from Duke University with a major in public policy. She worked at JPMorgan and Biztravel.com before attending Harvard Business School, where she received her MBA in 2001. She joined Siebel Systems as a product manager and a year later left to found Remote Clinical Solutions Inc., a provider of hydration monitoring systems.

> "You have to be passionate about what you're doing. This passion drives the quality of the team you can recruit and the number of obstacles you can overcome."

My grandfather founded a film distribution company in his fifties, which he operated until he was 87. Shortly before his retirement, he sent a card to his friends declaring, "Helen and I are off to see the Grand Canyon." But my grandfather's health declined quite dramatically following his retirement, and the Grand Canyon trip proved to be an elusive dream. His legs grew weak to the point that he needed help rising from his chair, and he often refused to shower for fear of falling. Eventually, he required 24-hour care. Some of the challenges my grandfather faced were inevitable and untreatable—the product of an aging body. Others, in my mind, were the result of gaping holes in the product landscape targeting seniors. In October 2002, I founded Remote Clinical Solutions Inc., whose mission at the time was to develop technologies that enabled seniors to live independently and with pride.

Over the next 12 months, as my husband will tell you, our home became a senior care institution of sorts. Our sofa held a seat cushion that propelled itself forward, helping those with mobility problems to stand. Our telephone was connected to a fall-alert service. I trialed various walkers, canes, and tools that helped individuals with limited flexibility to tie shoes and scrub backs, medication reminders, sleep apnea and bed sore sensors. Most of these products were inadequate for the problems they proposed to solve. After interviewing over 90 people for the position, I brought Charles—a biomedical and industrial design engineer—on board. Together, Charles and I looked broadly at the factors that force seniors from an independent to an institutionalized setting.

Among these, dehydration was a condition of particular interest. Dehydration represents one of the top 10 most frequent causes for hospitalization among seniors, and 50 percent of those hospitalized die within 12 months as a result of medical complications related to dehydration. Diagnosis is difficult outside of a hospital environment because the symptoms are nonspecific. And once diagnosed, the condition is difficult to treat because, while restoring hydration involves restoring blood sodium levels, sodium replacement requirements are unknown and vary dramatically across patient populations. So the old mantra "just drink more water" doesn't cut it, and in fact, in individuals with compromised renal function, drinking too much water (depleting blood sodium levels) can be fatal.

In the second quarter of 2004, we identified just-published, groundbreaking research that correlated saliva sodium with blood sodium, the gold-standard marker for measuring dehydration. We asked if we could develop an accurate rapid results, low-cost monitor that diagnosed dehydration and, further, could we develop a rehydration container that tailored the sodium concentration of the solution based upon the monitor's reading. The answer at the time appeared to be "no." Neither Charles nor I possessed the skills to develop a chemical assay or biosensor that quantitated sodium in saliva. But Dr. Allen Arieff, the former chief of clinical nephrology at UCSF's Veterans Affairs Medical Center, agreed to meet with us, and he jumped out of his seat when he heard our concept. According to Dr. Arieff, a saliva sodium monitor could dramatically improve quality of life for independent and institutionalized seniors, improve health outcomes for young children suffering from gastroenteritis, and improve physical and cognitive performance for athletes and military personnel.

I believe it is Jack Welch who describes the importance of risk-taking—of taking bet-the-farm risks—in building companies. Our decision to focus our development efforts on a hydration monitor, and to file away our lower-tech product designs without owning the financial or human capital resources necessary to address this challenge, was a bet-the-farm kind of decision.

For four months, we worked to identify a scientist who could give our idea wings. We crafted a nontraditional job posting: we needed someone who could develop a diagnostic test measuring an analyte in saliva with a reaction time of X, at specificity and sensitivity levels of Y, at a cost per unit of Z. This job listing was strategic in that it applied a strong filter to the candidate pool (those who cannot accomplish *exactly* this need not apply) and it forced applicants to conduct substantial research during our interview process. In fact, because of his extensive research during the interview process, we filed our second patent within two months of bringing David on board—a PhD chemist with some 20 years experience developing diagnostic tests for Abbott and SmithKline Beecham.

In addition, we recruited some of the nation's leading medical authorities in fluid and electrolyte disorders to the company's advisory board; we hired a regulatory consultant; and we recruited partners from two of the nation's leading law firms to provide us with legal counsel. We evaluated various business models (including selling directly to the consumer and licensing our technologies to larger medical products companies). We confirmed end user demand for our dehydration monitor. We secured interest from the executive directors of nursing homes, home health care companies, assisted living facilities, pediatric health care providers, lead trainers of professional sports teams, medical directors of marathons and triathlons, health and safety directors of mining companies, and advisers to the Department of Defense. And finally, we attempted to lay the groundwork for a Fortune 500 company by conducting substantial research into additional disease categories to which we could apply our technology platform.

This brings us to December 2004, when we approached the funding community. To our surprise, investors said, "We don't care about a strong product portfolio, we don't care about end user demand, what we want to see is a working prototype." Having gone to business school during the dot-com fever of the late 1990s, when crafting a business plan, much less building a prototype, was considered a waste of time, I was flabbergasted. A prototype?

Bill Sahlman, a professor of mine at Harvard Business School and still an important adviser today, defines entrepreneurship as the "relentless pursuit of opportunity without regard to tangible resources currently controlled." My accountant would certainly take issue with this definition. He might agree to define what I do as the "*reckless* pursuit of opportunity without regard to resources currently controlled." This is to say that in February of 2005, with the help of American Express, RCS negotiated an agreement with a contract diagnostics developer for the development of 100 test prototypes of our hydration monitor.

Over the course of the next two months, weekly conference calls with our diagnostics partner would read like a medical soap opera of sorts. Initial lab results were quite positive—our reagent produced a signal in the presence of sodium—and our team celebrated with champagne. The challenge—to reduce time-to-reaction and increase sensitivity of the assay—was one we believed we could overcome. Eight weeks later, our diagnostics partner reported that time-to-test-results was holding strong at 28 minutes—approximately nine times longer than what the market would bear, according to our research. Two weeks later, after conducting substantial research on what had gone wrong, we discovered a new substrate that we felt might have potential. Our diagnostics partner agreed to extend the contract—unpaid—to test it. Three weeks later, our partner reported that the substrate was "magic." Time-to-test results was one minute, and correlations between color development on the diagnostic strip and sample sodium concentration exceeded 99 percent. We leapt around the office.

I presented our findings to an audience of 150 venture and strategic investors just days after securing positive lab results. Two days later, we secured some initial seed capital. And we are now in initial licensing discussions with several very large medical products providers.

Are we out of the danger zone? Not even close; and we may never be. The reader for the diagnostic assay needs to be developed, funding needs to be raised to support salaries, patients need to be tested, 510(k) applications need to be submitted to the FDA—and failure to execute along any one of these fronts could cripple the company. I recently read the book *Ultramarathon Man: Confessions of an All-Night Runner*. In his book, Dean Karnazes, who has completed over ten 100-mile endurance races, maintains that his success strategy depends upon breaking up the challenge. During a 100-mile race, he often mutters something like, "I'll just run to the next stop sign and then re-evaluate." Without question, we at RCS are running a 100-mile race, and at each stop sign, we cannot be sure we will make it to the next. But, at the present time, our pace is strong and we recommit ourselves each day to winning the race.

MANDEE HELLER ADLER
AND TAMARA KING STARK

Mandee is a graduate of the Harvard Business School and the University of Pennsylvania. Tamara is a graduate of the Harvard Business School and the University of Michigan. These two Florida natives, who grew up 20 minutes away from each other, met at Goldman Sachs in 1995.

> "Let's give credit where credit is due. Our company was launched by women, for women, and with the support and encouragement of women from Harvard Business School, Goldman Sachs, and others we met along the way."

Starting with Goldman Sachs and then at Harvard Business School (HBS), we gained an ever-expanding network of successful female friends who encouraged us to pursue our business idea and helped us to succeed. In particular, we had, as far as we know, the first and only all-female study group at HBS. Although unanticipated, membership in this group provided us with the basis for understanding the financial needs of businesswomen. One would think that any woman who attends Harvard Business School would be financially savvy. As we entered our second year at Harvard, we were shocked to find that many of our female friends and classmates did not actively manage their savings. In fact, many had signing bonuses sitting idly in their checking accounts. Even with their deep financial and business educations, many were risk averse when it came to individual financial planning. We were determined to understand why this was the case and we set out to find a solution.

After graduation, our circle of friends became a network of women who were succeeding in diverse areas. Of the original seven women in our study group, four started businesses following graduation, and all prospered. We believe one of the critical ingredients of our success was the ability to leverage our friends who had gained expertise in various areas—marketing, legal, etc.—and were happy to lend a hand.

Initially, we had taken jobs in the retail and executive search areas. In the evenings and on weekends, we continued to work to refine our business plan. Gradually, the need for a company that addressed the individual financial planning needs of women through education became clearer and clearer. Four months after business school graduation, we both quit our jobs and founded our own company, HerDollar. The goal of the company was to help large financial institutions attract and retain female customers. When we first proposed the idea of marketing financial products and services to women back in 1999, many banks thought that they were already addressing women's needs by making areas of their websites pink. They had no plans to focus on increasing their share of profits from women. Seeing this void in the market drove us to pursue our goal even more—we wanted to raise the level of respect for women as owners of capital. We built HerDollar to correct this gap in the market.

Through networking in the New York area, we met even more women, who began to see the merit of our idea and supported us along the way. Rather than keeping our business plan to ourselves, we spent a lot of time sharing our ideas with accomplished businesswomen, asking for opinions and advice; most liked the concept, offered new ideas, and introduced us to other insightful women.

The business plan was gaining speed by December 1999 and through consistent networking, we continued to meet and receive support from women in the financial community, many of them quite senior. For example, as we expanded our business model, we leveraged our relationship with one woman who ran a market research firm. She helped us with focus groups. Another woman who is an investment banker helped us structure our capital raises. Networking was a skill strongly encouraged and developed by our mothers. Whether it was fund-raising for the high school swim team or selling Girl Scout cookies, we were encouraged to plan, organize, and communicate our desires.

Our mothers' cold-calling advice came in extremely handy in early 2000. A cold call to Muriel "Mickie" Siebert turned into the sale of our first company. Mickie is a pioneer as far as women and finance are concerned, having been the first woman to hold a seat on the New York Stock Exchange and the first woman to own a member firm. Good fortune comes from hard work and a lot of luck. We were pitching Mickie's assistant on our idea and trying to get a meeting. Mickie happened to be in the office that day, overheard the conversation, and the next morning at 9 a.m. we had a meeting with Mickie and her team. Working as a senior woman in the financial services industry since the 1960s, she immediately saw the importance of HerDollar and tried to figure out a way for us all to work together. After a few months of negotiating, we determined that it made sense to combine HerDollar's educational platform with Mickie's investment and transactional capabilities. Mickie's company, Muriel Siebert & Co. also acquired a company called WFN.com—Women's Financial Network—a company that had established a strong financial content and community site for women. The three components combined to form what is now called Women's Financial Network at Siebert, capitalizing on two great brand names in the consumer marketplace. Though we had not yet reached our 28th birthdays, we were asked to run the newly formed Women's Financial Network at Siebert, under the ultimate direction of Mickie Siebert.

HerDollar was a wonderful learning experience, both personally and professionally. We attribute much of our success to the support we received from the women to whom we reached out. By never being afraid to ask, we succeeded at enlarging our circle of contacts through networking with women (and men) who were in positions to offer guidance, contacts, and in some cases, financing.

MOUSUMI SHAW

Mousumi is the founder and CEO of Sikara & Company (www.sikarajewelry.com), a new retailer specializing in Modern Fusion Jewelry, a trademarked concept that celebrates the influence of cultural diversity through modern design. Mousumi founded the company while pursuing her MBA at Harvard Business School.

"My mother has always told me, 'No experience goes to waste ... you can learn something from everything you do and every person you meet.'"

I was thrown into the world of entrepreneurship at the age of 10, assuming responsibility for loading the Coke machine and handing out quarters to the customers at my family's laundromat. Shortly thereafter, my parents sold the family business. My mother, an immigrant from India, tired of working part-time jobs in retail that garnered little respect and small economic incentive, was determined to take fate into her own hands. Her passion was jewelry and she decided to open her own 200-square foot jewelry store in Corpus Christi, Texas, which was precisely where I began to learn the fundamentals of customer service and business.

Fourteen years later, after having work experiences that ranged from consulting, to starting an Internet services company, to working at the White House, I had an epiphany, similar to my mother's, that it was time to follow my heart. This led to the launching of Sikara & Company. Sikara's tagline is Modern Fusion Jewelry™ and is a reflection of my life as a first generation

Indian-American. Although my ancestral roots are from Calcutta, India, I have been influenced by a multicultural world. Traveling and experiencing life in over 30 countries is now engrained in my personality, my sense of style, and who I am. I am modern and I am fusion.

I believe the term *fusion* represents our lives as modern women living in America. It is a blend of our past heritage and a new modern spirit. The name *Sikara* also speaks to this fusion. The company's name is a derivation of an Indian word, meaning "houseboat." It symbolizes the journey we take in life that results in a fusion of experiences. Sikara is fusion, Sikara is edgy, Sikara is unique.

As an entrepreneur I've often been asked what motivates me. I realize that entrepreneurs can be motivated for many different reasons: seeing a burning need for a product or service, discovering an untapped opportunity, craving independence, or simply being frustrated with their current job. My own personal motivations have changed as I moved from one venture to the next.

As I mentioned at the beginning of my story, while my real entrepreneurial journey began in my family's laundromat, a number of life experiences and people since then have shaped my entrepreneurial genetic makeup along the way, influencing my decision to create Sikara & Company. My mother has been my entrepreneurial role model, my most prized mentor, and source of great inspiration. She lives life with such energy and drive despite the challenges she has experienced in life. Back in India, she was barely 20 years old when my grandfather decided that she was to be married off as soon as she finished her finals at her community college. Luckily, my father wasn't as controlling as my grandfather had been and he allowed her more liberties. Shortly after she arrived on U.S. soil, not knowing a soul, she decided to venture out as an Avon door-to-door saleswoman.

After my mother gave birth to my brother and me, she took on several jobs over time as a bank teller, a salesperson for a large department store, and a librarian in order to help my father provide for us. Over time, they invested their savings to purchase a laundromat. After years of hard work, my mother used the profit to make a foray into jewelry sales. Today my mother successfully runs two jewelry stores, thanks to her terrific memory and her ability to connect with just about anyone. My mother has always told me, "No experience goes to waste...you can learn something from everything you do and every person you meet." With that advice, I have learned to appreciate every experience, every person I have met, every job I have held, and every day that I live.

My mother's own taste for adventure has been an asset to me in my personal and professional life. Between our family road trips across the United States, camping, and travels to the Far East, my mom has taught me not only to have a love for our ancestral Indian culture but also a deep appreciation for other cultures. A passion for travel is embedded deep in my genes as well. I've visited over 30 countries in the past 10 years, opening my eyes to foreign culture, history, and politics, oftentimes not found in the textbooks. My travels have inspired me to work with a network of international designers to present a truly unique collection of jewelry. Each jewelry collection is a mix of pieces that are inspired from countries such as India and Mexico or regions such as Eastern Europe. When a person purchases a piece, they also learn about the history and culture pertaining to the country where the designer of the piece originates.

REBECCA ZUCKER

Rebecca is a widely respected career and executive coach and is principal and cofounder of the leadership development firm, Next Step Partners. After earning an MBA from Stanford, Rebecca began her own career at Goldman Sachs where she worked as an investment banker.

"I love being my own boss and collaborating with my partners to create what we envision."

It was a nine-week, cross-country journey at the age of 15 with a group called Man and His Land (similar to Outward Bound) that paved the way for the rest of my life. The height of this trip was climbing to the summit of Mount Rainier in Washington's National Park. This experience opened my eyes to all that I was capable of achieving and allowed me to see that I could create a life that I wanted for myself. Reaching the summit provided me with the self-actualization and inspiration to both excel in school and later succeed as an entrepreneur.

After graduating from college as valedictorian of NYU's Leonard N. Stern School of Business, I worked for The Equitable in a management training program, rotating through several business units. From there, I earned an MBA at Stanford, which opened my eyes to even more possibilities. After business school, I went to work at Goldman Sachs as an investment banker in the Financial Institutions Group. Other than at Mount Rainier and Stanford, I had never been around so many amazing, capable people, many of whom are still close friends. I had been working at GS for a few years on several M&A and corporate finance deals when I realized something was missing.

From my early days in school, I had acquired a fascination with France and I dreamt of living and working there. While I was still at GS, I went on a two-week vacation to France and decided to set up some interviews to check out how feasible it would be to get a job there "some day." The day before I left Paris, I met the woman who was to become my future boss. She granted me an interview with Disney Consumer Products doing strategic planning for the European, Middle Eastern, and African region.

I wound up playing hooky from the annual Goldman Sachs Investment Banking Conference back in New York to attend a second round interview at Disney in Paris. Two months later, I was living in a centuries old apartment on Ile St. Louis. While it was a dream come true to be living in Paris, I found myself still working bankers' hours well past midnight. I realized that I was sacrificing the food, culture, and fun—precisely what I had moved to Paris to enjoy—for yet another high-profile, demanding job. After finishing my contract, I turned down a promotion, five-year working papers, and a chance to move anywhere in the world with Disney, to just enjoy life in Paris.

I took full advantage of a year off in Paris to decompress and think about what I really wanted in my life and my work. I realized that just because I was good at finance, I didn't need to do it for a living. It wasn't something that I was passionate about and it really wasn't all that satisfying.

Initially, as a way to subsidize my living expenses in Paris, I started coaching Europeans part time. Little did I know that this was a pivotal experience that would put me on the path to my dream career. One day, I stopped myself on the sidewalk outside my Paris apartment and realized that I came out of these coaching sessions with an absolute high and thrived on the one-to-one interaction. I was fulfilled knowing that I was supporting other people in achieving their goals; it was something that truly meshed with who I am as a person.

When I finally moved back to the States from Paris, it was the height of the Internet boom in Silicon Valley. I ended up accepting a great job running training for over 300 investment banking professionals at Robertson Stephens in San Francisco, serving as an internal coach to many of them. It was a terrific, fast-paced environment, and every day I had people coming into my office yelling, screaming, and crying about all of their career and work-related problems. The funny thing was that I loved this part of my job and knew I was good at coaching these people through the issues they were facing. It was then that I began actively investigating the field of coaching.

When the economy tanked in the spring of 2001 and I lost my job, I knew that this was the time to plunge head first into coaching. I ran into a woman, who is now one of my business partners, who was also starting her own coaching practice, and asked if she wanted to meet for coffee. During this meeting, we both realized that we could do more together than individually and joined forces to cofound our firm, Next Step Partners. We have since taken on another principal and added four associates around the country to deliver programs we have created.

Initially focused on career-transition clients due to the nature of market demands, more than half of our business is now in leadership development and organizational effectiveness, areas that I find both exciting and rewarding. We work with clients at the individual, team, and organizational levels to help them be more effective at what they do and to move forward to reach the next step in performance.

My long-term plans are to continue to grow this business and, hopefully one day, have a family—and a *pied à terre* in Paris! I love what I do, the people I work with, and thrive on the variety of projects that I work on. Most of all, I love being my own boss and collaborating with my partners to create what we envision. On the top of Mount Rainier, I learned that I could control my own destiny and create whatever I wanted, and so I have.

MELINA HIGGINS

Melina Higgins grew up under economic adversity as the fifth of seven children. Her athletic ability helped her initially in getting a scholarship to college, but it was her academic achievement that paved the way for her future success. She graduated from Colgate in 1989, began her career as an analyst at Goldman Sachs, received her MBA at Harvard Business School in 1994, and returned to Goldman Sachs where she currently manages its North American mezzanine funds. Melina became a partner of Goldman in 2002.

> "My parents just kept saying, 'Yes, you can; you just have to figure out how to make it work.' That kind of positive attitude is very empowering."

My life has been great, and it didn't necessarily have to turn out that way. There was a lot of financial hardship in my family in the early years, but there was also a lot of strength and support. I am the fifth of seven children. My mother is Korean and my father is Irish-American. They met and married during the Korean War. When my father got out of the army, my parents moved to Northern California, where I was born. While in junior high school, the economic cost of the Bay Area had become too high for us, and we moved across the country to the Adirondacks in upstate New York, where my father had grown up. I graduated from the same high school as my father.

One of the first major challenges that I faced was figuring out how and where to go to college. My high school record was very strong. I've always performed well academically, was valedictorian of my class, and played four varsity sports in school and Empire State Games during the summer. My high school didn't have a lot of resources, and when it was time for me to apply to college, my guidance counselor thought my college prospects were very limited since my family was not in a position to help me financially. So I researched various options and applied to schools that offered volleyball scholarships. My father drove me to Colgate University in the middle of the winter and I tried out for the volleyball team. I was awarded one of the two volleyball scholarships that they offered. Shortly thereafter, I received a call from the coach saying that I was to receive one of Colgate's largest academic scholarships and therefore she was going to award the athletic scholarship to another student. So I went on an academic scholarship, which proved to be a big advantage because it allowed me to study abroad. I did play volleyball my first two years, but I spent my junior year abroad studying in Spain and Switzerland.

When I arrived at Colgate, I had to catch up to the other students who had attended terrific high schools. One of the first courses that you were required to take at Colgate was called General Education. My roommate, who had gone to boarding school, had already read every single book on our list, and I hadn't even heard of most of them. In the end I did fine, graduating in the top 1 percent of my class, Phi Beta Kappa.

One of the most defining events for me during that time involved a good friend of mine at Colgate who had grown up in Korea. She arranged for me to spend half of the summer between my freshman and sophomore year living with two of her friends in Korea. That experience gave me a wonderful chance to learn about my Korean heritage, and it opened up a whole exciting world of travel. Since that first experience, I have traveled to over 40 countries and try to visit new places at every opportunity.

At Colgate I completed a double major in economics and Spanish and wrote two honors theses: one on economics and the other, in Spanish, on the works of Jorge Louis Borges, the Argentinian writer. I liked analytical as well as creative thinking. Math was one of my strong subjects but I also loved to read.

By the time I was ready to graduate and begin my career, I had lots of work experience behind me, albeit very little of it relevant to a career in finance. I had a paper route when I was nine years old, a full-time babysitting job during the summers and after school by the time I was eleven, and waitressing experience in high school. I seem to always have had a job. During summers in college, I continued to waitress; and I spent the summer before my senior year as a nanny with a family in Spain, taking care of five kids, in order to become fluent in Spanish. While studying in Switzerland, I had an internship at the United Nations.

During my senior year January term, I completed an internship in government bond sales and trading at Lehman Brothers. A Colgate alumnus was head of bond trading, and he gave me a nonpaying job for a month. Though I had taken economics in school, it was my first exposure to finance. I loved my internship, loved finance, loved the fast pace. While at Lehman, I learned about two-year financial analyst programs, which sounded like the perfect opportunity for me.

At the time I graduated from college, investment banks like Goldman Sachs did not interview at Colgate. I thought it would be great to get a financial analyst job, but I had missed all of the application deadlines. The first few companies that I called said that it was too late for me to apply. So I called Colgate's alumni office and asked for a list of all alumni who worked in finance in New York City. I got on the phone and started cold calling, going down the list, introducing myself and explaining that I was looking for a job in finance. One person I spoke with was a second-year analyst at Goldman Sachs who worked in M&A. She told me to send my résumé, which I did. Fortunately for me, at the time there were two partners in M&A who were from Colgate. I ended up getting an interview, even though I had missed the deadline completely. I went in on the last day of interviews and Goldman offered me a job. At the time, I had no idea how unconventional my job search had been or how fortunate I was.

My parents are, and always have been, wildly supportive. My mother honestly thought her children could accomplish anything. If I had said I wanted to be an astronaut, my mother would have said, "That's great, go do it." The word "no" was not in her vocabulary when it came to her kids. All of us were very athletic and our parents came to almost all of our games. They would even come to some of my games when I was at Colgate. Their support was incredible. My parents just kept saying, "Yes, you can; you just have to figure out how to make it work." That kind of positive attitude is very empowering.

I loved Goldman and stayed for a third year as an analyst, but eventually decided to go to Harvard Business School. That was a terrific experience. I made lots of friends there with whom I continue to stay in touch. A group of girlfriends and I still go away together every year. When I was finishing my MBA, I had an offer to come back to Goldman Sachs in M&A, which is where I had worked as an analyst. I had worked during the summer at McKinsey, and I had an offer to go there as well. Where I really wanted to work, however, was Goldman's private equity group known as the Principal Investment Area (PIA). The problem was that private equity was a really hot area and there was a lot of demand for very few positions. During recruiting, I met with one of the coheads of investment banking. I explained to him that my first choice was PIA and that my second choice was to rejoin M&A but not right away. (My third choice was to go to McKinsey.) I proposed that I spend one to two years in PIA, maybe a year in corporate finance, and then go back to M&A as a third-year associate. Given that I had already spent three years in M&A as an analyst, I wouldn't be behind, and I would be a much more well-rounded banker having spent time in other areas. He thought this was very interesting and told me I could do it. I asked if he needed to check with anyone, but he was the boss, and he said not to worry about it and to assume it was done. I immediately got calls from recruiting saying that this was not possible, not how they ran the associate program. I told them that the co-head of investment banking said that I could do this, and if he wanted to tell me now that I couldn't, then I would like to hear it from him. They later called back to say that I could have the spot in PIA.

I've now been in PIA for 11 years. Probably what set the track for my career was when, as a fourth-year associate, I asked to specialize in mezzanine debt. (Mezzanine is privately negotiated debt, sometimes with an equity component such as warrants, which is often used to finance leveraged buyouts.) At the time, specialization seemed the way to go. The firm was starting to specialize, investment banking was specializing; even within PIA, we were moving from a generalist model to a specialist model.

Mezzanine was an area that few people wanted to specialize in. If you look at the returns, mezzanine often has a better risk/reward return than equity does today. From an investment standpoint, I think a lot of people want to invest in mezzanine, but in terms of actually working on it, equity is a bit more high profile. But I thought mezzanine had a very promising future and that we could build it into a big business. I thought it would be a great platform and something I could be responsible for. I went to the head of my department and said I wanted to specialize in mezzanine, and he thought this was a great idea. I was the first full-time person dedicated to mezzanine and now run our North American business. We now have a full team in the United States and in Europe, and we are the largest mezzanine fund in the world. We have raised over $6 billion in capital, and we are currently investing our third fund of $3.5 billion.

In terms of my career, things have gone well. I am 38 years old, and I have been a partner for four years. I serve on the investment committee for PIA, which oversees both equity and mezzanine investments. I have a terrific team in the mezzanine business and a wonderfully supportive boss. He is the head of mezzanine globally and was instrumental in developing my career as well as my making partner. I see myself continuing to play out my career in PIA and am already planning our next fund.

ANDREA MILLER

Andrea is a recent graduate of Columbia Business School, where she was a summer associate at Goldman Sachs and the managing editor of The Bottom Line. *Before business school, she spent three years working in project finance for Enron in India.*

> "Networking is all about connecting with people and building a community, both of which are essential to my sense of well-being and wholeness."

Dreams do come true, especially if you put your heart and soul into it. After spending the last three years developing a new magazine called *Tango*, we celebrated the publication of our first issue in February 2005, and our second issue in May. You have never experienced such exhilaration as taking a concept and turning it into a commercial venture. I had observed a huge gap in the magazine market and reasoned that a smart, new lifestyle magazine focused on love and relationships would be extremely popular. Whether the topic is communication, sex, career, culture, stress, travel, home, or money, *Tango* approaches it from a unique point of view, offering a rich mix of expert advice, in-depth reporting, dramatic personal narrative, and entertaining opinion.

I had a terrific experience at Goldman, but I didn't develop a passion for the work. I decided to pursue the entrepreneurial publishing path because I felt it had vast commercial potential and would fulfill my desire to be passionate about my career. Choosing the entrepreneurial path was a relatively easy decision given that I hail from a long line of entrepreneurs.

In developing *Tango*, I realized that I am passionate about the creative process, about telling stories, about connecting with people, about pushing beyond my (perceived) limitations and becoming more fulfilled, more whole, as a result. My biggest challenge was getting my venture financed. I overcame this challenge by continuing to fund-raise but also by making the deal more attractive through lining up partnerships, signing up additional advertisers, etc. I was also able to make this happen by support from members of 85 Broads, my extended network.

Networking is all about connecting with people and building a community, both of which are essential to my sense of well-being and wholeness. I am specifically enthralled with 85 Broads because of the concentration of incredibly talented, accomplished, bright women, where there is a shared desire to connect and commune with one another. While this has an important social component, it also has an important practical and professional component. I always leave 85 Broads events uplifted and inspired. I am in awe of the speakers and always grateful that I can apply their examples of passion, courage, brilliance, and tenacity to my own life and work.

LILIAN ALMEIDA

Lilian was born and raised in Brazil. She first flew solo when she was 18, and she founded her own air taxi company, LNA Taxi Aereo, when she was 24. Lilian graduated from MIT's Sloan School of Management, where she also attended airline management classes.

> "I faced the challenges of being a female commercial pilot, manager, and entrepreneur in the male-dominated aviation industry because I am passionate about challenges and I'm passionate about flying."

Starting my own air taxi company and being a young woman flying in the countryside of Brazil came with a lot of dreams and challenges. My hometown of Divinopolis, Brazil, and its vicinity had a lot of industry—such as textiles, fashion, shoes, and metals—but at the time, no airline. I seized the opportunity to connect local businessmen to their partners and customers elsewhere in the country. Business grew as our reputation for reliable and efficient service spread. I dreamed big when I started planning the introduction of an innovative operation with a Cessna Grand Caravan aircraft to become a regular operator in the future.

I come from a family of pilots. My uncle Cauby learned how to fly when he was 18. He introduced flying to my father, Vinicio, his best friend at school and brother-in-law-to-be, igniting a lifelong passion in him. Flying lessons were expensive, so my father had to wait until he was 44 years old to pursue his passion for flying. To make up for lost time, he bought a single engine plane the same year!

My mother Ieda was terrified of having her children flying with my father. She was so afraid that something would happen to us all that she begged him to give up flying small planes. As positive as my father is, he persuaded her instead to get her license, which she did one year later, when I was 10. She was so brave in achieving that!

My solo flight was on my 18th birthday. My brother Lester, then 17, did his solo flight on the same day. After landing, we celebrated it in local Brazilian tradition, "banho de oleo," an oil bath. Friends were invited to our birthday party at the airport. We put on some old clothes and they covered us with black oil. People were clapping, laughing, and cheering us on. When we were ready, someone yelled, "Go!" and we ran over to our friends to get grease on as many of them as possible.

A few months later, I moved to the state capital, Belo Horizonte, to study engineering. Five years later, I returned to my hometown and worked for my father's engineering company. By this time, I had already gotten my commercial pilot's license and my youngest brother, Licinio, had gotten his. So, we were a family of pilots!

I started flying my father's friends on weekends. Local businessmen began asking me to fly them to several places. I decided to start a business flying my father's four-seat single engine plane. I soon added a six-seat, twin-engine plane, from Dad's engineering company. I always had my father's support and encouragement in these initiatives.

It took about a year to get the company operating and in November 1995 I piloted LNA's first flight. This would be a good marketing tool to attract passengers. After all, I was the first and only woman to start and operate an air taxi company in Brazil.

Most of my flights traversed 300 miles of countryside. My clients were mainly businessmen, and they visited everyone from ministeries to fashion shows, and everywhere, from São Paulo to small villages and farms. And I got to go with them. I met many interesting people, got to know many industries, and saw much of the country by flying.

Year after year, my company experienced growth. The most challenging part was to convince users of the large commercial airlines to utilize air taxi service instead. Many times I had one single passenger for São Paulo, and renting the plane alone would not be cost-effective. One way to become profitable was to sell individual tickets in "systematic links" between Divinopolis and São Paulo. I had to get permission from DAC to apply this innovative approach in such a small company. I had studied the regulation carefully and knew my company was likely to qualify. My company was the first of its category to be granted the Air Transport Certificate, and in January 1998, I started operating regular flights from Divinopolis to São Paulo. To test the market, we used the small plane we had, though we aimed at expanding the operation and buying a Cessna Caravan. The plan was to connect Divinopolis, Pouso Alegre, and Pocos de Caldas to Belo Horizonte, my state capital, and to São Paulo, the biggest city in South America. In this process, I learned how difficult it is to manage a company within a highly regulated market, especially for women in a male-dominated industry.

During Brazil's economic crisis, I had to make major adjustments to my company's operations, and realized that I needed to learn a lot more about management and finance in order to do that successfully. After receiving my MBA from Sloan School of Management and taking classes in Global Airline and Airline Management at MIT, I am now more prepared for an executive career in aviation. I am also challenging myself again as an entrepreneur by launching Mitsie (www.mitsie.com), a new venture that brings Brazilian swimwear and shoe fashion to the United States. But as passionate as I am about new ventures, I am still most passionate about flying—so much so that I am back in flight school learning to fly helicopters!

MARIAM NAFICY

Mariam started her own company called Eve.com, an online cosmetics retailer, during the height of the dot-com era. Her company was eventually bought by Idealab in 2000. Mariam began her career at Goldman Sachs where she worked for a few years before joining Gemini Consulting and then a California restaurant chain. She earned her MBA from Stanford University. Mariam is currently working at The Body Shop and is committed to balancing her passion for her career with her love for her family.

> "The magnitude of the decisions you make before you are 30 is amazing—what career you will follow, who you will marry, what type of person you will be."

I felt like a country bumpkin showing up on the trading floor at Goldman Sachs for my first job out of college. For someone with absolutely no business training, I was tremendously lucky to have my first career experience at Goldman. After working there for awhile, I realized that my passion was on the operational side of the business and decided to work for Gemini Consulting, creating strategies for Fortune 500 companies.

Upon landing in California, I realized that this was exactly the place that I was supposed to be, because the environment was so entrepreneurial. I had learned at Goldman how companies raised money, but consulting introduced strategy and business process change. I came to the professional realization that I could take my operational understanding of business and apply it across a variety of industries.

After awhile at Gemini, I realized that I wanted to do more business-to-consumer work and knew that an MBA would help me make the migration to B2C. I applied to Stanford and was rejected, with the school encouraging me to reapply after taking the time to raise my GMAT scores and to do something "sexy" to beef up my résumé.

Not long after receiving that advice, an opportunity came knocking. It was an entrepreneurial opportunity to join a new restaurant chain. I signed on. Day after day, my boss Maurice coached me in the art of thinking like an entrepreneur. I watched him do everything from raising money to dealing with restaurant critics to handling operational crises. Maurice boosted my self-confidence and became not only a role model, but a mentor as well. I realized that I wanted to become an entrepreneur myself.

My second time around applying to Stanford, Maurice wrote my recommendations and I was accepted. My husband and I decided to go to business school together which was a great experience for us to share. Even before I began at Stanford, I was itching to do something entrepreneurial; I came up with an idea for a book and pitched it successfully to publishing firms. I began writing the book and completed it while at Stanford. The book is called *The Fast Track* and is intended to help aspiring bankers and consultants learn the ropes of the business world before setting their foot inside. To date, the book has sold over 50,000 copies and has received acclaim from recruiters, candidates, and businesses alike.

I skipped the whole recruitment process upon graduating from Stanford as I knew that I wanted to start my own business. I was willing to take a risk and I didn't have a lot to lose. Shortly thereafter, I met my business partner who was working at McKinsey at the time, and we began brainstorming about potential business ideas.

The two of us decided to start an online cosmetics store called Eve.com and became enormously successful signing up major cosmetics companies. We quickly grew to about $10 million in sales and had convinced 250 major brands to sign on to us. Having never managed a soul before in my life, we had 120 people working for us. We raised $26 million in three rounds of venture capital from some of the other VC firms. We were way ahead of the competition.

In early 2000, Idealab approached us with an offer to buy our company. We sold our company to them in May 2000 just before the markets went sour. Eventually, Idealab sold many of the Eve.com assets to LVMH, which owns Sephora. I stayed with the online cosmetics company the entire time, riding every wave of change. We created a huge return for our initial investors and all of our employees.

After working on an Internet joint venture for five major movie studios, I was invited to join The Body Shop to help launch their Internet channel. At the same time, our son Alex was born. I have found managing work and family is one of my biggest challenges yet. It is like having two emotional eggs in two different baskets. And while I would like to start a business again, I know what it takes to do that. It would take too much from my family life. I'm glad to be investing in my knowledge of retail through my work at The Body Shop right now, and I am sure that if I keep learning and keep thinking creatively, at some point an idea will come and the time will be right to start something new. You never really stop being an entrepreneur.

5

PARENTS

Parents have a profound influence on our lives, our values, and our passions. Sometimes as role models and sometimes as "reverse" role models. Sometimes as believers and other times as doubters. Sometimes because of their presence and sometimes because of their absence. Always because—no matter how close or distant, appreciative or antagonistic, loving or challenging—the relationship is *absolutely unique.* Parents are our very first partners, and we are our children's very first partners. What kind of partners are we? Will we be? Should we be? These are the questions that the women in this chapter, and throughout our global network, are trying to answer on their own terms and in their own time frames.

Many of the women in this book admire, and have been influenced by, their mothers—crediting them for much of their own success even though their lives and their choices have often been extraordinarily different. We even have a section on our website, 85broads.com, featuring "Mothers Who Rock!" Last year we held an event in London with the same title, and we've received a great many phenomenal tributes as a result.

From the hundreds of emails I get through 85 Broads each week, as well as our network events, I know that many of our members spend a lot of time thinking about how their children's views of them will mirror or potentially differ from their own views of their parents based on the choices and trade-offs they are making in their careers. What will my daughter (or son) write about me? Am I, will I be, a "mother who rocks"? Many other members who don't yet have children wonder how parenthood will mesh with the visions they are developing of their own futures.

One of the biggest reasons I started the 85 Broads network is that I didn't want anyone to feel as isolated or disconnected as I did when I first left Goldman Sachs. Returning to Goldman after almost three years at home and away from the markets wasn't the right answer either. It wasn't until I launched my own business—which my entire experience at Goldman had given me the skills and professional confidence to do—that I would start to build a foundation that could support my personal, professional, and philanthropic vision of myself, all at the same time.

There is no question that owning your own business is one of the hardest things you can ever imagine doing. Some days it's great; other days it's gut wrenching; it's always a high wire act. The stress is never-ending and the responsibility can be overwhelming. But the choices are your own, not someone else's. For the first time in my career I felt that I was truly in control of my own professional and personal destiny. This doesn't mean that there still aren't tough trade-offs and decisions to make. Change in careers and change in personal lives is now almost a constant. Just when your financial life and family life and career life seem to all line up in sync, something can happen that throws the whole cycle "out of balance" in an instant, no matter how well balanced you thought you were.

While "work-life balance" is a concept that can prove to be very elusive, I do believe in the idea of living what I like to call a *partnered life*. Sharing both the upside rewards and downside risks and taking the long-term view are what partnership is all about. Finding solutions that are *optimal* rather than balanced allow you to replace compromise with *teamwork*. Partnering with your spouse, partnering with your children, partnering with your parents, partnering with your bosses, colleagues, classmates, and clients are all part of creating win-win solutions that are strong enough yet flexible enough to allow you to *build* something truly exceptional, not just balance something. I think being an entrepreneur or working in an entrepreneurial environment—or even viewing yourself with an entrepreneurial mindset—allows you to better integrate your life, career, family, friends, and passions in a way that is uniquely your own. In many respects, parents are entrepreneurs. There is no blueprint for success and no easy trade-offs. Parenting, like partnering, is about building.

Being part of a network and learning how to build relationships that strengthen your focus both personally and professionally is also a key element of parenting, as we'll learn from a number of the stories in this chapter. Networks provide critical community connections that survive career moves, relocations, the birth and raising of children, and other life events.

They also can help you leverage the true power of the "story"—learning how others make parenting decisions can help you make your own decisions and define the dimensions of your own "partnered life" that make the most sense for you. As women lead increasingly global lives both professionally and personally, a strong network can literally become an extended family community for current and future parents to draw on when making these decisions.

This leads us to the last common thread in the stories of the parents we're about to meet. As in all the other chapters of this book and in the many dimensions of our members' lives, there is no "one-size-fits-all," no cookie-cutter approach. It all comes down to *individual choices and decisions*. No organization or community can create a policy or strategy or solution that works for every woman or parent in optimizing all of the dimensions of an "integrated life." The challenge for companies and workplaces is not just to formulate policies or programs that result in this elusive work-life balance, but to create work environments and cultures that allow women to make individual decisions that are right for them in strong partnership with their managers, spouses, children, and the other people in their lives. The women in this chapter may not have all the answers all the time, but they are making decisions based on their own definitions of success and of happiness—not just for themselves but for their families or future families. These are mothers and parents who rock!

MARIA MERRILL

Since graduating from Wellesley in 1992 and receiving her MBA from the University of Pennsylvania in 1997, Maria became a vice president in leveraged finance at a prominent investment bank, where she worked from 1997 until 2001. She is now a managing director of The Royal Bank of Scotland in New York and the proud mother of two young daughters.

> "Motherhood is such a joyous time, a time to be celebrated. You shouldn't have to worry that you will lose your job."

In my late twenties, my career in investment banking was sidetracked by the birth of my first daughter. Although I didn't realize it at the time, there was an unwritten rule that said you should wait until you make partner to have kids, and I naively thought that I was different and that my skills and value to the bank would help me circumvent any potential pitfalls. Although I had been on an upward path where I worked, I was asked to change my job shortly after having a baby, to a more "mommy track" position. My intelligence hadn't changed, my work ethic hadn't changed; so what exactly had changed? I knew that I was not going to throw in the towel so early in my career after having invested so much in my education and carefully calculated career steps.

I was very proud of my position, having reached for the brass ring and grabbed it! I was proud that I ended up in investment banking, with a top firm, and all without the benefit of any connections or direct role models. Although my parents were wonderful and supportive, they were teachers who came of age in the 1960s and had an entirely different frame of reference. They couldn't pull any strings to help me navigate the banking world. They recognized my analytical skills and ease with numbers and thought accounting would be a good career fit, as they knew nothing about investment banking. They are proud of my professional accomplishments, but I'm not sure, to this day, that they fully understand what I do.

I worked very hard in my first job as a financial analyst on Wall Street. I wanted to move up the career ladder as soon as possible. While puzzled with the course of events following the birth of my baby, I maintained faith in my abilities and felt that I deserved to be given more responsibility and more opportunities to prove myself. Fortunately, I had built a strong professional foundation, both in hard skills but also in relationships forged.

My former mentor from my analyst days called me as I was deciding to leave my job. How fortuitous! It was in that moment that I saw an important textbook career lesson illustrated in living color. It's vital that you make a good impression with everyone you work with, even in your very first job, when you think that you are having a minimal impact and you will never see these people again. While I didn't walk into my first job as an accounting wiz or experienced stock investor, I had a strong work ethic and a positive attitude. Those are the things colleagues remember—not how many models you can crunch out in the middle of the night. Lady Luck shone on me as my former colleague was building a new group at a large bank and was anxious for me to join the team in a senior client coverage capacity. It was the career leap I had been hoping for. The more I spoke to him, the more I realized that I would really enjoy working with someone who was a friend and who also had a lot of faith in me as a professional. The job became not just about meeting goals for the firm but also living up to his personal expectations of me. If I failed, it would not only hurt the bank's bottom line but it would also damage his respect for me and for my abilities.

Now, four years later, I still work with my friend, and I think I have surpassed all expectations he had of me. And, importantly, I couldn't be happier in my career. I have been promoted twice, I have direct revenue generation responsibility, and I have 15 clients that are my sole responsibility to cover. It is an intense and challenging position. I found an institution that did not prejudge my family status but let my results speak for themselves. I discovered that corporate brand name is not as important as the character of the people I work with. Regarding my decision to start a family at age 29, I have no regrets. In fact, I had another daughter eighteen months ago and my deal flow never slowed a bit; I have more traction in my business than ever. Clients don't care in the slightest as long as you are delivering the capital and the services of the bank.

As a result of my personal career twists and turns, I find myself being very vocal about equal opportunities for women in the workplace. It's hard to believe in this day and age that women are still not treated fairly. I always thought it was a problem for "them" and it would not happen to me. And there are so few of us, especially as you climb the ranks. My team at work is made up of 20 men and one other woman, a junior banker (a Wellesley alumna whom I recruited). As I climb the ladder and look around, I find there just aren't many women out there! I miss the mentorship from above, and the camaraderie of women peers. After 10 years in investment banking, I still have not found a good model for having a high-powered career and being a mother. None of my business school peers who are moms are still in banking. A close friend was told she was on the fast track but then she had children. She wanted to go back to work part time but was turned down because the firm didn't want to set a precedent for other women. So she stayed home. What a waste. Many other senior women bankers with children have stay-at-home or work-at-home husbands.

Women need to be aware of these challenges early on so they can take control of their careers. I think one of the mistakes I made in my career was that I didn't network enough. I thought that everything was a meritocracy, so I spent too much time with my head down doing the best job possible on my tasks. You have to position yourself for success and actively manage your career, and, yes, this means the political aspect too. In that area, my husband gives me a lot of advice. I think that men can be better at political maneuvering through a company than women are. They are not shy about asking a senior colleague to put in a good word or requesting a raise and importantly, they have an established network through which to navigate. Women are looking upward for political support and someone to pound the table for them in large corporate institutions, and there just aren't many people up there that will do it.

PAT DECKER

In 1980, after completing two master's degrees at Cornell University, Pat began her Wall Street career, trading commercial paper at Goldman Sachs. Years later, making choices that allowed her to work part time so she could spend more time with her husband and three children, Pat was charting new territory, where creative and determined colleagues proved to be invaluable.

"The most important things in life are relationships with other people."

Although my father was a professor and my mother a teacher/social worker, they readily supported my goal of becoming a professional capitalist, something unheard of in our family. Business school proved to be exactly what I wanted and led me upon graduation to New York City, where I began work as a corporate lending officer for Chemical Bank. Not only did I have a great job, I lived the New York fantasy in meeting my future husband, Marc, on Memorial Day weekend at a bar in the Hamptons where he had come for the summer to be the head tennis pro at Westhampton Country Club. Marc was the subject of my dreams: a handsome, caring guy with a great sense of humor who liked to read and to dance. What more could one ask! He proposed to me outside of the Federal Building on my last day of working at Chemical Bank. It was March 1980. A week later I started a new job at Goldman Sachs and began to plan my wedding.

With interest rates soaring to 18 percent, working on the commercial paper (CP) trading desk was like riding a roller coaster. Rates were jumping around so much that we had to check the prime rate every day. I loved it. Those were "the good old days" back at 55 Broad Street, when the whole Fixed Income Department was about 400 people. Jon Corzine was the long bond trader, John Gilliam and Jack Curtin ran the corporate syndicate department, and John Whitehead and John Weinberg would come down to the floor to discuss Penn Central's CP program with George Van Cleve and Roger Lynch.

Because there were so few of us, the women on the trading floor became a close-knit group, establishing friendships and professional relationships that have lasted for 25 years. Janet Hanson sat right behind me. We worked on the first master note transaction together with Prudential (her client) and Procter & Gamble (my issuer). I was also one of the architects of the first paperless CP transaction with Union Carbide and Bankers Trust.

Soon after that, I felt that I was ready for a new challenge. I consulted Roger Lynch, partner in charge of commercial paper, who was very supportive, allowing me to look at other opportunities within the firm. I chose to move into the area of tax-exempt money markets, and thanks to Phylis Esposito's masterful sales job on my behalf ("There's this fabulous woman in fixed income who is *willing* to make a change..."), I moved over to the municipal short-term trading desk. I arrived there in June 1985, and in the next six months Goldman did more municipal underwritings than had been done in the previous 10 years combined. It was like having a whole new career.

One of the most special things for me about working in the Municipal Bond Department was that, as a result of the client base and equal opportunity guidelines, there was an amazing community of talented women in that department. In addition to Phylis, an inspiring mentor and friend, I had the good fortune to work with Deb Buresh, Ann Kaplan, Debbie Ciampi, and many other incredible women in muni finance. Managing the short-term trading desk was exhilarating, but when my second child, Andrew, was born in 1987, I began to feel that I was missing out on many aspects of my children's lives. Part-time work was unheard of at the firm, but Phylis, full of optimism said, "We can work this out, Decker." Although the partners considered her proposal for a several months, they ultimately said no. I then turned to Jon Corzine, who was head of Fixed Income at the time. He said, "Let me work on this," and a few weeks later I got a call from Jack Curtin to see if I would be interested in joining him in Money Markets as the departmental administrator. I was able to work three days a week. It was a perfect solution for about 18 months until that department was absorbed into capital markets. Since there was already a full-time administrator in capital markets, I knew it was time for me to make a change. I decided to leave the firm and take some time to contemplate my next move while I spent some welcome time with Megan and Andrew.

During that time I had an opportunity to teach a course in securities and investments as an adjunct professor at Fairleigh Dickinson University. I have always enjoyed teaching so that experience was very rewarding. During that semester, I got a call from Karen Cook, who, after leaving Goldman, had started AlternaTrack, a business that helped find flexible work arrangements for former Wall Street professionals. I ended up working for a year in the Municipal Department at Muriel Siebert & Co. After Molly was born, a call from Mark Stitzer led me to join First Boston's Municipal Department as a part-time internal consultant. I did that for a year and a half until they withdrew from the municipal bond business. Along with the rest of the department, I was laid off in May 1994.

At this point, my husband Marc and I were both looking in new career directions. He had worked for years in the brokerage business on Wall Street, but he had come from an entrepreneurial family and he had always wanted to own his own business. Since he had been in the tennis business and it was my avocation, we decided that we should explore the idea of building an indoor tennis club. As we did some research and actually talked to several club owners, it became apparent that it would make more sense to buy an existing club. Six weeks after I was laid off, we were on vacation in Canada and Marc got a phone call from his boss's assistant telling him that everyone in Marc's department had been laid off. We decided that if we were looking for a sign, this was surely it!

We spent the next six months on unemployment and explored every opportunity that we could find. We made offers on two clubs, but neither of them came to fruition. Eventually we realized that one of us had to take a job temporarily until we could find a club to buy. Marc took a job in Stamford, Connecticut, and commuted from New Jersey. In November, we finally found a club for sale in Middlebury, Connecticut. It proved to be just what we were looking for—six indoor courts and a pro shop in the kind of community we were seeking. We submitted an offer, and six months later became the proud owners. The only sadness was that my father died during this time and that was really difficult for me. My dad loved tennis and he never got to see the club. He would have been so excited to see it.

Owning the club meant that we were able to do much more together as a family. Marc and I were able to arrange our schedules so we could attend our children's plays, their awards ceremonies, and all of their games. Marc coached soccer and baseball. As they got older, Megan and then Andrew started teaching in the junior tennis program and working on the front desk at the club. Molly helped with mailings and the computer database. The club became a second home for them, and in the 10 years since we bought it, it has grown to be an amazing community with over 3,000 players and four full-time teaching pros.

In February 2004, Marc died suddenly following a massive heart attack with virtually no warning signs. The grief and shock were at first overwhelming, but our many friends from the community helped the children and me through this traumatic time. In the next month, I composed a letter to go out to all of our members reassuring them that I had no intention of selling the club and thanking them for all of the love and support that they had given to our family. I was very fortunate that Marc and I had run the club together for the past nine years. While the workload was intense, the transition was smooth, thanks to the help of our manager, Deniece, and the wonderfully talented and conscientious staff at the club. The business thrived and in fact provided a much-needed continuity for my children and me. It also allowed me the flexibility to run the business while still being able to spend as much time as I could with Megan, Andrew, and Molly. Megan came home for the summer after her sophomore year, which was a great help both emotionally and in terms of getting things done at the club. I tried to plan a lot of special things for us to do in order to get through the holidays, birthdays, and anniversaries in the first year. Grieving is an ongoing challenge, and we feel fortunate to be part of a community that has become an extension of our family.

If we are to successfully survive life's greatest heartaches and challenges, it will be because of the relationships we have made with other people throughout our lives. I remember at Goldman watching a junior colleague invite one of the partners to go out for a drink and thinking that I would never have the nerve to do that. I thought it would be presumptuous of me to try to socialize with someone that senior. Now that I am the sole owner and head of operations at my club, I welcome the opportunities offered by the younger people on my staff to socialize with them. I increasingly recognize the degree to which the interchange between generations is beneficial to everyone, and senior people are much more receptive to this than one might think.

Co-mentoring is one of the greatest achievements of 85 Broads, because it brings all generations of women together: women in their twenties and thirties who are at the beginning of their careers and women who have been in the business for 25 years or more. It is a two-way street that benefits everyone. On a personal basis, as I watch my children become young adults, I am grateful for the relationships that they have with their friends and with adults with whom they are perfectly comfortable. These relationships become an invisible net that holds us as we go through life. My parents gave me a tremendous gift by their example of welcoming and cherishing all of the people who came into their lives. If Marc and I have given this same gift to our children, we will have succeeded at an aspect of parenting that will last throughout their lifetimes.

Beth Stewart

Beth graduated from Wellesley College with a BA in Economics. She worked for two years as an analyst in the Corporate Finance Department at Goldman Sachs and then earned her MBA at Harvard Business School. Beth returned to Goldman Sachs and worked for 10 more years in the Real Estate Department before leaving to raise her family and launch a start-up business. She is currently a director of three public companies.

> "I can't really tell you why the kids seem to be doing so well (so far) other than that we love them and pay attention to them."

About 15 years ago I attended an event organized by the Harvard Business School of New York Women's Club. The speaker was one of HBS's first female graduates. She spoke about her career and about her two sons who were in their early twenties. She started to cry as she told us how she wished she had spent more time with them. Her message went to my heart. I was a working woman with a baby at home, and I did not want to be working my way toward that kind of sadness.

First, it is important to say that there is no single path that is right for everyone. If you're lucky, you get information from the outside and the inside that helps you sort out what's right for you. Hearing that woman talk about her regrets didn't make me want to quit my job. But hearing her made me think that I might want to retire or work at home some day. This is my first bit of advice: When you are young, find a job you love so you don't mind working extremely hard and acquiring the skills, resources, and experience that will give you the flexibility you will want in later years.

I have five children. My daughter is 7 and her brothers are 10, 12, 14, and 16. They're great kids, healthy and happy and all doing well in school. People used to marvel at the way we managed everything when they were younger, and I realize in retrospect that maybe we didn't manage as well as it appeared. It is truly hectic with five kids. The biggest challenge is to keep them all motivated and give each of them the care and attention that they need. I make lists every day and probably 90 percent of what is on my list relates to my children. I arrange my schedule around school plays and concerts, meetings with teachers, doctors' appointments, and even cafeteria duty—anything related to my children that I feel is important. The fact that my husband is home when I am not frees me to work and travel when it's necessary.

Things have gotten a bit simpler now that we have "outsourced" some of the tasks to New Hampshire where our two oldest boys are attending school. It's like what Hillary Clinton says, "It takes a village." At a certain point you begin to release them to other adults who will capture their attention, inspire them, and help them set and achieve their goals. Kids will always look to their parents for the love and support they need. You never outsource the emotional aspects of parenting.

Back in 1982, when I was graduating from business school and thinking about where I wanted to work, I deliberately chose to go into real estate because there are many things you can do in that field that are entrepreneurial, and I knew that would allow me the kind of flexibility that I'd want when I became a mother. I was thinking about this before I was even married, so I guess I had an idea of where I wanted my life to go. I worked for four years as an associate in the Real Estate Department at Goldman Sachs and then was given responsibilities for deals and clients. During that time I was exposed to many senior people in the real estate industry, which was very important later in my life as I tried more entrepreneurial activities. I left GS late in 1992 when my third child was almost a year old.

I now work from an office in my house, and I schedule all my work calls for 9 a.m. to 3 p.m., when my children are at school. My primary business work is with an Internet start-up company called Storetrax.com where I am now the chairman and CEO. Storetrax was a marketplace concept for the retail real estate industry; we planned to build a database of all vacant retail real estate listings in the United States. Since we were not successful in building that database, our focus changed. We now offer technology and marketing services to over 100 clients in the retail real estate industry. It has been a struggle from the beginning, and although we're proud to have survived the dot.com collapse, I still go back over our original business plan and think about what I could have done differently. One reason the business has survived is that there weren't any venture capitalists involved, so we've been able to keep it going and control our destiny. However, the future for Storetrax is still uncertain. The investors all have faith in the business and are staying with me. That is a tremendous endorsement, and it makes me work harder so we can all succeed. They remind me that start-ups often struggle at the beginning as they find their place and a way to be profitable in a developing industry.

There are many things that I don't do because I have five children and a start-up—I don't play golf or tennis; I don't participate in as many not-for-profit activities as I could; I am a den mother and homeroom mother but I don't get an "A" for brilliant execution in either of those areas; I try to exercise three times a week (but mostly don't); I don't shop for groceries or cook dinner. I decorated the house once a couple of years ago, and I hope I don't have to do it again!

BRIGID DOHERTY

Brigid graduated from Boston College in 1996 with a BS in Finance. She worked at Goldman Sachs as a mergers and acquisitions analyst. She then went to Harvard Business School for her MBA and upon graduating joined Bain & Co as a strategy consultant. Now the mother of two children, Brigid works part time for a private school, finding that to be the perfect solution for managing her career and raising her family.

> "Life is full of compromises when you want to have a career and a family. When I do work, I want it to be in the most fulfilling capacity. By 26, I already knew that as a woman I had a lot to contribute, but I wanted it to be on terms that I could live with."

Commuting to see my husband for almost eight years made me realize the importance of focusing on work/life trade-offs when we had children—one of our jobs had to come first. Now, after having my second child at 30, I have finally found the ideal situation for me, a part-time job that I love. Anyone faced with the challenge of work and family must be constantly rebalancing and reshaping, testing the boundaries to come up with a plan that works. It also helps to keep meeting people, growing and tending to a network of friends and colleagues, and staying engaged with what's going on in the world.

My first experience in networking was trying to get a job on Wall Street without having gone to an Ivy League school. I went to Boston College where graduates weren't strongly recruited by Wall Street firms, but once I discovered the pocket of BC grads who worked on Wall Street, I found them to be an especially tight group who were glad to help me in my career.

I loved working at Goldman Sachs where the bar is raised high for work ethic and work product. I highly recommend that young people, early in their careers, work at a top-notch firm like that, because for the rest of their careers they'll know what a good work product looks like. I see it, I know it, and know it's important.

At that point, my husband-to-be and I had been having a long-distance romance for four years. I have always said that he is a patient man. He waited for me while I finished Boston College and then waited for me while I worked at Goldman in New York. It was time for us to live in the same city. He was in Buffalo, my hometown, and although we preferred Boston—he is from Boston—he had a great job in Buffalo that he wanted to keep. I moved back to be with him. It took a little getting used to. Even though I was from Buffalo, I had never worked there in a professional capacity. I had been spoiled by all the high-profile deals that I had worked on at Goldman with such high-caliber people. I went from working on deals with Daimler Benz to working on deals with car part manufacturers.

After one year, I decided that I wanted to get an MBA from Harvard, the school that seemed to offer the best program. At this point, I was not sure what direction I wanted to move in professionally, but I knew Harvard would broaden my horizons, open up new possibilities, and increase my tool kit. So despite having enjoyed less than a year of being happily married and living under one roof, it was back to commuting and back to Boston for me. I was thrilled to attend the MBA program at Harvard. I enjoyed my time there immensely; learning so much and forming lifelong friendships.

I did my summer internship at Bain and I enjoyed that work, though I knew strategy consulting was probably not where I'd be long term because of the travel and the intense work environment. But similar to my thoughts about Goldman, I felt it was important to put what I had learned at Harvard into practice at a premier firm. At this point, I needed to decide which firm I wanted to work with. Upon graduation, I had offers from both Bain and McKinsey but chose Bain mainly because it is run by women. The chairperson is a woman. The Boston office was run by a female partner, one of several in that office. Also, I knew that at some point I wanted to have children, and Bain worked hard to make it possible for people to have a family. Although I knew that being able to balance consulting with a family was a long shot, if there was anywhere I could do it, it would be at Bain. Even so, when I did become pregnant, I found that being on the road four days a week, a requirement of being in this client-driven consulting business, was just too much. Besides, I was in Boston and my husband was in Buffalo. We decided that the best move was for me to move back to Buffalo, again.

When I moved home and had my first child, I thought that I wanted to be a stay-at-home mom. But after 14 months at home, I decided that I needed an outlet. Winters are long in Buffalo, and I couldn't find the right parent group. I didn't feel whole and I didn't feel like myself. I did do some part-time consulting work at M&T bank, and after three months there, an interesting networking event happened that led to my current position. A colleague at M&T suggested that I pursue a position at Buffalo's oldest private elementary school where she happens to be on the board. It is amazing how one job leads to another. I never would have looked for a job at a school; it just never occurred to me. Networking in the traditional sense of the word—putting on a plastic smile, handing out business cards, and chatting with strangers—had never come easy to me. It made me uncomfortable. But networking can also be about embracing opportunities to meet and talk to people—this is something I am good at. Also, networking possibilities are everywhere.

As I interviewed for the position at the school, I realized that it was perfect for me. My experience at Goldman in M&A was very strategic and transactional. At Bain, I did a lot of cost-cutting projects and got more experience working on fine-tuning the operational aspects of a business. Now, the challenge I wanted was to implement a business plan.

I am proud to say that we are soon to be opening an enrichment center that will offer traditional tutoring and enrichment programs. The center will be open to all children in Buffalo. It's called "Achieve." It has been great fun because I have been able to use a broad range of skills: putting together a business plan, obtaining funding, putting together an advisory board.

And the best part is that I was able to negotiate a flexible arrangement where I only work three days a week. One advantage of living in a small city, where there may often be talent holes, is that if you have a lot to bring to the table, people will give you flexibility because they really need you. Being a larger fish in a small pond can make a huge difference in your career and in finding a way to balance your life.

HOLLY ISDALE

Holly joined Goldman Sachs in 1999 to create the advisory business within their private client group. In the fall of 2002, she moved with her family to work for Goldman Sachs in Philadelphia. She left Goldman in 2004 to join Lehman Brothers in New York.

"We had two kids, two jobs, two commutes, and it was just too much. You have to take a look at your life when things don't all fit together. Then you have to reshape it so it works for everyone."

Tony Ryan and I met in college in 1984 and were married in 1988, after my first year in law school. Tony had a master's in engineering from Cornell and was building a great career in Boston. But the job market for me was strange. I had offers from top firms in just about every city in the country, except Boston. We decided to go to New York so I could get started in my career, thinking we'd be there for two years and then move back to Boston. When I graduated, I was hired at Fried, Frank in downtown New York, where I worked in the Tax Department.

For the first couple of months in New York, Tony didn't have a job, and he stepped up to the plate doing all the work at home although it was just the two of us. We moved out to Long Island when he got a job at Brookhaven National Lab helping them build their newest particle accelerator. We both commuted an hour to our jobs in opposite directions. When Abby was born in 1994, I had just moved to JPMorgan and neither of us was comfortable leaving Abby with a nanny while we were both an hour away. There was onsite day care at Brookhaven National Lab so Tony would drive an hour each way with Abby in the car, drop her at the day care, and then go to work. He would take off whenever she got sick; we alternated a bit but he had more flexibility in his job than I did at the time. Abby thrived in day care and it all seemed manageable. Things got exponentially more complicated when Jack was born in 1996. Two kids, two commutes, we never saw anybody, we had no friends because we were never at home, and if we were home, we were dragging ourselves around just getting the basics covered.

I had been working at JPMorgan since 1994 as the chief tax strategist, doing tax advisory and product development in their private banking group, and getting frustrated because I wasn't moving ahead. Tony was ending his project in early 1999 so we figured he'd stay home with the kids through the summer. Our plan was to move back to Boston or "elsewhere" in 2000 but in March 1999 I got a call to go to Goldman Sachs.

The opportunity at Goldman was too good to pass up. However, part of our determination to have a parent home with the kids full-time stemmed from another development. In 1998, Tony's niece Rachel came to live with us through a series of unfortunate events. We had a 3-year-old, a 5-year-old, and then this 16-year-old appeared on our doorstep.... In some ways a teenager needs more attention than a 4-year-old. Whereas young children are eager to tell you right away the most exciting thing that is happening with them, or why they're upset, teenagers will chat aimlessly with you for hours about clothes or what's on TV without mentioning their thoughts or concerns. At 11:30 p.m., after hovering half the night, they'll finally tell you what's really bothering them. We saw with Rachel that you do have to be around your kids more as they grow older.

Rachel has been a tremendous gift to our lives and a wonderful addition to the family. It has been a great treat to watch her mature into a lovely young woman. But it did make us recommit to having a parent home with the kids. So, when I moved to Goldman Sachs in the spring of 1999, Tony left Brookhaven and stayed home full time. I really do have a "rocket scientist" taking care of the kids!

The first few years at Goldman were a total whirlwind of activities with the markets booming and the team building. Making managing director was a tremendous accomplishment and had been my focus for two years. I was running at an unsustainable pace and it showed in work, my family life, and my health. By 2002, my role at Goldman had changed with the markets and I opted to take a different role within the firm's Philadelphia office. While we loved living in the Philadelphia area, I was miserable with the new role, with the team I worked on, and with the experiences I was having at work. I hired an executive coach (best money I ever spent on myself!), and she helped me regroup and say: "I really like doing x, y, and z; that's where my strengths are. Now where do I find that and how do I bring that role to fruition?" Soon the perfect opportunity came in the form of a position with Lehman Brothers in New York, building their advisory practice. The management team was amazing, the timing was perfect, but the job required me to be in New York....

When we were figuring out if I should take the job or not and later, whether to relocate back to New York City, Tony said to me point blank, "If you're home from work at 5, I'll move back. If you're home at 7, I'll move back. But if you are coming home at 9 p.m., and you are on the road a few nights every week, I want to stay here where I have a network and a support system for the kids and a lifestyle that we all love." I realized that we could not uproot the family again, especially for a new job that would have me working long hours and traveling as I got the team started at Lehman. Over the last 14 years Tony has sacrificed for my career, so opting to do the New York to Pennsylvania commute is not that much of a sacrifice in the grand scheme of things. We put a lot of effort into being together as a family when we are together, and I love living away from the hassles of New York. I have been exceedingly fortunate throughout my career to have managers who have mentored me and been willing to let me juggle a bit as needed to maintain a work–life balance!

We are giving our kids a very different view into how roles can change within a family and how workloads can be shared within a marriage. I think that's a really wonderful thing to give them.

Ana Chapman

Ana is the mother of twins, Audrey and Max, born in April 2003. Prior to the birth of her children, she worked at Goldman Sachs in the Equities Division for six years. Ana made the difficult decision to leave a job that she loved at Goldman to stay at home with her children.

> "Having stepped off of the proverbial treadmill, I have a new and better perspective on my life. I have confidently defined success on my own terms, realizing that this doesn't necessarily mean becoming a partner at Goldman Sachs. I make my own rules."

I was a typical "type A" career woman up until very recently. I loved my job at Goldman Sachs and had every intention to go right back to work after giving birth to my twins. Minutes before my caesarean section, I called my boss and told her not to worry about me and that I'd be back checking voice-mail in a few hours. The notion of having kids and a career didn't faze me.

We had a baby nurse for the first six weeks. She helped me care for Audrey and Max while I spent a big part of my day checking email and voicemail and even attending some meetings at the office. When our nurse left after six weeks, everything changed. My husband and I didn't really know what we were doing. We decided to pack up and take a two-month vacation with the twins, taking advantage of my maternity leave. Being with Audrey and Max day and night, I quickly began to figure things out and became completely attached to them. I fell in love.

During our time away, I continued to take conference calls, intending to return to work full time after I was finished with my maternity leave. I was even offered an exciting new position in Equities Management at Goldman. I accepted and was absolutely blissful about going back to work.

But after returning to New York, the new job immediately began to dominate my life. It wasn't working out as I had imagined, and I found myself terribly conflicted.

I talked to several people at GS about my situation and was asked to consider part-time, job-share, and other flexible work arrangements. Given my all-or-nothing attitude about my career, I knew that this wouldn't work. The part-time alternative wasn't right for me so I made the difficult decision to leave Goldman and stay at home with my children.

For the first time in my life I put someone else's interests ahead of my own. While I terribly miss the markets and the pace and energy at work, I love my twins and know that they need me full time. I have stayed close to my former GS colleagues but have supplemented that daily support system with other social networks: 85 Broads, Cornell and Columbia Business School alumni, and members of the Manhattan Mother of Twins Club. I have met other women and grown closer to friends who are going through similar situations. I rarely feel like I am alone. I do refuse to get caught up in the "mommy world" of constant playgroups, never-ending classes for the kids, and thinking that the road to Harvard begins at four months. Most of my best friends are working moms.

Having stepped off of the proverbial treadmill, I have a new and better perspective on my life. I have confidently defined success on my own terms, realizing that this doesn't necessarily mean becoming a partner at Goldman Sachs. I make my own rules. I watch CNBC and read *Business Week* and *The Economist* religiously, keep up my business network, and find time for other intellectually stimulating activities. I exercise more regularly and am healthier than I have ever been.

I am fortunate to have my mother as an amazing role model. My mother ran her own business and controlled her own hours, enabling her to maximize the time she spent with her children. She was there to make me breakfast in the mornings, put me on the school bus, and open the door for me when I got home in the afternoons. Yet she had a fulfilling career while I was at school. She was always there for me and still is. I aspire to be that kind of mother for my children so that they can confidently say, "She was always there for us and I am so proud of everything that my mom has accomplished professionally and personally."

My recipe for sanity as a stay-at-home mom:

1. Appreciate the privilege to have the choice to fully dedicate yourself to your family. Enjoy it.

2. Discipline your children. They need structure. Set limits and stick to them.

3. Love your children unconditionally. Let them know that you do.

4. Don't overschedule yourself or over-rely on caregivers. You left your job to be with your children, so be with them.

5. Don't overschedule your children. They're kids. Let them be kids.

6. Always take your children outdoors on a beautiful day.

7. Pamper your spouse, your children, your pets, and *yourself!*

8. Strengthen ties with family and friends.

9. Take time to listen.

10. Indulge in hobbies.

11. Stay physically fit. Practice sports you love. Challenge yourself to improve.

12. Stay mentally fit. Keep up with current events and business events. Manage your finances. Read, write. Seek the company of interesting people. Attend lectures and conferences.

13. Avoid alcoholic beverages before sundown.

14. Keep a sense of humor (you'll need it to avoid alcoholic beverages before sundown).

15. Contribute to a charitable cause.

16. Celebrate: birthdays, anniversaries, spring, leaving town, coming back, and anything in between.

17. Have a game plan. Where do you want you and your family to be in one, five, ten years?

18. Realize that you're making a conscious choice to stay at home every day. Feel confident that you'll be able to return to your career or design a brand-new one if and when you want to.

DEBORAH BURESH JACKSON

Deborah spent 21 years as an investment banker, 10 years at Goldman Sachs, and later worked at her own firm. She also served on the boards of many charitable organizations such as the Heart and Soul Fund, Citizens Budget Commission, Project Sunshine, and Legal Momentum, among others. She has two daughters, age 18 and 15.

"Vision is key. If you don't have one, it is like driving a car without a destination."

I am pleased with the way my life has turned out despite the many obstacles. I can't say that I followed a master plan, but I can certainly say that I followed my passion.

Since I was a young girl, I have been able to visualize in advance what I wanted out of life. My mom chose to stay at home with her five kids. Imagine all those meals! From the age of nine, I decided that being a home-based mom wasn't for me. I wanted to work and earn my own money. I remember being in math class and fantasizing about working in an office as a secretary. I had a limited frame of reference at the time; 40 years ago, those were the only options open for women. I didn't know that I would work on Wall Street for 21 years with complete motivation and self-directed drive.

Some people had a very limited vision for me and thought I was aiming too high. A high school guidance counselor recommended that I take a typing class instead of math because, for a woman, typing guaranteed employment. Limited thinking on the part of others created in me a rebellious desire to succeed. It propelled me to challenge myself even more. I achieved what I set out to do despite the many naysayers, obstacles, and disappointments. Eventually, I broke "their" mold and went to Columbia Business School. When I graduated, I still wasn't sure exactly what I wanted to do. But I knew the key elements that were important to me: stimulating colleagues, fast-paced environment, high level of independence, and a field that I could be challenged in over the span of my career. By the process of elimination, I chose investment banking and went to Goldman Sachs. I spent years running from airplane to taxi to airplane serving clients around the country, traveling first with a senior banker, and soon after by myself. I really liked my clients and am proud to say that I retained them for many years. I reached my goal of independence, excellent income, and an intellectually fulfilling job.

But I wanted other things as well. I remember the realization that occurred when I was in a cab going to LaGuardia airport for a business meeting. I spotted a woman meeting her daughters after school and walking arm in arm and chatting about the day. I decided that I wanted that too. When I told the partner in charge at Goldman Sachs that I was pregnant, he was surprised and said that I didn't strike him as the motherly type. Obviously, I did not meet all his expectations of what a mother should be. I went on to have two children while working the whole time.

After 10 years of working at Goldman, a group of GS women and I thought about starting our own firm. No one believed that we would leave GS; we had great clients, great reputations. What more could we want? We shocked everyone at the firm by walking in at the same time and resigning.

They tried to talk us out of it but we were determined. We founded our own firm called Artemis Capital. This was one of the highs of my career. There is no other experience like owning your own firm. It is both exhilarating and debilitating all in one day. You learn to become confident in your own abilities when you don't have a brand-name firm behind you.

During this time, a devastating event happened in my personal life. My husband at the time and I ended our marriage of 13 years when he decided he was gay. Soon after, I had my first bad experience with the courts. I had been the major breadwinner during the course of our marriage, despite my husband being a Harvard-trained litigator. I became the children's custodial parent. Not only did I have to cope with my breakup and support my children alone, but I had to bear the financial burden also. I was devastated but did not give up.

Having children is hard. And being a single parent is unbelievably hard, but I wouldn't trade my daughters for anything. I learned a lot about myself over the years. I learned to have patience and be totally forgiving—of my girls and myself. I was anxious to be a good mom while working full time in a demanding, male-dominated environment.

Three years ago, at 49, I stopped working in an office, though I didn't stop working full-time. Throughout my 21 years as an investment banker, I found a lot of personal satisfaction by providing financial guidance in the nonprofit sector. As a child, moving around a lot in the northeast, the west, and midwest, I had experienced firsthand what it was like to live in an affluent neighborhood as well as a disadvantaged neighborhood. I knew that I wanted to live well but I also wanted to help those less fortunate. I did this by helping in many different ways: I served twice as the chair of the annual fund-raising auction for the Heart and Soul Fund which provides grants to community groups. I helped a recent college graduate realize his dream of establishing a nationwide organization that helps families whose terminally ill children are in the hospital. I am on the national board of Legal Momentum (formerly called the NOW Legal Defense and Education Fund), which is the organization responsible for major landmark legislation and litigation on behalf of women, such as Title IX for women in sports and the employment rights that women have today. When you contribute your expertise and time, you can see the impact you make on someone's life. You are free from focusing on money and can just revel in the contributions you are making and the many good things that can come from them.

Lessons for my daughters: You need to have perspective. The issues that you have today will be replaced by other issues tomorrow. When you're getting through today, just ask yourself, "Will this matter in 10 years?" In addition, you have to evaluate your life on many levels. People, especially those starting out, tend to focus on only one dimension of their lives. It is usually work. For a successful life, it needs to be well-rounded and consist of many things. Former colleagues who admit they were workaholics are now looking back on their choices with regret.

I missed having a husband and life partner. Friends at church kept telling me about this wonderful man. We met and found we had similar life experiences on Wall Street and both wanted a strong family. Once again, I was able to get what I was able to visualize. I have a wonderful marriage and full life. And my daughters could not be more inspiring and different. Lucy, 15, is a fabulous athlete and played on an elite girls' basketball team, complete with college-level coaches. She's physically competitive and could qualify for a scholarship that was unavailable to prior generations. Selby, 18, is multitalented; she designs her own clothes and loves modern dance. She is great at math, very mature, and self-aware. So in my hardest job of all, being a working mom, I guess I am doing just fine.

CHERYL KATZ

Cheryl began her academic career by graduating from SUNY Purchase. After earning a law degree from Case Western Reserve, she accepted a position working at the office of the District Attorney in the Bronx. She practiced law for 10 years before deciding to attend Columbia Business School. Upon graduation, Goldman Sachs offered Cheryl a job in their Commodities Division. After four months at her new job, Cheryl learned she was to have triplets.

> "I thought having triplets was hard. Raising them while working full time has been the hardest job in the world."

Being a working mom is the hardest job there is. You need a lot of personal drive. Work must give you a real boost. If it doesn't, you should go home. There are some certainties: You will always feel guilty that you are not home with your kids. You will always struggle with your decision to go back to work. You will always feel that you are falling short of providing for your children in some way. You will always compare yourself to the stay-at-home moms and look wistfully at their spotless homes. A neighbor recently commented that my daughter might be allergic to dust. I told her that my daughter might have to find a new family. I'm over feeling guilty.

To be a happy and fulfilled working mom, you have to get your energy from inside. And getting some praise from the outside doesn't hurt. Closing a deal feeds my head. A hug from my child feeds my heart. It's ironic. If I didn't work and put myself under so much pressure, I probably wouldn't have as much energy as I have. I'm energized by doing many things that interest me, such as tackling a new obstacle at work or taking my children to a new museum exhibit. Most of all, I get my energy from a job well done. Of course, some of my energy is biological. But the busier I am, the more I do. I'm sure that is true of many people. I get home exhausted, but I always get my second wind when I see my three kids—two girls and a boy. I am very lucky because I have the support of my husband, whom I have known for over 20 years.

My husband and I met working summers at Bloomingdale's. So much for a quick summer romance! After 10 years of practicing law, I got my MBA from Columbia and started working at Goldman Sachs. Four months later I became pregnant. It was tough. The hours were long. I didn't have an easy pregnancy and gave birth to triplets early. I was lucky that my immediate boss accommodated me a lot—he let me put my feet up on an upside down garbage can. The medical benefits were great. But people are always concerned that you won't come back after you have a baby. They don't come out and say anything but you know because it shows in their actions.

Having just completed my MBA from Columbia, I thought everyone knew that I was serious about pursuing my career. I had been so thrilled the day I received my offer letter from Goldman. It was such a prestigious company and they wanted me! I worked in commodities and learned a lot. Before I started there, I thought gold was just something that you put on your finger. I built a skill set that will keep me in good standing.

Now, six years later, I've moved on to a new company with new challenges. Even though Goldman had benefits such as a back-up child-care center—where, when your normal child-care plans fall through, you can bring the kids to a center downstairs from work—juggling my professional life and personal life was still hard. But it was great that the first few days I was back from having my triplets, I was able to leave them downstairs at the center. It really helped my transition back to work after four months' leave. And I'm confident that it boosts productivity because you can focus without worrying. As the kids get older, it helps them understand where you go every day.

They start to believe that work is a good thing and that their parents get to go have fun at work every day. And your kids will learn that you're more than just a mom. It makes them a partner in your work and then they don't feel resentful. Now they would understand if I were to miss their ball game. Before the kids really understood the concept of my going to work, they used to say things like, "Mommy, we don't need money for new toys. Please don't go to work. Stay home with us." Statements like that broke my heart. But now the triplets are six years old, and they understand work. In fact, they help me get ready, even for trips. They put pictures of themselves in my suitcase so I won't be lonely in a hotel far away.

I have learned a lot from my motherhood experience that I would like to share. First of all, think carefully about your decision to have children and about going back to work. Sit down with a spreadsheet and figure out the financial and then the emotional benefits. Going back to work is not for everyone. You are the only one who can make this decision for yourself.

Don't apologize to anyone for the decision you reach. There will always be someone who tells you that you made the wrong choice. Pay no attention to them. They do not know what decision is best for your situation. You always have to manage other people's expectations. You will be pulled in a thousand different directions. If you like working, stick with it. I know many people who have left work, and then have had trouble getting back into the workforce. If you do choose to leave, you have to understand that you may have an unusual career path later on. You have to know your own priorities.

Be flexible. I've been taking my triplets with me grocery shopping since they were very small. When I couldn't carry packages and push the stroller, I would have the groceries delivered. Now, we enjoy our time shopping and everyone has a job. One scans, one packs, and one carries.

Nobody is Superwoman. Many successful professional women want to do everything perfectly, and they feel guilty if they don't. Be willing to invest in some extras. Get help with the housecleaning. I take my daughters with me to get a manicure. If I didn't, I wouldn't get to go. My son comes too and he supervises, making sure that everything's okay. Be good to yourself.

Be creative. Many women spend a lot of time worrying about squeezing in fun activities for the weekend. Join organizations such as your local zoo so that you don't have to plan as much. If you're a member, you won't feel guilty just spontaneously heading down for the afternoon. You won't feel the drive to get your money's worth, and you always have special events in your back pocket.

But most of all don't give up being a person. You can be all of these things, but it's very important to remember to be you.

JUDY SCINTO

Judy received her BA in English and Spanish literature at Tufts University and then joined the Federal Reserve Bank of New York as a bank analyst, where she worked for five years before going to the University of Chicago Graduate School of Business to pursue her MBA in Finance. In 1998, Judy joined Goldman Sachs in London as a summer associate in the Equities Division and then worked in Equity Sales in Boston after graduation. Since late 2001, Judy has opted to be a full-time mom.

> "It's amazing how motherhood can come along and change you. While my profession is now listed as 'full-time mother' according to the forms at my son's pre-school, I definitely look for ways to keep the achievement-oriented part of me active and alive because I do miss my career. I'm definitely a 'work in progress.'"

My greatest passion in life is my family. Being a mom has been, without a doubt, the most challenging and most rewarding job of my career. After all my years of studying hard and working hard in the finance world, most recently in Equity Sales at Goldman Sachs in Boston, I never expected that I, being the type A woman that I am, would choose to opt out of the work-force to be a stay-at-home mom. In my mid-twenties, one of my best friends had a baby and decided to stop working. I remember thinking, "How lame. I could never be that person. How can she just abandon her career and her education?" And now *I am that person* and quite happy. It's amazing how motherhood can come along and change you just like that—and I'm so glad it did. But it's still a constant struggle for me. Some days I feel so lucky that I can be at home to raise my three young children and be a part of their every-day lives. Other days, I just feel like I'm drowning in diapers, and I wonder whatever happened to the "me" that I used to be? So I'm definitely a work in progress. When the kids get older, I know I will find greater balance in my life—the trick will be how!

Being a University of Chicago alumna and an ex–Goldman Sachs woman is still an important part of my identity, even though I'm out of the workforce for now. I much more identify with working women than I do with the traditional Connecticut moms out here in suburbia. While my profession is now listed as full-time mother according to the forms at my son's preschool, I definitely look for ways to keep the achievement-oriented part of me active and alive. And I really do miss working. Not the long hours, politics, or stress of work. But I definitely miss the mental stimulation and camaraderie, not to mention getting a bonus at year's end! The whole notion of being a "cost center" within the family is something I still don't like to admit to, because I feel like I am working hard—harder than ever. But it's a process. I no longer feel the need to have my résumé taped to my forehead so that people will know that I'm more than just a mom. At some point, I'll emerge from the sidelines and get back out there. For now, I'm just trying to enjoy my babies, and that is wonderful and exhausting!

I do wish that early on in my career someone had sat me down and talked with me about my personal goals in life, not just my career goals. I've always known I wanted to have a family—more than anything—but it was never part of the plan. As young women, we're brought up to be achievers—to get good grades, win at sports, choose a profession, become well-rounded people, and so on. There are plenty of advice and discussion around those topics. But what about motherhood? How about considering that before you turn 30? I don't know, it just seems like it shouldn't come as such a surprise or dilemma. It would be great to be more prepared—young women should definitely think about it before they get to Wall Street, business school, and even college. If you know a family is going to be important to you, then it should become a conscious part of the choices you make. I know that when I was in business school there was absolutely no time spent on anything having to do with motherhood or integrating family priorities with career priorities. I was completely single-minded at Chicago. I was there to learn as much as I could, get the best job I could, and have fun. So I did all of those things. But now, some of my closest girlfriends from b-school have said to me, "Judy, I can't believe that you have three kids and stay at home, I never would have expected that." And why would they—we never even discussed it with each other then—forget about it being part of the curriculum or something men considered. But I think that's changing now in schools and at work, which is good. Because the topic of motherhood is universal once you get to a certain age. It's one that I now discuss with all my friends—whether or not they work and whether or not they have families.

After leaving Goldman, I found out about 85 Broads from a Chicago classmate and former Goldman Sachs woman. It's been a great network for me to be involved with because I'm able to stay in touch with working women even though I'm at home. And the women in the network are all achievement-oriented on some level, which is something I really appreciate. Next week, I'm very psyched to attend a discussion about "Achieving Work/Family Balance," which is being sponsored locally by HBS's alumnae group and which I heard about through the network. It'll be great to meet with women from my own community who are living these same issues, hear their perspectives, and understand their choices. And at some point down the road, I hope to tap into others' advice and experience when I transition back into the workforce. I'm not sure what my strategy is yet, and I know that it won't be easy, but I know that I'll definitely benefit from talking to other women.

My mom is a lawyer who went back to graduate school in the 1970s, when I was a toddler, which was rare at the time. She was my role model. The 1970s were all about feminism. But now that these women have helped us kick though the glass ceiling, how do we manage it all? Many workplaces still lag behind in creating solutions for women. So you have to think it through for yourself and make the choices that are sensible for you. But the good news is that women aren't so alone in making these choices—we have each other, and the network is growing.

JULIE YAO COOPER

Julie received her AB from Harvard University. She worked as a financial analyst for Goldman Sachs before returning to Boston to obtain her MBA at Harvard Business School. Julie then became a doctoral candidate in marketing at HBS and later a research associate there. She also worked for two years as a marketing consultant for Monitor Group. As the mother of a young daughter and infant son, she currently works part time, teaching marketing and quantitative methods at Hult International Business School.

"None of us knows what the next change is going to be, what unexpected opportunity is just around the corner, waiting a few months or a few years to change all the tenor of our lives."

Kathleen Thompson Norris,
Hands Full of Living, 1931

"There is a lot of noise in the background as I speak to you. I'm growing used to sharing phone conversations with my toddler." I'm over 40; my daughter just turned 3 and my son is 5 months. I met my husband when I was 36; got married at 38. I feel lucky I didn't hear my biological clock ticking—it made it easier to wait for the right person. My husband and I had both lived full and fun lives before we met. When we made our commitment to each other, we were ready to start a family. In my twenties, I thought I was in control—that I could plot my life path. Well, I learned that you don't have control over when you meet the right person or have children. Life meanders much more. Even careers have serendipity. After a few shifts in direction, I am now a full-time mother juggling two young children and a part-time career in teaching and consulting. I love it all, even when those many balls in the air threaten to drop.

I really loved my first job as an investment banking analyst at Goldman Sachs. I fed on its intensity. After three years there, I wanted to take my career and education to the next level. I applied, was accepted, and attended Harvard Business School. Upon graduation, I was considering offers from some top management consulting firms. I thought, however, that I had found my passion, so I did something rather unusual for a debt-ridden business school student: I decided to pursue an academic career and stayed on to do a doctorate in marketing. The lure of a paying job made me give the financial factors a lot of consideration. Still, I thought pursuing my dream to be a professor at a leading business school was worth living the "starving grad student" lifestyle a few more years. Not that I was really starving; HBS helped out their doctoral students with scholarships and forgivable loans.

So then I started my doctoral studies and loved the intellectual rigor and debate of the program. I also reawakened my passion for teaching. I had taught since I was in high school; I had twelve piano students before I left for college. This was even more fun: teaching at the graduate level brings you into contact with a large group of highly motivated overachievers who share your same interests. Teaching, however, is often not the major portion of an academic career. Instead, much of one's time is spent doing research. And research is a solitary endeavor. After a few years, I found that this solitary environment was not right for me. In contrast, I liked the more social milieu of consulting. While in school, I got to work on consulting projects for certain Fortune 500 companies. I remember thinking at the time, "Am I having my cake and eating it too?" Consulting offered collegial work in an intellectually challenging environment.

After several years of school, it was finally dissertation time. My professors were telling me it would require another two years, at least. By then, I was deeply aware of the mismatch between my passion for marketing and my decided lack of passion for the solitary endeavor of paper writing. I did a lot of soul searching and decided to leave academia for "industry." Such transitions can be hard. I looked for a career where I could match my academic work in marketing with my desire for a team-oriented atmosphere. After re-exploring some of those well-known management consulting companies, I discovered one that had a specialized marketing practice that suited my interests. It seemed to be the perfect fit. Naively, I thought that the switch back to the corporate world would be a piece of cake.

It wasn't. People had warned me about the long hours and extensive travel, but having thrived on both at Goldman Sachs, I did not expect things to differ. However, being a jet-setter in your twenties is a lot different from being a jet-setter in your mid-thirties. And as luck shines on busy people, I met my future husband. For the first time, personal life significantly intruded into professional life. I would be on a plane flying home from a long week away and be looking forward to having dinner with my then boyfriend. I got really mad and frustrated when I was delayed. It didn't get easier once we got married. Then, when you're thinking, "Wouldn't it be nice to have a kid?" you realize that it is a biological impossibility because the two of you aren't even in the same city.

What I learned from this experience is that there are distinct phases of your life, and what mattered to me most at that time were my family and the proverbial work/life balance. It was a real awakening for someone who previously scorned those who did not give their careers "their all." The lesson really came home when a family health crisis arose. Every family handles these types of things differently. This one brought my husband and me much closer. I remember thinking that we lived many years of marriage through those several months of fall and winter, when my full-time job was nursing my husband back to health. I had left the management consulting rat race by then, and was running my own market research practice from my home. There was no debate and no guilt about putting my professional life aside for my personal one.

I really feel blessed now that I am able to choose to stay home with my children and not feel pressured to work full time. I joined a mothers' group in my neighborhood. I met so many mothers who wanted to stay home but felt compelled to return to full-time work because they needed the second paycheck. We make financial compromises and have tightened our belts, but frankly, our quality of life is better. For instance, when I was a management consultant, I never had time to cook. Now, making dinner is routine. It's great on the budget and it improves my cooking skills.

Becoming a mom has launched me into a new phase. The flexibility of independent consulting, valued before, became a burden. Being in a client-service industry means ebbing and flowing with the client's needs. But, how can one plan for child care when one week I need 2 hours, and the next 40? I would turn down work, especially projects that had strict deadlines, hoping that clients and business partners would not write me off. So, again, I re-examined my professional goals. My life has come full circle. I am teaching again.

Talk about the power of the network. One of my former classmates recommended me for an academic position that wasn't advertised yet. I now teach marketing and quantitative methods at Hult International School here in Cambridge. How it happened is a funny story. I went to the interview doubting I would be really interested in the position, originally fairly limited in scope. The interview went so well that they expanded the job description into one that really suits me for now. It offers flexibility with predictability, mental stimulation with manageable responsibility. I am staying in the professional game by doing something that keeps my career moving. And my outlook on life has changed.

If you had told me five years ago that I would be back to teaching, but not gunning for tenure, I would not have believed you. For now, I accept that I can only do one or two things really well. My ambitions have altered; I suspect they probably will again. My professional identity has altered, too. At school, I'm the only female professor with young children, and I try to do many things via phone, such as attend faculty meetings. I remember cringing once when an older faculty member brusquely asked who was babysitting, after my daughter loudly overcame the mute button. Still, I am learning to let go of, or rather, reshape my professional aura. I remember wanting to attend an 85 Broads reception and feeling nervous about bringing my daughter since I had no one to care for her. Would others view it as unprofessional? Was it even practical? After all, what was the point of going to a networking event when I might spend much of the time chasing an energetic toddler? It was reassuring when Janet Hanson, the founder of 85 Broads (who brings her own children to network events), showed how thrilled she was to meet my daughter. And I still got to talk to great people, even with a child in tow.

I'm new to this world of juggling jobs and kids. Right now, I am happy with the balance. I continue to network, meet new people, and I hope to meet other moms, be they stay-at-home, full-time professional, or somewhere in between. I do have one bit of advice, especially for stay-at-home moms. It is so critical to develop a network, to know that there are other women out there like us. Networking helps for every career situation but especially when you do not work outside the home. I can't stress how important it is to build connections, even if it's just once a month. If you're willing, it can work. Be daring; be creative. I threw out my five-year plan a long time ago. I have no idea what I will do professionally in the longer term. Maybe I'll really go full circle and complete my doctorate. In the mean time, my daughter wants to babble on the phone. Care to listen?

ANA CABRAL

Ana is a native Brazilian who moved to the United States originally to engage in graduate studies toward a PhD in economics, which she gave up to join Goldman Sachs in New York in 1994. Since leaving Goldman Sachs she has continued to work in investment banking in New York and in London. She received her MBA from Columbia Business School.

"While my months-old baby was getting in and out of NICUs in hospitals during his first two years of life, I was working 16-hour days, delivering impeccable results, while maintaining a tough and professional attitude. I kept my armor on. By looking at the placid 'outside façade,' no one at work could ever imagine the turmoil sweeping through my personal life, resulting from all of the uncertainty about whether my son was going to live or not. I was driven to work hard during that period because work gave me an enormous sense of control over my life, and that was somewhat comforting. Although I could not control my son's fate, I could surely control whether my deals would be successful. This certainty and the overall sense of reward brought by my work was what kept me going in the darkest and saddest moments, giving me purpose and direction. Later on, partly because I thought my son was never going to live a full life, his survival became a huge blessing, which I saw as a hidden message to fix my unbalanced life."

I was simultaneously coordinating the execution of three very large privatizations of more than $28 billion in size when I found out that I was pregnant. I had mixed feelings about my pregnancy: I was one year away from a coveted vice president promotion, and I felt that my ill-timed pregnancy would completely derail my career. I remember being so consumed by professional concerns (such as people are going to think now that I am pregnant that I do not care about my career; I will be placed on the mommy track) that I barely enjoyed my pregnancy. I was so worried about "perception" that I almost forgot about "reality." I worked until the day before I gave birth, and I clearly remember walking home to begin my maternity leave that evening, endlessly worrying about some loose ends in one of the privatizations and thinking that maybe I would have to go back to the office (after giving birth) to fix it. Well, little did I know that just a day later, my entire life would take a dramatic turn upside down—forever.

Labor during my son's birth was extremely complicated and medically traumatic. I almost died at childbirth. He was born without his vital signs; technically he was dead. He could not be resuscitated and was immediately admitted into the NICU. He was on a respirator, his kidneys did not work, he was being fed by IV, and his heart and his brain were failing him. We almost lost him three different times in his first week of life. One night, I dragged myself and my IV stand from my hospital bed at 4 a.m. to sneak into the NICU, because I had dreamed my son was dead. When I got to the NICU, dripping blood from my legs and looking like a ghost, the nurses did not know whether to scurry me back to my room or whether to feel sorry for me; he had indeed already seized 18 times that night. He was not going to make it through the night, I was told. I touched his hand from the hole in the incubator and feared becoming emotionally attached to a dying baby. Strangely enough, I had not yet cried. In hindsight, all of it was like an "out of body" experience; it was not happening to me; I was just there witnessing it all, not yet feeling the full extent of the pain.

In the following weeks, after the first MRI to assess the full extent of our son's brain damage, my husband and I were told the prognosis by a neurologist. It was bleak, and there was nothing we could do to change his fate: cortical blindness, cortical deafness, severe motor impairment, and mental retardation. The magnitude of the damage was such that the neurologist was at a loss for words. I felt a pang of profound sadness and for the first time in my life I was afraid of the future: my future, his future, the future of my marriage. I was still in the hospital, far away from my routine, and I was becoming increasingly apathetic as my hopelessness gradually metamorphosed into depression. I thought I was never going to be happy again. How could I?

But I could not possibly spend my entire maternity leave watching my newborn die in an incubator because I would gradually die too, as my core, my eternal optimism and passion for life, would disappear. That is when I realized that I had the choice of sinking into profound depression or swimming to the surface in the midst of all of these events. I needed something to pull me out.

That is when I threw myself at my career. As soon as I got out of the hospital I fell into the routine of waking up in the morning, going to the NICU, going to work for as long as I could, and going back to the NICU in the evenings. I asked to focus in media and technology so that my international travel could be decreased and it all worked well. At the time, my work was the only thing in my life that I could control. It provided me with other things to focus my energy on. My deals gave me a gigantic sense of achievement. Work was rewarding, and it kept me going by providing some direction and momentum for my life at that time.

Finally that spring, my son came home, though diagnosed with severe quadriplegic cerebral palsy. When I got the news I was at a meeting on the West Coast and did not flinch. I went back into the room, delivered my pitch as if nothing had happened, and took the red-eye back to New York. Although I was profoundly sad about the news, I was back to my old optimistic self and tried to focus on the "good aspects of it": now that he was sent home, it meant that he would live, so there was hope. The damage to his brain had been done already, so going forward there would only be improvements, I thought. On that plane ride back to New York, it dawned on me that working so hard during that interval had energized me to tackle "the biggest deal of my life."

From then on, I would spend the days in banking and the nights researching motor impairment and neurological papers. My work at the bank stayed impeccable while my personal life was crumbling. I was in the office 16 to 17 hours daily and bringing in millions in revenue for the firm by securing precious IPO mandates. In the meantime, in my parallel universe of reading, I learned about the "plasticity of the baby brain" whereby the nerve cell connections (synapses) are formed around the damaged areas, thus potentially minimizing the effects of the initial damage. Therefore, if I had any hopes of my son benefiting from the effects of the brain's plasticity, I had to get him started on all sorts of early intervention and intense physical, speech, and occupational therapy. That is when for the first time in my life, I started to think that I should take time off from work to get my son set up with the best team of specialists and place him on the right track to recovery.

But change does not happen overnight and, not having the courage to quit, I still spent most of that year working like a horse. Maybe I was waiting for something bigger to happen. Finally it did: one day returning from San Francisco, I realized my son did not recognize me at all. Not because of his disabilities, but because I simply was not spending nearly enough time with him. My breakneck schedule and relentless bicoastal travel were finally taking a toll on my attempt at motherhood. Only when my marriage was showing signs of distress did I finally decide to leave banking after almost seven years. So the day I took home my year 2000 bonus, the largest sum of money I had ever earned in my life, I flew six hours to tell my boss my full story face-to-face and asked to leave the firm. There was nothing he could say to make me change my mind. Since the birth of my son almost two years before that meeting, I had kept such a professional attitude and had worked so hard that my boss did not really know the the full extent of the turmoil sweeping through my personal life. He was amazed at my strength, and on a handshake, he told me that I could come back to the firm any day.

I spent 2001 as a full-time mother, focusing my energies toward placing my son on a path to recovery. Ironically, I was not working but this turned into the most difficult period of my life. My son started to have seizures and, as a result, the once remote possibility that he could die was again a reality. I was on a quest to find the right mix of therapies for him. The list of doctors was endless. My son and I spent a lot of time traveling to see specialists everywhere in the United States and around the world—New York, San Diego, Michigan, London, Brazil, Poland, and Hungary—looking for the right mix of therapies. I tried everything from hyperbaric oxygen therapy to horseback riding therapy, to intensive physical therapy (a method used by Russian astronauts), to daily swimming classes and music therapy. All that effort made investment banking look like a walk in the park most days. It was all too emotional. Personally, it was also a very difficult time: I lost another baby and my marriage fell apart. I missed my career tremendously because this time, unlike the other difficult periods of my life when I focused on my work through my "tough patches," I had very little left to hang onto. I had lost the keys to my parallel universe.

By mid-2001, I realized that I needed to tilt the balance in my life away from motherhood a bit and back toward my career. (Isn't balance the Holy Grail of investment bankers?) and I gradually returned to work by consulting to several private equity firms and to my previous banking clients. As a banker, all that hard work had helped me build truly exceptional relationships with my clients within the media industry, which led to some high-profile consulting assignments. Later, they would prove invaluable when I decided to reenter the banking industry. Also, my timing was good, with the markets melting down in the second half of the year; some of my previous media clients could use my help either in debt restructuring or in acquiring targets at lower valuations.

By January 2002, the markets were in "full bear territory" and although I was very busy with client restructurings, I decided to continue my graduate studies (which had brought me to the United States in the first place), enrolling in the MBA program at Columbia Business School with the goal of continuing into the PhD after that (the markets will not get better anytime soon, I thought). However, later that year, while still in school, I took on a full-time position at the investment banking arm of a European commercial bank, focusing on restructurings/M&A. We made an arrangement— they were absolutely fantastic—where my employer allowed me to carve out weekends and from time to time to leave work to attend class. After all, as a single parent, I needed to be with my son; as a graduate student, I needed to study. It was an insane period of my life, juggling school, work, single motherhood, and a nasty divorce battle in the U.S. courts. But I had to take that opportunity at that stage. After all, as a divorced mother, my job was now more important than ever, as I had become the head of my household and had a disabled child to support. That period also taught me an invaluable lesson: not to feel guilty about my juggling act. Since I was deprived of the choices that "plague" most women, I stopped feeling guilty about less than perfect parenting. Losing the guilt about my "choices" (or lack thereof) at that crucial stage made an incredible difference in my whole attitude about my career into the future.

After I graduated from Columbia, I was ready once again to take one more major step for my career, and I accepted an offer to return to my old employer in capital markets in London. Professionally, it meant that I would be back to the pressures and rewards of life in a top-tier U.S. investment bank. Personally, I had mixed feelings, as moving to London meant leaving more than a decade of my life behind in New York. But London offered two things: the quality of life in capital markets is infinitely higher than in investment banking (once again, searching for the Holy Grail of balance), and my son would be able to attend one of the best schools in the world for children with his disabilities.

On the surface it seems that my life has come full circle from 2000, as I am back at the same firm. But I became a very different person. All that I have been through has made me extremely resilient and thick-skinned. I can pretty much handle any crisis at work, with the cool-headedness of those who have lived through the real "worst case scenarios." I have also gained a different prospective about my role in our ever-changing industry, which ironically makes me a much better banker in these ultracompetitive times. I still work intensely; I am extremely committed to my career; I still absolutely love what I do. To this date, I still often stay in the office for 13 to 14 hours, putting in some of the longest hours in capital markets. The difference is that I have become very selective on how I actually spend those hours: I am incredibly focused during the day, barely stopping for anything, almost like a machine. And I make time for my clients, occasionally squeezing in a game of golf on weekends or a dinner. But I completely avoid wasting time in some of the "extras" of this profession, such as: the endless after-hours internal socializing, the politics, the internal gossip, the glitter, and the pointless internal competition. I learned over the past 10 years that I can be just as successful without any of those "extras." And more importantly, I now have a six-year-old brave little boy waiting for me at home every night.

6

GIVERS

This chapter goes to the heart of the 85 Broads network. Giving is an integral part of connecting within our community. "Women helping women" has always been the purpose and positive message of 85 Broads. It is the reason I started the network. It is the reason the network has grown beyond industry, geographic, cultural, and generational boundaries. Giving means getting beyond yourself, beyond your own focus and priorities, beyond your own challenges and perceived barriers. Giving can take on many forms—philanthropy, healing, co-mentoring, parenting, and even entrepreneurship—as we'll see in the stories of the exceptional "givers" profiled in this chapter. Virtually every aspect of our professional and personal lives provides opportunities for giving or helping others, and I believe that it is one of the key ingredients of living the kind of "integrated and partnered" life we heard about from the parents in the previous chapter. To introduce our givers, let's look at just some of the many facets of "giving."

The 85 Broads network has always had this incredibly positive energy, optimism, and passion. I strongly believe one of the biggest reasons for this is because we haven't isolated or shut out any of our individual voices, including the voices of the next generation, who are too often told to "wait their turn" just when they have the most to say and contribute. 85 Broads has moved these incredible women to the front of the stage and given them the podium. We've co-mentored with them and partnered with them in redefining leadership for women. We've always wanted to show that women are passionate about helping each other—not just in formal mentoring programs or when they are "supposed to," but completely serendipitously and spontaneously. And guess what? We have younger women helping older women; women from different cultures and backgrounds starting businesses and philanthropies together; and women realizing that their "return on life" has increased exponentially because of the connections they're making through a network like 85 Broads.

Women Helping Women

Many times in my career I have seen and sometimes experienced exactly the opposite. Women thinking and acting individually rather than collectively. women being "siloed" and increasingly isolated from the start of their careers. Women who, as they advance in their careers, focus only on themselves and not on helping the other women beside them or coming up behind them. As one of my male colleagues once said: "If women aren't willing to help other women, that gives men an excuse not to either!" As you now know, one of the reasons I started 85 Broads was because I had vowed that I didn't want anyone to feel as isolated or alienated from their own professional identity as I had when I left Goldman Sachs to start a family and stay at home. That's why the network now connects us with each other across lines that many others consider "barriers"—current employees *and* former employees, women *and* men, current students *and* alumnae, those still in the workforce *and* those who don't work or who are trying to return to their careers. The feelings of isolation that many women express, both in heavily male-populated workplaces and at home during leaves or periods of career transition, are being replaced by a greater sense of connectivity and community. How is this being accomplished? Co-mentoring relationships with younger women is one way; it allows more experienced professionals not only to give much-needed advice and feedback but to keep their own professional skills sharp and to identify the new skills they will need to advance in their careers, return to the workplace, or transition to other careers.

Strategic and Personal Philanthropy

Many of the women whose stories are in this chapter and this book, and many more women throughout our global network, are finding and using their voices through philanthropy. For the 85 Broads network, this was a very personal lesson as well. I have already told you the story of how our network learned we had lost one of our members, Cathy Chirls, in the attack on the

World Trade Center on 9/11. We dedicated our global event that fall to Cathy and called it "What's Your Gift?"—raising money to help Cathy's family establish the Cathy Chirls Fund. This also has inspired us to find literally thousands of other ways over the past five years to weave philanthropy and cultural understanding into the connections we are making at our events, online, and around the world.

The nonprofit organization which 85 Broads set up that same year—Miles To Go—is now a public charity dedicated to humanitarian, educational, and economic empowerment for women and their families around the world. As we learned in our Adventurers chapter, 85 Broads has partnered with our members and other philanthropic organizations to build two schools in Nepal that today educate over 1,200 children in a country where the illiteracy rate among girls is historically 95 percent. We're also now building a school in Vietnam, supporting an orphanage outside of Moscow, working with Broad2Broad members at Harvard and Wharton to fight AIDS in South Africa, and launching our most exciting new global venture called Angels Abroad, which is creating network-based venture philanthropy partnerships in seven different developing regions around the world. Teams of 85 Broads members are "investing in women who invest in themselves" by giving female entrepreneurs the resources, network co-mentors, local partners and start-up capital they need to start socially responsible businesses and new philanthropic initiatives in Africa, Asia, Eastern Europe, India, Latin America, and the Middle East.

Generosity has become one of the greatest passions of our network. Not just generosity with our wallets, but generosity with our time, our talent, our vision, our teamwork, and most of all, our spirit. This kind of strategic and personal philanthropy has helped us take our passion for "women helping women" to a completely different level. It also has led us to once again redefine how we think about our global community and the power we have to be true agents of change through the cross-cultural connections we are creating.

GIVING AND GETTING

Another common theme of givers is that giving is a two-way street. Each of our givers has herself been the recipient of many gifts and generous giving on the part of others in their lives. These gifts come in many forms, sometimes even in the form of adversity or life-threatening illnesses. Whatever the gift, givers integrate giving into their lives, careers, and passions; it's not some-thing we defer anymore until our careers are on track, our finances are in order, or our family lives are settled. As we'll see in this chapter, many of our most "gifted" and passionate givers are women in their twenties and early thirties.

They also have taken to heart what I like to refer to as a "tough love" mes-sage that our network got early on from one of our many male "friends of 85 Broads." Pete Kiernan is a former investment banking partner of Goldman Sachs who has led many extraordinary philanthropies like the Robin Hood Foundation, the Christopher Reeve Foundation, and World T.E.A.M. Sports. His work with disabled war veterans on both sides led to the Emmy Award–winning documentary *Vietnam Long Time Coming*, chronicling the extraordinary bicycle trip they made across 1,200 miles through Vietnam. After 9/11, Pete and his colleagues at Robin Hood produced the Concert for the City of New York, one of the largest-grossing charity events in history. But what the 85 Broads network remembers most about Pete are the rousing challenges he has given us to put philanthropy into action. The speech he gave at our "What's Your Gift?" event in 2001 perfectly captured the win-win essence of giving:

"OK, 85 Broads, here's the message. *The world runs in boardrooms.* What makes you think you're going to know how to sit in a boardroom, act in a boardroom, and serve in a boardroom if you've never been in a board meeting? This opportunity is right here for you, right now. There are hundreds of board memberships and thousands of leadership positions with philanthropies available right now in this city and hundreds of other cities where they are dying to have any one of you— *dying to.* Organizations within five miles of where we're sitting that don't know how to do the things you know how to do just like 'that'—just like you know how to get up in the morning. *Places where your involvement could create instant and total change.*

By the way, the people who are on boards also tend to be the influencers, the shapers, the leaders, the hirers, the firers, the determiners, and the strategists. If you sit next to them day in, day out, and you solve a really Gordian riddle—some complex problem, some horrendous wrong you help right—then first you develop as a professional, and second you are at the center of a group of people with tremendous influence who will sincerely appreciate the fact that you are someone who can bring about change. You are labeling yourself as a leader. You are making the world better and, in the end, that is the definition of leadership. I also can tell you, by the way, that there is no person on this earth—absolutely no person—that you can fail to meet under the banner of philanthropy."

Thanks to constructive challenges like Pete's and the examples of women who we'll meet in this chapter, our members are joining the boards of nonprofit organizations and getting involved in starting or running nonprofit organizations all over the world. They are following their own hearts in finding unique ways to give and to benefit from that giving, both personally and professionally. The scale of the giving doesn't matter. The form of the giving doesn't matter. The women of 85 Broads are totally committed to defining and pursuing our passions on our own terms—and equally committed to helping or being helped by others who are as passionate as we are.

SARA M. GREEN

Sara is the founder of Art for Refugees in Transition (ART), a non-profit organization that develops programs enabling long-term refugee populations to preserve their traditional art forms and transmit them to younger generations. Revitalizing indigenous arts provides a catalyst for rebuilding displaced communities and helping to heal the wounds of war, famine, flight, and other trauma. Sara graduated from Columbia Business School in 2001 with a degree in finance and economics.

"When I doubted myself, I remembered the words of a Columbia professor who insisted, 'How could you have a dream and not make that dream come true?'"

After spending 10 years as a professional dancer and working in various nonprofit organizations, I knew that I needed a change. I no longer felt challenged and was eager to reach out to help others and to make a difference in the world. At the time, I was watching the war in the Balkans unfold daily on television. As battles raged, refugees flooded into provisional camps for safety. Every day I saw the pictures of the refugees, and I could not help but be moved by the plight of thousands of children fleeing their homelands. Their faces were etched with a pain, a fear, and a hopelessness that they did not deserve to know.

From my experience as a dancer, both in performing and in teaching dance to children, I knew that every child loves to sing, to dance, to play, and to be free. Perhaps, I thought, these children could overcome their pain and regain their lost childhoods through song and dance. The arts would be a way for them to find freedom, to connect with their elders, to preserve their indigenous traditions, and to rebuild their shattered sense of community.

That is why I founded Art for Refugees in Transition, a vehicle for using art as a healing agent to empower communities in need. My vision was to help refugee communities cope with the trauma of dislocation by engaging them in arts and traditions drawn from their own cultures.

Having spent a decade working with nonprofit arts organizations, I knew that in order to make this vision become reality I needed the skills and credibility that business school could provide. When I started at Columbia Business School, I wanted to learn everything. I was surrounded by extraordinary people—intelligent, passionate, and interesting—and the student body was extremely diverse. Working with two other classmates and a professor in Columbia's entrepreneurship program, I developed a strategic plan to launch ART, which was eventually chosen to be part of Columbia's "greenhouse," an incubator for entrepreneurial projects.

Using a simple model that would involve as few outside "consultants" as possible, ART's mission is to encourage community elders to pass their cultural traditions on to future generations, not only preserving fragile traditions that can be so easily lost in times of trial, but also rebuilding the links between generations that are vital to maintaining communities.

At Columbia I was introduced to one of my mentors, Janet Hanson, who helped nurture my project. Janet was an inspiration, encouraging me to pursue my dream. She introduced me to Mary Diaz, who was executive director of the Women's Commission for Refugee Women and Children, an organization which took me on a two-week trip to Kosovo with the International Rescue Committee so that I could examine programs and policies for children in war.

Just as ART was getting off the ground, I suffered a traumatic life-changing head injury, affecting my short-term memory, eyesight, ability to focus, and balance. For months, I was barely able to stand. I persevered with my work through a long recovery, graduating from Columbia Business School in 2001 and determined to make ART happen. When I doubted myself, I remembered the words of a Columbia professor who insisted, "How could you have a dream and not make that dream come true?" The classmates with whom I had developed ART had found other jobs, and I was left to develop the organization on my own.

I wanted to go back to Kosovo to put ART into action, but the situation in Kosovo had improved so the IRC sent me instead to two camps in northern Thailand to launch ART's pilot program in a community of more than 23,000 Burmese refugees. The program has been a stunning success, with a daily curriculum of classes for the community, including instruction for the younger generation in weaving, instrument making, folklore, singing, and dancing. The Burmese refugees have shown a real and proven appetite for rebuilding their communities and restoring their traditions. Now, two years after implementation, the program is run solely by the refugees and is fully self-sustaining. The momentum of ART's success in Thailand continued when I was approached by a New York–based foundation that helps to fund and implement humanitarian programs in Colombia, focusing on the country's three million internal refugees. After several trips to Colombia, ART implemented its first Latin American program in a displaced community in Bogotá. There are over 180,000 members of this community, and their enthusiasm and excitement is overwhelming. I was able to partner with Universidad de los Andes, which has assigned several students from their anthropology, literature, music, and fine arts departments to work with ART to implement, manage, and evaluate the program; the students receive credit for their work and ART has an ongoing stream of employees. Government and UN agencies are also climbing on board. It is incredible!

There are more than 17 million refugees around the world, almost half of whom are children, now living in camps or "temporary" settlements. Most of these refugees will never be able to return to their homes, and they are in grave danger of losing all contact with their roots and of losing the sense of community that is their only identity, and frequently, the only possession they can pass on to their children. My vision for ART is to create an adaptable curriculum that can be implemented in refugee camps and other communities in need all around the world, offering an array of classes, recording facilities, music, newsletters, folklore, and opportunities to organize traditional festivals. ART has plans to create training manuals and film documentaries to assist the elders in teaching the younger generations their cultural traditions.

The true reward in this work is the response I receive from the refugees themselves. ART is the light in their eyes. Tearful elders explain that without ART, their traditions would have died with them. One of the refugees said to me, "You have returned meaning to our lives. We had lost so much." With this affirmation of our work together, I am ready and eager to expand ART to the next level.

JUDITH AIDOO

Judith was born in the United States and moved to Ghana, West Africa, when she was 12. She gained interest and confidence in the world of business through the independent, entrepreneurial women in her family. With degrees in Business Administration and French from Rutgers and a Juris Doctor degree from Harvard Law School, Judith started her career at Goldman Sachs and is currently an independent investor, specializing in media and entertainment in the United States and Africa.

> "You never know who you will meet next, or how that person will affect your life. From some you receive and to others you give."

It was 98 degrees in the shade. I watched the tall African man stoke the fire, trying to get the bread to bake faster. The sweat poured down his face as the line of women to buy bread grew longer and longer. I watched this daily routine from my "office," a wooden kiosk under a nearby mango tree, and I was relieved that it was my job to simply count and record the cash collected and loaves sold. At 14 years old, I had already decided that I liked the money side of the business, and I have been a committed capitalist ever since.

I am an African American in the truest sense of the word; my father was from Ghana, West Africa, and my mother hails from Charleston, South Carolina. Since each place was at the opposite end of the trans-Atlantic slave trade, I have assumed that it is my destiny to bridge these two worlds.

Starting my career at Goldman Sachs provided me with an excellent foundation for my future work in private investment. At Goldman, I learned several important lessons, including how capital moves, how risk is assessed and priced, and how to make money on market inefficiencies. While there, in my free time, I was able to combine my passion for making money with my love for Africa by advising the World Bank and African governments on setting up capital markets and by privatizing state-owned assets. It was a great experience because during a two-week vacation from Goldman, I would literally fly into a major African country, work for its finance minister, and meet its senior business leaders. Consequently, my advisory work was a wonderful way to obtain access to the most senior capitalists in Africa, and I could do so quickly.

I continued to do this work in Africa for two of my four years at Goldman, and for the following eight years of my career. We literally made history, both in establishing African capital markets, and in raising capital for African companies in the U.S. capital markets. To convince U.S. investors to give us the capital required, we focused on investing in assets that American funds could easily understand, even if they didn't trust the African market per se. We gained a reputation for acquiring undervalued licenses or franchises, from Coca Cola bottlers, to cellular and satellite licenses, to financial services companies. Having gone to law school, I am comfortable with licenses and contracts, and Goldman taught me to manage downsize risk, a useful skill in a place like Africa. We decided to deal in financing assets that American investors could readily understand and value, so investors could price the investment opportunity properly and commit capital.

I loved working in Africa, largely because I felt that we could make money and do good at the same time. Our investments really helped improve the economic situation for many Africans, and that makes me proud. But, after 11 years, the 12-hour plane trips caught up with me. My ideal situation would be to have a toehold in Africa but to do more work here in the United States. I began looking around for a small business to buy; of course, something with a license or a franchise because that is the business I understood from my African days.

As it turns out, the last black-owned radio station in Charleston, where I decided to settle, was struggling and in need of capital. It was owned by a local leader who focused on informing and educating the community. His motivation was wonderful, but the business side needed some work. I met him on a Thursday, and he needed money by Tuesday to keep the station afloat. Even though I knew nothing about the radio business, I thought to myself, "Why not?" and I got him the funds he needed.

I was now a major lender to the company, and I had an option to acquire the station if he failed to repay the loan. Was I in for a shock! Ten days later, the station burned to the ground and he had no insurance. I had made such an emotional investment that I had to make it work. I increased my investment significantly and took over the business. I quickly figured out that the only way to make money in the radio business is to achieve scale, and quickly. I therefore looked for a way to consolidate lots of mom-and-pop–owned radio stations in the southeast that hadn't already been acquired. Fortunately, managing this radio station gave me important contacts and an inside look at the industry.

I quickly learned that communications companies, as opposed to service businesses, need millions of dollars in start-up capital. Everything that goes wrong costs tens of thousands of dollars. I needed to raise at least $10 million to play, more than I had ever required before for any of my other ventures. So, for the first time in my career, I had to ask people to back me. I also quickly learned that it's really hard to raise money, especially for a woman. I started calling Goldman alums and friends on Wall Street. A friend with ties to MSD Capital, Michael Dell's private office, put me in touch with someone else who was running a hedge fund. This financier told me that if I decided not to run radio stations, we could form a joint venture to finance media and entertainment companies together. Even though I eventually raised the capital that I needed to consolidate radio stations, I decided that the cost of capital was too high and I would need to be an exceptional operator to win. Remembering my African bakery days, I decided to return to my strengths on the finance side, which I had discovered long ago, and I formed a joint venture with that hedge fund.

I am now a full-time investor, and I manage a small portfolio of investments in media and entertainment. One of our recent investments is a new movie network on broadcast television called the *Uptown Movie Network* (www.uptownmovienetwork.com). In just our first two months of operation, we have become a leading syndicator of urban programming in the United States. With any luck, we will be able to leverage the millions of people we reach on a monthly basis to become a major distributor of urban television and movie programming on broadcast TV, cable, the Internet, and any other platform that makes sense.

I believe that my competitive advantage is that I'm willing to take calculated risks. Specifically, I'm willing to invest some of my own money in the beginning in order to learn the business from the ground up. But, in order to play a big game you have to have real capital, and that means that you have to ask others. Until I invested in broadcasting, I had never felt the money crunch personally. In fact, I'd invested a lot of money in many nonsensical ventures and slowly learned the investment business. Not having enough money to expand and run my own media business made me much more dis-

criminating with my money, and it also taught me to appreciate the importance of access to capital.

This insight goes way beyond my own business; it applies to the very social
fabric of this country. Democracies without capital cannot work. The reason
that America is a great country is that it is commonly understood that you
can have a dollar and no contacts, yet work hard, use your creativity, and
make it big. Many of the wealthiest people in America have all created their
own companies. But if you can't get the funding, you can't get your company
to the next level, and society, as a whole, can't rise. I was lucky enough to
overcome the capital raising issues through my Wall Street contacts, and I
learned to never say die.

But it also affirmed in me the need to help others who have no access to
capital or contacts. That is the reason that I recently stopped to help a young
Nigerian woman sitting on Wall Street with a sign that read, "Hello! I'm Mary.
I'm brilliant. Columbia University agrees. All I need is a loan. Name your
interest rate." It took only 60 seconds to speak to this young woman, Mary. I
was taken with her chutzpah. So smart, but she had no idea how she would
come up with the $40,000 in annual tuition. I respected her for coming to
Wall Street to get the money she needed. When I was 19 and really fearless, I
would have done the same thing. However, I was wary, so I told her to prove
to me her situation was true. She faxed me a copy of her Barnard documen-
tation, including her acceptance letter. See www.sendmarytoschool.com.

The next day, I put the word out to my friends and colleagues, and when
I called later that evening, I had already raised $5,000 for her. Within two
weeks, Barnard's Bursar's office had received more than $20,000 from a broad
network of people around the world, just enough for Mary to register for
classes. We have since been on *Oprah*, CNN, and in many major daily newspapers, as this story has resonated so strongly around the world. Even more
important, not only have we funded Mary to go to college, we have recently
helped four other women pay for their college tuition as well. We have raised
nearly $250,000 since August 2004 through our project, which we now lov-
ingly refer to as the Wall Street to Hollywood Network and Opportunity
Fund, which is administered by the Twenty-first Century Foundation (see
www.21cf.org for more information). All this from a random walk down Wall
Street…!

I consider myself blessed that, at this point in my career, I can put my
capital and time into those projects that I am most passionate about. The
amazing part of it all is that you never know who you will meet next or how
that person will affect your life. From some you receive, and to others you

give. You just have to remain open, seize every opportunity to play a big game, and help someone along the way.

Sheila C. Cavanaugh

Sheila began her career in the financial services industry in the mid-1980s at Chase Manhattan Bank and has held a variety of positions in international banking in Japan, Switzerland, and the former Soviet Union. She spent a sabbatical year teaching English for the United Nations at a Vietnamese refugee camp. After several years as a consultant with Coopers & Lybrud, Sheila joined Fidelity Investment in Boston, where she is currently a senior vice president. Sheila and her husband are the parents of three children from South Korea.

> "Don't aim at success—the more you aim at it and make it a target, the more you are going to miss it. For success, like happiness, cannot be pursued; it must ensue, and it only does so as the unintended side effect of one's personal dedication to a cause greater than oneself or as the by-product of one's surrender to a person other than oneself."
>
> Dr. Viktor E. Frankl,
> Nazi death camp survivor

On an otherwise obscure Saturday morning during my first year at Chase, I was doing sit-ups on my bedroom floor in preparation for a run across the George Washington Bridge into New Jersey. I had been a runner in high school and college, and kept at it while living in New York. About 20 minutes into my workout, I lost feeling in my right hand. It simply went limp. Moments later, I lost feeling and movement in my right arm. It hung lifelessly by my side. I couldn't will it to move. I sat on my bed wondering what was going on when suddenly I fell on the floor with a loud thud. I couldn't get up. My right leg was paralyzed.

There are some things that just can't be planned and this was one of them. I was living with two medical students and a nurse; my roommates came running in only to discover me in a panic on the floor. By the time the ambulance arrived, I had lost my ability to speak. I was admitted to the Neurological Institute of New York and diagnosed with a blood clot in my left brain. The doctors said, "You've had a stroke." I was 26 years old.

The blood clot I had that day took away my memory, my ability to speak, my ability to comprehend. When you can't speak, people assume you can't hear...or think. And they treat you that way. Beyond not being able to speak, I was paralyzed on my entire right side: arm, hand, leg, foot, face. It took me several years to fully recover my speech, although I still don't have any feeling on my right side.

My recovery from the stroke gave me a powerful sense of gratitude that motivates me every day. I am happy to be able to walk and talk. It is a gift to be able to express my thoughts. I am highly motivated to share what has been given back to me. My experience has made me acutely sensitive to the visible and invisible challenges that countless people carry with them every day. I try to help others embrace the belief that life can get better by embracing that myself.

My stroke also injected my life with an intense sense of urgency. We pass through this world just once. We have no knowledge of how long that passage will be. There is no time to delay in taking action on our dreams. Today may be all we have.

I learned firsthand that life is an immense gift. Its greatness is shaped by its boundaries; we only get one and, whether we're on board with this or not, it ends. Once we wake up to the power of our own lives, to the greatness stored within ourselves, to the vast possibilities available to us to shape our lives in profound ways, we can embrace our experiences as the opportunities they are: lessons designed to instruct, ripen, and renew.

Christopher Reeve said there are many able-bodied people who are paralyzed in other ways. I came out of a paralyzed state like a sprinter going for the gold. I couldn't wait to extract life's riches by pushing myself beyond my comfort zone. I decided to break away from the familiarity of my life as a banker in New York and move to the furthest point on the planet from my hometown. I bought a one-way ticket to Singapore. I wanted to be challenged by living with people who were ethnically, politically, culturally, and spiritually different from me. I enrolled in the National University in a graduate program in economics and joined the United Nations as an English teacher. I was assigned to work at a Vietnamese refugee camp in Sembawang, Singapore.

Six weeks after I arrived in the country, I took a weekend boat trip to one of the 13,000 islands that constitute Indonesia. During that trip, I met a fellow on one of those distinctly remote islands and discovered that he was also living and working in Singapore. I have to admit I was swept. We got engaged on our third date and were married in Massachusetts in 1989. We are now raising three beautiful children from Korea. I'm a fanatic about taking risks. The wonderful thing is we don't have to take big steps to go far.

My students at the camp didn't have much, but what they had in abundance was hope. They were eager to start new lives. They were hungry for a language that would help transform them into citizens of new societies. They had all the ingredients of success: enthusiasm, a deeply-rooted work ethic, a reverence for learning and knowledge, and a belief that life can and will get better. They also shared an intense sense of community, which helped sustain them through the trauma of escaping their homeland. I came to respect an entirely new dimension of risk-taking through my students, and I recognized the powerful role many of us can play in helping to transform lives, including our own.

A couple of years into my career at Fidelity, I had another life-altering experience. I was working for the vice chairman at the time. I discovered rather quickly that every time an executive's name was published in the paper, it served as a catalyst for countless letters of complaint. I managed a lot of "problem resolution" cases, and wondered why so few people took even a fleeting moment of time to praise. The complainers were vocal, and understandably so. But from a sociological point of view, I found it distressing that so few people chose to take a moment to praise. Then I realized that I had never written a letter of praise for good service, and I chastised myself for complaining that others hadn't either.

I committed myself to finding an opportunity to praise. Not long after that, I left my office at lunch one day and walked across the street to Macy's Department Store. I was waited on by a lovely young woman who spoke with a heavy Eastern European accent. I asked her where she was from. "I am from Bosnia," she said. She had arrived in the United States as a refugee from the Bosnian war.

She was delightful and engaging. I enjoyed her immensely. I went back to my desk and wrote a letter of praise to the head of Macy's in Boston. Management sent her to headquarters in New York City as a sign of their gratitude for her good work. They gave her a shopping spree and wrote to her parents, neither of whom could speak English. The young woman, Aida, was supporting them on her clerk's salary. She was 19 when we met.

I befriended Aida. I visited her family's apartment north of Boston and discovered they only had one lamp. We had to transport it from room to room as we moved through the apartment. I went back to Fidelity and asked my colleagues if anyone had an extra lamp. I could've lit the city of Boston with the number of lamps I received. I did the same with clothes. I ended up with nine boxes of beautiful clothes. Unknown to me, my Bosnian friends shipped some of the clothes I gave them to Sarajevo.

I traveled to Sarajevo to visit my friends during the summers of 2000 and 2004. Women came up to me to show me that the clothes they were wearing had been shipped to them from Boston. I told my colleagues at Fidelity, and they were delighted that their donations had made a transatlantic trip. There was joy on both sides of the world.

I helped Aida apply to college and mentored her through four years at the University of Massachusetts, Boston. She graduated in May 2003, having spent six semesters on the dean's list. My one letter of praise has transformed the lives of two people and two families, one Catholic and the other Muslim. My family celebrates Ramadan with Aida's family, and they share in the joy of Christmas.

When I went to Bosnia in 2004, my Muslim friends offered to drive me to Medjegore, a Christian pilgrimage site buried in the mountains of Croatia. We drove for hours through the mountains to get to this tiny village where we came upon people of every race and religion praying to a universal God. This is what world peace ought to be about.

KENDALL WEBB

Kendall graduated from Harvard College in 1986 and began her career at Goldman Sachs. From there, she worked for the World Bank as a way to merge her financial background with her desire to make a positive social impact on the world. Kendall went on to work in small African villages and then to an orphanage in Poland for three years. Upon her return to the United States, Kendall worked on the founding team of a company called More.com, a health and wellness Internet drugstore. Kendall has since started her own nonprofit organization, JustGive.org, which connects contributors with their chosen charities by leveraging the efficiencies of an online website.

> "I am convinced that I am finally at the place where I am meant to be. Simply put: Each and every skill and passion that I have acquired in the course of my education and career is now being engaged."

I began volunteering in a high-security prison in Boston, teaching men and women rudimentary math and reading skills when I was barely 16 years old. I was struck by the stark contrast between the lives of the prisoners and the lives of people in nearby communities—how people living in such close proximity can live in such disparate economic and social worlds. As a volunteer in the prison and other area schools and hospitals, I was conscious and curious about people less fortunate than myself and knew that I would eventually work in some capacity to help others.

After graduating from Harvard College in 1986, I received an offer from Goldman Sachs to work as an analyst but chose to defer for a year to get a sense of the "real world." I took the time to travel around the world, spending six months in Asia. One day, I saw a large group of children running and playing in a field and couldn't reason why they weren't in school. When I asked, the reply that I received was that the village had no school and, even if there had been, there wouldn't have been an adult capable of teaching.

Upon my return to the United States, I helped launch WorldTeach, an organization that sends students to remote villages in Africa and China to serve as teachers. WorldTeach carried teachers, books, and pencils to villages that otherwise wouldn't have had any access to these resources. As my first professional experience in the nonprofit sector, I discovered that I loved the opportunity to make a very real, positive difference in the life of these communities. However, I became profoundly frustrated by the inertia and lack of momentum. Time almost seemed to stop altogether.

After my year of traveling and working at WorldTeach, I started at Goldman Sachs and quickly realized that time definitely did not stop altogether at this firm. The environment was both intense and extremely fast-paced which was terrific training for my future work. The intellectual environment was incomparable and there was tremendous opportunity to work directly on fascinating and diverse financial projects. This was the purest form of capitalism—prodigious profit for both the firm and its clients.

Goldman taught me the standards of excellence in work, which I have carried throughout my entire professional life. I joined the World Bank a few years later as a way to combine finance with making a positive social impact on the world. It was a highly intellectual atmosphere, and I had the opportunity to work on Latin American private debt restructuring.

In time, I became frustrated with this indirect level of social support. The restructuring of debt was only decreasing the tremendous amount of debt that the countries already owed and wasn't putting money into the hands of those families who needed it the most. So while we lessened the amount of money that Brazil's government owed and its overall financial burden, we were not addressing the country's hunger and poverty issues. I wasn't satisfied with a job that seemed more or less like number-adjusting on paper, and

I couldn't help but notice the incredible chasm between the institution's mission and the lack of aid that was actually filtering down to the people. I became more and more aware of the enormous gap between American institutions with tremendous wealth and influence and the huge and immediate need to meet basic living standards in countries throughout the world.

So I quit my job at the World Bank to get in touch with the heart of the matter and spent time working in remote African villages planting tomato and cabbage seeds and educating Ugandan women on the need for these foods in their banana-only diets. After Africa, I moved to western Poland to work in an orphanage that was achingly devoid of even the most basic human necessities. My memories and mental images from these experiences strengthened my commitment to find a way to bridge the unfathomable gap between tremendous wealth and tremendous need.

After working in Eastern Europe for three years, I moved to California to become involved in the Internet, which was still in its infancy at the time. In Poland, I had started a western business in a communist country; in California, I was interested in seeing how the Internet could redefine and creatively challenge western business. I joined the founding team of More.com, a health and wellness Internet drugstore that grew from 5 to 300 employees in three years.

Our initial business at More.com was based on educating consumers on the benefits and warnings of herbal drugs. With our success, our venture capitalists pushed us to come up with more products to sell, sell, sell, and we began selling everything from toothpaste to toilet paper. One day, after categorizing specific toothpastes, I realized that the creative challenge was diminishing for me. I instinctively turned my attention to the social sector to see if the Internet could enhance philanthropy. What I found was more disturbing than the toothpaste sales…many companies were trying to make a profit on the nonprofit sector. A quote by one individual to his venture capitalists was "let's take the poor public."

With the words of that venture capitalist resonating in my mind, I witnessed three of my lifelong passions collide at once, setting off sparks of inspiration on how I could most effectively and positively impact the world. My vision was to combine my passion for charitable giving, my experience with entrepreneurial finance, and my expertise with the Internet to create an organization that connects people with charities in an easy and efficient manner to greatly facilitate charitable contributions.

I launched JustGive.org in 1999 with the intention of providing a logical and successful alternative to traditional charitable giving by using the technological possibilities of the Web. Our services make it convenient for donors to give to multiple charities in one transaction, with the ability to designate, give a gift card, or simply donate anonymously. Individuals can buy Charity Gift Certificates for their family or business colleagues, and the recipient can redeem it for any of the one million charities that we list. Individuals can even donate their accumulated credit card reward points to their favorite charity. Our most popular service is Charity Wedding Registry, where wedding couples can choose their favorite cause in lieu of gifts. Each donor retains a giving history of all their giving activity that they can use for tax purposes. Last year we generated over $6 million for thousands of charities and our services are doubling every year. As our government is decreasing its public support and individuals are living increasingly busier lifestyles, I am focusing on modernizing philanthropy to make it an exciting, easy, and fun way to give back.

JustGive.org was my attempt to start a nonprofit with financial accountability *and* entrepreneurial leanness and drive, which is the new direction of charitable giving. We don't just solicit money. We inspire individuals to give. We analyze the way people live and, through our innovative online programs, encourage giving through everyday services. I am convinced that I am finally at the place where I am meant to be. Simply put: Each and every skill and passion that I have acquired in the course of my education and career is now being engaged.

Kelly L. Close

Kelly is founder and principal of Close Concerns, Inc., a consulting firm devoted to diabetes and obesity research, which she launched in 2002. She writes Diabetes Close Up, *a newsletter focused on the business of diabetes and obesity, as well as an adjunct newsletter for Close Concerns. Kelly lives in San Francisco with her husband John and their daughter Coco, who was born on New Year's Day 2005.*

> "Today, one out of three children will develop diabetes. After generations of progress, the generation of our children may have a shorter life span than *our* generation because of this disease. It is my mission to provide actionable evidence to patients that diabetes is manageable—even reversible—and certainly a completely preventable problem for the vast majority of patients."

I was diagnosed with diabetes my first semester at Amherst College. I made the best of it, continuing my studies at Amherst and later completing an MBA at Harvard University. After building a career working in investment banking at Goldman Sachs, consulting at McKinsey, and equity research at Merrill Lynch, I decided in 2002 that I'd learned enough to strike out on my own—that the world was calling! To various degrees, health care had come into play in all these roles, most of all in equity research, where I covered medical technology companies. However, I realized that being a specialist was something I do better than being a generalist. This is a surprising realization, given all the broad roles I'd had. Rather than try to be an expert in cardiology, orthopedics, cancer, and metabolic disease (plus a slew of related therapies), which was what was called for in my equity research role, I decided to focus on two areas of personal interest to me, diabetes and obesity. By doing this, I also felt that I could work myself to a level where I could help patients in addition to businesses— how inspiring that vision was to me!

Being diagnosed with a serious disease like diabetes has been a gift in many ways. I've learned to take nothing for granted. I look around and see that for the vast majority of the world, even a job standing with a broom in your hand or behind a counter all day is a true privilege. I see sickness all around—and poverty—and I think: I haven't really had *any* challenges; in the scheme of things, I've been incredibly lucky. And even though my illness has its ups and downs, I live in a place where I'm fortunate enough to have health insurance and live close to major academic medical centers. In a word, it's magical.

If I do have a sorrowful day, my husband John will take me to the museum, or even around our home, and put me in front of a wonderful piece of art and ask me to breathe deeply and just look and not speak. It works incredibly. We're so lucky to have so much around us; sometimes what's most important is remembering to be still and to watch and appreciate! My late father taught me this long ago, and I know he must be so happy that I've become better at stopping and taking time to think and feel and be, to relish in how lucky we are, and to think of how we can best contribute to helping others on this great big earth of ours.

In my spare time, I must say, I've focused a lot on spreading education in ways I like to think have been creative. I have spent a total of, collectively, five years on the 85 Broads and McKinsey Bay Area alumnae boards, and I have really enjoyed my time helping to bring engaging speakers to our groups. The 85 Broads and McKinsey groups do so much together, and I've been so lucky to engage with such incredible women; moreover, I love the connection it had to my early career. John and I also run a lecture series from our home—CPS Lectures (www.cpslectures.com). If you are ever in San Francisco, please register and come over!

LUANNE ZURLO

Luanne spent nine years working on Wall Street, ranked as one of Institutional Investor's top Latin American telecommunications analysts. She recently left her job at Goldman Sachs to found the World Education & Development Fund, an organization that supports quality education in impoverished Latin American communities. Luanne received her MBA from Columbia Business School.

> "Education is key to individual and community development, and in the developing world, particularly in Latin America, basic education is not receiving the funding and attention it deserves. It is also not an overly difficult service to provide."

September 11, 2001, was a turning point in my life. It led me to step back to ask myself, "What is it all about?" In answering that, I kindled enough courage within me to begin thinking very broadly about how to use my talents to make a difference in the world. For me, it meant walking away from Wall Street to found the World Education & Development Fund (WEDF).

At the time, leaving Goldman Sachs was clearly the right decision. It was obvious that the telecom bubble was deflated. Things were just not as much fun on Wall Street, and people were being let go with increasing frequency. It just so happened that during this period, I went on a business trip to Mexico City, where I visited a Mano Amiga school that was located in an extremely poor area of the city. The school was beautiful, the teachers engaged, the children clean and happy to be there. Here was a school that was committed to reaching out to students with limited financial resources. It was an absolute success.

Upon returning to New York, a priest from the Catholic congregation that founded the school I visited in Mexico, approached me and said that he wanted my help expanding the Mano Amiga school system, from a current 18 schools to a targeted 50 throughout Latin America. The time was right, so I left my job and returned to Latin America for several months visiting the schools and other community and literacy outreach programs for both children and adults. I spent time with the directors of the schools to develop a unified organization and a growth plan to spread the Mano Amiga school system.

I was passionate about equipping children with the skills they needed to become contributors to their local and national economies. In Latin American countries, a severe lack of funding, a lack of qualified teachers, and other difficult social issues haunt the school systems. Over 70 percent of students in developing countries never make it past the sixth grade and, as a result, these children become caught up in the vicious cycle of poverty and unemployment. When I was working on Wall Street, I used to visit these large corporations in developing countries and was surprised to learn that one of the biggest challenges for these companies was to find high-quality workers. There were lots of available people to work but, sadly, many of them just didn't have the proper education or skills (i.e., basic reading and writing) to perform these jobs.

After spending a few months doing the necessary fieldwork to begin our project, it became obvious that the most significant impact that I could make would be to create an organization to raise money to build the Mano Amiga schools and to raise the profile of the project. I discovered that there were no other organizations dedicated solely to providing quality education in Latin America, so I decided to start the World Education & Development Fund (WEDF).

Our organization became incorporated in December 2002. The concept and the launching of the WEDF was relatively easy for me. What has been a much more daunting challenge has been figuring out how to grow and institutionalize WEDF without exploding our cost structure. We have been successful by maintaining a low overhead, returning 90 cents on every $1 to the Mano Amiga school system. We are fortunate to have had our office space donated and to have only one salaried employee with the rest of our staff working on a volunteer basis. Keeping our administrative costs down allows us to maximize the returns on the money we raise. Needless to say, each donation that we receive is critical.

At the very beginning, the Internet was the single most important tool that allowed us to spread our word to a wider audience. I was open-minded and willing to meet with almost anyone who offered advice. Suzanne Nora Johnson at Goldman Sachs and Janet Hanson at 85 Broads were two influential women who provided me with contacts and encouraged me to hold a large-scale event to raise the level of exposure for WEDF.

We held our inaugural black-tie fund-raising dinner in June 2004. Carlos Slim, the Mexican telecommunications entrepreneur, was our honoree and Sandy Weill, the chairman of Citigroup, was one of our speakers. We involved most of the big banks and a number of corporations to sponsor the event. One of the most moving moments of the evening was when one of Mano Amiga's graduates spoke about her positive experience and the opportunity she was given to come to the United States, where she is now attending business school. The 500-person audience rose to give her a standing ovation. The event was a success, raising over $700,000, but just as importantly, it provided critical relationships and the momentum needed to expand the mission and impact of WEDF into the future.

ELEANOR BURTON STURDY

Eleanor Burton Sturdy joined Goldman Sachs after graduating from Oxford in 1988. She worked in finance for 10 years before leaving to become a nutritionist. She was then given the opportunity to manage McKinsey's banking team in Europe, which involved extensive traveling. Eleanor is now working with several clients to build new schools in some of the most deprived areas of London.

> "One of the greatest gifts that I have received in my life is realizing that I had to change my behavior, my thinking, and the way I communicate with others in order to be happy."

I view education as one of the most powerful ways to support disadvantaged children. I am currently working with a major investment bank in order to build a brand-new school in the East End of London, a traditionally underprivileged area. The community was initially suspicious of this corporate show of goodwill, although it is now beginning to embrace the school in the East End. The school itself has a unique approach—emphasizing both math and the arts, to encourage the students to use both sides of the brain and to thereby develop superior decision-making skills. Another project that I am working on will build a performing arts school on the west side of London. The students that graduate will continually refresh London's talent pool, assuring the vitality of the city. Being a catalyst for projects that genuinely affect other people's lives is a rare privilege.

At one point in my life, I was reluctant to trust anybody to do anything, which in hindsight was somewhat arrogant of me. I realize now, that once you have achieved a level of self-confidence, you can let go and have faith in others, handing responsibility to them. It is at this point that everyone does a better job and work becomes both liberating and wonderful. This self-confidence is not easy to maintain, but it seems to be the key to much of my personal happiness.

One of the greatest gifts that I have received in my life is realizing that I had to change my behavior, my thinking, and the way I communicate with others in order to be happy. My Buddhist practice and my continued study of this path on a daily basis has been a positive force in my life, and it has helped me find a way to love and trust myself. I have realized that nothing is achieved instantly but every action we take will have its effects later.

Dasiaku Ikeda, the president of the Buddhist organization Soka-Gakkai International has been an incredible mentor and provides encouragement by his example of overcoming great criticism, and even imprisonment, for his views. Mahatma Gandhi is another person I look up to as a leader of ordinary people determined to make changes on a grand scale. And Eleanor Roosevelt's enduring strength and endless hope in her efforts to improve the lives of so many people is equally inspiring.

Leadership is about trusting others while taking complete responsibility for one's own actions and not blaming other people when the inevitable obstacles appear. In this sense, leadership is one of the ultimate forms of "giving." My advice to all women is to learn to ask for more information before making a decision and to learn to say no and to let others have opportunities— another form of "giving." Form your own vision of yourself and what you want to be, and always see beyond others' expectations of you. I've found that you first must give to yourself in order to have something to give to others.

Lastly, despite working for years in the financial industry, I have found that the best rewards are not financial. Determining what you are good at and then making a difference in the world is happiness. Being happy with yourself is the only way that you can give to others, and similarly, it is the only way that you will receive the real riches in this world for yourself.

NATALIA MLOTOK

Natalia Mlotok was born and raised in one of the most northern cities in Russia—Severodvinsk. Natalia graduated from the St. Petersburg State University of Economics and Finance and went to work at McKinsey in Moscow. She is currently in her second year at Harvard

Business School and plans to return to Russia to contribute to the further development of her country. Natalia is deeply involved with the Murzik organization, which supports Russian orphanages.

> "What I am most grateful for is how this experience helped me to develop a proactive attitude toward life. I realized that even if something seemed impossible, with daring and hard work it is possible to realize one's dreams."

I find it astonishing, looking back, to see how much my path in life was determined by the city that I was born in. Located nearly at "the end of the earth," Severodvinsk is on the coast of the White Sea in northern Russia. In its prime, the city was dynamic and run by young, ambitious, well-educated people united with a common goal: to build a city from scratch out of the swamp that was to become a base for nuclear submarine manufacturing. These people came from all around the Soviet Union to build the city in the unfriendly northern climate where we joke that winter is 12 months a year and the rest is summer. They volunteered to endure these inhumane conditions because they were not just building a city around a defense enterprise, they were protecting the communist principles that they sincerely believed in.

While succeeding generations might not have been as enthusiastic about the Soviet system, there had always been these almost tangible feelings of patriotism, pride, and sense of a bigger purpose in the old Severodvinsk. I remember the city as being filled with friendly, smiling people and sunny, green avenues with snatches of navy songs carried by the wind. But then the collapse of the Soviet system and *perestroika* brought an end to the thriving economy, and the vibrancy that I once associated with Severodvinsk has been reduced to a mere mosaic of my teenage memories.

In a city of 300,000, nuclear submarine manufacturing was the sole industry and there were only two plants. One of them, SevMashPredpriatie (SMP), built the submarines, and the other one, Zvezdochka, repaired them. Almost every adult in Severodvinsk was employed by one of the two plants that were owned and financed by the government. After the "successful" market reforms in the early 1990s, there was virtually no money in the budget and the government basically stopped paying for the submarines it had ordered. It didn't even have enough money to pay the salaries of the employees. The inhabitants of Severodvinsk were trapped as they lost all their savings through hyperinflation and could not move to another city. The employees still went to work every day, and they were officially employed but not paid. Among several other efforts, the plants tried to provide basic support by purchasing bread on their own accounts and giving it to the employees against the salary in arrears. As there wasn't any money left in the household coffers either, people could be found reading by candlelight and sleeping in fur coats, as they didn't have money to pay for utilities.

By the time Severodvinsk reached this dire state, I had already left the city to study at the St. Petersburg State University of Economics and Finance. It was a very prestigious university. The overall income level of the student body was high, and most of the students were paying for their education out of their own pockets, whereas the government was paying for mine. The greatest challenge for me then was to not feel inferior to my peers as I could not afford the fashionable clothes everyone was wearing or even afford to join them for dinners out. In fact, I could not even afford to buy meat at the university canteen and had to ask for some gravy to be put on my rice so it tasted a little bit like meat.

I decided to take charge of my purse in order to remedy my impoverished situation. As a student, it was very difficult to find a decent job since I could not work from nine to five. I had the opportunity to become a Mary Kay sales representative and operate as an independent entrepreneur. In order to do this, I had to borrow my older sister's passport because you cannot run a business until you are 18 years old. During my time with Mary Kay, I was awarded the "Excellent Start" recognition for reaching high sales volumes— all the while working "undercover," as I had trained myself to react and respond to my sister's name of Lena.

During the summer holidays after my third year at the university, I found a full-time job as an assistant investment project manager and became relatively well paid as an investment analyst. I was able to keep the job when the next school year began since most of our communications were with the United States and, due to the time difference, didn't interfere with classes. I would be at the university from 8:30 in the morning until mid-afternoon and from there would run to the office and typically stay until midnight. My weekends were spent catching up on homework and writing papers, so I didn't have much time to rest. Probably more difficult was not having enough time for extracurricular activities and finding myself deprived of the "true joys of life." It was all very hard for me. While my friends were going to cafés after classes, I found myself heading off to work. Yet, I was proud to be making enough money to support not only myself, but my parents as well.

No matter how tough this experience was, I am glad to have had the opportunity to help my family through difficult times. Additionally, I learned a lot and was prepared to handle hard work in the future. However, what I am most grateful for is how this experience helped me to develop a proactive attitude toward life. I realized that even if something seemed impossible, with daring and hard work it is possible to realize one's dreams. I came to believe in myself and have the self-confidence that will help me to reach even higher goals.

As I gained experience with the leading companies at McKinsey, I came to realize that the chances of turning around SMP were slim to none. Severodvinsk had lost its greatest asset: the people. They had left SMP and the city altogether. More importantly, I realized that the government would never privatize SMP, further reducing the opportunities to attract a top-caliber team to turn the plant around. This realization made me reassess my mid- to long-term goals, and I decided to apply to business school.

After abandoning a dream that had been driving me for many years, being accepted into business school couldn't have come at a better time, as it is the perfect place to start a new chapter in life. With Harvard Business School on my résumé, I hope that I will once and forever overcome the credibility issue I encountered at earlier points in my career. Living in Boston is my first time being abroad for longer than a two-week vacation, and I'm also enjoying the amazing international diversity of the student body at HBS. Being exposed to all these different cultures helps me to see the situation in Russia from multiple perspectives.

My experience at HBS also increased my commitment to contribute back to society. I have continued and intensified my support of Murzik, the charity organization I got involved with while I was still in Russia. Murzik focuses on helping orphanages, which is a critical role as the government is not financing them adequately, and the concept of corporate citizenship is unfamiliar in Russia. Murzik is an amazing organization in that it circumvents corruption and bureaucracy by delivering all the goods directly to the orphanages and basically tearing off labels and putting clothes on children (you can find photo reports at http://www.murzik.ru/english/photo.php?secti=14). In Russia, corruption is a huge problem, so Murzik makes sure that it is the children who actually get the benefits, rather than orphanage directors or staff. Furthermore, Murzik doesn't have a full-time staff. Volunteers run the entire organization. Thus, the overhead costs are zero and all donated money goes to the children, unlike other charities where overhead can be 30 to 40 percent. While I'm in the United States, I'm focusing on raising money for Murzik, but when I go back to Russia, I aspire to get even more involved with it. Currently, Murzik is covering several orphanages at a driving distance from Moscow—in Russia, that means up to five hours driving each way over dirt roads to reach an orphanage 200 miles from Moscow, as the volunteers need to deliver the goods themselves. I believe the Murzik model can be scaled up, and I want to help expand Murzik's coverage. This is one of my many dreams.

YOUNGHEE MICHELLE KIM WAIT

Younghee Kim emigrated from Korea to America with her parents, two sisters, and brother when she was 17. Younghee was chief of staff and chief administrative officer in the Fixed Income Division of Goldman Sachs Asia and GS Japan. After returning to the United States she began pursuing her interest in holistic healing and now works as a wellness educator.

> "I find being a healer and serving as a spiritual guide is a way of life, a way of being. It is a state of mind, an attitude you bring to your interaction with others."

Each of us can be a healer. We are born with that gift within us. To become a healer, you have to first heal yourself and explore healing from within.

During the process of studying ancient alternative healings, I came to understand that healing is about the active participation of those who seek to be healed. A healer is a coach, a catalyst, and a transformer. A coach in athletics can give strategies and feedback to athletes, but cannot win a game for them. In healing, a "healer-coach" shows a pathway, but an individual has to be willing to walk down that path. As a catalyst in the process of healing, a healer facilitates and supports the self-healing process.

My father moved my family to New York from Korea in 1976. Years later, when I was working through my grief after my sister died and faced the questions of my actions and inactions, I found I had a lot of anger and resentment toward my parents. I was angry that they weren't there for us. They were absent parents and never understood what we had to go through in schools struggling with English and a strange new life in America. Then one day I realized my father had come to this country with four children at the age of 44 having given up everything in Korea that he built for himself. Given how challenging I found life here, even having gone to the best schools and having great jobs and economic security and having a network of friends, I was astounded to realize how courageous my father had been, how life must have been very hard for an immigrant father of four children in a new country with a wife so sheltered she knew nothing outside of her homemaking. I was so focused on making my own life count that I never thought about my father's life. I had a chip on my shoulder because I had to work every summer and use work-study to pay for tuition that wasn't covered by scholarships. I felt that what I had accomplished, I had accomplished on my own. I was resentful of my parents. I was resentful for what they did not do rather than being grateful for what they had already done or recognizing that my parents did the best they could under difficult circumstances.

I am now my father's age when he first came here. I am a mother of two children. I have greater appreciation for the sacrifices he has made for us. He gave up his life's dream for us. That is more than any child can ask for. When I walked a mile in my father's shoes, I cried for him and I was grateful. I found healing in my relationship with my parents and that expedited my own healing. I now find more peace with those around me as I begin to walk in their shoes a mile before I judge them by my own expectations.

This is not necessarily unconditional love like that which you find between a mother and a baby. It is still conditional, as we expect people to treat each other with honor, decency, and respect. But first recognizing my set of expectations around values that were important to me broadened my understanding of other people in their own context.

Healing is a lifelong journey. I am now working on how to do more work with interfaith communities. I have come across children from interfaith families in need of spiritual healing and comfort in the face of fighting terminal illness. My desire to serve these families led me to be ordained as a nondenominational Christian minister last year. Accepting and acknowledging different spiritual heritages and being able to serve as a healer allows me to do work that is much needed today. I find my own faith deepening. I find grace and blessing in my daily life.

My healing came slowly. But grief and anger no longer define me. I am able to move on with my life and focus on the present moment knowing that all of my past and what it contains have shaped me and made me who I am today. I no longer worry about the future much either. I have found a peace that does not depend on anything.

DONNA CHILDS

Donna started her career as a research associate at the Harvard Business School, then became an investment banker in the financial institutions group at Goldman Sachs and subsequently relocated to Zurich, Switzerland, where she was a director and member of senior management of the Swiss Reinsurance Company. With her personal savings, she established her own Wall Street firm, Childs Capital LLC, where she serves as president and chief executive officer. Her business is the result of "parallel" careers of pro bono projects and a more traditional finance path. Following the 2001 destruction in lower Manhattan, Donna co-wrote the book Contingency Planning and Disaster Recovery: A Small Business Guide, *which was published in 2002.*

"Work is love made more visible."

Kahlil Gibran

I credit the Harvard Business School with having a profound influence on my career. My first professional position was working there as a research associate, with responsibility for the financial institutions course. My duties included researching and writing business school case studies for use in teaching MBA students. The cases developed at Harvard are taught at business schools worldwide. For me, it was a great opportunity to develop skills, such as research and writing skills, to learn about the financial services sector, and to make senior contacts in the industry.

I had the opportunity to put the skills I developed at Harvard to very good use. While I was employed as a research associate, the Pioneer Institute together with then-Governor William Weld sponsored the very first "Better Government" competition, which was so successful that it has been held annually to this day. The Pioneer Institute is a Boston-based think tank dedicated to improving civic life in Massachusetts. Would-be "armchair governors" were invited to submit five-page executive summaries outlining how they would improve the efficiency of public services. Finalists selected by the Institute had the summer months to flesh out their ideas in complete business plans.

Summaries of the final business plans, which satisfied stringent judging criteria, were published in a compendium of all of the winners. Governor Weld promised to personally read each one to consider the feasibility of implementation. Together with a ranking legislator, John Bradford, I developed a plan to provide home care to the elderly of Massachusetts at no incremental cost to the taxpayer. This plan addressed a particularly important need, as home care services were discretionary, subject to the availability of resources, but publicly funded programs for nursing home care were an entitlement. Incentives existed for frail seniors to spend down to a level of impoverishment such that they qualified for institutional care. The result was a lower quality of life for seniors, who would surely prefer to avoid institutionalization and higher costs for taxpayers. Our home care plan was one of the 11 winning plans in the 1991 competition.

After graduating from Harvard Business School, I joined the financial institutions group of the investment banking division of Goldman Sachs. I worked on corporate finance and mergers and acquisitions for banks and insurance companies. Because I am fluent in several languages, I had the opportunity to work on major international transactions, such as the privatization of the French insurance company L'Union d'Assurances de Paris. As I had done at Harvard, I continued to volunteer my time and business skills for projects that were important to me. For one such project, I contributed my entire annual vacation allotment, four weeks, to work in Russia.

I traveled to Stavropol, which is on the Volga River, some 600 miles east of Moscow. I went as a volunteer on a project for the U.S. Agency for International Development. The major employer in Stavropol was Avtovaz, the manufacturer of Lada cars. Following the collapse of the Soviet Union, Avtovaz and the local economy were in serious trouble. Avtovaz was unable to compete in a global market and lost export sales in the former Eastern bloc, whose consumers were eagerly buying Volkswagens. Unemployment in the region reached 40 percent. I provided training to the managers of Avtovaz Bank, the finance affiliate of the car manufacturer, to help ready them for raising needed capital. It was one of the most rewarding experiences of my career.

I then relocated to Zurich, Switzerland, where I worked as a senior executive of the Swiss Reinsurance Company. With proficiency in French, German, and Italian, this was a great experience for me. As I had done at Harvard and then at Goldman Sachs, I availed myself of every opportunity to learn, to develop specific skills, and to make industry contacts. I also continued my volunteer work in my spare time. While working at Swiss Re, I served on the Board of Governors of Opportunity International, a not-for-profit organization that sponsors microfinance operations in 25 developing countries. Upon my return to the United States, I had to take some time off from both work and volunteering. My mother, who was then in her mid-fifties, suffered a cerebral hemorrhage as a consequence of a ruptured aneurysm. The bleeding was extensive and few people survive a traumatic brain injury of that magnitude. My experience with insurance companies was very useful as I negotiated for her inpatient and outpatient rehabilitative care. I stayed with my parents, caring for my mother and reassuring my father, who was understandably devastated. We are very blessed. My mother survived and recovered.

When I went back to work, I started my own business, one that marries my past volunteer interests with my business experience. I am putting the skills, experience, and contacts I have developed in service of this business, which also gives me the flexibility that I need and the quality of life that I want!

HEATHER ZEHREN ALBINSON

Heather is the co-founder of the Adelante Development Group and the vice president of development/marketing, where she worked while getting her MBA at Berkeley. Heather briefly worked at NextMonet before returning, in 2001, to the World Wildlife Fund, where she is now the Bay Area Regional Director.

> "I followed my passion for conservation and am so happy knowing that every day I am helping to ensure that we leave a living planet for the generations that follow us."

I recently traveled through Asia and Europe, where I visited several field sites and country offices managed by the World Wildlife Fund (WWF). I was greatly impressed by the widespread evidence of WWF's reach and impact, and my travels throughout some of the world's most spectacular landscapes reinforced my belief that I had made the right decision to return to a career in environmental conservation. Everywhere I went, from small villages in India to mountain towns in Nepal, from Beijing to Europe, I saw evidence of our work. The panda logo was everywhere, indicating parks and reserves under WWF management, education programs we established, and community-building projects we run.

One of the most inspiring and moving moments of our trip was in southeast Nepal's Royal Chitwan National Park. I had always dreamed of seeing an Asian greater one-horned rhino in the wild. The species was on the brink of extinction in the mid-1960s, when the Chitwan population had dropped to approximately 60—extremely worrisome as this was one of the few protected populations in the world. Even today, the species is extremely rare with numbers estimated at less than 2,000 individual wild rhinos.

Upon arriving at Temple Tiger Lodge in Chitwan, we found an elephant saddled and waiting for us, and we climbed aboard. Within half an hour, we had seen 16 rhinos, many with young babies, some within a just few feet of us! These creatures are truly awesome to behold. They look absolutely prehistoric, with great folds of skin reminiscent of armor plating, and yet they have an unmistakable equine quality. Thanks to WWF's work, the Chitwan greater one-horned rhino population is now so healthy that in the past year, we have been able to successfully translocate 87 individuals to Royal Bardia National Park in the southwest of Nepal. Witnessing evidence of this real conservation success story up close gave me tremendous satisfaction and a great sense of pride to be working for an organization that is making such a positive impact.

Another of these inspiring moments occurred in the Peruvian Amazon, where I traveled last year with some WWF donors. The Amazon is absolutely filled with life—it breathed all around me. In fact, there was so much oxygen in the air that I could literally feel its richness, and I gained a real understanding for why the Amazon is called the "lungs of the planet." One afternoon, while paddling in a dugout canoe up a freshwater tributary, we saw a dolphin dive out of the water immediately in front of us; it was cotton candy pink! It showed little fear of us, and in fact acted very curious. It resurfaced several times around our boat. Amazon freshwater dolphins are frequently pink, they are quite rare (the IUCN officially lists them as "vulnerable"), and seeing them up close is absolutely magical. The knowledge that something this fantastic exists in the wild, and the fear that they may not exist for my children to see, drives me forward in my work and makes me absolutely committed to doing everything I can to leave a living planet for the generations that will follow us. The Amazon is being destroyed at a frightening pace, but WWF has recently helped to establish the Amazon Region Protected Areas Project, a 10-year $370 million program designed to triple the size of protected areas of the Brazilian Amazon, creating a network of fully protected and sustainable-use conservation areas that will exceed 200,000 square miles.

My passion for the environment has always been with me; nature has always stirred my soul. My parents like to tell the story that I literally learned to walk while we were camping in northern Minnesota. Growing up, we lived on a remote ranch in the mountains of Colorado, in a stunningly beautiful valley surrounded by high alpine meadows and aspen forests. We lived miles up a dirt road. Ours was the last house to have running water and electricity, and nature was all around us. Elk came frequently to feed from our haystack, and one summer my sister and I watched a family of beavers build their dam in the creek outside our front door. Sadly, the valley where I grew up has been developed. There's now a resort about a mile from my family's ranch.

I earned my undergraduate degree in environmental conservation because I wanted to protect the natural splendor that had surrounded me as I grew up. Soon after graduation, I spent three months in the wilderness in British Columbia's Waddington Range, developing practical outdoor survival skills and mountaineering techniques. I was as close to heaven as I have ever been, standing on a glacier and watching moose pick their way through tall scrub beneath us, while a bald eagle circled above. For me, being in pristine wilderness is truly a religious experience.

7

SURVIVORS

After maintaining six weeks of "radio silence" with the network during the fall of 2002—for reasons that will become immediately apparent—I sent this email out to the entire 85 Broads membership:

To: The Members of 85 Broads
From: Janet Hanson
Date: October 29, 2002
Subj: TIMING IS EVERYTHING

A few weeks ago, the only stressful event happening in my life was that our kids' nanny of 10 years had run off with an unemployed mechanic and ex-con with tattoos. He was "madly in love with her"—having met her just the prior week. What he meant to say was that he was in love with her bank account, as she had saved all her paychecks and was extremely "liquid." Out of the blue, we received a call one Sunday afternoon from our nanny and her tattooed boyfriend informing us that they were starting a new life together in a trailer park in Florida. I figured running a business and being a full-time mother was a challenge but manageable—for the most part it meant cutting my day a little short at the office and making it back home in time to pick up my son and daughter by 4:30. The one day that looked challenging was September 26, when my husband Jeff had to go to Miami and I had to race into the city for my annual mammogram. I drove down to New York City in the pouring rain, figuring I'd be in and out in an hour tops. Wrong! After cooling my heels in the reception area, I let them know that I'd have to come back some other time, as I couldn't leave my kids stranded at school.

Finally, after having all those breast-crushing x-rays done, I raced back to the dressing room to throw on my clothes and head for my car. The technician stuck her head in to say that my mammogram was "clear" but that Dr. Drossman wanted to do an ultrasound. I said "NOW??!" I grudgingly agreed and 10 minutes later went from being stressed but happy to being terrified. The ultrasound had picked up a growth in my right breast which the biopsy four days later confirmed was malignant. That weekend, I drank most of the scotch in our liquor cabinet as my whole world had been turned upside down. My diagnosis was "invasive ductile carcinoma," which sounded very fatal to me. In the next week, I consulted two breast surgeons and made an executive decision to have a bilateral mastectomy—given the appalling history of breast cancer on my mother's side of the family. Last week I had surgery and although my chest feels like it got hit with a hand grenade, I am lucky that it was caught when it was before it advanced to a stage that would indeed have been fatal. Here is some quick advice to all the wonderful women in 85 Broads/Broad2Broad:

Currently, there is tremendous controversy over the accuracy of mammography and monthly self-examinations as effective measures in the detection and prevention of breast cancer. I am 100 percent sure that my doctor would not have elected to do ultrasound if my chart hadn't been stamped "high risk," which was due to my family history. Had she not done ultrasound, I would have walked out of her office and would not have returned for another year. MY ADVICE TO EVERYONE: add ultrasound to your annual checkups even if you aren't considered "high risk!" In my case, there is no doubt that having the test done most likely saved my life.

"HEALTHY BROADS" will be a new resource on our website where we will post useful information re: health/wellness issues that pertain to women. In the first three weeks of October, I had to absorb a great deal of information and make several enormous decisions extremely quickly—for better or worse. I hope that you will send your suggestions, recommendations, and referrals to us so that we can build a "portfolio" of world-class doctors, hospitals, and medical information that will benefit our entire network worldwide.

What I didn't know when I sent out my "upbeat" email was what was in store for me next.

My postsurgical biopsy showed that the cancer was not just in my right breast, but had spread to my left breast as well, so in hindsight I was very happy that I had instinctively rejected the original medical advice I received urging me to consider a milder form of surgery/treatment. Of course, I also was now terrified by what else might have been "missed." Because my family history and genetic profile significantly increased my chances of developing ovarian cancer, I was back in the hospital six weeks after my first surgery having my ovaries removed. Let me tell you, they don't call it "traumatic menopause" for nothing. For the following year it felt like I had lost most of the hard drive in my brain while my mind and body tried to rewire themselves. Shortly after my ovarian surgery I went through four rounds of skin cancer surgery on my face, legs, and, where else, my chest. As I am fond of saying, "What a joke—I don't even have a chest!"

Throughout this entire time I was running our business, managing a $2 billion fund, and parenting my then 13-year-old daughter and 11-year-old son through an adolescence that now included having a mother with cancer. As a teenager, I had been absolutely traumatized when my own mother was diagnosed with breast cancer. When my mother, Patty Tiebout, celebrated her 80th birthday by parasailing 400 feet over the ocean with us on a family vacation last year, you can imagine what that did for morale all the way around! In my own case, I've now had a series of "all clear" six-month checkups on the cancer survivor roller-coaster ride. There's nothing like the high you feel right after that checkup or the anxiety you feel right before the next one.

Which is why the 85 Broads network has taken on a whole new dimension and direction since my email of October 2002. There was an overwhelming and passionate response to that email. Not only from all the women in our "cyber clubhouse" who wished me well and offered phenomenal advice/resources—an absolutely critical part of my recovery—but from the many, many women with extraordinary health stories and challenges of their own. What was shocking was how many women, as young as 21 and as old as 58, emailed me back to say thanks, as they had also been diagnosed with cancer. That was the moment when I realized how passionate I was about each and every single woman in the network, particularly when I realized that I had never even met most of the women who emailed me to tell me their stories.

Just as 85 Broads had given women a platform for finding their own professional voices and pursuing their own personal or philanthropic passions, the network now amplified the voices of the survivors. Stories of courage and humor and heartbreak poured in, especially from the younger generations of women in our network who often found it difficult to confide in their colleagues, classmates, or companies about their struggles with cancer and other debilitating health issues. Cancer rates among younger women professionals are rising at an alarming rate, a disturbing trend that is mirrored in our network. Their stories often echo my own experience—too little time to make life-or-death decisions with too little information, too few resources, and way too much uncertainty.

But there also is a strength in these stories that can come only from facing down your disease or tragedy—and ultimately your own self. Life-threatening situations and illnesses are the extremist forms of adversity, but the cycle is the same: How can you transform adversity into a challenge that you are ready to face? How do you create success out of that challenge? How can you convert your success into real happiness? And how do you do it again and again and again? Nowhere in our network community has the "power of the story" had a greater or more profound impact than through the voices of women like those we'll hear in this chapter.

Meg Berté

Meg is a former All-American soccer player and graduate of Harvard University. After teaching high school biology for a year and then working on Wall Street in the analyst programs at NatWest and Credit Suisse First Boston, Meg returned to Harvard to pursue an MBA degree. Following her graduation, she returned to Wall Street and now works in the investor relations group for a prominent hedge fund in New York City. Meg has survived two battles with Hodgkin's disease.

> "I firmly believe that any man's finest hour, the greatest fulfillment of all that he holds dear, is that moment when he has worked his heart out in a good cause and lies exhausted on the field of battle—victorious!"
>
> Vince Lombardi

I have always loved sports. I will play anything and everything that involves a team and a game, but my first love is soccer. I started playing when I was six and I found myself on numerous club teams, travel teams, state teams, and school teams. My passion for the sport continued when I attended Harvard College and was captain of the Varsity Women's Soccer team. After Harvard, I spent a year teaching high school biology and coaching boys' soccer at a small private school in New York City. I loved working with the students, but I realized that sports had fostered in me a passion for competing. I needed a career that would provide that same kind of intensity and thrill. And I found it.

Shortly after the school year ended, I joined the financial analyst program at NatWest Bank and began my career on Wall Street. It reminded me of competitive athletics, with a suit as the uniform—the hard work, competition, and intensity—I loved it. A few months into my new job, I came down with what I thought was mono. With a brand-new job, I certainly didn't have time for something like this! Didn't my body, which had never let me down in sports, comprehend that I was really busy? How surprised was I when the doctors diagnosed me with Stage IIB Hodgkin's Disease—cancer of the lymphatic system.

I told myself that if I had to get cancer, at least Hodgkin's was known to be very treatable. The doctors assured me that this was the case. My competitive drive kicked in. I kept working despite chemotherapy and radiation treatments. Thankfully, my wonderful new career on Wall Street kept me busy enough that I had little time to worry about my illness. However, I was only 24 years old and I was certainly not living the life of my peers. When I wasn't at work, I was pretty tired and run-down, not dancing on the bars at New York City clubs! My body was worn out, but my spirits were good. This was just a small bump in the road of life.

The day I completed my final radiation treatment at Memorial Sloan Kettering, I almost skipped out the door. When the radiation oncologists bid me adieu, they told me that they would most likely never see me again, and that was a good thing. I dove back into work. I started a new job at Credit Suisse First Boston in the media and telecommunications investment banking group and ramped up to 100-hour weeks. My life was buzzing along again. A few months later, as part of my post-treatment, I had a routine CAT scan at Memorial. The next day, two days before Christmas, I received a phone call. The doctors insisted that I come into the hospital. When I arrived, they asked me if my parents were planning on joining us. This was obviously not a good sign. The doctors told me that the cancer had returned, which is never good news, but when it is within six months of the last course of treatment, it is especially bad news.

The cancer was very aggressive. I had to undergo a stem cell transplant, which is intense to say the least. The treatment consisted of very powerful chemotherapy followed by daily radiation treatments for one month. Chemo and radiation treatments are dangerous because they suppress the immune system. The more aggressive the cancer, the stronger the treatment required, and the more significant the immuno-suppression. As such, during the most intense period of my treatment, I was put into isolation for almost a month, with only family and very close friends allowed to visit my hospital room.

My life felt as if it was in a tailspin and I was scared. The first time I battled cancer, I dealt with the physical treatment of the illness, never doubting that I would get better. This time, however, I struggled with the fear of dying. But my desire to fight and win took over, and I battled my disease head on.

While I was in the throes of my illness, I was physically and emotionally consumed with fighting the disease. However, when I walked out of the hospital as a "cured" patient, I had many challenges to face in reentering normal life. For a number of months I couldn't work. I was bald, jaundiced, and I had lost 30 pounds. For awhile, I couldn't even climb stairs. I could barely walk 10 steps. Although I hated asking for help, I needed it. My mother moved to New York City to help me out and provide support; she and the rest of my family were there for me every step of the way. They were my lifeline.

Because the treatment left me physically weak, I needed to stage my comeback—not a return to competitive sports, but a transition back to a normal life. I readjusted my goals and focused on accomplishing my best each day. One day, I focused on walking from my apartment to the end of the street. Two weeks later, my goal was to walk around the block. As with my former sports training, I did a little bit more each day and slowly but steadily my body became stronger.

In a matter of months, I started to get my life back. I began working half days, then full days, and exercising again. However, my perspective had changed as a result of my illness. I knew that I had to make life changes, especially with respect to my career. I didn't want to work such long hours and jeopardize my health, which was now a top priority. I made a decision to go to business school because I thought it would give me more career flexibility and a wider set of opportunities. I was thrilled when I was accepted into the Class of 2000 at Harvard Business School. My health was improving and I was looking ahead to a new chapter in my life. Goodbye, Hodgkins. Hello, Harvard Business School!

Fast forward several months. During my second week of business school, I felt a sharp pain in my back while jogging along the picturesque Charles River in Cambridge, Massachusetts. I didn't realize it at the time, but my left lung had partially collapsed (most likely as a result of my chemotherapy). It completely collapsed during Christmas break. Repairing the damage involved a chest tube, surgery, and two weeks back in the hospital. My other lung collapsed during spring break. The doctors told me I would most likely never play competitive sports again. Now it was not just my body that was being attacked, but my spirit and my whole way of life as well. I was angry. But I learned to channel that anger into an even more intense fighting spirit.

Relying again on my sports training, I recuperated both physically and mentally over the next few months by building up my strength day by day. One more minute on the bike, one more lap around the track. Eventually, I was back in business! My second year of business school was fantastic because I felt great. I hadn't had that much energy in a long, long time. I looked forward to graduation and my subsequent two-month trip to Southeast Asia. I had so much to catch up on, and I was seeing life through a new lens. I was so happy to be alive, and it was a gift to feel healthy and strong each day. I had a hard-won understanding of the importance of health, and I enjoyed even the most mundane aspects of life more than ever.

After graduation, I took a job at Goldman Sachs managing investment portfolios for high net worth families. This job was intellectually stimulating, and it didn't entail the brutal hours of investment banking. Getting sick had forced me into balance and off the treadmill. Keeping that perspective is hard to do, but becoming ill (or having any serious challenge) gives you permission to live a balanced life. All of us want to have these amazing careers. Sure I can work 16 hours if I choose to, but I don't want to anymore. My health and my life are too precious to me. I now work at a hedge fund in an investor relations capacity. This side of the business allows for a somewhat more "normal" lifestyle, but it also has the intensity and excitement that I will always crave.

My sports goals now center around cycling, my new sports passion. I was recently chosen to join Lance Armstrong's 2005 Bristol Myers Squibb Tour of Hope Team, and I will personally ride 800 miles as we travel from San Diego to Washington, D.C. After my stem cell transplant I could barely walk ten steps, and now I am preparing to ride my bike across the country!

Having cancer was like being sent onto the field in the championship game of a sport that I had never played. It's scary, intense, and huge. You have to learn quickly, and you have to rely on your team. My learning continues to be about thriving with a healthier, more balanced perspective on life. It's about embracing life's toughest challenges with determination and embracing every day with hope. I will never win races on my bike, but I'm grateful for every mile I can go and everything in me and around me that cheers me on—that sees winning as accepting the challenges, doing one's best and having a great time along the way.

Christie Millard Tully

After graduating from the University of Vermont in 1997, Christie spent two years on the mutual fund sales desk at Goldman Sachs, and later worked for Thompson Financial. She currently works at General Electric in the Corporate Treasury. Christie lives in Connecticut with her husband Mark and their son Andrew.

> "For some reason, I was unusually happy that day. I had just recovered from a nasty virus, and I was excited to be going back to work on such a beautiful Tuesday morning."

Sunday, September 9, 2001. I attended a bridal shower for my wedding, which was set for November 17, 2001. Family and friends surrounded me with love, excitement, and anticipation of the wonderful event to come. I felt as happy as I could ever feel. The buoyancy of the day carried me through the next day, when I was at home, sick, and into Tuesday, September 11, 2001. I went to work happy as ever and the day was spectacular—the most beautiful blue sky and such a clear day. Little did I know that the events of that day would be with me for the rest of my life.

I worked for Thompson Financial on the 78th floor of Tower 2 of the World Trade Center. We had a national sales conference going on in our office; the office was packed. For me, it was a day like any other. I was going through my usual routine, eating my morning bagel while preparing for the day ahead. I had just sat down when my boss ran down the hall yelling "Get the f... out of the building—now!!" Something had happened in Tower 1.

I grabbed my purse and my bagel. Thinking it was a fire drill, we all made our way toward the stairs—no rushing—things were still calm at that point. While we went down the stairs, rumors began to spread. We heard that a plane had hit the other tower. Our reaction, above all else, was surprise. "It must have been a really small plane. How terrible. The pilot couldn't have just hit it; the sky was so blue, the weather conditions so clear. He must have had a heart attack."

There was still no panic. Everyone was calm. We had no idea what was in store for us. As we approached the mid-40s floors, we heard announcements telling us that everything was fine in our building and that we should go back to our offices. We were a few floors above the 44th floor, where we knew there was an express service elevator, so we decided to go there and return to our office on the 78th floor. An elevator came, the doors opened, and we were just stepping on when my managing director grabbed a few of us by the elbows and told us not to get on the elevator. He wanted to think about this for another minute. "Let's wait for the next one." Other people pushed their way onto the car and the elevator left. We stood and waited for direction.

When the elevator returned, we all piled in; it was stuffed like a cattle car with at least 30 people. Because I had gotten on first, I was standing all the way at the back of the elevator as the people crammed in. The doors started to close and at that exact moment, the plane hit our building. Debris, fire, heat, and smoke immediately shot down the elevator shaft. With a sudden boom, the ceiling of the elevator collapsed, the lights went out and everyone was thrown to the floor. Debris showered down on us from above. In emergency situations like that, elevators are designed to close their doors and to keep them closed.

Miraculously, two men in the elevator with us were able to pry the doors open with their bare hands. I was one of the last people to get out. The air was thick with swirling dust and debris. You couldn't see a foot in front of you. Crawling on my hands and knees, I made my way out of the elevator and finally hit a wall. When I looked up, I bumped into someone who turned out to be a coworker. Holding hands, we made our way hurriedly to the stairs. I had lost my shoes in the impact and was running barefoot down the stairs and out of the building. But my body was numb. I don't remember feeling a thing. In fact, I don't remember much about running down the remaining 44 stories. When we finally arrived in the lobby, the police directed us to go underground through the subway and head north. Going underground did not seem like the right option to us. We wanted out of there. We ran up some stairs nearby and came out by the Borders bookstore. The police stood in the middle of the street ducking the huge chunks of building that rained down from the sky and directed us to where we could cross Church Street. We ran, but they stayed there, guiding others to safety.

Now there were four of us. I don't remember where we found our other two coworkers but there they were standing with us, looking up at the carnage that was still the World Trade Center. I remember looking at the burning tower thinking, " It is going to take a lot of work to fix these buildings." Our cell phones weren't working, we didn't know what was going on, and we wanted to get as far away from there as possible. One of the women with me had a loft in Tribeca, not far from where we were. Picking our way through the falling pieces of building, abandoned cars, and shattered glass, we made our way up Church Street. In the middle of this chaos, a woman who noticed

I was barefoot offered me a pair of shoes. Random acts of kindness in the midst of terror still strike me as the greatest acts of love I have ever witnessed. Now, I think back and see her as my guardian angel, and I am so grateful to have been so watched over. Although my coworker's apartment was only a few blocks from the WTC, it seemed like we had walked for hours. She had a landline and we all tried desperately to call our families and friends to let them know we had survived. While one of us was making a call, we all watched in horror as Tower 2 collapsed. The sound of the crushing steel will forever be etched in my memory; it was the worst noise I ever heard. We had a perfect view through her front window. We were dumbstruck. The overwhelming tragedy of the situation was beginning to hit us.

Over the next few days, the trauma of that day began to sink in. I counted the casualties, both known and unknown to me. I lost several colleagues and one friend from high school. Our office intern's father was a captain in the FDNY, and he was one of many heroes who died trying to save others. One of my sweetest, dearest colleagues perished. We are not exactly sure what happened to him. His wife was three months pregnant at the time. It was, and still is, heartbreaking.

I heard stories of people who were physically, mentally, and emotionally paralyzed. Although I was still in shock, I made a determined decision to "get back in the saddle." Steadily, I recovered. I had to recover because I had a lot to look forward to. My wedding had been planned for November. Our honeymoon was scheduled for Europe but neither of us was comfortable with getting on a plane at the time. In the end, we took a road trip to Canada immediately after the wedding and enjoyed a vacation in Europe the following summer, when things had calmed down a bit.

But I felt like I was on the road to recovery. I tried to reach out and help people afterward. Mark and I spoke to a youth group that was struggling with this tragedy, and since we were 26, still relatively young, they could open up to us. I felt privileged to be able to help others come to terms with the situation, especially the younger ones.

It took about two years to fully come to terms with the whole tragic event. I went back to all the things I used to do in an anxious situation when I was younger. I did a lot of cooking and baking during the months that followed. It became a way for me to focus my emotions on things that I loved to do, and it really helped with the healing process. Long-distance running was also very therapeutic. I finally now feel that I'm healed.

Before this, I had spent endless time and energy worrying about issues like whether the flowers at my wedding would match the bridesmaids' dresses and what songs the band would play. I always thought that I had strong values, but the lessons learned from this experience strengthened me emotionally and spiritually and will stay with me, and those close to me, for the rest of our lives.

I don't define myself only as a survivor. I define myself as a person, a wife, a mother, and a friend. Surviving this tragedy is only a part of my life. I won't allow it to control me. It changed me in a way few experiences in life can change a person, but it's only one of many experiences that have shaped me into the person that I am. I see some people who have not gotten over it, and it saddens me greatly to see their struggles. I remind myself every day that life is too short, and I tell myself that I cannot and will not let one event, no matter how devastating and disastrous, take over my life. I have been through hard times since, and I'm sure life has a lot more to hand me, but with every new experience I just put one foot in front of the other and try to move forward, even if it's one very little step at a time. And I always remind myself to look back to see where I've been and to be proud of what I have endured.

Miracles do happen. I gave birth to our first child Andrew in February 2004—bringing incredible joy but at almost the same moment another enormous and immediate challenge. Andrew underwent emergency kidney surgery two weeks after he was born. Seeing my seven-pound baby in intensive care was so physically and emotionally trying, I felt completely hopeless again. For the next few months, we went to his urologists frequently for more tests. He will be fine in the long term and you would certainly never know any health issues exist based on his high-octane nature and enthusiasm for every moment of the day!

VEDRANA VASILJ

Vedrana was born and raised in Bosnia-Herzegovina and spent her time during the civil war as a volunteer in the hospitals while attending the Medical High School in Tuzla. Her father died during the war and Vedrana was wounded during a shelling. She was airlifted out of Bosnia in 1995 and came to the United States, where she received a full-tuition scholarship to attend Phillips Exeter Academy. After graduating from the University of Chicago, Vedrana went to work for Lehman Brothers and is now applying to business school to pursue her MBA.

"That night, I reported into the Tuzla Medical Clinic and witnessed the worst occurrence of my life. A shell had been launched into the town square, killing 72 people, mostly teenagers. I was sent to the Pathology Lab where mounds of mangled bodies were piling up waiting for identification. Some of my friends were lying there among the dead. I worked through the night assisting the doctors on numerous procedures—wrapping wounds in bandages, taking blood. The most difficult task was facing the families who were looking for their missing daughters, sons, husbands, and wives. Many of these people I had known for years. How could I tell them that many of the bodies couldn't even be identified? Many of them were my friends too. How could God let this happen?"

In 1995, during my third year at the Medical High School, the Yugo/Serbian army surrounded our city, cutting off food supplies from outside of Bosnia. Our food was rationed. I remember opening a can of hamburger meat with a 1984 expiration date stamped on the lid. We would bake the meat and then fry it again in lard, turning hamburgers into meatballs, trying anything to make the food go down.

That winter was extremely hard, and I was working almost full time at the hospital as the fighting had grown out of control. We didn't dare leave the house. On days of heavy shellings, we would tune into "Radio School" from home to listen to our professor's lecture over the radio. We were without electricity and running water so we studied by candlelight at night. We had it down to a candlestick science after awhile. If I had three exams the next day, I knew that I could get by with using only two candles.

After the tragic May 1995 shelling, a wonderful thing happened to me. A U.S. outreach program was offering to airlift a select number of Bosnian students out of the war and send them to live with host families in America. I was one of only two students in my high school chosen to submit an application for the program. Almost two months to the day after the fateful massacre, my aunt received a letter in the mail addressed to me. I had gotten my papers to leave Tuzla and move to Roanoke, Virginia, to live with the Hunt family.

Deciding to leave my family in Bosnia was one of the most heart-wrenching choices that I have ever made. I was 16 years old. Just the thought of getting out of Tuzla was terrifying. I had never even left the country. I would have to travel by myself on the tiny mountain roads knowing that guerrillas were hiding in the forests nearby. It was my mother who really urged me to make the decision to go, telling me that it may be the best opportunity I might ever have.

I arrived in Roanoke on July 16, 1995, and was welcomed into a household of total strangers from a completely different culture. Overnight, they were to become my family. They never treated me as merely a foreign student, residing with them temporarily, but truly treated me as one of their own children. I hadn't spent more than a few months with the family when a man named Robert Azi made an unexpected telephone call to my host father that had a lasting impact on my life.

An application had come in the mail a few weeks earlier to spend a summer term at Phillips Exeter Academy in New Hampshire. My host mother and father were incredibly generous people, but didn't have the financial resources to spend that much money on their own children, much less a child who had just arrived from Bosnia. The application landed in the garbage can almost immediately without any of us giving it much thought.

We were sitting around the kitchen table one evening when Robert Azi called again. He spoke with my host father for awhile, encouraging him to let me apply for the summer program at Exeter. Robert lectured at Exeter often and made it his mission to encourage individuals like me to apply. My host mother and I literally fished the application out of the garbage can.

While I struggled with English, my math, physics, and science scores were apparently just what Exeter was looking for, and I was admitted to the summer program with full-tuition aid. One of my greatest challenges was trying to fit in with the other students. I looked up and saw them all arriving in U-Hauls with their futons, televisions, clothing, and books. I looked down and saw my single suitcase in my hand. Buildings were everywhere; I didn't believe that I would ever find my way.

During the summer term, I managed to impress enough of my professors with my math and science skills, as well as my knowledge of European history, to receive a full-tuition scholarship to return full time in the fall. It took a long time to fit in. My peers were busy researching and applying to colleges while I was challenged just checking out a book in the library. I had no idea what an essay was, much less how to write one. I couldn't even begin to think about colleges when my adviser called me into his office one day to begin discussing the admissions process.

Instead of handing him my list of top-choice schools, I reached out to him for his advice. I researched all of his suggested schools' academic programs, professors, and financial-aid packages. Wellesley seemed like the closest thing to perfect. My boyfriend's jaw dropped when I told him that Wellesley was my top choice. He was shocked that I was going to an all-women's college. I assured him that no, that wasn't the case. I assumed he was just correcting my broken English. He insisted that it was pronounced, "Wesleyan." Ah, of course—he must be right. My English was so bad at the time, I really didn't know one from the other. I had done all of my research, but had managed to overlook one detail: Wellesley was indeed an all-women's college.

Not long after receiving my admittance together with a full-tuition scholarship to Wellesley, I was at a cocktail party with my new host family in New Hampshire, the Morozes. Mr. Moroze was telling everyone how proud he was of my efforts this past year at Exeter and how perfect it was going to be for me to be going to an all-women's college next year. I think I choked the moment that those words came out of his mouth, confirming what my boyfriend had said months ago. That night, I ran straight back to the library and read it with my own eyes. I was indeed going to "Wellesley," the all-women's college.

A real turning point in my life took place the fall of my sophomore year at Wellesley. I had spent the prior summer doing research at Harvard Medical School. While the experience was truly phenomenal, I became a bit disenchanted with the hospitals in America. Everything was so different than it was in Bosnia, and I was frustrated with the bureaucracy that I saw crippling the physicians. At the same time, while Wellesley had been an ideal place for me to begin my college life, I realized that it lacked the choices and resources that only a full-scale university could provide. I quietly decided to fill out an application to transfer to the University of Chicago. My friends and professors at Wellesley were truly amazing, but I knew that I wanted more.

When my University of Chicago acceptance letter came in the springtime, complete with a full-tuition scholarship, I made the choice to transfer. After my summer at Harvard, I decided that I would begin to look away from medicine and into other fields to study. It was in Chicago that I fell in love with economics. The department was revered throughout the world as one of the best, and I knew it was right for me.

I spent the summer doing an internship at Mercer Consulting, working on a Johnson & Johnson study that was fitting, given my health care background. When Lehman Brothers came to campus to recruit the following fall, I was intrigued by their analyst program, which boasted three 8-month rotations through finance, supporting three different areas within the firm. I realized that this was a great opportunity to learn more about exactly what I wanted to do.

I have since graduated and have been working at Lehman for four years. Ten years ago, I never thought I'd even be in the United States, much less analyzing long-term and short-term debt rates in an investment bank. My next goal is to go back to school for my MBA.

My role model is my uncle, an economist who was unjustly charged with fraud during the communist regime in Bosnia and thrown into jail. He spent six years in jail sharing his cell with Alija Izetbegovic, a man who would later go on to become the president of Bosnia and Herzegovina. My uncle never stopped believing in himself while he was imprisoned, and upon his release he started his own bank. After the fall of Yugoslavia in 1990, my uncle opened his banks throughout a region that was in dire need of an honest banking system. He passed away a few years ago, but I will always look up to him as a father figure to me after my own father passed away.

I have lost a lot of loved ones in my life, yet I believe that they are with me in spirit, living through my experiences with me. I was lucky to have the opportunities that did come my way, and I was prepared to seize them. My approach to life is to be open-minded and willing to give other people a chance to express their own love for life. Humor carried me through the war, and I believe that it is so important to laugh every day. One time when I was returning home to Bosnia after spending my first few years in the United States, my uncle asked me one question and that was, "Vedrana, are you content?" He didn't need to ask about my friends, classes, host families, or culture shocks back in America. Instead, he realized that was ultimately the most important thing in life—transcending cultures, ethnicities, and religion. I couldn't agree more.

LISA BISSETT

Lisa is only 35 years old, but she has already had three careers and started a business. She studied geological engineering at the undergraduate and graduate levels, first at Queen's University, Canada, and later at the Colorado School of Mines. She worked in environmental consulting for several years before returning to school. Her life as she knows it today really began in 2000 when she graduated from Wharton with an MBA in international marketing, accepted an associate position with McKinsey & Company, and was diagnosed with breast cancer. After leaving McKinsey in 2002, Lisa worked as director of corporate strategy for Clean Harbors. She then

*used her entrepreneurial drive to found Blooming Color, Inc.,
providing floral arrangements to corporations and corporate events.
Today Lisa is involved in various charitable organizations and enjoys
her many hobbies and life at home with her husband while she
continues to take care of her health.*

> "People often ask me what to say to friends or loved ones
> who are going through very difficult illnesses or injuries.
> Tell them how important they are to you. Remind them
> of a time they did something that made a difference to
> you ... I know I need to know that I'm important to the
> people around me. I need to know I was important before
> I ever got sick."

I finished my MBA at Wharton in 2000. That fall, I moved in with Matt,
the man of my dreams, and started work at McKinsey & Co. On my very first
day there, I discovered a large lump in my right breast. I was only 31, had always
found many lumps, and had no family history of breast cancer. I wasn't overly
concerned, but two months later I was diagnosed with breast cancer.

By the time we got this diagnosis, the cancer had already spread to 18 of
my lymph nodes and I was going to need some very aggressive treatment:
surgery, chemo, radiation, and years of hormonal treatment. It's a little
strange, but my first question wasn't whether or not I would die, but if I'd be
able to have children. Chemotherapy—especially aggressive chemotherapy—
can do irreparable damage to the ovaries. We heard varying opinions, but
ultimately decided on one round of in vitro fertilization and froze four
embryos before beginning chemo. Perhaps concentrating on fertility was a
coping mechanism, a way to focus on something other than my own mortality during that very scary time.

Six weeks after my diagnosis, Matt proposed, and we were married during a lull in my treatment. It's amazing what a very good makeup artist and
a quality wig can do! I actually looked (and felt) beautiful and healthy as I
walked down the aisle.

Matt's background is in biology, specifically cancer research, so I have my
own translator in the doctor's office. He has helped me sift through volumes
of information and think through some very difficult decisions. One of the
biggest decisions we made was to participate in a clinical trial involving a
stem cell transplant. This involved a very high dose of chemotherapy (a 96-
hour-long infusion) given in an isolation room. Hopefully, the dose would

kill my cancer, but it carried with it the side effect of killing all my bone marrow. After the chemo, the doctors transfused stem cells, which had been taken from me two weeks prior and frozen, back into my blood stream, and we all waited for the bone marrow to grow back. This was by far the most difficult of all the treatments I've had, and it took a long time to regain my strength. But I did, and every year I bring something for the nurses on that floor around Christmas to thank them for taking such good care of me.

Ironically, I had asked for mammograms for years during my regular physicals, but the doctors had always refused. As I now know, it wouldn't have done any good, because the mammogram I had *after* diagnosis didn't show the tumor at all. It turns out that the younger a woman is, the firmer her breast tissue is, and the more difficult it is for abnormalities to appear on a mammogram. There are no good screening methods to detect growths in young women. There are tests that can be used once an issue is identified, but screening everyone requires a simple, inexpensive, and accurate test. Sonograms are very helpful, especially when there is a specific lump to investigate. MRIs are also proving to be quite useful in very high-risk young women and research is ongoing in other areas. But the only screening method we have for young women is the good, old-fashioned breast self-exam. Please do them regularly. You're looking for any change—in lumps, in density, or even in something you can't quite describe. You are the one who knows your body best.

Treatment for breast cancer is, of course, very difficult. What few people know is that it can also be quite absurd. I remember walking to work one icy February morning during chemo (yes, I did work through much of my chemo treatment). I was wearing a beautiful wig and a very heavy coat and walking with two canes because I had a broken foot (one of my more fun winters!). As I had no free hands, I had my purse slung around my shoulders. When I got to my office I took off the purse, felt a draft, and looked down to see my hair on the floor! I instinctively ducked behind my desk and had the biggest belly laugh I'd had in a very long time. It didn't take very long before the wig, hats, and scarves were left behind and I decided bald was, indeed, quite beautiful.

Unfortunately, some stories are not so funny. Just a couple of weeks after my diagnosis, a technician in my dentist's office decided to tell me all about the two people she knew who died from breast cancer. Not really the kind of uplifting story I was looking for at the time.

Sometimes well-meaning people say things that they have no idea might bring me down. For instance, I don't like hearing how a great attitude has so much to do with how well someone battles cancer. I realize that this is said with great kindness because the speaker thinks I have a wonderful attitude. But, first of all, there is some scientific evidence that this is probably not true; second, my attitude is not so great 24 hours a day; and third, if you continue that stream of logic, it suggests that if I don't get better it may be my fault for not keeping my spirits up. Don't get me wrong, I do think a great attitude is important; but I believe its importance lies in *quality* of life.

I returned to McKinsey four days a week after my course of treatment. I think I needed to prove to myself that I could still work in such an intense environment. I could and did. But I no longer enjoyed it enough to continue with such a difficult lifestyle. McKinsey had always been and continues to be very good to me, and they helped me to find my next position in corporate strategy. I was restless, though, and wanted to work for myself. I wanted to do something that made people smile. As a small child, my grandmother had taught me Ikebana, Japanese flower arranging. I took a professional course in floral design, and I began providing flower arrangements for corporate clients.

I had been in remission during the three and a half years since my initial diagnosis, and the flower business was starting to take off. At this point, I'd been having some neck and shoulder pain. Sure enough, the cancer was back. This time it was a small tumor in a vertebra high up in my spine. The good news was that it was small and isolated and could be treated with a few weeks of radiation. The bad news was that this meant the cancer was now metastatic—it had spread to another organ, the bones. Breast cancer caught early is generally very treatable, but metastatic breast cancer is not considered curable. It can often be controlled for many years with various treatments, but it's very rare for it to go into a permanent remission. I closed my business; it was too difficult to run a small business under these circumstances.

I had about seven months of remission after the radiation. In the eighth month, an MRI found some spots in my liver. As I write this, I'm about two months into chemotherapy to treat this recurrence. I feel a little tired and my hair is gone again, but otherwise I'm quite well.

Everyone needs a safe place to explore and vent the fear, anger, hopelessness, frustration, and pain that comes with a serious illness. I've found a wonderful support group of young women who are surviving breast cancer. We're all in different stages of this disease, but have so much in common with each other. We're early in our careers, have young families, or are enjoying single life, and generally don't know many—if any—other people our age who have faced such serious illnesses.

I'm no longer working and doubt I ever will again; at least not full-time. I have several hobbies I now have time to pursue. I love cooking, and now Matt and I actually sit down to a healthy, home-cooked meal several times a week. I've been sewing all kinds of beautiful quilts, drapes, and pillows for our home. I'm even learning to crochet and knit! I have more time to visit with friends. Yoga is becoming quite an obsession.

People often ask me what to say to friends or loved ones who are going through very difficult illnesses or injuries. Tell them how important they are to you. Remind them of a time they did something that made a difference to you: perhaps a sister who helped you duck out of a really bad date, or a friend who brought you cookies when you didn't feel well, or a neighbor who shoveled the driveway when you threw out your back. I know I need to know that I'm important to the people around me. I need to know I was important before I ever got sick.

What's next? I'm speaking with a few people about various types of volunteer work that will be flexible enough and meaningful to me. A photographer friend of mine chronicled my initial treatment. Perhaps we'll turn the pictures into a book. I always have a special event to look forward to. Right now that's a trip to China this summer for my brother's wedding in Shanghai.

Living with breast cancer is not what I expected at 35. But then, the idea that we have any real control over the events of our lives is an illusion. My grandparents have always loved a poem by Kalidasa, a Hindu poet from the fourth century CE. I've always loved the poem, too, but perhaps it took cancer to help me really feel it.

THE EXHORTATION OF THE DAWN

Look to this day, for it is life, the very life of life.
In its brief course lie all the verities
and realities of your existence:
The bliss of growth,
The glory of action,
The splendor of beauty;
For yesterday is but a dream,
and tomorrow is only a vision;
But today, well lived, makes every yesterday
a dream of happiness
and every tomorrow a vision of hope.
Look well, therefore, to this day.

The only thing I know for sure about my future is that now that I have come face-to-face with my own mortality, I will be more passionate about enjoying my life and cherishing the people I love than I ever could have imagined.

KATHLEEN BRIANO

Kathleen has over 14 years of experience in Management Information Systems, working for such firms as Goldman Sachs, JP Morgan, and Coopers & Lybrand. She grew up in Staten Island and received her Bachelor's of Business Administration from Pace University. Her two daughters, Emily and Julia, are eight and six years old.

> "I was at the height of my career and I didn't want any-one at work to know that I was sick. I wanted to be just like everyone else."

In 2002, I received an email from a woman telling me that she had been diagnosed with breast cancer. I couldn't believe that she was reaching out to me—much less to all those other people. I didn't know her very well, but it created an immediate bond between us because that same disease had ravaged my body two years earlier. I was only thirty years old and had two daughters, ages 2 and 4. The woman who sent the email is Janet Hanson, who inspired me to reach out even more to other women afflicted with this disease.

When I was diagnosed, I was stunned. My mother had died of breast cancer, but she was in her sixties when she was diagnosed. I was so young. She had lived a full life by then and had seen her children grown and married. I know it sounds horrible, but I couldn't help but think how unfair it was that I had been stricken with this disease at an age when my life held so much promise.

I was at the height of my career, and I didn't want anyone at work to know that I was sick. I wanted to be just like everyone else. I wanted to show that the disease that ravaged my body hadn't affected my brain. More importantly, I wanted some control over my life. Work was the one area of my life where I still had some control, and I still wanted and needed to work. I couldn't afford to lose my job. So I suffered in silence.

And now someone else had this disease and was reaching out to me. Without delay, I wrote to Janet and shared my experience of beating breast cancer in 2000. Hoping to motivate her, I explained how I developed a proactive approach to conquering the disease.

Looking back, I have to credit my husband with "declaring war" on the disease. When I was first diagnosed, I was so caught up in the unfairness of my predicament that when I chose a treatment option, it was something convenient and close to home, a local hospital in Staten Island. My husband, leveraging his anguish for more power, convinced me to move out of my comfort zone and seek a hospital with more innovative treatment methods. Reluctantly, I went to Sloan Kettering in New York City. It turned out to be the best thing that my husband could have done to help me fight the disease. My doctors at Sloan supported a proactive strategy too. Taking a "positive" stance against the disease made me emotionally and psychologically stronger. I was able to face the disease head on.

The diagnosis was not good. I had a lump and calcifications in my right breast. In the spirit of pursuing an aggressive method of fighting the cancer, I told the doctor to remove the breast. With that decision behind me, I thought that perhaps the worst was over. But it was just beginning. My cancer was estrogen positive, which meant that a third pregnancy would put my life at risk. Also, too much estrogen would increase the risk of the cancer returning. I really struggled with that one because we had always wanted more children. Having to leave behind this wish, I thought about how blessed we already were with our two girls. Determined not to leave them motherless, I asked my doctor to perform a hysterectomy. His suggestion was that a hysterectomy would be too radical, but that if I removed my ovaries, this would drastically decrease my estrogen production. I didn't care what they did to me at that point; I just wanted to survive. I was up to five doctors now. They agreed that just removing my ovaries was the more prudent solution. So with another decision made, I learned that there was a slight chance that the cancer would show up in my other breast. I saw no reason to hang onto it—knowing my luck, the cancer would have eventually shown up in the left breast and then I'd kick myself for not having gone ahead and had the double mastectomy when I had the chance. After they had removed three major pieces of my anatomy, how weird it was to look at myself in the mirror and see so many pieces missing. Despite my preventive measures and six months of chemo, my cancer was still aggressive.

Then, a few things happened that struck me as some sort of divine intervention. A national cancer research institute was planning to conduct new research on a cancer drug called Herceptin. Normally, Herceptin was only used to treat people in their second or third stage of cancer. It proved so effective with that, however, that the institute wanted to see if it could be used in a "preventative" fashion. Desperate to find a solution, I waited for weeks, postponing standard treatment, to be included in the study.

Experimental studies are tricky because they can offer false hope. When you participate in a study, no one in the medical community can give you guidance about the best course of treatment. Doctors cannot tell you whether participating will actually help you because it would skew the study. That, and because they don't actually know how much it will help. So the ultimate decision for treatment is up to the patient—in my case, someone who has no medical training and no experience with this sort of thing. So, not only are you sick but you also have all these responsibilities and decisions heaped upon your shoulders. To make matters worse, these drugs all carry side effects. Just the mention of most of them can make your hair (if you have any!) stand on end. With Herceptin, the main risk in most patients is complete heart failure. OK, I thought, either the cancer or the heart failure will do me in.... I woke up one morning and decided to go for it. I was psyched, my body was ready, I was completely confident that I had reached the right decision. Bring it on. For the next six months, I went in for chemo treatments. Thereafter, I underwent a year of Herceptin treatment, once a week for 30 minutes.

I got the hang of it pretty quickly. With my IV planted firmly in my arm, I walked around the hospital, soothing the nerves of newcomers who were beginning treatment. When I was done, I'd head down to work just like nothing was wrong.

Every three months I had to have a heart scan because of the drug's potential side effect of weakening the heart. Initially, my doctors were surprised. Instead of weakening, my heart actually improved slightly. It was strange, but I don't think it had anything to do with the drug. I was just exercising to make myself feel better, and it must have helped me build up my cardiac muscle.

After the two longest years of my life, I had my last treatment on Labor Day weekend of 2002. It appears that I have beaten my cancer, at least for the short term. However, this was not the only outcome. I have learned many things from this ordeal that I would like to pass on to others. I had never considered myself part of a "network" before. Because I was the first person at Sloan to undergo this treatment, I became a resource to other women. At first, I just gave information. Soon, I found myself actively providing support and reassurance to newly diagnosed women embarking on this treatment path. Now, after doing this for several years, I realize that I have been a vital source of support for some women. My illness has inadvertently given me one of the most rewarding experiences of my life—women telling me that I have inspired them by sharing my experience. They were so grateful and so am I. As a young cancer survivor, my message is that the battle is worth fighting!

While I was sick, I didn't really reach out to anyone for support. I felt so alone when I was suffering with cancer. Ironically, I never went to a support group during the course of my treatment, but I have now become an advocate. When I received that email from Janet back in 2002, I was inspired by the courage she showed in sharing her story with so many people. At that point I had not even told my coworkers.

But I did reach out to my family. My husband was my pillar of strength, and together we did our best to explain my illness and the effects of the medicine to our young daughters. Although my illness must have been devastating to my father and siblings at the time since we had lost my mother to cancer, they were also a tremendous source of support.

For almost four years I have kept my cancer at bay. Statistically, a woman is only regarded as healthy when the cancer does not reappear for five years, so I am not out of the woods yet. While I was dealing with the cancer I just kept my head down and fought it. My efforts to stay positive during the illness have remained with me. I have a healthy outlook on life. Life is way too short to argue with loved ones or to be stubborn. I now focus on sharing my experiences with others, and I have been trying to raise money and awareness. I ran as a member of the 85 Broads team in the Race for the Cure. It was truly uplifting. So many people gave me encouragement along the way. That's a gift I'm happy to pass along.

KATHY MATSUI

Kathy grew up in California and received her BA at Harvard. She then studied in Japan as a Rotary scholar. Kathy entered the Johns Hopkins School of Advanced International Studies in 1990 and received her MA in Japan Studies and Finance. After working for four years at BZW Securities Tokyo, Kathy was offered a job at Goldman Sachs Asia. Since 1994, she has worked for Goldman in investment research and currently is Chief Japan Strategist and Co-Director of Investment Research. Kathy lives in Tokyo with her husband and two children.

> "So many people I see are unhappy—at their jobs, with their relationships, where they live. Still others (and I was certainly one of them) simply procrastinate, thinking, there's always tomorrow. But the reality is that there isn't always a tomorrow."

At age 36, shortly after the birth of my second child, I was diagnosed with Stage II breast cancer. Since my mother and both grandmothers had it, I knew that I had a predisposition to the disease, but naturally I never expected to be diagnosed at such a young age. I was vigilant about getting mammograms, but the disease still got me. As soon as I was diagnosed, I flew back to California for treatment. The incidence of breast cancer in Japan is only a fraction of what it is in the United States, so I felt I might have better treatment options in the United States. As luck would have it, one of my younger brothers is an oncologist, so he provided me with a lot of helpful information and advice. The most difficult part was that my husband and son (then age four) had to stay in Japan during my eight months of treatment in California. However, I was fortunate to have my baby daughter with me for most of the time. She was far more therapeutic than any of the medications I was prescribed.

My husband was an absolute star and managed to come visit me every month (without getting fired!), bringing our son for extended visits. Though I was fearful about how to explain what I was going through to my son, I decided that it was best to be honest. I took him to my chemo and radiation treatments, and he saw me without any hair. He used to ask, "Mama, are you going to die?" And all I could say was, "Well, Mama's very sick, but all the doctors and nurses are helping me get better, so don't worry."

Although there were some difficult moments during this period, I must say that there were also many silver linings. First, I was lucky to be blessed with a loving and nurturing family that took excellent care of me. Since I had left home for college when I was 17, it was actually nice to spend extended, quality time with my parents after nearly two decades of separation. Second, the outpouring of love and concern from so many friends was overwhelming. Shortly after sending an email about my predicament to one of my college roommates in Washington, D.C., she was immediately on a plane coming to visit me. Unbelievably, even several clients and colleagues from Japan stopped by to see how I was doing.

When I finally recuperated, I faced one of the toughest decisions of my life. Should I return to work? Should I return to Japan? I did a lot of soul searching during that time. I went to support groups and sought counsel but none of the women in the group had the same experience as I had. They didn't work in the type of stressful job I did, with extensive travel, and few had ever lived overseas. People unanimously thought that I was crazy to return to this lifestyle. Many cancer survivors follow their passions after they recover—become an opera singer, write a book, or use their talents in some other way. If I possessed such talents, perhaps I would have pursued another path. But nearly five years later, here I am, back at Goldman Sachs.

I decided to return because (a) coming back to a routine would be therapeutic since it would help take my mind off the disease, (b) I felt a responsibility to help so many of the young and talented women in GS Asia succeed, and (c) I wanted to show others that breast cancer survivors don't necessarily have to "give everything up."

So far, I have been able to make this work. In the beginning, I didn't want to tell many people about my illness, but now I'm quite open about it with colleagues and friends as I think the awareness level about the disease in Japan is dangerously low.

The biggest lesson I learned from my experience with cancer is that you can't take anything for granted. Right before I was diagnosed, I had achieved a number one Institutional Investor ranking, I was made a partner of the firm, and I had just delivered my second child. I remember thinking, "Life can't get much better than this." Until I heard those three dreaded words from my doctor. "You have cancer." Now, every day I wake up and thank God for giving me yet another day to enjoy life. Little things that used to annoy me are inconsequential now.

As I was recovering, I read a book for cancer survivors that said, "If you were told you were going to die in a month, make a list of 10 things you would do and do them." At first I scoffed at this, but having faced my mortality at age 36, I realize that few people in the world approach life like this, and it's not a bad idea. So many people I see are unhappy—at their jobs, with their relationships, where they live. Still others (and I was certainly one of them) simply procrastinate, thinking there's always tomorrow. But the reality is that there isn't always a tomorrow. Many people fail to realize they have the ability to change their situations. In this respect, I almost feel lucky to be a cancer survivor because it's taught me to embrace life and not leave a minute wasted.

KATHY KUHNS

Kathy joined the Fixed Income Sales Division at Goldman Sachs in 1982. After leaving Goldman 12 years later as a vice president, her twin boys were born. Kathy returned to the workforce in 1999, joining the Directorship Search Group, where she was an executive recruiter specializing in financial services and women board members. She is now a realtor for William Raveis Real Estate in Greenwich, Connecticut.

"Life will throw you some curve balls, such as an illness, that you just have to deal with."

When I joined Goldman Sachs in 1982, it was the beginning of a challenging and magical journey. I immersed myself in Goldman's culture. Every day, I arrived at work at 7 a.m., and my evenings and weekends were often spent with colleagues and/or clients. I even met my husband-to-be on an airplane while on a business trip.

My approach to life has always been: "Give it your best shot!" This philosophy guided me through my years at Goldman and is why I ultimately left Goldman. I wanted desperately to have children. Achieving this goal at age 43 was becoming a career in itself. I felt that to ask for a leave of absence to get pregnant would have derailed my career. Very reluctantly, I resigned.

A year later, I gave birth to twin boys. A whole new chapter of challenges began. Without the luxury of my salary, we sold our co-op in New York City and moved to our weekend house in northwestern Connecticut. Dreams of life in the country soon gave way to feelings of isolation, depression, and frustration. I missed the intellectual and competitive nature of work. When the twins turned four, educational issues arose and we decided that country life was not for us. We moved to Greenwich, Connecticut. This move provided me with the opportunity to rejoin the workforce. At age 49, I was forced to reinvent myself. I became an executive recruiter at the Directorship Search Group founded by Russell Reynolds after he sold his eponymous firm. Although my specialty was financial services, I became involved in putting women on boards of directors. I met many fascinating people and reconnected with former colleagues, including Janet Hanson, who was always a great source of ideas and has a vast network of connections.

My family was happy and thriving. Life was good. Then, I was thrown a major curve ball—I was diagnosed with Stage III colon cancer. Having just had a routine colonoscopy, still groggy from the medication, the doctor informed me that she removed four polyps but there was still a mass in my lower intestine, which had to be removed with major surgery. It was cancer. Several hours later, a surgeon removed a foot of my colon. Three days later, I was told that the cancer had spread to my lymph nodes but so far had not invaded other organs. The fight of my life had just begun. With the help of a friend, I was able to get an appointment with Dr. Saltz, the guru of colon cancer at Sloan Kettering. Seven months of chemotherapy ensued.

Cancer is now not automatically a death sentence but it does change your life. Determined to be a "normal" person, I stoically went to work every day at the expense of my family. I returned home in the evening exhausted and nauseous, said good night to the housekeeper, crawled into bed, and tried to read to the boys. I would fall asleep and the boys would play with their PlayStation II until my husband came home. My son Dylan stopped focusing at school and eventually confessed that he was terrified that I would die during the school day and that he would never see me again. On a positive note, my husband, after hearing a heartfelt lecture from a friend whose wife was a cancer survivor, cut his workday short and learned to use the microwave and dishwasher. Friends and family became my cornerstone. They brought over meals, attended soccer games, and offered to drive me into Manhattan for my chemo treatments.

Eventually, fighting cancer and dealing with the physical side effects and the fallout on my family became my full-time profession. I resigned from the Directorship and rearranged my priorities. I channeled my energies into my sons' school. My boys were very happy to have me involved with their everyday lives. Up until then, I had been an "invisible parent." Afterward, I became a "class parent." I reclaimed my family, my health, and my confidence.

It was time for another reinvention that would allow me to work, putting my family first, yet enabling me to be a producer. Skill set: relationships, listening, keeping a deal together. I am now a real estate broker in Greenwich. I am with a firm that has great training and mentoring, a model that worked well for me at Goldman Sachs. I work with many high-caliber people, a number of whom are former Wall Streeters. It is fun and rewarding—both mentally and financially.

I am a private person who rarely talks about herself. I undertook this task of telling my story so that I could share my experiences as a "survivor"—physically, mentally, professionally, and most importantly as a wife and mother. Do in life what excites you! As a woman, I think there often comes a time (or times) when your priorities change. Part of my identity has always revolved around my work, and I think that, after over 20 years in the workforce, I have finally achieved a balance between my family and my profession that works for me and for us all.

CARA MORENO

Cara graduated from Columbia Business School in 2004 and recently relocated to London with her husband. Prior to attending Columbia, Cara worked in investment banking at Gleacher & Co. and in private equity at Saunders, Karp, & Megrue. In 2001, Cara lost her mother to cancer.

"Throughout my life, I have never viewed the challenges I faced as either insurmountable or out of my control. In 2001, I was confronted with a unique situation where I had absolutely no control. My mother had been diagnosed with stage-four pancreatic cancer and was given less than one year to live."

I have always considered myself a fighter, seeking out the biggest challenges, toughest competition, and most difficult jobs—and then setting my mind to achieve success. When my mother was diagnosed with cancer, I instinctively began to fight for her survival. I took a leave from my job on Wall Street and moved home to be closer to her. I contacted every hospital, research clinic, and doctor that I knew. I spent countless hours researching the disease, exhausted every last Western and Eastern medicinal option available, and searched everywhere for hope. As months passed, my mother's condition worsened and she became frustrated with my relentless fighting. She begged me to accept that which neither she nor I had any control over and focus on her journey. While it was contrary to the way I had done everything in my life up to that point, I had to let go.

With the fear of losing out on the quality time that remained, I resolved to change my behavior. We focused our energies on the things that really mattered the most, making these last moments of my mother's life as fulfilling as possible. We spent the last few weeks of her life reminiscing about the past and planning for the future. My fiancé and I sped up our engagement so that my mother could participate in this momentous time, and we began planning for the future welfare of my youngest sister and her higher education.

The loss of my mother was an awakening for me. I developed an acutely strong sense of compassion and an understanding that not everything in life is within my control. My family grew closer to each other and each person stepped up to fill part of the void left by my mother's passing. My stepfather, who had never had children of his own, took on the responsibility of raising my youngest sister and my middle sister moved home after college instead of taking a job in Washington, D.C., to aid him in this role. My mother's siblings, parents, and close friends spent countless hours supporting the family, and her nurses did everything they could to make our lives easier.

At times, my grief consumed me, and each day was a struggle. Over time, however, I learned to cope with my grief by building a support network among my own friends who had also lost parents, staying in close touch with family, and joining an official support group at Sloan Kettering. My fiancé also became my daily sounding board for all struggles and triumphs. My mother's words, insisting that "good always emerges from bad," resonated in my mind during this tragic time as I came to fully appreciate and value the support of my family and friends.

After the loss of my mother, I realized that I needed a change in my life. Remaining at my current job was not an option, as I was burned out and had lost my focus. I thirsted for an environment with constant stimulation where captivating and motivated people would surround me. Business school seemed like a logical step, so I applied and spent the next two years at Columbia Business School. Columbia provided me with a forum to channel my energies, passions, and motivation to take on a leadership role. I became the co-chair of the 2004 Columbia Women in Business Conference, which gave me the opportunity to take a 30,000-foot view of an organizational process. From this perspective I realized that I didn't want to be stuck in the details over the long term. Instead, I decided to embark on a path that I hope will someday lead me to run a company, big or small.

I recently moved to London with my husband, where I accepted a job at the Boston Consulting Group. It was certainly a challenge to leave the immediate support network that I had built for myself in New York. However, I am enjoying the opportunity to develop new relationships and interact with exciting people. My husband and I are planning to have children in the future, which I have no doubt will be the most important thing I do in my life. While I know that I will never be "just a mom," my family will always be priority number one.

Given my experiences in my life, I believe that I am prepared for the challenges that lie ahead of me. Although I would do anything to have my mother back, I have come to terms with my loss and find additional peace in my life every day. Losing my best friend, confidante, supporter, and mother all at once has certainly made me a stronger person. I challenge myself to think and react on my own without needing to depend on anyone else for approval. The loss of my mother also motivated me to strive for success using the strength of my inner spirit. Finally, I have come to understand that I will never have control over what will happen tomorrow, so I must take every opportunity to cherish what I have today.

8

OFFICERS

When 85 Broads held our "What's Your Gift?" event in November 2001, we asked a second-year Harvard MBA student who was a member of our Broad2Broad co-mentoring partnership to speak about her leadership experiences as a graduate of West Point. Her name is Gail Seymour, and she is one of the extraordinary women officers whose stories we'll hear in this chapter. After graduating from West Point, where she had been second-in-command of 350 cadets, she was commissioned as a second lieutenant of the Quartermaster Corps and served as platoon leader of an all-male platoon in Germany, among many other responsibilities. After Gail graduated from Harvard and joined Bristol-Myers Squibb, we stayed in touch with each other through 85 Broads. She sent this email to me in August 2003.

Hi Janet,

I was perusing the website because a close friend of mine has started an organization called Women of West Point for alumnae that's along the same lines as 85 Broads. It's a web-based network of women graduates of the U.S. Military Academy in whatever phase of life they are—active duty with or without kids, professionals, and stay-at-home moms. I think there are some interesting additional challenges for women in the military that women in industry might not face—deployment, inability to separate work and personal life, limited access to professional or combat roles, perhaps even fewer female role models, and so on. But as I said, this group is intended to be broader than active-duty military women. In fact, my friend got the idea for starting the group based on an article she read about 85 Broads!

Anyway, she just sent me her "business plan" to review as she'd like to get recognized by the Association of Graduates, an umbrella organization for all West Point alumni organizations, societies, etc., and I thought it might be good for her to talk to you in person. Would you be willing and interested in talking to her and sharing some of your ideas on how to build a successful organization? I figure you're the most qualified person I know in this area due to the success you've had with 85 Broads and all of the subsequent related groups in your organization. Let me know what you think.

Take care and talk to you soon,

Gail

Before the end of that summer we met with Gail's friend and classmate whose name is Niave Knell (pronounced "Neeve"), a first-generation American who entered West Point a few weeks after graduating from high school in 1988. She was a member of the first Army women's crew team and went on to serve as a battle captain in Bosnia. When we met with her, Niave, her husband, and two young sons were preparing to move from Fort Meade in Maryland to Fort Leavenworth in Kansas where Niave has since completed the Army's senior tactical course. Like 85 Broads, Niave and a small group of other women in the military wanted to create a network for women across all branches of the service. Because they shared a common bond as graduates of one of the military academies, they wanted to have a way to stay connected with one another throughout their careers and lives. Here was a chance for 85 Broads not only to help women in our own community connect with each other but to use our network platform to help other networks get started, grow, and ultimately create very powerful network-to-network connections as well (something we've now done with networks in banking, consulting, and across a number of other professional sectors). Their network became Academy Women, which today has over 650 members who stay connected through academywomen.org, a community-based website developed using 85 Broads' network technology. The success of Academy Women and other women's networks built by entrepreneurially spirited women is one of the reasons I'm so passionate about 85 Broads—the potential for creating new networks and connections among incredible women all over the world has never been greater!

But the story doesn't end there. Gail's email and Niave's visit got me thinking about women in the military within our own network, so I did a "member search" on 85broads.com and found many of the amazing women whose stories we are about to hear in this chapter.

The 85 Broads' "Women in the Military" event later that same year was one of our most successful ever, featuring the stories and voices of these and other remarkable women who had chosen career paths which started, and in some cases continue, with service in the military. All of these women have held positions of awesome, sometimes overwhelming, responsibility. Each has had her character, courage, and confidence tested to the extreme, and every one of them has had to find her own unique answer to the fundamental question raised throughout this book and our network: How do you turn adversity into challenge, challenge into success, and success into happiness—again and again and again?

More than anything else, these are stories about transitional leadership. How do you take the leadership lessons you've learned in one setting or context and apply them in other areas of your career, education, and life? The women in this chapter have embraced, not just accepted, leadership in virtually every way imaginable and used their incredible experiences to move forward—into business school, professional and managerial positions, philanthropy, entrepreneurship, and in some cases further service in the military. In many ways these women display virtually all of the character traits reflected in the stories of this book. They are at once trailblazers, adventurers, entrepreneurs, parents, givers, survivors, ambassadors, visionaries, and rockets. If you look up *officer* in the dictionary, one of the definitions you'll find is "someone who holds an office of authority or trust." These remarkable women have learned to exercise their authority to create the greatest common good, and they have earned the trust, respect, and loyalty of those around them—classmates, cadets, colleagues, and all the members of our global network. They most definitely are *officers*.

BRIDGET ALTENBURG

Bridget decided to join the Army during her senior year in high school when her father's Army unit deployed to Desert Storm. In the spring of her senior year she received a nomination to the U.S. Military Academy at West Point. She graduated from West Point in 1995 and was commissioned as a second lieutenant in the Army Corps of Engineers. She was deployed three times to the Balkans, the last of which she served as the V Corps aide-de-camp during the war in

Kosovo. When Bridget's five-year commitment ended in August 2000, she enrolled at Columbia Business School. She graduated in May 2002 and began work with Bally Total Fitness Corporation. She continues to work there as the director of project management at the corporate headquarters in Chicago. Bridget has completed five half-Ironman triathlons, and she completed her first full Ironman in November 2004.

"Take care of your troops, lieutenant!"

In 1990, I was 17 years old and we were still living in Germany when the entire local Army division of 15,000 people was deployed to Desert Storm. I remember the silence the most. The base was silent, the halls were silent, and some kids were left raising the younger children because both parents were deployed. I was fortunate that my mom could stay with us. A few of my classmates were left raising their siblings alone. My mom took care of lots of families during the war. I remember her talking to young spouses all the time, giving advice, consoling, helping them get through 6 to 12 months alone raising their kids. She was amazing, completely unflappable. Some of my best leadership lessons are from her during Desert Storm. It was amazing to see the community come together to provide comfort for the residents on the base. It was then and there that I decided that I wanted the military to play a major role in my life. It's more than just a job!

Before graduating from the American Army high school on post, I went to visit my older brother at West Point. Immediately, I felt the same sense of community that I had experienced on the Army base in Germany. I knew that West Point was the place for me. During the academic year, school was held as normal. During the summer months, we had training. First year was basic training; second year, field training; third year, drill cadet; and fourth year, cadre for cadet basic training.

In the military, you get a lot more respect if you're in good physical shape, and I found that my triathlon experience really came in handy. If you're a woman *and* you're in good shape, the men totally respect you; if you're not, the men really don't respect your opinion on any subject. Sadly, the same standards don't apply to men. If a guy's in bad shape, it doesn't really matter, his opinion still counts.

Between my junior and senior year at West Point, I went to the Lake Placid Olympic training camp to be an "intern." We had to work in a formal sense, but we also got to "work out" at least three times a day. A typical day went something like this: Wake up, swim, go to class, bike, go to another class, and so on. Needless to say, I went into my final year at West Point in top physical form.

"Cooperate and graduate" is the unofficial motto at West Point, which means helping out your fellow cadets and helping each other make it through. At West Point, having teammates looking out for you helps you avoid being hazed by upperclassmen on the way to class. You could definitely spot the students who had played team sports. Sports and training helps you handle the mental stress in the military and teaches you how to make a decision in a split second.

Upon graduating in 1995, I wanted to be involved in a "combat" branch. It was the epitome of leadership. It not only appealed to my adventurous side, but I wanted to challenge myself with the most difficult thing out there. Unfortunately, most of the combat branches are closed to women, so I pursued Engineers, one of the branches that wasn't. I learned tactics, which combined engineering with combat. Our mission was to provide mobility by breaching obstacles, building bridges and roads, as well as to provide countermobility by creating obstacles for the enemy. We were also responsible for survivability, and built bunkers and fighting positions as well as support.

I happened to be the only woman in my platoon who was deployed to Bosnia, and I am proud of being a good platoon leader given the circumstances. I lived in a tent with 10 guys and had about 2 feet of personal space; pretty tough to keep a senior-subordinate relationship when you're changing in your sleeping bag. I was deployed three different times to the Balkans, where I eventually worked as an aide-de-camp for CG V corps as a first lieutenant. However, this was the first time the Corps headquarters had been deployed since World War II. The conditions were very austere—thigh-deep mud, no showers, no wash, MREs three times a day.

In 2000, after returning to the States, I enrolled at Columbia Business School and was able to combine my drive, discipline, and the team building skills that I had learned in the military with a new set of business skills. After graduating, I joined Bally Total Fitness, happily meshing my love for sports with my newly acquired business training. Working at Bally is my absolute dream job. I am lucky to work with people dedicated to improving fitness. They encourage and understand fitness. My boss is a former triathlete who gave me the flexibility to train up to 20 hours per week (primarily on the weekends) to prepare for my first ever Ironman, which I completed on November 6, 2004. I'm pretty happy with my performance, finishing in 12 hours and 51 minutes and making my dream of finishing in 14 hours.

I'm still trying to figure out what my next career steps are. It's been a challenge adapting to the civilian world. I have gone from completing missions to improving freedom of movement so that locals could vote for a democratic government to "creating shareholder value." One thing I have recognized in the civilian world is that there is a need to encourage and develop women leaders. I don't know how I will make an impact, but it is something I'm passionate about. Somehow I'd like to teach civilian women what I learned in the Army—to give them the confidence in themselves, in their instincts as leaders, and in pursuing leadership opportunities.

Molly McCabe

Molly received an Air Force ROTC scholarship to Princeton University and graduated in 1996 with a BS degree in civil engineering as well as a certificate from Princeton's Woodrow Wilson School. Instead of serving in the Air Force, Molly was able to cross-commission to the U.S. Navy. She graduated in the top of her class as the regimental commander, and served in the Navy for five years. Seeking a civilian international experience, Molly enrolled in the MBA program at Stanford, with the expectation that she would eventually work for an international corporation. After a summer internship at McKinsey in Dallas, Molly decided to return to the Navy. She is currently a combat systems officer on a ship in Mississippi.

> "As a Navy officer, my goal is to command a warship. An unusual career path for a woman? I don't think so…women are natural leaders."

If you haven't been in the military, you may have a hard time understanding this: the military taught me to be a leader. It shaped my concepts of fairness, ethics, friendship, and accountability. It has taught me to see competencies I didn't even know I had—such as motivating people to superior performance when they've hardly seen land for six months while out at sea.

I consider myself lucky to have been exposed to the military at a young age. When I was seven, I decided upon two things: I would go into the military and I would go to Princeton. Both institutions were in my blood. My father served during and after Vietnam and both grandfathers fought in WWII. Learning of their service as a young child created in me a passion to serve my country.

I put all my energies into getting into Princeton on an ROTC scholarship with the Navy, like my dad. Disappointingly, I learned that Princeton didn't have a Navy program so I applied to their Air Force program and was accepted. The first year I learned the core curriculum. The second and third years taught me to be a squadron commander, getting firsthand experience leading teams and passing inspection. If you succeeded through the first three years of grueling tests, both disciplinary and academic, you learned military strategy—how and why the great leaders won, how to recognize and appreciate a good leader. It gave me a new framework to make decisions and pushed me to think beyond my normal frame of reference.

All four years, my discipline was tested. We had to get up early for drills. We had to behave under a code of conduct. We had to wear our uniforms twice a week on campus. This evoked interesting discussions from my fellow classmates, which made me think hard about my decisions and direction. But I was convinced that I was on the right path. I finally finished the program but in an unusual career move, I switched over to the Navy.

If I thought the ROTC program was tough, being a woman in the military was even tougher. I respected my fellow officers but there were very few women. I had no role models and few people to turn to for advice. I traveled for five years with the military—from Rhode Island to the Panama Canal to San Diego. I really enjoyed the excitement and the exposure to new things. On my first assignment as strike officer aboard the USS *Decatur* (DDG 73), I was responsible for the Tomahawk and Harpoon missile systems, as well as the Phalanx gun and the fire control system for the 5-inch 54 gun. The *Decatur* was still under construction when I arrived, so I spent the first year of duty in the shipyards of Maine developing, along with my phenomenal division of sailors, requisite operating procedures to ensure that the ship passed its initial sea trials. On my second assignment I was stationed in Hawaii and deployed to the Middle East and South East Asia as a Tomahawk mission planner on the battle group staffs of the USS *Lincoln* (CVN 72) and the USS *Kitty Hawk* (CV 63).

There's no questioning how exciting it was. But there were challenges specific to serving in the Navy. We went out to sea for six-month stints, with few windows and close quarters. I slept only 10 feet away from my boss. Despite the close quarters, you feel a kind of isolation out at sea. Thank God for email; it kept me connected to the outside world. That piece of technology has made a world of difference to people in the military, helping them stay linked to friends and family during long deployments overseas.

There were other challenges. It is very important to respect, and be respected by your boss, given the strict career paths in the military. I had a bad experience with a superior and because I was so young, I let myself get beaten down; I had no enthusiasm left. When I look back, I was also very idealistic at the time, but I think it's good to feel that way in your twenties. This bad experience was an early motivator for me to look outside the Navy for a career path.

In addition, I had always wanted to serve overseas. The Navy offers some interesting international opportunities, but, as a woman, there are fewer possibilities because some foreign navies don't always allow women on a ship. For example, I was accepted to a foreign posting in Berlin, Germany, but then they turned me down when they realized I was a female officer. That was not only a major disappointment and waste of time and effort, but it made me feel vulnerable because of my gender. That was the clincher for me. I wanted out. I had a severe case of the "grass being greener" syndrome. I wanted to be stateside—immediately. So I decided to go back to graduate school for a degree in business. I considered East Coast schools, but I had "been there, done that." I decided to try for the best of the West Coast—Stanford University.

I started business school in 2001. During my orientation, the unthinkable—September 11—happened. It's amazing how that tragedy roused my sense of duty. I spent many nights thinking/hoping that I would be called to duty because I had undergone Tomahawk mission training. I was prepared to go. But I wasn't called, so I continued my education.

Business school was a different world for me. The stories I heard at b-school about the obnoxious sexual behavior of investment bankers certainly outdid anything I had experienced in the military. On my first ship, there were people who had never worked with women before, but they just wouldn't think of sexually harassing anyone because the Navy takes significant steps to educate people against this kind of behavior. I was surprised to learn that this sort of thing was apparently still tolerated at some Wall Street firms.

After completing my first year, it was time to test my "grass is greener" theory. I landed the plum summer internship assignment—working for McKinsey in Dallas, Texas. I lived the high life for 10 weeks: interesting projects, with a superintellectual and well-mannered team. I had the corporate experience that almost every b-school student yearns for. At the end of the summer, however, I knew it wasn't for me and told the partners of my decision not to return.

Why? Because I missed the camaraderie and identity of the military, being part of a larger community. I also missed the leadership of the military. Leaders in the military endure thorough scrutiny before getting the opportunity to lead because lives depend on their ability. Their competency but also their character is taken into consideration. I know that what's inside a person determines the true character that emerges during dangerous times. We are also taught to be loyal to our teammates, to those we lead, and to those we follow. I think that all of these characteristics are important to me, especially as a woman. And I missed the diversity of the military—all Americans were represented. I had given corporate America a try but my heart just wasn't in it. Surprising even myself, I set my sights back on the military.

Okay, so here I am, back in the Navy, a combat systems officer on a ship in Mississippi, and I love it. The only downside is the continued lack of female role models or mentors in the military. Professionally, I have a few former officers to turn to but they are men. I look to my peers and friends from business school to give me advice. In one way, it's great because it's outside the military, but it's not really professional guidance. For real advice, I have to use my own contacts. I still keep in touch with women from my first ship. You can only imagine how close one gets when rooming 10 feet away from someone for six months. But I tend to look at everything positively. So maybe my female peers and I are the trailblazers, setting out to become role models for a new generation of military women of the 21st century!

GAIL SEYMOUR

Following her graduation from the United States Military Academy at West Point in 1992, Gail Seymour was commissioned as a second lieutenant in the Quartermaster Corps, the logistics branch of the Army. After graduating first in her class at the basic officer training course, Gail got her "jump wings" before going on to her first duty assignment in Germany. When Gail returned to the United States, she attended the combined logistics officer advanced course and was next assigned as the supply and service officer of the 101st Corps Support Group. During this tour, Gail was the honor graduate of her air assault class and served as the primary logistics liaison for the 3rd Infantry Brigade during their joint readiness training. After serving on active duty for over five years, Gail left the military to join Bristol-Myers Squibb as part of the company's corporate associates program, a leadership development program bringing "retired" talented junior military officers to the corporation.

"Leaders are made, not born. Leadership comes from gaining the respect of others through the actions you take and the decisions you make. The leader that I have become is due in large part to my experiences at West Point, as well as serving on active military duty. I thrive on being challenged and knowing that I'm making a genuine difference."

As a child, I never dreamed I would go into the military, not to mention West Point. I knew nothing about the Academy until I met an incredibly interesting woman who had graduated from there herself. West Point isn't just your typical academic experience. Instead, the school focuses on developing its students academically, physically, and mentally—with a "sink-or-swim" mentality. The Academy has a systematic approach to leadership: plebes (known as freshmen everywhere else) follow the lead of the upperclassmen, and cadets are gradually given more opportunities to lead as they progress through to their "firstie" or senior year in school. Leaders are expected to lead by setting the example. The more I learned about West Point, and its sense of history and tradition, the more I wanted to go.

West Point proved to be the most challenging four years of my life, yet it made me a strong person and an even stronger leader. When people find out I went to West Point, they often ask me, "Was it difficult being a woman at West Point?" And the truth is, yes it was. But, it was difficult for both men and women at West Point. Because of my experiences there, I now know I can achieve anything to which I set my mind.

During my junior year, I was assigned to be a squad leader for nine new cadets during their basic training. While it was expected to be a transformational experience for them, it was equally or more so for me. I was completely responsible for my nine new cadets—for both their successes and their failures. Their ability to perform as a team was representative of my accomplishments as a leader. By the time I graduated from West Point and had become an army platoon leader, I already had numerous cadet leadership positions under my belt and had learned that teamwork, effective communication, and leading by example were necessary tools for the success of any team.

My first commissioned position was really quite daunting. I was 22 years old and in charge of 26 male soldiers and noncommissioned officers (NCOs), many of whom were older and more experienced than I was. Although I was accustomed to being the only woman in a classroom at West Point, this was the real world and these soldiers were waiting to see what I did. I was responsible for the development, training, morale, and overall welfare of my soldiers, in addition to accomplishing our day-to-day mission of being fully prepared if called to action.

Based on what I had learned at West Point, I was able to gain the trust and respect of my soldiers early on by showing respect for their experiences as well as my own. I sought out the advice of my senior NCOs regularly. I took the time to learn about each soldier individually, and I set high standards for all of us.

Not long into my position, I wanted to take my platoon on a weeklong field training exercise in order to build unit cohesion while training for our military mission. For our "fun" activity, I arranged for us to learn how to rappel, with instructors teaching us how to tie off properly and how to belay. When it came time for the actual descent of an 80-foot cliff, the platoon looked to me to go first. To put it mildly, I'm afraid of heights, but I knew that this was a defining moment. I needed to set the example as their platoon leader and show them the way down. I knew on that day that I had earned their respect.

In the military, there is a pervasive perception that a woman won't perform to a man's standard. The fact that I was a female platoon leader required that I go to additional lengths to prove myself. Consequently, I was always setting the standards higher for myself, to earn the respect of the men in my platoon, as well as the men in senior leadership positions. Coming out of the male-dominated environment of West Point, I was well prepared for this situation. What is interesting is that this approach has not only served me well in the military, but it continues to benefit me in my professional life today.

While I've learned a great deal from the successes I experienced both at West Point and on active duty, I've probably learned more from my failures. A few years later as a captain stationed at Fort Campbell, Kentucky, I was tasked to go on a deployment exercise with two senior NCOs. Having just returned from another month-long deployment, I wasn't all that happy about being selected for this assignment, and my attitude probably showed in the way that I communicated with my NCOs and relied on them to pack our equipment without double-checking their work.

Upon arrival at our destination in Virginia, I realized that we were missing key pieces of equipment and were ill-prepared to conduct our mission. As a unit, we were compromising the success of the operation because I had failed to exercise my responsibilities as a leader during the planning and preparation for the deployment. Fortunately, we were able to borrow the necessary equipment because of our convenient location at a stateside Army post. Had our assignment been a real deployment to an overseas location, our lack of preparation would have had a serious impact on the larger organization's success.

After my failure as an officer to provide for my unit's readiness, I learned that as a leader I couldn't take even the briefest break from my responsibilities. No matter how I felt personally about the deployment, I should neither have shown it to my soldiers nor let a lack of enthusiasm and interest compromise my duty to accomplish our mission. I was fortunate to have had access to backup equipment and to have had the opportunity to learn from this lesson. I realized that there will always be projects that I don't want to do, but as a leader it is important for me to suck it up and get them done, because others are looking to me to provide leadership and direction. When I now find myself with one of these projects in hand, I remember my lesson in the Army and I get the job done.

I left the Army with more than five years of active duty experience. Leaving the military was a difficult decision for me to make, but I am convinced that it was the right one in the end. I left primarily because I knew that I had already learned a great deal in terms of leadership, responsibility, communication, and teamwork, and the learning curve just wasn't as steep any longer. Second, when it comes to promotions, the army is still behind corporate America. In the army, officers are promoted primarily on time-in-grade, as opposed to performance and potential. Finally, the trade-offs between family and career can be tremendous in the military because the military's needs always come first. However, in corporate America your personal life doesn't have to be tied to your professional one. My husband Scott, also an army officer, and I decided that we wanted to be able to make work-life balance decisions for ourselves instead of having the military make them for us.

In 1998, I was recruited into the corporate associates program at Bristol-Myers Squibb (BMS). The company developed the program in order to bring junior military officers into the company's leadership development pipeline. As a corporate associate, I spent two years in rotational assignments in different business functions both to gain a better understanding of the pharmaceutical business and to make important work-related contributions. The goal for Bristol-Myers Squibb with this program has been to build future leaders for the company by leveraging our military leadership backgrounds.

Despite differences on the surface, I was surprised to find how similar corporate America was to the army. While I didn't have to wear camouflage, low crawl through the mud with an M-16, or wake up for physical training at 5:00 each morning, the fundamentals of the two institutions were similar. Additionally, although there were many more women working with me at Bristol-Myers Squibb than I had been used to in the army, there were still very few who had made it to the top.

After spending over two years at BMS, I had the opportunity to go back to school for my MBA. I was accepted at Harvard Business School and interestingly enough, I found yet another fairly natural transition as both HBS and the military have a mission to train successful leaders. In fact, HBS was home to the Navy Supply Corps School during World War II and has continued to be supportive of the military. Dean Clark at Harvard states, "Harvard educates general managers—individuals who possess the talent to lead and the capacity to learn throughout their lives."

While at HBS, I was elected copresident of the Women's Student Association. It was interesting to me that many of the women on campus thought there were so few women represented in the student body. While having come from both West Point and the Army, I felt like we were a well-represented group. However, that didn't stop me from working on initiatives to bring more women to HBS, to have more case studies developed featuring female protagonists, and to provide opportunities for students to meet dynamic and successful women leaders.

It was in this capacity that I met Janet Hanson, who had come up to HBS for a talk about the importance of networks and who was just beginning the Broad2Broad partnership with women at business schools, presenting an opportunity to have a comentoring relationship with members of 85 Broads. Janet was very interested in my background and invited me to speak at the next 85 Broads event, "What's Your Gift?," in New York City. I have to admit I was hesitant about speaking about my background in front of such a large audience of incredibly successful women. But Janet convinced me that I had a compelling message to share about leadership.

After graduating from HBS in 2002, I returned to Bristol-Myers Squibb, and I am currently doing marketing for the Oncology Division. I'm enjoying the work, especially the interaction with patients who are so appreciative of what companies like BMS do for them. There are definitely new and different challenges that I face in the corporate environment. However, as Dean Clark told us, an important part of growing as an individual is the capacity to learn throughout your life.

Having never perceived myself to be a natural networker, I realize that it is something that I have had to work on at Bristol-Myers Squibb. Staying connected to people is a critical component in any career. Sometimes, even when I think others know I'm doing a great job, they might not. And, although it's not my style, I've had to become more assertive in promoting my accomplishments to others in the organization. I've always believed that if you do great things, then great things will happen to you. Perhaps that's a little naive in today's business world, but I'd like to think it's still true.

I think that eventually I would like to run my own business, which doesn't necessarily mean being an entrepreneur per se; it could be a business on my own or becoming a general manager within a larger organization. I've still got a career stretching out in front of me and I've still got a lot to learn.

As I just finished duty in the inactive ready reserve during the summer of 2003, the military was, until recently, very much a part of my life. Yet, the legacy of those experiences stays with me. One of the most important things I acquired in the military is a personal leadership style that has continued to evolve as I learn from other people in leadership roles. I've learned that it is hard work being a leader, but it can also be a lot of fun. And, regardless of the structure or nature of the environment in which you find yourself, the fundamentals of what makes a good leader are the same, and if you practice them, you will succeed.

GRACE PARK

After graduating from West Point, Grace served in the Army as a military intelligence officer. She was deployed to Korea, her parents' homeland. On returning to the States she was promoted to captain and served in a Pentagon think tank. At the completion of Grace's five-year commitment, she joined Bristol-Myers Squibb, where she was selected for the company's fast-track leadership development program. Grace graduated with a dual degree from Harvard Business School and Harvard's Kennedy School of Government. She is currently on a Fulbright fellowship in Singapore, under the mentorship of the permanent secretary to the prime minister.

> "What ties all of my life's pursuits together is a love for challenge and exploration. I consider myself to be a life-long learner. It is when I am in the midst of a challenging new adventure that I learn something deeply meaningful about others and myself."

I was born into an incredibly strong, tight-knit family, which is very important to me. My sister Alice is one year older than me and my brother Thomas is one year younger. My parents emmigrated to the United States in the 1960s and, with humble beginnings, my father became very focused and disciplined in order to succeed. He instilled those same values in his own children. My parents sacrificed much in order to provide their children with the best education possible.

At West Point, I was tested academically, physically, and militarily each and every day. Having the physical stamina to carry a 40-pound rucksack and an M-16 rifle and march 12 miles in three hours, rappel, or parachute was no easy feat. I was given an opportunity to be the first West Point cadet to spend a semester at the French Military Academy. I spent the entire summer prior to going to France training extremely hard because I was nervous about what awaited me across the ocean. In the French Military Academy there were only going to be two other women in my class, and I was aware that the culture was less accepting of women in the military.

The first day at the Academy was really a defining moment. No one could figure out how to treat me. I was a woman, and they wanted to treat me well, but they just weren't all that happy that I was a woman in the military. I knew immediately that I had to prove myself.

They started us out on day one with a 10-kilometer run, and I was able to keep up with the fastest runners. Rather than ending the run right there, everyone was expected to do three sets of 10 pull-ups. I held my own and completed my sets. The male cadets actually started clapping when I finished, applauding me for my accomplishment as a woman. It was really somewhat bizarre. I don't think they had ever seen a woman even do one pull-up in their entire life. And I didn't do the pull-ups in order to draw special attention to myself; instead, I just wanted to show that I was as strong as any other male cadet.

The challenges at West Point, such as leading 120 cadets in the U.S. Army Air Assault School and all 4,000 cadets in the school's athletic program, were daunting at first. Yet with the support of my family, I did not give up. I looked to the inspiring wisdom of individuals like Calvin Coolidge who said,

> "Nothing in the world can take the place of persistence. Talent will not; nothing is more common than unsuccessful men with talent. Genius will not; unrewarded genius is almost a proverb. Education will not; the world is full of educated derelicts. Persistence and determination alone are omnipotent."

Victories such as placing third with All-American honors at the national judo championships all four years, which then led me to train with the national judo team in preparation for the 1996 Olympic judo team trials, are the results of persistence and determination toward reaching my goals. More importantly, I felt that I gained the respect of other cadets by demonstrating that women were capable of meeting the physical demands of the military. Just as many prominent American leaders were graduates of West Point, I was inspired to lead and become a proud member of West Point's long line of graduates.

With the leadership skills gained from West Point, I served in the United States Army as a military intelligence officer. While assigned with the 10th Mountain Division at Fort Drum, New York, I led a 46-soldier general support intelligence and surveillance platoon with ground sensor and radar capabilities along with counterintelligence and interrogation support. As the first female to take the helm of this organization, the majority of whose members were male soldiers with up to 15 years more experience, I periodically reminded myself of an inspiring quote from Eleanor Roosevelt, who said, "No one can make you feel inferior without your consent." My first priority was to build trust. By having compassion for others and pursuing collective goals with integrity, I earned the respect as their trusted leader. Rather than making sweeping changes upon my arrival, I listened to others' ideas. Based on this experience, I discovered that showing care and understanding each person's values are attributes of an effective leader, regardless of gender.

I volunteered to serve in South Korea for my next military assignment, despite the wishes of my commanders at Fort Drum. It was important for me to chart my own course and not to let the limitations or expectations of others confine or define me. With a Korean heritage, it was great to be able to live in Korea for a year to learn more about the country's history and to connect with some of my relatives over there whom I had never met. I learned a lot about the Korean War while I was living there, which was meaningful because both of my parents had lived through the war at a young age and I had the desire to understand the gruesome history, present capabilities, and future possibilities of the two Koreas.

After my yearlong deployment in Korea, I was promoted to captain and served as the most junior officer in a think tank at the Pentagon, where we were tasked to reengineer Army intelligence based on 21st century technology. Besides creating innovative solutions to transform the Army's effectiveness and gain a more strategic outlook, I worked alongside many of the brightest Army generals and colonels, who were brimming with years of accumulated experience and knowledge. Rather than avoiding contact with these rather intimidating and powerful senior Army officers, I persistently sought them out as my mentors. I had often thought that if I were talented, then mentors would come to me. Little did I realize that I must make just as great an effort to facilitate these mentoring relationships, many of which I still keep today.

With five years of service in the Army under my belt, I embarked on a path of fresh challenges in the private sector that would allow me to build on the foundation of my family upbringing and my military experience. Bristol-Myers Squibb, one the world's largest pharmaceutical manufacturers, hired me to take part in an intensive general management grooming program.

After gaining hands-on experience in marketing and sales, I entered Harvard Business School to hone my technical skills in business management. Soon afterward, I decided to pursue a joint degree at Harvard's Kennedy School of Government to develop practical public policy skills. Given the close interrelationship between business and government, gaining both business and government degrees would enable me to maximize my breadth of understanding and effectiveness.

After graduation, I co-founded a fellowship program to develop the next generation of entrepreneurs and venture capitalists in the United Kingdom. By targeting women and minorities in order to create a more competitive pool of applicants and selecting fellows based on merit, I am striving to help others reach their full potential and pursue their passions.

Now, as a Fulbright fellow in Singapore, I am working under the mentorship of the permanent secretary to the prime minister. My research focuses on analyzing leadership through two lenses: fostering creativity through entrepreneurship, as well as engaging the youth in public service leadership. What ties all of my life's pursuits together is a love for challenge and exploration. When I am in the midst of a challenging new adventure, I learn something deeply meaningful about myself and about others.

Nana Adae

After graduating from the United States Naval Academy in Annapolis, Maryland, in 1991, Nana served as an officer in cryptology, working with communications specialists, linguists, and signals analysts as she led one of the largest military communications centers in the western Pacific. Following her tour of duty in Japan, Nana attended the Defense Language Institute in Monterey, California, where she studied Arabic. Her language training prepared her for additional tours of duty in Spain and Greece, leading specialized teams onboard Navy reconnaissance aircraft. She was awarded the NATO Medal and Air Medal while leading her team on missions over the former Republic of Yugoslavia. Leaving the Navy after more than seven years of service, Nana enrolled at Columbia Business School to earn her MBA. Upon graduation, she worked at

Goldman Sachs before moving to Stonewater, a start-up focused on consolidation in the day-spa industry. Nana recently joined Lehman Brothers' Investment Management Division.

> "The military taught me a lot about dealing with change, since I could be in Spain one minute and Greece the next."

I hadn't given much thought to joining the military until a letter from the United States Naval Academy arrived at my house describing the unique experience it had to offer its students. It wasn't like any of the other letters that I had received from colleges, and I was intrigued. Knowing that I wanted to do something different, I began to research the Academy. The school was known for its academic excellence and at the time, I wanted to be an engineer. I was blown away by my first visit there. Watching the students in uniform march in formation and talking to the midshipmen about everyday life was fascinating. Everyone whom I encountered appeared to be doing such extraordinary things and had more exciting postgraduation plans than students at other colleges I had visited.

After my visit to the Academy, I tossed around the option for awhile before finally deciding to apply. As part of the application process, I had to meet one of my state's congressmen to obtain an appointment to the Naval Academy. After I was admitted to the Naval Academy, I started to think of my academic major and had visions of becoming a naval architect or aeronautical engineer. While I knew that my academic strengths lay on the right side of my brain, loving English, poetry, and literature, I challenged myself to study something practical for the military. Nevertheless, my first elective class in English, the interesting coursework, and one professor, in particular, provided me with a refreshing break from the rest of my science and engineering courses at the Academy.

At 17 years old, I was still a kid and had been thrown into a very new experience at the Naval Academy. A lot of it was difficult, and I tried hard not to complain, especially to my parents, during the time allotted each week to call our families. My parents were incredibly supportive. While proud of my choice, they always said I could come home at any time. I was grateful to them for not adding stress to an already stressful situation, like some parents did to their children. I was determined to stick it out and knew I would only leave upon graduation. Not being that athletically inclined, I found it a struggle to awaken each morning at 5:30 for PT (physical training). With all of the challenges, the thing that I relished most about the Academy was the camaraderie. There wasn't any room for pretense in that raw environment, so it was easy to bond and form strong relationships.

After graduation, as a newly minted officer, I went to Japan and became the head of the Communications Department at one of the Navy's cryptology stations. Among the 80 communicators that worked for me, there was an especially senior warrant officer named Randy who had been in the Navy for 27 years. I was 23 years old. I thought that it was going to be great—I had an old, salty dog working for me who would share all of his pearls of wisdom. I was wrong about that and in for a rude awakening. On my first day, Randy took me around to meet all of the people in my department and then brought me into his office and shut the door. He leaned over his desk and said to me, "I don't want you here." I remember thinking that this comment wasn't really about me; Randy had probably just woken up on the wrong side of the bed. Besides, it was my first day, I hadn't been there long enough to do anything wrong; this couldn't be about me. But he continued, "I don't know why the captain keeps filling this billet. They keep bringing in junior officers like you who don't know a thing. I have to train you and you just make messes. I could run this department with one arm tied behind my back. If you just stay out of my way, like the last guy, everything will be fine."

In time, I proved my professionalism and Randy realized that I wasn't there to be a threat to him. I was just there to do my job. We became very good friends. I learned a lot from him and gained confidence in my own ability to overcome obstacles in future endeavors.

After seven and a half years in the military, I realized that I was ready for a change. Business seemed like the next logical step, so I applied to Columbia Business School to receive my MBA. After graduation, I joined the Private Wealth Management Group at Goldman Sachs where I worked for a year before joining Stonewater, a spa company where I focused on strategic development and operations. I have recently joined the Investment Management Division at Lehman Brothers.

Life throws a lot of curveballs, and I've watched some of my best laid plans get thrown by the wayside. Ten years ago, I would have never guessed I'd be here, but it's a good spot to be in nonetheless. While I would like to eventually take a stab at starting a company, writing a book, and having a family, who knows what's in store. The military taught me a lot about dealing with change, since I could be in Spain one minute and Greece the next. I learned that each situation was a finite experience and instead of focusing on future changes, I tried to enjoy the moment that I was living in. Instead of dwelling on how much I missed the life I led at my last duty station or becoming anxious about my next assignment, I had to learn to be present in my current situation. We tend to make life much more stressful than it needs to be by mulling over the past and worrying about the future. Instead, we should try to accept the things that we can't control and revel in the things we can!

SHANNON HUFFMAN

Shannon grew up in Anchorage, Alaska, as the eldest of three children, enjoying swimming, running, debate, and piano. After graduating in 1993 from Duke University, Shannon spent eight years as an Army aviation officer and attack helicopter pilot. In addition to staff positions in personnel, logistics, and intelligence, she held operational positions as an Apache platoon leader of two platoons and company commander in Bosnia and Korea. Shannon then went on to Dartmouth's Tuck School of Business to pursue her MBA, graduating in 2003. After completing a management training rotation at Guidant Corporation, she is currently working as a marketing program manager at Microsoft Corporation.

> "Leadership comes from combining a love for your mission with a love for your people. Real leadership comes from the heart, not from a sense of wanting glory for oneself or even one's company. If you and the people with whom you work are part of something bigger than yourselves, you can strive to understand their values in terms of the mission as well as in terms of each individual. You then inspire them with this understanding of their values as people and professionals. That is leadership."

Apaches sounded like fun: 15,000 pounds of metal capable of flying over 200 miles per hour, highly computerized, and equipped with more firepower than I ever could have imagined. I thought I was unstoppable. Upon graduation from Duke in 1993, I volunteered for active duty in the Army and was in one of the first classes of women allowed to fly combat aircraft. My first assignment was at Fort Bragg, North Carolina, where I was one of 120 pilots in the 229th Aviation Regiment, and the first woman assigned as an attack helicopter pilot in the XVIII Airborne Corps.

While I felt fortunate to have a few supporters, for the first time ever, I was in an environment where some people did not want me to succeed. Some did not believe that I could succeed, and some even wanted me to fail. In all fairness, the 120 guys had done things a certain way for up to 20 years and had done it very well. All of a sudden, a woman showed up, and they were supposed to change. It was difficult for all of us. It wasn't only a gender issue, but an issue of learning the ropes as a new lieutenant with the requisite attempts, successes and failures, and at least as many of the latter as the former. That in and of itself is challenging enough, and the gender issue added a layer of complexity to an already challenging equation.

I was halfway through my first platoon command when I requested a transfer to our sister battalion to take a new flight platoon to Bosnia. At the time, it was a country with nine million unexploded landmines, the simmering anger of masses of people, and the constant threat of hostile fire. We flew daily armed reconnaissance and aerial escort missions over entire towns that had been destroyed in the forested mountains of Bosnia. At one point, I remember seeing a newspaper clipping of an illegal Serbian checkpoint that had been neutralized by the NATO force overflown by Apache gunships. I realized that the article was referring to my wingman and me. We were part of history.

As we departed Bosnia, my back-seater and I were the flight lead for 18 other helicopters. As the front-seater, I was personally responsible for providing all primary navigation and communication across several tense international borders. We flew north into what became a dense fog, requiring an emergency landing prior to reaching our airfield in Hungary. Any misstep would have been catastrophic. The responsibility was breathtaking and fantastic, and the challenges were real. Throughout my experience in the Army, I had to learn to keep my emotions to myself, at times necessitating a sheer act of will.

After returning from Bosnia, I was sent to Korea—first as a logistics officer and then as company commander where I was responsible for eight helicopters as well as the pilots and mechanics. I was the first woman to command a line company of Apaches in the Second Infantry Division. One of the more challenging missions was planning and executing attack aviation support of an air assault, with live artillery rounds hitting north of the landing zone and multiple Black Hawk helicopters flying in proximity to my company. We flew into the dark hills of Korea without lights, risking collision but crucial for mission reality. As a result of the careful planning and skillful execution of my pilots, the mission went like clockwork.

The ribbons and medals in the Army didn't matter after the first one. What did matter were the people I served with, the missions we undertook, and the situations that reinforced our sense of purpose. Returning from a weekend trip to Seoul during my first week in Korea, I was preparing to disembark the train when a tiny elderly woman who didn't stand much higher than my ribcage grabbed my hand tightly and demanded, "You GI, you GI?" Oh no, I thought; now I'm in trouble. You could never be sure which way political currents were running. She held my hand tightly as we got off the train. I said, "Yes, GI." She looked at me with tears in her eyes and said, "Thank you GI, Korean War, thank you GI." I was dumbfounded. Talk about purpose.

After eight years full of adventure, excitement, challenge, and hardship I still feel passionate about having a purpose. It is crucial to live for something outside of yourself, something bigger than yourself, in order for life to be worthwhile—believing in an ideal and striving for that ideal, even when you see yourself and others falling short of it. This is such a simple, yet difficult concept. The challenge is to discover what you truly believe in, what you are truly willing to live for. I believe in the Army, our country, the people I served with, and my duty. This is what made the difference for me between execution of the mission and collapsing under stressful situations—like flying along a hostile border in Korea, knowing that if we strayed off our navigation, we would be shot down. I had to do what I was doing, and moreover, it was an honor to do so.

I have found this to be true in all facets of life and in my professional life beyond the military as well. Finding a sense of purpose in one's professional work as well as in social and volunteer activities, and valuing the people with whom we are fortunate enough to share these endeavors, are the keys to a fulfilling life. I am extremely grateful to have learned this lesson of returning one's blessings, loving those around us, and living life to the fullest from the most important person in my life, my dad, who was the greatest example of all these things I can possibly imagine throughout all of his short but vibrant life. And I am blessed to have connected with these important things through: my work with corporations that are committed to social benefit and change, as well as with 85 Broads; the Seattle Symphony Chorale; overseas missions with University Presbyterian Church and the Agros Foundation in Seattle; and monthly Inner City Outings trips benefiting disadvantaged youth through the Sierra Club. Look for your own way and commit yourself to live your passion!

9

AMBASSADORS

In 2004 I emailed the following "BroadCast" out to all the members of 85 Broads, marveling at how diverse and global our rapidly growing network had become:

WHY WE ROCK!

In just the last month, we have had new members join from Ethiopia, India, Romania, Bulgaria, Russia, Pakistan, China, Vietnam, Turkey, Australia, and South Africa. In a world that feels increasingly "threatened" and "threatening," we have the unique opportunity to help discover what unites rather than divides us through the community of women in our network who are from every corner of the globe.

Equally incredible are the women in our network who are leaving their home countries to go abroad—whether to help small village farmers in Africa, or to assist refugees in Kosovo and Thailand, or to teach Math and English in Nepal, or to venture to remote places on the planet to raise money and awareness for charitable organizations.

One of the most frequently asked questions is whether 85 Broads is just a network for "women in finance." The answer is an emphatic "NO" as our members work for over 500 different companies and choose many different career paths throughout the course of their lives!

Our network is a rich and vibrant "tapestry" of remarkable women. Our members are launching new businesses, collaborating on community projects, and finding new co-mentors and friends. These women have become outstanding role models for other talented, ambitious women around the world.

With the addition of college women from leading undergraduate colleges and universities through our Broad2Be co-mentoring partnership, the 85 Broads network has now become even more global and more diverse in the year since I sent out that email. And as is often the case, many of our youngest and newest members are the ones whose voices are leading us toward a new paradigm of global understanding and community responsibility which transcends cultures, generations, and geographies. These are voices of women who not only are traveling out into the world to define success on their own terms but who are also deeply committed to generating extraordinary returns on their investments in themselves, often by literally returning to their home countries and cultures with the education, experience, and relationship connections to now make a true difference. For the women featured in this chapter, and throughout our network, being an "ambassador" is not a one-way street—it's not about being on a mission to spread a particular world view or a crusade to create change based on a single perspective or on narrowly held beliefs. While being an ambassador often starts with a journey of self-exploration, as we will see in the stories that follow, it really involves traveling beyond yourself, your own views, and your own reality. Connecting and learning how to partner with others —whether through education, business, philanthropy, investing, raising a family, or by any other means—who look, sound, act, and think completely differently than you is the ambassador's passion.

I truly believe that one of the greatest strengths of the 85 Broads network is our diversity—not just in terms of culture or background but also how we think, what we value, and how we envision our futures. And ambassadors, whatever their age or profession or personal profile, understand how to tap into this diversity in ways that strengthen the bonds of community while respecting and even celebrating our dramatic differences. Not all the voices in this chapter, or this book, or our network as a whole sing in unison. They're not even singing the same song in the same key! They define success differently, happiness differently, family values, and aspirations differently. Not all the stories and voices in this book agree with one another on the best path to take, the right way to handle career decisions, the best way to think about blending personal and professional priorities, the ingredients of a truly fulfilled life, etc. Some think they have found answers that work for them, others have found completely different answers, and others are still asking questions. The power of the network and the power of the story are two things that ambassadors really "get." How to be *different but connected at the same time.* How to listen to the stories and understand the unique perspectives of others, but at the same time to take clear action in creating positive change within their own lives, companies, and cultures.

One of my favorite stories about Goldman Sachs is from my very first year at the firm. I was struggling as a new salesperson, trying to learn the business and find new clients. Whenever I was lucky enough to do a trade, usually a tiny little "nothing" trade that didn't make any money for the firm, I would make a copy of the ticket, write across it "I did this trade," and send it up to John Whitehead, then co-chairman of Goldman whose daughter Anne I had gone to college with. John finally called me one day and said, very simply: "Janet, at Goldman Sachs we never say 'I,' we always say 'we.'" Then he hung up the phone. I *never* forgot that.

The power of "we" has always been the foundation of 85 Broads. As the network has grown from 1,000 members in the year 2000 to nearly 3,000 members in 2002, 5,000 members by 2004, and now over 10,000 members before the end of 2005, we all are discovering just how powerful the message of "we always say 'we'" can become. Every single one of our members, in that sense, is an ambassador—a strong, smart individual, an "I" who chooses to speak, see, and live as a "we." It's not surprising that John Whitehead is a hero and true champion for many of us in 85 Broads—and not just because of the Goldman Sachs connection or John's strong support of our network since the very beginning. It was under John's leadership, in partnership with his co-chairman John Weinberg, that Goldman became a truly global investment bank in the 1980s. And after "retiring," John went on to serve as Undersecretary of State, to serve on the boards of numerous philanthropic and international humanitarian organizations, and most recently—at 84 years young—to serve as the chairman of the Lower Manhattan Development Corporation, helping New York to rebuild and renew itself after 9/11. John has lived his life as a true ambassador, combining understanding with action to help make his "home" a better place by making the world a better place. He is a great role model for all of the ambassadors in our network and a great reminder to always say "WE."

SIMI SANNI NWOGUGU

Simi was born in Nigeria, where she lived until she moved to the United States to attend Mount Holyoke College. She worked in investment banking at Goldman Sachs in New York before returning to Nigeria to begin Junior Achievement Nigeria, a youth program partnering business with education in over 110 countries worldwide. Simi obtained her MBA from Harvard Business School and is currently the director of business development and strategy at Nickelodeon.

> "I genuinely believe that a nation's development begins with women's development. To raise girls to be leaders, you have to show them what it takes to be leaders."

After two years of working in investment banking for Goldman Sachs in New York, I made a trip back home to Nigeria. The trip was a turning point in my career as I decided to quit my job in banking and return to my home to help revitalize its economy. Nigeria had been through two decades of military dictatorship that plunged the country into devastating poverty and corruption. Most people were disillusioned about the state of their future, especially the youth, as the school system had collapsed. The young adults were graduating from secondary schools and universities without the requisite skills and knowledge for survival in the real world. I saw this as an opportunity to return to my home country and contribute toward its redevelopment.

Having been a volunteer for Junior Achievement while living in New York, I knew that introducing its economic educational programming to the young people of Nigeria would be the ideal way to begin rebuilding the country's economy. Educating the youth on the environment, social issues, and the global economy would help to shape and inspire Nigeria's future business leaders. I decided to start Junior Achievement Nigeria (JAN) in 1999, believing that the programs would serve as essential and practical real-world supplements to what the students were learning in schools.

At the time, most of the nonprofit organizations in Nigeria were funded by the government or international charities and riddled with corruption and mismanagement. My idea was to merge private sector funding with the governance of JAN to maximize efficiencies and operate a successful organization in a developing country. It was a challenge to get the buy-in of the private sector, as they were typically wary of corrupt nonprofits. I was grateful that my background at Goldman Sachs and the development of a comprehensive business plan gave investors enough confidence to allow the organization to succeed.

In 1999, JAN became the first Nigerian nonprofit organization to be fully funded and governed by the private sector. I was able to convince several major donors and corporate leaders to be on the fledgling organization's board after giving a speech at a luncheon hosted by the U.S. Ambassador in Lagos. Through an aggressive and relentless marketing campaign, we were able to get 12 of the nation's leading businesses to join our board of directors. We were the first nonprofit organization to publish an annual report accounting for every single donation that we received. This accomplishment went a long way toward helping us to garner the necessary trust and funds that we would need to expand. By the time I left Nigeria in 2002, JAN had programs running in four major cities and had reached out to more than 15,000 students from over 50 schools.

After running the organization for three years, I left to obtain my MBA at Harvard Business School. I still sit on JAN's board of directors, and I'm proud to say that the organization has gone from strength to strength since I left. In July 2005, JA Nigeria won the Fuqua Global Excellence Award presented to the member nation that best demonstrates excellence in all operations.

I am now married to my best friend Obi Nwogugu. We have a one-year-old son, Emeka, and are expecting our second child in April. I am currently working as a director in the business development and strategy group at Nickelodeon, the leading network for children, where I combine my business skills with the joy of inspiring children through entertainment. My goal is to help expand MTV Networks in Africa. I believe that its youth need a forum in which they can discover and express themselves and communicate across cultures. I also have decided to finish a novel I started in college about three young Nigerian women, which I hope to publish in both the United States and Nigeria. It is my dream to continue inspiring Nigerian youth so they can reach their full potential.

JUNKO YODA

Junko enrolled in the MBA program at Columbia Business School and received her degree in 1984. The following year she was hired by Goldman Sachs and moved back to Japan to work in Goldman's Fixed

Income Division. Junko joined Deutsche Bank in 1996, first in money market trading and fixed income portfolio management, and later as regional treasurer in the Singapore office for fixed income portfolios. She is currently located between Australia, the United States, and Japan, where she is managing investments.

"Remember to take a few quiet moments to think."

When my father decided to send me to an international school instead of a traditional Japanese school, he was opening the first of many doors for me. He was ahead of his time, believing that his daughters should grow up to be independent. This was Japan in the early 1960s, and local officials would come by the house and question my father, reminding him that to get a good job in Japan a child had to attend an accredited Japanese school all the way from kindergarten. I started international school without a word of English. I ended up going to Sacred Heart University in Tokyo, the same university that the Empress graduated from. I studied African literature.

My father's decision to send me to the international school not only gave me a good education, but it gave me a global perspective, free of the limits of traditional Japanese culture. This new perspective included exciting new roles for women in society, particularly in the workforce. The many friends I made from all over the world greatly enriched my high school experience, giving me a feeling of world citizenship and opening more doors to possible careers and places to live.

Some of my American friends suggested that I get into business. I entered the field of advertising, selling American products in the Japanese market. My "value added" was my language ability, but I could also understand the cultural nuances and various factors that would predict the success of products in the Japanese market. When Procter & Gamble introduced paper diapers in Japan, I knew that they would not be easily received. Research showed that Japanese women demonstrated their love for their children by working hard as mothers (including washing cloth diapers by hands). They were not looking for ways to make their lives easier. It would be very difficult to try to change their opinions via advertising. In addition, Japanese competitors made really good consumer products. So I began searching for a U.S.-based product that I could really believe in. That's when I got into finance.

I thought that my path should be to get into investment banking. I got into Columbia Business School in 1982 during a big recession with high unemployment. Upon graduation, the only people obtaining investment banking jobs were those who had already completed analyst programs. As I searched for opportunities, I noticed an ad for a summer intern in the Japanese fixed income business. I interviewed and got a summer job at Goldman Sachs, which at the time had only 5,000 employees. It was great work experience. With that background, I got offers from everywhere. I had the opportunity to stay in New York or go back to Japan. Thinking that the Japanese market would take off, I chose to return to Japan in 1985 to be part of the GS fixed income team. I became the rookie again. All the experienced guys took the great clients, and I got what was left. But that was the rest of Asia, which was huge! Eventually I hired male colleagues who had experience in financial institutions in Japan, and I ended up heading the sales group that covered financial institutional sales.

During this time, there were many funny stories. I was one of the female pioneers, even by Wall Street standards. In Asia, it is critical to have a good relationship with your colleagues and clients. I had to go to hostess bars. I had to learn to play golf. And I had to learn very quickly. We were going out with colleagues and clients every night. Plus in Asia, we had to be awake when the market traded in the United States, so I would pull two all-nighters a week.

In 1994, the bond market crashed and there was a lot of restructuring that had to be done. By then, I was a senior member of the Goldman office. We felt that things were changing—that the culture was changing. I was recruited to Deutsche Bank where I did fixed income portfolio management and asset liability. After the Asia crash, Deutsche Bank asked me to move to Singapore to become regional treasurer for fixed income portfolios. Talk about cultural diversity! I was responsible for 14 countries, from New Zealand all the way to Pakistan.

We survived the Indonesian crisis, the riots, and the killing of ethnic Chinese, though our staff was caught in the midst of that crisis. When Pakistan couldn't repay the money they owed due to capital restrictions, we held emergency asset liability meetings, and I was in the difficult position of being the tough old treasurer from the head office debating with the local staff for hours over decisions on rates and restructuring.

After 20 years, having met all of my goals in investment banking and having worked a few years managing alternative assets in Hong Kong, I moved on. I am currently managing investments and living between Tokyo, Sydney, and Honolulu. I am a forward-looking person, seeing my life as a progression and as a series of opportunities.

Being part of a network like 85 Broads that helps to reverse the "old boys club" mentality on Wall Street and elsewhere, and that supports women in helping other women, is really important. If I were to give advice to a woman who was going to Wall Street today, the most important thing would be to keep your financial goals in sight. Another is to plan ahead—at least three years ahead—always having a clear picture of what you want to steer yourself toward. I always take some risks, either with starting a small business or focusing on something that needs to be fixed.

And on a very personal note, remember to take a few quiet moments to think. Otherwise, you'll look up and 20 years will have gone by!

NOOR SWEID

At a very early age, Noor was routed off the traditional path of an Arab woman by being given the opportunity to live and travel all around the world. She was born in Boston, moved to Spain at age two, to London at three and a half, to Saudi Arabia eight years later, and then on to Dubai. She came full circle, receiving her BA in finance and economics from Boston College, and spending two years at Accenture doing strategy consulting. In June 2005, Noor received her MBA from MIT's Sloan School of Management.

> "I believe that education teaches you that it is possible to modernize without becoming Westernized, and that they are not one and the same. It is important for countries undergoing modernization to realize that it is still possible, and imperative, to keep their culture and traditions while they do this."

This past year MIT hosted the Dubai Entrepreneurship Conference, and I organized a trip for 35 of my fellow classmates to attend the conference and explore Dubai and the region. I received incredible feedback from the group and as a testament to their marvels, five Sloan classmates, all of non-Arab origins, are currently seeking internships in Dubai and about ten others are hoping to move there on a more permanent basis. Introducing my peers to the city's companies and culture has been one of my greatest personal accomplishments, and it was this trip that became the clincher for me in deciding that I would return to Dubai after graduation.

During the summer of 2004, I worked at the Dubai International Financial Centre. The premise of the DIFC is to fill the "financial center" and time zone gap between London and Hong Kong, creating a link so the world's markets can be truly open 24/7. The Dubai International Financial Exchange, a 110-acre complex, opened in September 2005 with the goal of becoming the "Wall Street of the Middle East." The Center is conceptually a "city within a city" and intends to attract foreign firms such as Goldman Sachs, CSFB, and Morgan Stanley. These international companies, building awareness among their regional offices and geared toward hiring locals and foreign qualified locals, are making the Center an incredible opportunity for young professionals of Arab descent, such as myself. It is a way for us to explore career opportunities in a location that offers a competitive advantage that we wouldn't realize in other parts of the world. I am convinced that over there I will start off with an edge that I wouldn't have in the States, where, as a foreigner, it will always be more difficult for me professionally.

It will be optimal for me to return to Dubai professionally not only because the economy is booming but also because my parents are settled there and I will have the chance to be close to them. My family has always been important to me and a source of stability in my life. The Arab culture preaches and practices high family and social values and maintains its traditions in our everyday life. When I went to the United States to study and work, the lack of these values and traditions was what I found hardest to adjust to. The culture shock that I experienced when studying, and continued to experience while working, was based on the lack of family orientation and traditional values and practices in comparison to the Arab world. Living in the States made me increasingly appreciative of the positive values in Arab society and helped me recognize the beauty of its life and culture. This part of life is what I miss most from home, and it is an important force in drawing me back to the region.

I recently had lunch with a role model of mine in Dubai, who shares my passion for empowering women. She discussed the conundrum that women in the Arab society face as they are allowed to obtain a formal education and are then not expected to work after receiving it. Men frequently tell her that they love the work she does but they would never let their own daughters do it. We need to convince the Arab society that women should work not only for monetary benefit but because it improves their self-esteem and mental development. It is also crucial to empower women and help them advance their independence by teaching them how to manage their finances. It has proved challenging to convince the Arab society of this because, as all societies do, they resist change. Additionally, they see female independence as a potential "Western influence" and do not wish to adopt it. I believe that education teaches you that it is possible to modernize without becoming Westernized and that they are not one and the same. It is important for countries undergoing modernization to realize that it is possible, and imperative, to keep their culture and traditions while they do this.

Queen Noor of Jordan is another role model of mine and of many other Arab women. She manages to preserve her culture and family values while living outside of the typical role defined for a woman. I personally believe that you cannot simultaneously have a full-time career and have a family while being successful at both. My personal views are very traditional and I believe that a woman's primary duty should always be to her family and that to do anything in life well (including raising a family), full attention and commitment are required. As such, I would ideally like to work full time for five or six years after obtaining my MBA and then shift my attention to having a family, while eventually also working part time. I would ultimately like to use my foreign education to do charity work in Dubai, teaching older women who haven't had a formal education, or teaching at an all-women's university as a way to give back to my community. I don't think it matters what I do, as long as I use my education and experience to empower women and give back to the region. Essentially, I think I am an example of a woman who has advanced and progressed academically and professionally without losing her roots, beliefs, or culture, and I want to show other women that this is possible—that the two are not mutually exclusive.

Arlette Vargas

Arlette grew up in Tijuana, Mexico, and completed her undergraduate studies at Georgetown University. She went to Goldman Sachs for three years and then accepted a full scholarship to receive her MBA at NYU Stern School of Business, graduating in 2004. Arlette is currently working at Lehman Brothers' London office in international fixed income sales.

"One of the best ways to promote growth in a country is through education."

When I arrived at Georgetown, I was interested in international relations and marketing. I didn't know a thing about finance, but I got my first glimpse into the financial markets through a required core class on corporate finance.

At the time, Russia and East Asia were experiencing a deep economic crisis that in many ways paralleled the Tequila crisis in Mexico, which I had felt first-hand in 1995. The resulting peso devaluation drastically reduced my family's finances and nearly jeopardized my ability to attend Georgetown. The peso devaluation really sparked my fascination with the mechanics of financial markets, their movements, and how systematic risk can create turmoil in a local economy while also having a profound ripple effect throughout the world.

While at Georgetown, I interned at the Organization of American States, where I worked on socioeconomic development issues in the Office of Cultural Development. The experience was invaluable and taught me that nonprofit organizations and NGOs were not the only avenues available to accomplish real change—it could be done through the private sector as well. I also had the opportunity to survey the World Bank and USAID in a thesis I wrote about microfinance for women in Latin America. This work exposed me to a range of methodologies for creating long-term wealth in communities. It also helped me formulate a plan: go to Wall Street on the "fast track" to learn and work on these issues, gain credibility, and use my knowledge and expertise to structure financial instruments that directly enhance economic development.

After completing my undergraduate studies at Georgetown University with a triple major in finance, marketing, and international business, I had a wonderful learning experience at Goldman Sachs in Debt Capital Markets. My work focused on financial advisory services and debt financing for emerging markets, in particular for Latin American corporate and governmental entities. After three years at Goldman, I accepted a full merit scholarship to attend the NYU Stern School of Business. Upon completing my MBA in the spring of 2004, I joined Lehman Brothers' international fixed income sales team in London.

Through my work with NGOs and at Goldman Sachs, I learned that the best way to promote growth in a country is through a long-term commitment and investment in education. Though the returns on these types of investments are hard to quantify in the short term, I firmly believe that education is a rewarding investment that must be the cornerstone for fundamental economic and social gain. The commitment and resources and ultimate financial implications are not only justified, but essential for healthy long-term growth.

This idea resonates strongly with me on a personal level as I challenge myself to be an ambassador for my country, my family, and my culture. And while I'm not given to trite sayings, the "think globally, act locally" maxim has inherent value for me. I work hard to stay involved in my local community. Currently, I am aiming to team up with other women in the finance industry to find new ways to assist the underserved elderly community. Most recently, when I was living in Kensington, I was a member of the Kensington Green Garden Committee, which spearheads the landscaping, environmental, and construction decisions for the community.

I also try to be involved with projects that benefit Mexican communities, because my homeland is always close to my heart. While at Georgetown, I was named by the Mexican Embassy's cultural attaché as the representative for Mexican youth in Washington, D.C. I have recently teamed up with my family to donate land and build an orphanage in Tijuana. I have also been invited to be an external advisor to the Municipal Finance and Planning Committee for the city of Tijuana, reporting to the city's mayor.

At Lehman Brothers I am now challenged to think on a macro level and am fortunate to have the opportunity to infuse passion into my involvement in the international capital markets. Sounds simple, but I feel so lucky to be able to do so.

I credit my parents—my generous and wise mother and my entrepreneurial father—who both taught me early on that "the sun shines for everyone." It was from my parents that I learned to push myself and be happy for others' success.

Ana Veruna Stanescu

Ana grew up in Romania and studied travel, tourism, and international management at the University of New Mexico, graduating in 2000. For the next two years, she was an executive team leader for Target Stores and also became a co-captain of the United Way Campaign. Hired by Goldman Sachs in 2003, Ana is currently a technical specialist at their Salt Lake City office, working closely with private wealth management operations to facilitate and support key initiatives. She also is currently pursuing her MBA at the University of Utah.

> "I'd like to make an impact. I'd like to help people understand that an open mind is a better mind."

It was January 1986. The line of people was moving slowly, cold and with hung shoulders, each was inching toward the countertop, holding a stub in her hand. The little girl, now seven, was also holding a stub. Curious, she was glancing at her fellow butter-shoppers—250 grams of butter each per stub, nothing more. "Mother, is this the crisis?"

I was born in Sibiu, in the middle of Transylvania, Romania. I grew up in a country characterized by corruption and a broken economy, and I am now working for Goldman Sachs in the United States. How can two countries be so different economically and politically? I went to work for Goldman Sachs because of its global position and because of its success at home as well as abroad. Even my parents, who are artists in Romania, have heard of them. This firm has been able to adapt its practices to foreign operations and create a leadership position in these markets.

My parents helped me immensely to get here. My mother is a curator in a museum and my father is a painter. It's hard enough to be an artist in the United States, but can you imagine what's it's like to be an artist in Romania? People in communist countries didn't have enough income to buy art. Having watched their struggle to follow their passion and live their lives as artists, I have the utmost respect and admiration for them. Their struggle inspired me to follow my dream, to study abroad.

One day, there was an announcement in the local Romanian newspaper. George Soros had set up the "Open Society Institute," and there were scholarships available to study in the United States or the United Kingdom. I had always dreamed about coming to the United States because there is so much access here—to information, to education, and to work. Granted, much of what I learned about the United States came from watching rerun episodes of *Dallas* or *90210* on TV, but still I wanted to come here. My mother urged me to apply for the Soros scholarship, so I started the application process, which consisted of a written portion and some high-level tests. I had to travel four hours away from where I lived, to Bucharest, to take the testing. There were 3,000 applicants for three scholarships in the United States. When I first got the letter, I didn't even open it because I didn't think I would get it. What my acceptance meant in terms of potential didn't hit me until I was on the plane flying to America. I was 16 and was embarking on the biggest adventure of my life! Open Society put me in touch with the Rotary Club, who helped place me with a host family. I had no choice over where I ended up and was surprised, and delighted, to be sent to New Mexico. I had only heard of Santa Fe because my parents knew of its art connection. I ended up in a town of 14,000 people. I come from a Romanian town of 250,000 people. So, it was quite an adjustment and not what I expected. I couldn't have done it without my host parents. I had been taught British English so I couldn't pick up on the slang. But I was very good at math and science. I tested out of my junior year of high school, so I went straight into my senior year and graduated at 17.

While all my friends were going to college career fairs, I thought that I would be going back to Romania. I asked my parents if I should come home to Romania and finish high school or go to college in the States. *That* was an interesting conversation! I decided to attend the University of New Mexico because they have a major in management of travel and tourism. I thought that I could combine my love of people with an industry that could blossom in Romania. If not Romania, then certainly I could work in the hospitality industry in Europe. After doing an internship, I found that the travel industry was not the place for me.

But I wanted to learn more about Europe. In 1999, I went on a semester abroad program to France. My roommate was Lebanese and lived in the United States. How ironic. The two of us, nonnatives, were representing the U.S. schools. When I finished, I spent my last months backpacking around Europe. Living in hostels or on people's couches, it was all a very eye-opening experience. I returned in 2000, and right after graduation I was recruited by Target Stores—a very hip, ambitious, and marketing-centric company. I was thrilled to be a part of their marketing program and to manage a store. Fresh from school, I showed up my first day on the job and learned that I would have to manage eight older men who were much more experienced than I was. That's a very interesting situation for someone young and foreign. Although I was thrilled with Target's corporate communications and marketing expertise, I became disenchanted with the career path—manage a store, manage a region. I would be just enforcing the corporate rules in each store, rather than making the rules. I considered a job at their headquarters but didn't have the necessary experience.

So, I decided to pursue an MBA at the University of New Mexico. In spring 2003 Goldman Sachs came to campus for the first time to recruit for their summer internship program. The campus recruitment officer forwarded my résumé to Goldman Sachs, and I was called for an interview. I wasn't sure it was the right thing for me, but I was impressed that Goldman was open to hiring people who didn't have a finance background. Instead, they looked for a certain skill set and attitude. I came to Goldman to work for the summer and never left! I had landed in a private wealth management team, and by the end of the summer, I was happy with my career path. Surprisingly, Goldman offered me a full-time position. Given the prestige of the job and the state of the economy, I decided to take advantage of the position right in front of me. I put my MBA on hold and began working full time.

After being at Goldman for a year, I started my professional MBA program at the University of Utah. I debated whether I should do it now or wait to get more work experience. But having learned that many things come up in one year, I decided that this was the time to work hard and finish it. I see some of my friends in school who have a family and I can't understand how they can do both.

There are a few possible career areas that I am toying with for when I complete my MBA. One is the financial fraud area, having been hit by it myself. Credit here is so important—it is precious and it is your own identity—and I like the idea of outsmarting the bad guys. I'd also like to make a difference in the world through my job. Another area that I'm interested in is diversity because as a Romanian living and working in the United States, I've had to adapt. I've met people from all over the world and realize the differences and similarities that we all have. I think that diversity is one of the most important corporate issues for the 21st century, and I would love to be part of shaping corporate responses to what is a very large challenge and at the same time a very exciting opportunity.

ERIN KEOWN GANJU

Erin spent her high school years living in both the United States and Asia. In 1992, she completed a five-year bachelor/master's combined program at Johns Hopkins University School of Advanced International Studies. After working for Goldman Sachs in Hong Kong and for Unilever in Vietnam, Erin followed her passion—transforming her volunteer work into a professional career. She joined Room to Read in 2001, where she is now chief operating officer for an organization which provides resources to help educate underprivileged children around the world.

> "We see ourselves as the venture capitalists of the non-profit world. We take a limited amount of capital and are able to create great change with it."

Halfway around the world, Bala Krishna Shresta is finishing his workday. He is headmaster of Pashpupati Kanya High School, a 600-student, all-girls' school in a bustling mountain village called Charikot in northeastern Nepal. The school is on a long slope of land, in the lap of one of the highest mountains in the Himalayas. Today, like many other school days during the past year, a handful of students arrive a good half hour before school starts. They come for the books, says Shresta, whose teaching career spans more than half his life. There is no public library. Our little room of books is the only place where students can go to broaden their knowledge. They are very curious, and they like the colorful pictures in the books. They have never seen anything like this.

And so began one of Room to Read's many projects. Room to Read is an organization that provides underprivileged children with the opportunity to gain the lifelong gift of education. Room to Read began with its first book donation in 1998 and was founded on the belief that education is the key to breaking the cycle of poverty and taking control of one's life.

After earning my MA, I went to work in the for-profit world for 10 years. I had lived in Hong Kong while in the 10th grade and in Taiwan while in college, so it seemed like a good idea to return to Hong Kong while working for Goldman Sachs. Eventually, I moved to Vietnam to work for Unilever. It was there that I realized my life's calling. My passion was my volunteer work. While in Vietnam, I had volunteered to teach English in a secondary school and was touched by the students' great desire to learn. At the same time I was concerned about the lack of educational materials and poor educational facilities they had. With Unilever's corporate support, I helped build a kindergarten and saw what a difference it could make for a community. As I traveled all over Asia doing business deals, I always wanted to do more for the kids. They were truly the future of these countries.

I must admit that I was afraid to pursue a nonprofit opportunity full time because I felt that nonprofit organizations might not be efficient or fast-paced enough for me, given what I was used to. That all changed when, through a mutual friend, I was introduced to John Wood, the founder of Room to Read. John is a former Microsoft executive who found his calling to the nonprofit world during a trek through the Himalayas in 1998. During his climb, he met a local schoolteacher who invited him to visit the school. There he found enthusiastic schoolteachers but a total lack of resources. The library had only 20 books, which were locked up in case someone might damage them. They weren't children's books anyway. He knew, at that point, that he could really have an impact on the lives of these children. When he reached a cybercafe in Katmandu, he sent an email to 100 friends, asking them to send books to his parents' house in Colorado. In the first month, they received 3,000 books. The success of the idea, combined with John's business training at Microsoft, helped us put together a new vision of how a nonprofit could be well managed. It could be results oriented, maintain a low overhead, and have strong project management by local citizens, who obviously want the best possible project outcome.

Using the educational model developed in Nepal by John and Dinesh, the Room to Read country manager in Nepal, I worked with my friend Nam to create Room to Read Vietnam as a volunteer project in 2001. Soon after, John convinced me to join him full-time to build Room to Read into a world-class nonprofit focused on international education. I became their first U.S. paid staff member in 2002. My friend Nam became the country manager of Room to Read Vietnam. We expanded into Cambodia in 2002, India in 2003, and Sri Lanka and Laos in 2005. My job as chief operating officer is to oversee all our programs around the world. My great pleasure is in figuring out how to spend our resources efficiently in each country, to constantly improve our work, and to monitor and evaluate our success.

My past corporate career in investment banking and business development prepared me for this work in several ways. I learned about the importance of a strong management team; how to globally coordinate offices and work on cross-cultural teams; how to operate on a thin budget and manage fast-paced growth; the importance of treating our customers/clients (essentially our beneficiaries and donors in the nonprofit case) as stakeholders in our work and listening to their input; and ensuring that all employees (or in our case now, our volunteers too) are motivated, well trained, and feel they are accountable and part of the team.

I no longer wonder if I am in the right job, as I did when I worked in the corporate world. I know that I am now doing what I love and am passionate about. Yesterday, I spent the day with some of the scholarship girls in Can Gio, Vietnam. One of the girls has polio, probably caused by Agent Orange left over from the war. Room to Read has put her on a long-term scholarship for only $250 a year that pays for her school fees, textbooks, uniform, and medical insurance. We even bought the first wheelchair she has ever had. When she and her mother smiled at me and told me how much they appreciated the help, I was determined to work even harder in helping to provide more children with educational opportunities in the developing world, where the help is so badly needed.

This desperate lack of resources has led us to develop a unique three-pronged approach to tackling the challenge of education in these countries: (1) partnering with villages to build schools; (2) establishing libraries and filling them with books and computers; and (3) providing scholarships for underprivileged girls. Grants and contributions have allowed Room to Read to expand its operations and programs into new countries. It takes

$9,000–$15,000 of outside contributions to build a school in the partner countries where Room to Read operates. This amount is surprisingly little for a successful American executive but an unimaginable fortune for a typical villager in Nepal, who survives on less than $1 a day. This is the beauty of Room to Read's unique formula. It challenges villages to contribute a significant portion of the project, sometimes up to 50 percent, through the donation of land, volunteer labor, materials, and cash before work begins on a project. In many cases, the process of meeting the "challenge grant" takes longer than the process of building the school. But Room to Read believes that it's worth the wait. The projects are about ownership. Challenge grants are as much about creating an educational infrastructure as they are about initiating social change. Room to Read is a dynamic, results-oriented organization. Since our inception as a nonprofit entity in 2000, we have touched the lives of over 800,000 children by building 200 schools, establishing over 2,300 libraries, publishing over 70 new local language children's book titles, donating more than one million books, establishing over 75 computer and language labs, and funding over 1,700 long-term girls' scholarships.

Several 85 Broads members have donated to Room to Read by supporting a girl's scholarship; by contributing money themselves to build a school; by doing fund-raising for us, as Alison Levine did with her climb; or by volunteering to teach English in one of our schools, as Kate Reid did. The 85 Broads organization has been a tremendous help by funding several key projects in the Dhading district of Nepal.

Many people ask why we are focusing on helping children outside of the United States. Our reasons are twofold: First, a dollar goes a long way in a country like Nepal. Second, we believe that it's in our collective self-interest to invest in education abroad. What do people in these countries know about Americans? They see our military bases, our TV shows such as *Baywatch*, and our products in their supermarkets. But what tells them that Americans are kind and generous people? If we help them build schools and libraries, we believe that the children in Asia will grow up viewing the United States in a much more positive light. This, we hope, will pave a path for better understanding, a path toward world peace.

RAMATOULAYE DIALLO

Rama left her home country of Senegal to complete her high school studies in New Mexico as part of the United World College program.

During her sophomore year at Bryn Mawr, she traveled on a peace mission trip to South Africa, an experience that had a tremendous impact on her thoughts and on her future. After graduating from Bryn Mawr, Rama began working for Morgan Stanley and eventually earned an MBA from Harvard Business School. She has moved back to Africa as head of Endeavor South Africa, a nonprofit organization that supports and accelerates entrepreneurial activities in developing nations.

"I realized that Africa was where the need was greatest and my contributions would have maximum impact."

In my junior year at Bryn Mawr, I headed up the African student organization. We weren't a large group, but we were very strong. We sponsored and organized cultural activities to introduce African culture to our fellow students. Interest grew over time, and I am so proud that we were able to share aspects of our culture with other students. During my four years, I had to work at a variety of jobs because I was financially responsible for myself. I was a waitress, a receptionist, and a bartender. I washed dishes and taught French, statistics, and algebra. Whenever I felt frustrated or felt like complaining, I remembered that many of the people who I worked with did this type of work full time. For me, this was just temporary until I finished school. Those work experiences gave me a lot of humility and perspective.

During the summers, I sought to strengthen my education by studying abroad and taking on internships. I studied Spanish in Madrid for a few months with a scholarship from the Economics and Spanish departments. Prior to entering my senior year, I obtained an internship on Wall Street through an organization named Sponsors for Educational Opportunity. That summer was a "baptism by fire" introduction to the professional world. I learned a lot but also got to discover New York City for the first time.

As a sophomore in college, I was selected to be one of Bryn Mawr's representatives on the peace studies mission. Three colleges—Bryn Mawr, Haverford, and Swarthmore—organized the mission annually to visit a different part of the world that had experienced conflict. That year, we studied South Africa, a nation struggling to define its postapartheid history. Our group of twelve students and three professors visited Johannesburg, Capetown, and other cities, where we met and interviewed people from all walks of life. In South Africa, I witnessed not only the horrible legacy of apartheid, but also the hope in the eyes of my generation. I was deeply touched and shaken by the experience. Prior to that, I was ambitious but did not know how to focus my ambitions. From this experience, I realized that Africa was where the need was greatest and my contributions would have maximum impact.

In South Africa, I witnessed contrasts that made me question whether I was in the same country. One morning, I visited shantytowns with neither running water nor a sewage system. At lunchtime, I dined with members of parliament in their opulent chambers under the portraits of previous apartheid leaders. I also met students and activists who were committed to do their part to rebuild the nation. While newspapers abroad crafted headlines on crime rates, the young people I saw went about crafting a better life. They inspired me to put my skills toward endeavors that would empower Africans to build a life on their own strength and resources. For me, that journey culminated in greater clarity and direction in life: a resolution to trace my professional path back to Africa was born. Today I have started on that path. But it was not a straight progression.

When I graduated in 1998, I went back to Wall Street into the investment banking analyst program at Morgan Stanley, where I learned that experience in life comes from your actual work and, more importantly, from the people you meet. Mentors and some really great colleagues made a huge difference in my experience as an analyst. After two years, most analysts move on to another position either inside or outside the firm.

I was about to board the plane, moving to Morgan Stanley's São Paulo office and another step in my international career, when I attended the Africa Business Conference at Harvard Business School. One of the speakers was a director at a newly formed private equity fund focused on investing in Africa. At the end of her speech, I wrestled my way over to her and managed to get her business card. I sent her my résumé the very next day, and I was on my way to Washington, D.C., a few months later. I joined the fund as an investment officer within the team responsible for investing $400 million in the African continent. The fund offered a rare opportunity to combine my interest in finance and African business. It was a new institution vying to provide equity capital to African businesses using rigorous financial analysis. It was neither charity nor foreign aid. The fund planned to be profitable, yet at the same time finance much-needed infrastructure throughout Africa. There was an ideological fit, and I had the skills to make a meaningful contribution to the organization.

I worked in small teams of 2 to 3 people. The fund overall had about 12 people. I stayed for two years and traveled across the continent evaluating businesses and working with entrepreneurs in a variety of industries. Again, I was lucky to have terrific mentors who encouraged me to think about what

I wanted to do long term. I knew that I wanted to go to business school at some point, and I knew that I wanted to broaden my options.

I ended up going to Harvard Business School, which turned out to be a wonderfully affirming experience. From a career perspective, HBS inspires students to find exciting, high-impact work and to strive for the next level. The business school experience opens students up to many new career options that they may never have considered.

If you had asked me a few years ago if I would be running a nonprofit today, I would have said, "no way." However, I am now heading up Endeavor South Africa—an organization that aims to be the leading nonprofit supporter and accelerator of entrepreneurial activities in developing countries. We believe that entrepreneurship and new ventures are the key drivers behind economic growth and innovation. This organization has had enormous success in Latin America, and we plan to replicate the model in Africa.

The road to getting this job was very bumpy. So many people recited for me the obstacles to getting here: I was possibly too young-looking; I wasn't from South Africa, etc. But I was so passionate and proactive that I networked my way into this position. And I know that we will be successful here. We have the right board of directors and many supporters. We are all motivated to make a difference. It's my dream job coming out of HBS because I get to put all the skills that I acquired before and during business school into action. My advice to everyone is to always pursue opportunities that excite you, as they will lead you to many more opportunities. But remember that the world is tiny, so when you undertake something, do it well, because you will run into the people you work with again. I'm glad that I never dismissed anyone because they didn't have an immediate impact on my career. You will meet so many people who are willing to help you. Just be open to them and remember to give a helping hand to others along the way.

VICTORIA LEGGE-BOURKE

Victoria was born and raised in England and educated at Oxford University. She began her career as the social attaché for the British ambassador in Washington, D.C., and then moved to become the director of junior tourism, running English language courses for foreign students. She then worked at a well-respected public relations company running one-off events such as product launches, royal visits, and other political events. Later she became the protocol officer

*for the American Embassy in London and is now working as the
director of cultural and social affairs at Goldman Sachs. Victoria's
series of talks, "Torie's Tips," teaches skills in networking and
manners designed to help decrease social anxieties in the workplace
and other social settings. Victoria has also served as a part-time lady-
in-waiting to HRH the Princess Royal for the past 30 years.*

> "Growing up as the daughter of a politician, I learned at
> an early age how crucial it was to have respect for and
> to get along with all sorts of people. We needed their
> votes! I was brought up to find common threads that
> interlace people across countries, cultures, and customs
> and to put myself in their shoes in order to make those
> connections. It all just became second nature to me."

I did not set out in life to travel down any specific career track. Instead, I
spent my time honing my social and professional skills, having faith that others
would recognize my value. The practice worked out in my favor, having been
offered positions to become everything from the social attaché at the British
Embassy in Washington, D.C., where I began my career, to becoming the director of cultural and social affairs at Goldman Sachs, where I am currently.

Having the good fortune to be born a gregarious person, these jobs have
all come seemingly naturally to me. I love meeting new people and have
found myself interacting with them on all levels in my professional career
and in my social life outside. I have friends in all corners of the globe and
from all different walks of life, representing the wide diversity of experiences
that I have had in both my personal and professional lives. I like to see myself
as a conduit for aligning individuals with similar interests but sometimes of
disparate backgrounds, who otherwise might never have met but who are
potentially useful to one another.

Young people these days often seem overawed when thrown into unfamiliar social settings, not having had adequate training on how to handle
themselves socially. My answer has been to invent a series of talks called
"Torie's Tips" which help those less confident by giving them a set of rules
on networking, appearance, handshakes, conversation, eye contact, language of emails, and so forth; essentially, the talks cover what is appropriate behavior and what is not. I have found an eager audience both inside
and outside of Goldman Sachs. Everyone from women's groups to new and
lateral hires finds that these tips help to relieve their anxiety about the

unwritten rules of networking and operating socially inside and outside of an organization.

With the speed at which business is conducted today, it is not surprising that the importance of manners is often overlooked. Yet, with the increasing sensitivity to gender and diversity issues in the workplace, employees are forced to reestablish certain formalities and manners—which really just comes down to having consideration for other people. In the workplace, proper manners translate into looking out for your team members and having empathy for what they are going through as individuals. Good manners should typically go hand in hand with being a successful leader. The sign of a true leader in my eyes is someone who has the ability to empathize with others and to encourage them to open up, relax, laugh, and gain confidence, thus enabling them to give the best of themselves.

One of my proudest accomplishments at Goldman Sachs was running the corporate events team and not having a single individual leave voluntarily. The team learned a mutual respect for one another and everyone enjoyed working together. By the time I relinquished my position as manager, there was a team of 24 women who, almost without exception, have remained good friends. Their relationships were founded on the keystones of trust, high standards, and unselfish teamwork.

Having been in the business world for a considerable number of years now, I take pride in facilitating the growth of younger individuals and helping them expand their horizons. I enjoy being a catalyst and aligning individuals with similar interests for their mutual benefit.

My advice to young women entering the workforce is not to fight their femininity. Women don't need to behave in a masculine way; we were made to be different from men for jolly good reasons. I believe that young women in particular can take themselves far too seriously. I have seen my own humor and genuine concern for others as being two of my strongest suits in facilitating my personal success. I encourage you to travel. Worldwide travel rests at the top of my list as one of the best ways to obtain an enriching education. When I am looking at stacks of CVs, it is travel experience that can set one qualified candidate apart from another. It suggests a natural curiosity and represents open-mindedness and openness to life-experience, which often indicates a potential employee of exceptional quality.

My advice to leaders and managers is to pay more attention to the needs of their peers and their juniors than they do to their seniors. The latter learn about potential good leaders from the former without any need for sycophantic brown-nosing. A leader must be fair and supportive of people not only when they do something well but perhaps more importantly, also when they err. Public praise is critical to developing team members as is introducing and praising them to senior colleagues. Leaders must learn to share the spotlight and to know that the only way to make it to the very top is to treat all people with the same empathy and respect.

Karen Premo

Karen majored in anthropology and French at the University of Michigan, and afterward served in the Peace Corps for two years in Togo, West Africa. She worked for BNP Paribas before enrolling at the Lauder Institute and the Wharton School, where, in June 2005, she received a master's degree in international studies and an MBA. Karen plans to work in consulting and eventually to return to international work in the area of economic development.

> "If you're open-minded, you can get so much more out of life."

I arrived in Togo in September 1998 and started to learn Mina, the local language. A main component of Peace Corps training is language. We also received training in accounting, bookkeeping, marketing, and feasibility studies—learning useful techniques in all of these areas. When I first started, I was really interested in microfinance and began to work with a microfinance bank on their impact study. The organization's training materials were intended for literate women who worked their market stands in the main market in town, but most of our clients were illiterate. I didn't like the fact that we were excluding these women, and I really wanted to bring them into the loop. I gathered a lot of resources and developed a training exercise, using some of the techniques we had learned in our Peace Corps training.

The training was a bit hard to get off the ground because everyone thought I was crazy to use a skit and role-playing. The field agents, the people who went out in the field and assessed the women, weren't on board with it at the beginning. They were the ones who were going to administer this training and they said, "What is this? This is not how we do things." I knew it was going to be hard. I told myself, "This is what I came here to do." I just had to keep trying. The field agents finally agreed to give it a try, and right from the first day it was a hit. The women were so excited that there was finally something that they could participate in and learn from, and the field agents loved it too. This was such a great moment in my working over there because everyone had been against me and I had to have faith in myself and push so hard to make this happen. It was a huge success.

While I was in Togo I lived in Lomé, the capital of the country. I was a bit surprised to see chickens running through the dirt streets of the capital, but I became accustomed to that and to the daily inconveniences and uncertainties of water and electricity. I didn't have hot water, and the cold water only worked in the middle of the night because there wasn't enough pressure to get it up the hill and into my house. Late at night I'd put water in a bucket so I could take a "shower" the next day, and I had jars of water everywhere that I'd collect at night; you never know when you'll want to wash your hands. I was sharing some of the difficulties that the local people had, and that helped me understand the challenges of their daily lives.

During my two-year stay I got involved with the Junior Achievement program. JA has outreach branches in over 100 countries; the program in Togo had been floundering, with money no longer coming in from outside agencies. On the other hand, some U.S. government officials, including then First Lady Hillary Rodham Clinton, had begun to see the benefit of encouraging business development through programs such as JA. I decided that I wanted to help this organization, so I wrote a letter to the ambassador, asking for some form of help, knowing that Togo had been sanctioned because of its government, and that the embassy could not provide funds. My letter went unanswered and my next step was to call. I got the secretary on the line and she said, "Oh yes, we got your letter, hold on a second," and then she clicked over and a woman answered. It was the ambassador! She asked what she could do for us and I suggested that she could do a reception at her house. She invited some business leaders and other people in the development community to come and hear a presentation on Junior Achievement. That was a real watershed for us in terms of getting legitimacy and attention.

In both my work with the microfinance bank and with Junior Achievement, I taught the "4 P's," the fundamentals of marketing: price, product, promotion, and place. These are very basic business skills, and fairly logical once you've heard them, but it helps to introduce these concepts when one is learning to develop a small business.

By networking with Peace Corps volunteers in other communities, we were able to expand our projects. The Junior Achievement kids were psyched at the chance to work on a newspaper, to do really creative work. When they published their first issue, they were arrested and spent a night in jail. It hadn't occurred to us that it was illegal to publish a nongovernmental newspaper, especially one in which the kids wrote an article asking when their teachers, who were on strike, would be paid so the students could go back to school. This is the environment we were working in. The parents didn't blame us. In general, the people in Togo were so grateful that there were people who were willing to spend time there, to hear them talk about their feelings about the world and about their country. They said, "We're so impressed that you want to come here and learn our language and eat our food and be with us." To me that was really motivating. If you're open-minded, you can get so much more out of life.

It was a really formative two years, and I learned that business actually helps people. These countries need economic development; it is at the root of all the other issues like the lack of health care. I decided I wanted to use business as a tool for development and social justice, and when I returned to the United States in December 2000, I planned to work for awhile in the for-profit sector and then get my MBA.

I interviewed for a job as a staff accountant at BNP Paribas. It was at the start of the downturn in the economy and I really had to convince the woman I spoke to that even though I had no relevant experience, she wouldn't regret hiring me. I was hired and after a year I was promoted to be the head of the group.

While researching MBA options, I read the profiles of students in the Lauder Program at Wharton. I was inspired by the kind of people who were in the program and by what they were doing. I applied and was accepted, and I graduated in the spring of 2005 with a degree in international studies and an MBA.

Last summer, I worked in Bonn, Germany, in the in-house consulting group of Deutsche Post, a logistics company that is the parent company of DHL. It was an opportunity to travel and to expand and apply my all-around business skills. Having just graduated, I plan to work in consulting and to eventually get back into humanitarian work, perhaps for a large nonprofit organization such as CARE International. I developed hard finance and other skills at Wharton so I can be as effective as possible in one of those roles. It seems that there is a lot of good will but not a lot of skill going into those organizations. That's a missing piece. The Peace Corps has many young people who are right out of college, with a lot of energy and good ideas, but lacking experience and essential skills. I'd like to return to the international scene as a real professional, equipped with the skills and confidence to do a great job.

10

VISIONARIES

What's Your Challenge? What's Your Destiny? What's Your Gift? What's Your Legacy? What's Your Passion? Each of these questions has been the theme of one of our 85 Broads global network events over the past five years. They are simple questions that often inspire not so simple answers. Our speakers and our members have looked inside themselves, outside and around themselves, and often ahead of themselves to search for the answers. How do you answer these questions? How do you create a vision of your own future or as we like to say in the 85 Broads network, "*read the ending first?*"

Often "visions" can be very serendipitous or the result of seemingly quite simple questions. Like the story I told you at the beginning of the book about the Harvard MBA student who raised her hand in the middle of my speech about 85 Broads in 2000 and basically asked why she should care about a network that she couldn't join. While many responses may have come to my mind that day, the one I gave on the spur of the moment—"You know, you're absolutely right"—would lead to one of the best things we have ever decided to do with 85 Broads, which was to create the Broad2Broad co-mentoring partnership with women on the leading business school campuses. I certainly hadn't walked into that classroom expecting to discover any new grand visions for the future of our network, but in an instant this student had changed my entire perspective. My reality was not her reality. Looking back today, it's almost impossible to imagine 85 Broads *without* our Broad2Broad co-mentoring partnerships—thousands of the most incredible women on the planet who are now connected with us and each other through the network. In fact, a number of the visionaries we'll hear from in this chapter joined the network as Broad2Broad members.

The same thing basically happened again several years later when I was at Dartmouth speaking with undergraduate women interested in business and women MBA students at Tuck (Dartmouth's graduate business school). These women had never really connected with one another. Creating role models and co-mentors among women who are closer in age with one another has had an incredibly positive impact both ways—for those still in college and those in the early stages of their careers or graduate business school. Broad2Be, which essentially started that day on the Dartmouth campus, has grown even faster than Broad2Broad did and now includes co-mentoring partnerships with undergraduate women at over 50 colleges and universities. In some cases, there are already women's business organizations and networks on these campuses for 85 Broads to partner with. In other cases, 85 Broads is partnering with teams of fabulous undergraduate women to help start these organizations and networks on their campuses for the first time.

For instance, this email, which I recently received from Allysen Hepp, an undergraduate student at Tufts University, was a total "day maker" for me and for all the women of 85 Broads:

Hi Janet,

I am writing to thank you on behalf of all the Tufts Broad2Be members for giving us the opportunity and support to form an undergraduate chapter of 85 Broads. Over 100 people are now registered as members of Tufts Broad2Be.... At the Fifth Annual Student Awards banquet, the University recognized the great strides Tufts Broad2Be has made and honored us with several awards. Out of 25 student groups formed this year, we received the Best New Student Organization Award. In addition, out of over 140 registered student groups at Tufts, we were recognized as the Best Student Organization—the first group to ever receive this award as a brand new organization. Finally, I was honored to be awarded the Legacy Award "for leadership and service that will leave a lasting impact on the Tufts Community for years to come."

Beyond the group's success within the University, our members have landed competitive internships at top firms such as Lehman Brothers, Goldman Sachs, Morgan Stanley, Bear Stearns, and CSFB.

So many students have already gained from Tufts Broad2Be. I want to personally extend our gratitude to you and 85 Broads for helping us help Tufts.

Very best wishes,

Allysen

So being a visionary often comes from asking simple questions and finding your own answers, and then being open to having everything change as a result. That's the hard part. Not just seeing things differently, but doing things differently as well. More than anything else, this is what the following stories have in common. Women who have truly moved beyond the safety zones—and often the constraints—of societal, cultural, economic, and familial status quos by finding their own unique answers to questions that others simply accept as reality.

The other thing that the visions of all these extraordinary women have in common is a unique sense of community. Whether it is a community they are building or changing or redefining, each of their visions revolves around how they are connected with others and how these connections can create positive change. When we first started 85 Broads, one of the most senior women partners at Goldman Sachs at the time summed it up perfectly in this email:

> "It took a wonderful and far-sighted community vision to establish 85 Broads. The network is organic, with a life of its own. It gives women something they didn't have years ago—a feeling of sisterhood. In younger women it instills the confidence one feels by belonging to something greater than oneself; in older women it brings the warm pride of still being part of something truly excellent."

GEORGIA LEE

Georgia Lee is a writer/director and is passionate about making films that portray people's complex life paths and choices. Georgia's first feature film Red Doors *premiered at the Tribeca Film Festival in New York and won the award for Best Narrative Feature. She has an undergraduate degree in Biochemistry from Harvard University and was a consultant for McKinsey after graduation.*

Along with two other women, Georgia has formed a production company called Blanc de Chine Entertainment.

> "My Harvard-McKinsey life was so safe, so respected, and so certain, but it was not the life I dreamed of. After considering all the ways I could leap and fall, I finally just made that leap of faith, and found myself flying!"

Sitting comfortably in my first-class seat on a return flight to New York from Paris, I thought to myself, "Wow! I've made it!" I was 21 years old, a high-flying McKinsey consultant, and proud of my work. But after that brief moment of self-satisfaction, a voice from deep in my heart asked, "Am I *really* happy?"

McKinsey had taught me a great deal: the broader skills of project management, organization, strategy, cost/benefit analysis, and the application of these basic business concepts across multiple industries and companies. McKinsey had turned me into a young woman who had the confidence to make presentations to CEOs all over the world. But was I happy? It was the emerging voice of my longing for a different life, one that allowed me to pursue a latent but growing passion for the art of filmmaking.

I was born in Philadelphia in the bicentennial year. My parents, who had come to America from Taiwan two years before and met at the University of Pennsylvania, had hoped that their first child would be a boy. Their preference reflects the patriarchal Chinese society they had left, and their choice of names reflects the country they had moved to. They were going to name their son after George Washington, so they named me, the first of their three daughters, "Georgia."

My mother loved films and borrowed all kinds of movies from the library—screwball comedies, classic dramas, 25-hour-long Chinese soap operas, grand martial arts epics, Ginger Rogers and Fred Astaire musicals (she loved music and dance)—and along with my sisters, Jennifer and Katherine, I shared my mother's love of films at an early age.

For a professional path, my parents encouraged me to study science. I was, in fact, a science geek and as an undergraduate spent all of my summer internships in molecular biology labs. My first passion in life was to find a cure for cancer, so I went to Harvard and studied biochemistry. Thanks to a wonderful thing at Harvard called the Core Curriculum, I took classes in the arts to complete my distribution requirements. Through Advanced Standing, which allows students who have enough AP credits to graduate in three years, I told my father I was planning to graduate early and spend a year studying film. My father thought this idea was ridiculous.

During my third year at Harvard, McKinsey came to campus to recruit, and on a whim I interviewed with them and they offered me a job. After my parents recovered from the trauma that their eldest daughter wasn't going to medical school, they gradually got comfortable with the possibility that I would have a successful career in business. Not long after, I began working for McKinsey in New York, but I soon discovered the city's extraordinary independent film scene and felt myself reaching for something else. I had never honestly asked myself if this career in business was what I truly wanted, and I knew at that moment that I wanted to explore filmmaking, my true creative passion.

There's no well-lit path to become a filmmaker, and initially I didn't have the courage to leave the very bright, warm, structured, civil, highly respected world I was in. But then came the epiphany (which, to my parents, was my decline). I asked McKinsey if I could have some time off during the summer to take a film course at NYU, and they agreed. The class I took was a most amazing experience. In a matter of six weeks, you write, direct, light, shoot, edit, and produce five short films with a bunch of other students. I'd be up until 4 a.m. editing—cutting and splicing real film—and I loved every minute of it.

My first short film from that class was *The Big Dish: Tiananmen 89*. I had watched *The Big Shave*, a short film that Martin Scorsese had made as a student at NYU. The film, about the absurdity and destruction of the Vietnam War, made me think about Tiananmen Square. I felt strongly about what happened there, the government massacring hundreds, perhaps thousands, of innocent civilians. The news coverage of that event, especially the image of the unidentified young man trying to stop the tanks, had a tremendous impact on me as a child. I was horrified, as were my parents. I chose that as the subject for my first assignment and made a very experimental short film. My professor watched it and said that I should send it to Scorsese!

At 21, I naively dialed 411 and asked for Martin Scorsese's address and phone number. The woman who answered the phone said, "Yeah, you want Robert DeNiro's too?" And she promptly hung up. So I sent my VHS tape to Scorsese's fan mail in LA, without great hopes that I would get a response.

Several months later, having returned to work at McKinsey, I was working on a cost-cutting project for a sports company in Florida when late one night I checked my voice mail and heard this message: "This is Gretchen

Campbell from Martin Scorsese's office. Marty watched your film. He really loved it and he'd like to meet you." I almost fell off my chair!

I visited Martin Scorsese on the set of *Bringing Out the Dead*. When I had a chance, I naively asked him, "How does one become a great filmmaker like you?" He kind of chuckled and said, "You have to keep making films. Keep on working ... that's the only way you can get better."

Taking that advice to heart, I again requested time off from McKinsey to take a summer class at NYU and made my second film, *Bloom*. At that point, Miramax had just green lit *Gangs of New York*, and Martin Scorsese asked if I wanted to go to Rome to apprentice with him during the shoot.

To me it was a fairytale. To my parents it was something that would surely derail my business career. The people at McKinsey have always been very flexible and supportive, particularly my mentor Lowell Bryan, who has always encouraged me to be a creative problem solver. I took a sabbatical from McKinsey and in total spent five months in Rome. It was an amazing experience! I learned more in those five months about filmmaking than I would have learned in three years of film school. I took copious notes and absorbed everything I could from the top craftsmen in the filmmaking business.

I returned to New York and in 2002 made another short film, *Educated*. The film channeled much of my frustration and confusion between following the straight and narrow path of being a respected businesswoman and following my dream of becoming a passionate filmmaker. *Educated* included images of children on leashes, dutifully following their parents around. Shown in over 30 festivals around the world, *Educated* received, among other awards, the Best Short Film Award at the 2003 Durango Film Festival. It was clear to me that my next step was to make a full-length film, but my parents insisted that I go to business school.

Harvard Business School had accepted me once, but I chose to turn it down in order to study under Scorsese in Rome. Honoring my parents' wishes, I applied again. This time when I was accepted, I reluctantly enrolled in the two-year MBA program. During my first semester there, I met a lot of great people and learned many valuable things. But I also went to New York every weekend and made two more short films. In my finance class, I would have one screen open to a finance valuation spreadsheet and another screen with Windows Media Player showing *A Clockwork Orange*. If ever there was a metaphor for my life, it was this split screen.

I had to make a decision, so I did a McKinsey analysis of the whole thing. I created a utility spreadsheet with all the relevant weighted variables, the different levels of happiness—a happiness spreadsheet! I realized that the like-lihood of my being successful in business was infinitely higher than my being successful in the film industry. However, when comparing the best-case scenario of a career in business—I'm the CEO of a Fortune 50 in my 99th-floor corner office—with the worst-case scenario in film—I'm making independ-ent films that I'm proud of, but only a few people see—I realized that I would be happier making films no matter what!

Facing this decision, I felt as if I were standing on the edge of a bottom-less canyon and not able to jump. My Harvard-McKinsey life was so safe, so respected, and so certain, but it wasn't the life I dreamed of. After consider-ing all the ways I could leap and fall, I finally just made that leap of faith, and found myself flying!

So after just one semester at HBS I took a leave of absence and moved to Los Angeles, where I set up an office in my friend Mia's kitchen. I slept on her couch, reminisced about my expense accounts while taking the bus and eating ramen noodles, and, with the greatest sense of urgency and excitement, worked on my script for *Red Doors*.

I wrote the script in about three months and joined forces with two amaz-ing women I had met during my undergraduate time at Harvard. Jane Chen, one of my producers, had been involved in the production of *Bloom*, and she also cowrote and coproduced *Educated*. She had worked at McKinsey too and had gone on to become the Vice President of Strategy at American Van-tage Media. Mia Riverton, my other producer and member of the *Red Doors* cast, had worked as a staff producer at Fox Entertainment. She is the founder and president of Harvardwood, a nonprofit arts and entertainment associa-tion for Harvard alumni. We are all Asian women who came from a tradi-tional culture that says keep your head down and make a good living—that's the American dream. But we also had the confidence and competence we gained as students at Harvard. When we got together in LA we said, "We're going to make this happen. We're going to make this film."

Making a film is a huge operations management puzzle. After analyzing the whole value chain of making a movie and trying to apply a very rigorous cost/benefit analysis, Jane, Mia, and I wrote a business prospectus. We then raised the money we needed, all from private equity investors.

Red Doors tells a story about modern American life through the experiences of a truly dysfunctional Chinese-American family. Our extraordinary cast includes Tzi Ma, Jacqueline Kim, Freda Foh Shen, Elaine Kao, Kathy Shao-Lin Lee (my sister), Mia Riverton, Sebastian Stan, Jayce Bartok, and Rossif Sutherland. Our enormously talented crew includes Zeus Morand (director of photography), Youna Kwak (film editor), Robert Miller (composer), Susan Jacobs (music supervisor) and Angelique Clark (production designer).

As soon as the final edits were complete we sent *Red Doors* off to film festivals. Tribeca Film Festival accepted the film and wanted us to premiere it there. Though we expected it to be just a little film that no one would pay attention to, we ended up winning the award for Best Narrative Feature in our category at Tribeca! Following that success, we went off to CineVegas, where we won the Special Jury Prize for Ensemble Acting. Another triumph awaited us in LA at Outfest, where I won the Grand Jury Award for Screenwriting and the film won the Audience Award for Best First Narrative Feature.

Jane, Mia, and I have formed a production company called Blanc de Chine Entertainment. (Blanc de Chine means "porcelain" in French and is a play on our East meets West sensibility.) We plan to raise a production fund and start producing a slate of movies, particularly those with compelling female protagonists. We want to continue making more and better films. We are putting the stories we want to see on the screen and are following our passions fully. And most importantly, I've finally realized that ultimately I can only be happy doing what I truly love. No more "split screen!"

CHRISTY JONES AND NADIA CAMPBELL

While attending Harvard Business School, Christy launched her third company, Extend Fertility, which aligns women with breakthrough science to freeze their eggs and proactively plan for future fertility. Nadia left Goldman Sachs after six years to join Christy at Extend Fertility.

> "Women in my generation were told we could have it all. Unfortunately, the reality is that our biological clocks—specifically, our eggs—haven't evolved with our opportunities. I decided to seek out medical options that might bridge the disconnect between 'having it all' and a biological clock that never got the memo."
>
> Christy Jones

CHRISTY

After graduating from Stanford, I co-founded Trilogy and spent the next 13 years working with software. During a year of soul searching following the

IPO of our company, I read an ironically sad book called *Creating a Life* by Sylvia Ann Hewlett. The message of the book was pretty hopeless for professional women, insisting that many would never have children. Infertility was a hot topic among many 20- and 30-something women, but all the news was frustrating; there were no solutions to combat the depressing data. Women felt almost powerless. So I began my research.

Egg-freezing had historically not been a viable option because of the early state of the science. However, I knew that it was high time to bring improved technology to market. I befriended the head of the fertility department at Stanford, who was working on egg freezing for cancer patients, and began my research with him. We identified breakthrough science allowing women to harvest eggs earlier in life, when healthy eggs tend to be produced, and then store them for later use.

In 2002, I launched my new company, Extend Fertility, which provides every woman with the possibility of having a future family. At the time, I was moving from California to Boston to complete my MBA at Harvard and "incubated" the company while I was at school. It worked phenomenally well. I incorporated my goals for Extend Fertility into my classes, developed marketing tools, got volunteers, and reached out to professors who advised me on the relevant health care issues, insurance issues, and government regulations. I even met my future business partner, Nadia Campbell, at HBS. She is now the chief operating officer of Extend Fertility.

I recently got engaged to my fiancé Rob, and we have moved back to California together. My goals are to continue to work with Extend Fertility and build it into a great company over the next five to ten years, and to one day have children with my husband.

NADIA

The signature on my emails while I was working at Goldman Sachs was a quote by Admiral Collingwood that read: "Do something today that the world may talk of hereafter." I often wondered what was stopping me from taking my own advice and getting out there to do something else. I knew deep down that it was my destiny as an empathetic citizen of the world to make a difference.

My ultimate goal has always been to experience both personal and professional happiness. One of my greatest milestones in achieving this was choosing to redirect myself professionally to join Christy so I could have a career whose cause I genuinely cared about, one that allowed me to have an impact on the world in a real way. It was a challenge to muster the courage to leave a financially secure, safe life at Goldman. It meant becoming comfortable with the tall order of creating a new market, affecting opinions, and educating others.

When Extend Fertility's first client had her own eggs frozen it became for me a culminating moment of a lifetime's worth of work. I was helping to create new hope among women in the way they think about fertility and their biological clocks. It was personally validating for me to witness my ability to execute an abstract plan.

I view passion as the key to my success. It was passion that enabled me to make the great leap into the unknown at Extend Fertility. I realized that a job was just not worth doing if I couldn't be passionate about it. I knew that I had to look for a career that I felt very strongly about because that's pretty much the only way to be taken seriously and create positive change.

Confidence has also played a huge role. Each accomplishment that I've had in my life has given me a real awareness of what I can do. Having confidence in myself allows other people to have confidence in me and in my ability to deliver results.

None of the successes I've achieved would have been possible without the support of those around me. My friends, family, and husband Brad have shown full confidence in me and have encouraged me to seize a tremendous opportunity in the name of passion and change. My husband stood by my side when I was leaving a comfortable and profitable job at Goldman Sachs, reassuring me that taking this big risk was in fact just taking advantage of my fullest possibilities in life.

85 Broads has been instrumental in providing positive support to me and other women who are trying to make changes in our lives. Women are easy and natural networkers, and you can build your career by networking purposefully in developing lifelong relationships. My extensive Rolodex, one of my greatest assets in business, has been built primarily from my HBS and 85 Broads connections.

My advice to other women is that knowledge and smart planning are the keys to "having it all." We at Extend Fertility want women to take into account *both* their personal goals (marriage, family, etc.) and career goals when thinking about their futures, so as not to wake up one day with "regrets." Integrating my personal and professional goals, and becoming passionate about both, has allowed me to feel successful and fulfilled in my life. My mentor at HBS, Brian Hall, hammered home the ideal to take our skills and knowledge and to "go forth and create value." I remember this almost every day—asking myself how I am going to create value not only for myself, but for all the women of the world.

MELINDA WOLFE

In 1999 Melinda joined Goldman Sachs to work on staffing and development in the Asset Management Division. Two years later, after serving on the firmwide Diversity Task Force, Melinda assumed her current position at Goldman as head of the Office of Global Leadership and Diversity.

> "I'm sure that growing up in Skokie, Illinois, one of the more homogeneous places on earth in the 1960s, fueled my desire for diversity. In many ways it explains the choices I've made today—from the city I live in, to my career, to my home—where I am married to a Japanese-American man with whom I have a truly 'multicultural' child."

I champion the interests of women and underrepresented people at Goldman Sachs. I am working to create a more inclusive environment, developing programs that address the needs of women, Blacks, Latinos, the LGBT (lesbian, gay, bi-sexual, transsexual) community, and non-U.S. citizens. All of these groups have had a limited presence on Wall Street, but they are the future labor force for any global company. Every day, I am trying to effect change, and fueled by optimism, tenacity, and possibility, I hope my efforts will improve our workplace and our work product.

I grew up in a white middle-class Jewish community (distinguished by a huge number of concentration camp survivors) with people very much like me. My parents restricted me to college choices within a small radius of my hometown, limiting me to the "safe" borders of the Midwest. I always loved the energy, excitement, mix, and mess of big cities. So, after studying both the making of cities and art history as an undergraduate at Washington University in St. Louis, I headed out of the boundaries of the Midwest, to Washington, D.C., to work for a nonprofit called Partners for Livable Places. My experience there, combining economic development and design concerns, landed me next at the Kennedy School of Government at Harvard. I knew I wanted to work for the public good.

But after graduating I ironically found myself headed toward Wall Street, where I would spend 15 years at Merrill Lynch in both banking and diversity positions, followed by three years in recruiting and professional development at Credit Suisse First Boston. After I joined Goldman Sachs, I focused on staffing and development for my division and also found opportunities there to address a diversity agenda through strategic hiring and mentoring programs. Nearly 18 months later, I was asked to sit on a firmwide Diversity Task Force that was taking a serious look at how effectively Goldman Sachs had made inroads to greater inclusion. Top down and across the firm, there was a deep desire to tackle this issue with the rigor we would apply to any critical business initiative. It wasn't long before my career path had come full circle once again. By 2001 I was leading the firm's Office of Global Leadership and Diversity.

Simply put, I love my work. The issues are complex, with no right answers, no silver bullets. The ethical dilemmas go to the heart of peoples' core values. I learn from others outside the industry and in the academic community. I have the privilege to work with talented people from an array of backgrounds throughout the globe. In addition to shaping policy and priorities, I can influence important decisions and use my skills as a mentor, coach, and connector to facilitate opportunities for others.

Truthfully, though the percentage increase for all underrepresented groups has grown significantly since my early days in the industry, the pace of change feels slow in a world that demands big profits and quarterly results. We have a long way to go. It takes a few courageous leaders to see both the moral imperative and business sense of a diverse workforce. Moreover, they must have the commitment and resources to drive these concerns into the fabric of the organization. Today, I'm surrounded by leaders who have a strong commitment to advance the cause. In my view, the stars are better aligned for change, and I am excited to be at the center of this challenge.

My career and life lessons on Wall Street have led me to see the power of great minds, great commitments, and significant resources. All of these must be tempered by an unrelenting desire to stay the course. In the end, it is extremely satisfying to know that I am working to make a difference and helping individuals gain access to outstanding opportunities in their lives.

Noreen Harrington

Noreen began her career on Wall Street in 1985 in the Fixed Income Division at Goldman Sachs in New York and then moved to their London

office to work with hedge funds. Over the next two decades she held
senior positions across a variety of trading and investment management
businesses. In 2002, while working for Stern Asset Management in New
York, Noreen identified what turned out to be illegal trading practices in
the mutual fund industry. After leaving Stern that year, she uncovered
more criminal trading activity and became the whistle-blower whose
report to authorities led to an investigation that eventually rocked the
industry. She is a founding partner of Alternative Institutional Partners
(AIP), a fund of hedge funds established in 2005.

> "I reported a crime that will forever give me the label,
> 'whistle-blower.' Fortunately, 95 million people bene-
> fited from my action and are thankful I had the courage
> to blow the whistle."

The crime involved some of the biggest firms in the mutual fund industry and affected many of the 95 million mutual fund investors. The majority of mutual fund firms would not allow these illegal activities to take place,
but the trust and faith in the entire industry was shaken to its core. Honest,
hard-working Americans from all walks of life were having their money stolen
by some unscrupulous people, and the stealing was so devious that the
investors were not even aware of it. I became aware of this criminal activity
through a series of fortuitous happenings. I was then faced with the decision
to report it or to remain silent. I came to the conclusion that the activities I
had uncovered were not taking place in the gray areas of SEC regulations.
Most of them were clearly well into the black of illegal activity.

I chose to report what I knew, and the mutual fund scandal investigation
began. This crime touched almost all of us—our families, our friends and
coworkers—Americans whose major asset for their future had been confidently invested in mutual funds. These investments represented the ultimate
safety net for millions of people. Unfortunately, some powerful families and
unethical investors were allowed to skim off just a little profit from many of
these funds. This taking of "just a little" from many unsuspecting investors
generated billions in illegal gains. It was truly a case of "reverse Robin Hood"
—the rich stealing from people with a lot less money to increase their individual wealth. It is difficult to fathom why a family entity worth an estimated
$3 billion has to engage in such illegal practices. It is estimated that between
$10 and $15 billion was skimmed each year. The amount was so staggering
and affected so many people that I knew I had to do something about it.

Every time you take a risk, there are consequences. But the moral code had been drummed into me as a child, and I felt strongly that as a senior executive, I had a responsibility to prevent the further spread of this already widespread fraud. Uncovering the dishonesty wasn't straightforward; it happened gradually while I worked at Stern Asset Management. I was in a separate building from my boss, Ed Stern, but slowly began to realize that some of the things being done there were highly questionable. Stern was in charge of investing $800 million dollars in private funds for the Stern family, the proceeds from the sale of their Hartz Mountain pet food company. I was the person responsible for the fund of funds—giving money to the individual hedge funds seeking out alternative investments. Ed Stern was mainly involved in the family hedge fund, Canary Capital, which was trading in the mutual fund industry. I was completely separated from these activities.

While working late one night, I was surprised at the cheers coming from Ed Stern's area. It was well past 9 p.m., and the small group was celebrating a trade they had just completed. How could they be trading at this hour when the mutual fund market closes at 4 p.m.? I became suspicious of these activities and confronted Ed with my concerns about what to me was certainly close to illegal. He replied, "Don't worry, the SEC won't come after me, they will go after the mutual funds."

I resigned from Stern in 2002, only to discover that what I had witnessed at Canary Capital was much more widespread than I had realized. At first I thought I had stumbled upon an isolated problem where one family was using its power and wealth to receive illegal late-day trading benefits from certain mutual funds in return for fees and deposits of "large sticky assets." However, the more I spoke to people in the industry and probed deeper, the more I realized that the trading irregularities in mutual funds were not limited to Canary Capital. They, and many others, had crossed a line that should never have been crossed.

The widespread extent of the crime forced me to place an anonymous phone call to the office of New York State Attorney General Eliot Spitzer. I had no idea that my call would spark a mutual fund trading investigation that has subsequently reached across the entire industry. Making that call was the scariest thing I've ever done, but I could not have lived with myself if I hadn't. Eliot Spitzer and his small team responded immediately and aggressively to protect the interests of the small investor. Within just three months they announced the indictment of Ed Stern, his settlement of $40 million, and his complete cooperation with the investigation of the mutual fund industry. To date, there have been fines assessed in excess of $3.5 billion, and many individuals have been barred from the industry. More importantly, the investigation by Eliot Spitzer, the SEC, and numerous states has created new and tighter regulations to help ensure that these activities will never take place again.

What has the personal cost been to me? Unfortunately, I found out that truly "no good deed goes unpunished." All of a sudden my 22 successful years on Wall Street were being judged only by my recent action in "black and white" terms. Some in the industry will never speak to me again—I broke "the code" by speaking to a regulator and inviting them into our business. Others feel that I am not a "team player" and can never be trusted again. But I do not believe that any of us want to be on a team that needs to steal to make money. I know that I don't.

In reflection, I discovered more positive things resulting from this action and learned that times of crisis reveal what people are truly made of. A great number of people in the industry picked up the phone or wrote telling me how proud they were of me and of what I had the courage to do. These are the individuals who stood up for me in numerous closed-door meetings within firms and who championed the internal changes that will make the industry stronger.

On a personal level, I was deeply touched by the thousands of ordinary people who wrote to thank me for standing up for them. A lot of the tension went away when some stranger would recognize me and give me a hug for helping them. The industry has also recognized me for what I have done, and I will always be extremely grateful for the awards I have received: Mutual Fund Industry Titan of the Year 2003; Fast Company Top 50 Persons of the Year; Compliance Person of the Year; The SIPA Award as The Truth-Sayer of the Year. (I much prefer being referred to as a *truth-sayer* than as a *whistle-blower!*)

I also discovered that I had greater inner strengths than I ever thought I possessed; my core values guided me through some really rough times. I am equally convinced that there are many people with outstanding ethics who approve of what I have done, and as we rebuild trust and respect for the mutual fund industry, these are the people our entire industry should reward.

As a whistle-blower, I will be forever linked with three other whistle-blowers: Cynthia Cooper at WorldCom, Coleen Rowley at the FBI, and Sherron Watkins at Enron—*Time*'s Persons of the Year for 2002. Their efforts rocked the organizations they worked for and affected the entire foundation of American business. There are many different theories regarding the fact that we are all women. Some of the research shows that women work in order to make a difference. They want to know that what they do truly matters and is valued. Other theories state that women are on the outside looking in, and by not being part of the inner corporate club, it is easier for them to take a step back and act on their own principles. Most women today are interested in climbing the corporate ladder and having their efforts rewarded—but just not at any cost.

All of the women involved in these major cases have cited some significant influences in their personal and professional lives that enabled them to have the courage to report the crimes and to have the strength to come out of the battles as stronger individuals. In my case, my father died suddenly when I was very young. I learned that life doesn't always last as long as you expect or hope for. You have to make sure that every day matters and every day you try to do what is right. Suffering a loss like that early in one's life also teaches you that life is not easy and doesn't always follow the path that you would like.

The other person who influenced me was my mentor and my boss, Jon Corzine, the former chairman of Goldman Sachs. He had an unbelievably strong value system and work ethic. We were always reminded at Goldman that if we do right by our clients, we would also do well. No matter how demanding our jobs were, Jon also reminded us of the importance of giving back to the community. He has been living that principle now as a U.S. senator from New Jersey and was recently elected governor. Jon also taught me the importance of making calculated career moves even if there was risk involved.

In 1993 I was faced with a difficult decision which involved a move to London and a change to a division where I had no experience or track record. I would have to give up everything I had achieved in New York, my clients and knowledge of the U.S. market. I would be learning by doing—hiring and training people when I was only two chapters ahead of them myself. Moreover, I would be moving to a country where I had no contacts or friends. On the other hand, I wanted to expand my knowledge and become more globally oriented. I gave this decision a lot of serious thought. Many people advised me against taking the risk. But Jon Corzine convinced me that it was the right move, one of those calculated risks that would pay off.

So I went for it and became the head of Hedge Fund and Non-Dollar Sales in London for Goldman Sachs. It was a fantastic decision; I grew exponentially in this role, losing the U.S.-centric approach toward markets and discovering my new clients to be some of the smartest and most intellectually challenging people in the world. The team I hired surpassed all expectations and the results were clear: We were the most productive sales group for

Goldman Sachs worldwide. And I was named a managing director of Goldman, an honor that made me one of the highest-ranking women internationally. I will always be grateful to Jon for encouraging me to take that risk.

In 1997, I decided to accept an offer from Barclays Capital in London to become Co-Head of Fixed Iincome, where I was named to the seven-member management committee, reporting directly to the CEO. After almost six years of missing my family and friends, I returned to America in 1999. I joined Janet Hanson and other women as the first members of 85 Broads. Our concept was to use the Internet to stay connected wherever our members were located. We had a vision of keeping this network together by forming a community whose members would share ideas and promote each other's career advancement. To have been there at the beginning and now to see the huge success that 85 Broads has become makes me very proud. The organization has been instrumental in giving back to the communities we live in as well as supporting good causes around the globe. I really enjoy teaching and derive an enormous amount of satisfaction from being able to help women shape their careers. I am active in 85 Broads through co-mentoring, and I look forward to more opportunities to exchange helpful creative solutions with other members of this extraordinary network.

I am currently setting up a new investment company, a fund of hedge funds, called Alternative Institutional Partners (AIP), with my partner, Margaret Towle, former CIO of Northern Trust. Our company will be built on the SEC best-practice guidelines and will serve institutional clients. In taking on this challenge, I am reminded of these words of encouragement that Jon Corzine gave to me after the mutual fund scandal, "Some doors will close to you now, but many more doors will open, and the ones that close you would *not* want to go through anyway."

SAFIA RIZVI

Safia grew up in Pakistan and moved to the United States to study chemistry in graduate school. She has since received a PhD in Chemistry and her MBA from Wharton. Now she is part of GlaxoSmithKline's corporate groups and leverages her scientific background and her business and management skills to make her mark on the pharmaceutical industry and help take modern miracles to remote parts of the world. She is the founder of a nonprofit organization, eLIT (www.elitonline.org), which focuses on electronic literacy for socially and economically disadvantaged women and children in many parts of the world.

> "I grew up in an environment where the average woman is not afforded many opportunities. I was fortunate enough to have access to education that opened a multitude of opportunities for me. I am passionate about giving women a voice and providing them with access to educational and economic opportunities. In raising my own daughter to become a citizen of the world, I would like to see a world where all women are empowered and able to make informed choices."

I was raised in a traditional family in Pakistan, where the men were educated and professionally accomplished and the role of a woman was to attend to the needs of the men in her family. A woman's worth was determined by how much she was liked by the men in her life. For more than two decades of my life, my brothers were like demigods to me, and I did not question the social order. Along with the rest of the girls in my social surroundings, I was expected to fill the gap between birth and marriage with school and college to become a better marriage prospect. The irony is that no one ever expected me to have a career or become part of the workforce.

After my final year at the Karachi University, I was awarded the opportunity to continue my education at a graduate school in the United States. As expected, my family reacted negatively to the notion of an unwed girl leaving home for the States. With an unbelievable amount of creativity, I repeat, "creativity," I persuaded my parents to let me go the United States to pursue higher education. Miraculously, they let me go under just one condition—that I would not be living in the United States as an unwed girl. Shortly thereafter, my parents found a "suitable boy" and arranged a marriage for us.

The marriage was not forced on me. I could have said no, but I was programmed to expect an arranged marriage. I am probably the only girl in the world who did not attend her own wedding. Marriage vows were exchanged over the phone with my groom living halfway across the world. Not surprisingly, we were also more than a world apart in our outlooks on life. My husband was a traditional Pakistani man who naturally was uncomfortable with my aspirations for higher education and a career.

I lived in the United States with my husband and pursued my graduate education. Eleven months after our marriage, I gave birth to my lovely daughter, Sheherzad. Without going into details, shortly after that I found myself a single mother in a foreign country with no support from anywhere. I was raised in very sheltered environments, and I had never imagined myself living on my own. However, I did the unthinkable for a woman of my upbringing and chose to raise my daughter with absolutely no financial or emotional support from any of the familiar sources. At the time, I was attending graduate school, taking and teaching classes, conducting research, and taking care of my daughter. I could have gone back to live in my ex-husband's house (with his second wife) which would have made everyone happy, but that would have meant raising my daughter without the opportunity to develop herself and her own self-esteem, something that every human being deserves. It was not an easy decision to make; it cost me dearly. My family disowned me for the shame I brought to them by becoming divorced, and my community practically ostracized me. However, giving my daughter a happy childhood, a safe and loving nurturing home, the ability to dream and fulfill her dreams, and a future that would not be limited by her gender was worth every bit the price that I paid.

As I experienced motherhood in graduate school, I became increasingly interested in the chemistry of life and decided to pursue the study of biomolecules, which lie at the interface of the cell and its environment. My interest and expertise in membrane protein structure led me to my position at the University of Pennsylvania, where as a fellow of the American Heart Association I studied the membrane proteins that bind with aspirin and ibuprofen to play a role in inflammation, arthritis, and the regulation of blood pressure.

My transition from the academic world into the pharmaceutical industry was driven by my desire to experience science in more application-oriented environments. I joined the Bioinformatics Department at SmithKline Beecham and supported the oncology discovery program. I feel fortunate to have been part of one of the best bioinformatics teams in the world at a unique time in the history of science when the human genome data were released. I also feel proud to be a small part of a process that worked to discover better and more effective drugs for the treatment of cancer. Two of the projects I was part of are now in clinical trials and will, I hope, make it to the market and help cancer patients soon.

I began to realize that a number of problems in this world can be more easily addressed from an economic perspective. I decided to acquire the tools of economics and pursued an MBA at Wharton School of Business in Philadelphia. Having a strong scientific background combined with business and management training from Wharton, I am uniquely positioned to evaluate and mobilize emerging medicine to move from the laboratory to patients and health care professionals. I am looking forward to making my mark on the industry and to eventually participate in taking modern scientific miracles to remote parts of the world.

I recently received an invitation from the White House to meet with President Bush and members of the National Security Council to discuss the situation in Pakistan and Afghanistan. The essence of my suggestion to the President was that sustained and constant provision of educational opportunities for women and children of all ages is a significant way to diffuse the political fragility of the region. I believe that terrorism is not the disease. Terrorism is simply a symptom of the disease. The disease is actually ignorance and intolerance that seem to worsen through poverty.

I remember hearing a poem written by a second grader in Philadelphia who writes about feeling scared of terrorism and feeling that he might not have the chance to grow up and reach the age of 22. I couldn't help but wish that he were writing poems about love, humanity, success, beauty, and other wonderful things that our children deserve to experience. We live in an increasingly global world. Its problems are our problems. By helping children in places like Pakistan and Afghanistan, we will actually be creating a safer world for our children right here in the United States. In my opinion, one of the best ways to help children across the world is to help the mothers and the would-be mothers in these societies. A mother can most effectively nurture positive values in a child.

Currently there are religious schools known as Madrasah in Pakistan where children learn to read and recite the Quran, and they are also implicitly and explicitly taught hatred for anyone who does not fit the mold of a specific brand of Islam. Madrasah are powerful because poor children attend them and can be assured of a steady income upon graduation. Unfortunately, the economic opportunity provided also includes inculcation of a violent temperament toward outsiders.

I proposed the radical idea of converting Madrasah into technology education centers. Building technology centers is a cost-effective way of pursuing the aims of education and creating economic opportunities. Information technology supports rapid communication and exposes people to a diversity of religions, governments, and cultures. Cyber-communities, email groups, community websites, and video teleconferencing are some of the ways in which technology centers may fundamentally support the drive to provide educational and economic opportunities and lessen the alienation and resentment among nations.

I have committed myself to this cause in South Asia by organizing an initiative to provide basic computer literacy to socially and economically disadvantaged women and children. With the help and support of like-minded people, I established eLIT, Empowerment through Learning Information Technology. eLIT was conceived in 1998 and shared publicly at a conference in Washington, DC. After two years, founding members managed to gather a critical mass of people and resources to officially launch. eLIT's mission is to combat poverty, ignorance, despair, and political/religious extremism through education. Its supporters believe that an informed, educated, happy, and fulfilled mother is critical for the 21st century. eLIT currently has four learning centers: one in West Philadelphia, one in KukutPally, India, one in inner city Karachi, and a fourth in Mansehra, northern Pakistan. To date, nearly 1,000 women and children have benefited from eLIT centers. Women who have graduated describe numerous positive outcomes that have come into their lives as a result. Some women found better jobs; others are better able to help their children do homework. Many others feel empowered by just being able to reach the world that was inaccessible to them prior to this training.

We are currently in the process of raising $150,000 to launch four technology and literacy community centers in Kabul to help Afghan women regain the opportunities that they lost during the Taliban regime. The University of Pennsylvania Alumni Club of Philadelphia has established a sponsorship to collaborate with eLIT and plans to leverage its alumni network across the globe to replicate the eLIT model. We consider the empowerment of women in any community to be a necessary and critical step in the betterment of the community as a whole.

DEENA BAHRI

Deena Bahri is a member of Reebok International Ltd.'s global leadership program. Deena received her MBA from Harvard Business School in June 2004 and is currently a regional chapter co-chair of 85 Broads in New England.

> "I hate hearing people say, 'Don't make your passion your job, because then you won't enjoy it anymore.' I don't believe in that. I really think you should love what you do, try to find a way to do what you love, and infuse it in as many parts of your life as possible."

As my college graduation loomed nearer, I began job hunting in the creative services industry. I interviewed at several advertising and public relations firms in New York that were ultra hip and paid absurdly low salaries. My father wasn't too excited about the prospect of subsidizing my rent. He told me, "You keep saying you don't want to work for 'The Man.' You have all these liberal notions about the horrors of finance and consulting, but you don't even know what these jobs are like. Maybe you should take just one traditional interview and learn a bit about that path before you shun it." My dad was right that my attitude was not particularly informed. I had decided against traditional recruiting options based on secondhand information and my own youthful idealism, but I was not going to admit that to him!

Soon after, a friend who was interning at an investment bank told me that he thought I would make a great banker. I just laughed. Banking was something I had never considered. Still, when he told me he could get me an interview at his firm, my dad's words echoed in my head. I agreed to give the professional services world just one try. As it turned out, it was all I needed to become hooked. I had great chemistry with the people I met, and I was impressed by their passion for their jobs. I was intrigued by the challenging environment and seduced by the dynamic pace and intense lifestyle. And so I accepted a position at a small regional firm in Philadelphia called Janney Montgomery Scott.

I remember at the time thinking that my decision seemed whimsical; I was curious, I knew I would learn a lot, I felt in my gut that it would be a fun ride. I had no suspicion that it would set me on a path that would include exhausting highs and lows, serious self-examination, and a Harvard MBA. After a year and a half at JMS, I felt I had gotten a taste for the banking life. But I wanted a more tailor-made experience that would satisfy my desire to be near the heart of the action (New York), to work with the sexiest companies in the market (technology), and to apply strategic analysis as much as possible (M&A). I took a job at Broadview International, where I learned an enormous amount about technology, finance, teamwork, and client service. More importantly, somewhere between the grueling hours and meticulous details, I figured out a lot about myself—my strengths and weaknesses, how tough I could be, and especially the kind of life I wanted to lead.

It's amazing how philosophical you get at 2 a.m. when you've been running numbers for hours. The big question for me was, "Why do I have to sacrifice so much of myself in order to have a 'successful' professional life?" I felt that there were huge parts of my personality and intellect—creativity, liberalism—that I was never able to bring to work because they were not valued. Furthermore, my job forced me to sacrifice too much in my personal life, whether it came to relationships, hobbies, or sleep. I also realized the industry required a certain amount of aggressiveness that I didn't want to be a part of my life. On an intellectual level, building models and pondering financial problems just didn't inspire me. And I felt that I was not being rewarded in a way that meant anything to me, given how much I was compromising. From early on, there were so many signs that finance was not the right industry for me. I just didn't face them right away.

I guess it's no big surprise that I sought out yoga while I was experiencing all of this turmoil. My romance with yoga began soon after I took my job at JMS. Between working until midnight, eating meals in front of my computer, and skimping on sleep, I needed some sort of outlet through which to undo the damage I was doing to myself. So I signed up for my first class out of necessity, not really suspecting that I was subscribing to a powerful practice that would offer me so much more than stress relief.

I remember that first class with total clarity. It was part of a 10-session course at Temple University, held in an old classroom with smelly gym mats and awful neon lights. The teacher fit my preconception perfectly, with her jangling silver bracelets, hippie hair, and flowing pants. Then she began to talk about the breath, leading us through some simple breathing exercises that involved noticing how the rib cage expands in three dimensions and how time seems to slow down when you breathe with intention. I forgot all my preconceptions, reservations, and concerns about who had sat on the smelly mat before me. An hour later, when I walked out of that first class, I felt everything had been fine-tuned; the cold air was crisper, the night sky was blacker, the stars were brighter. I was not exactly sure what had happened to me, but I felt plugged in, energized, and connected in a way that convinced me I had to go back the following Monday.

I think one of yoga's most valuable lessons for me has been mindfulness of my actions. It starts on the mat, as you move through the postures and try to stay focused. *Try* is the key word. Over time you learn how to switch on the mindfulness and how to keep it on. It does get easier — that's why it's called yoga practice! And then you start to apply yoga qualities in other contexts. Simply noticing how I behave at work, for example, observing what pushes my buttons, how I react under stress, how focused I remain while performing a task or attending a meeting. It's amazing how many times I let habit dictate my actions or I simply go through the motions. Once I started to pay careful attention to what happens and why, I felt I was able to get and give more, as well as begin to change the things I didn't like.

It's funny how the physical spills over into the intellectual, emotional, and spiritual realms of my life. It's all connected—another great yoga lesson for me. Early on, I noticed that the more involved I became in yoga, the less inclined I was to go running or to lift weights. I started to realize that these other activities were aggressive and goal-oriented; things I didn't need any more of in my type A existence. What I did need was an activity that would help me tune in, find my center, connect with joy and grace, express myself fully, and balance out the aggressiveness and goal-orientation that were rampant in my banking life. I still marvel at those perceptible moments when I see how living my yoga makes me choose more wisely, act more efficiently, or listen more closely.

And that's how, after four years, I made my way out of banking. I started to pay more attention and realized I needed a creative, liberal, and diverse work environment to be happy. I was unsure where I could find such qualities: which functions, companies, industries? Because I didn't want to jump into a new job without knowing what I hoped to accomplish, I felt I needed to do some deeper exploration of my personal and professional objectives. So I applied to Harvard Business School, which seemed to be the perfect forum for me to explore those questions and obtain career clarity.

Before business school, I worked in a job that was at odds with fulfilling my passion to live a good life, as I define it. Now I feel I've chosen a professional path that will help me to get there. During school, a lot of people who contemplated a similar transition would talk jokingly about "losing the edge." Imagine the conversation: "I used to be so tough and so hungry that I would compromise my health, my dreams, and my happiness to get the job done, but now I can't rationalize that sort of insane, thankless devotion unless it's for my own company. I guess I've just lost my edge." They should call it "gaining a grasp on reality" or even "finding a pot of gold at the end of the rainbow." I think it's a real gift to have had the time to think about what will make me happy and now to have the opportunities to pursue that happiness.

I am really excited about my next several years at Reebok. I chose an environment where I am expected, and want exceedingly, to perform. At the same time, I am encouraged to have a balanced life. I chose a company whose business is at the intersection of two of my passions, wellness and fashion. This job is such a great fit for me because it marries my passions with my goals; I'll even have the chance to teach yoga again, at the corporate fitness center. I hate hearing people say, "Don't make your passion your job, because then you won't enjoy it anymore." I don't believe in that. I really think you should love what you do, try to find a way to do what you love, and infuse it in as many parts of your life as possible.

In the big picture, my relationships are the most important part of my life. I think my most significant accomplishment in life is being a great friend, sister, aunt, and daughter. I hope that list grows to include wonderful mother, wife, manager, and mentor.

ANA ESCALONA

After graduating from the Instituto Tecnológico Autónomo de México (ITAM), Ana joined the Goldman Sachs office in Mexico City, where she worked for two and a half years until moving to Boston to pursue a masters of science in finance at Boston College. Graduating in 2000, Ana worked for Goldman in New York and later joined Pro Mujer, a nonprofit microfinance organization that provides small business loans and training to women living in poverty in Latin America.

"I was flipping through the ads in the newspaper when this posting caught my eye: 'Nonprofit organization, seeking financial manager, fluent in Spanish.'"

I was born in Mexico City and lived there until I was 12 years old, when my parents relocated my family to Houston so that my sisters and I could learn English. My father eventually started a business in Houston, where I stayed for junior high and high school. I have a traditional Mexican family, and when it came time for me to begin selecting colleges to apply to I was encouraged to return to Mexico, which I did. I enrolled in Instituto Tecnológico Autónomo de México (ITAM), where I received my undergraduate degree in economics. My father wanted me to work for the family business, so it was a tough decision when I chose to accept an internship opportunity at Goldman Sachs in Mexico. I started as an intern in the Equity Operations Department and then accepted a full-time position while attending my last year of college and completing my thesis.

After working at Goldman in Mexico for over two years, my fiancé and I decided that we both wanted to further our studies in the United States. Goldman Sachs offered to relocate me to the Boston office, but I was ready to take a break and explore graduate programs exclusively. I was accepted to Boston College's master of science in finance program and my husband to

Harvard Business School, so we went to the States to earn our respective business degrees.

After graduating from BC, I decided to work for Goldman.com in New York, which was a big project for Goldman Sachs during the Internet boom. While I wouldn't be working in microfinance, I wasn't concerned, as I knew that I would be in a challenging role that would undeniably move me toward my goal. During one of my trips back to Mexico I ran into a friend from Boston whose mother knew of a microfinance organization in New York called Pro Mujer, which provided loans and training for women starting or operating small businesses. Pro Mujer already had three programs operating in Latin America and had plans to start another in Mexico. It was exactly what I was looking for and I expressed interest in learning more about the organization, although nothing came of it at the time.

I never thought that I would find a job in *The New York Times* but just a couple of weeks later I was flipping through the ads in the newspaper when this posting caught my eye: "Nonprofit organization, seeking financial manager, fluent in Spanish." The listing was for a microfinance organization for women in Latin America called Pro Mujer, the same organization that I had heard about just a couple of weeks before from my friend. The next day I sent an email to Pro Mujer indicating that I was currently an associate at Goldman Sachs but was interested in learning more about their organization and the financial manager position. I received an email back the following day from Pro Mujer's executive director thanking me for my interest in their organization and warning me that the salaries at Pro Mujer couldn't compete with GS salaries, and if, after knowing this I was still interested, I was encouraged to call them to set up an interview. I wrote back assuring her that my interest in Pro Mujer "goes beyond compensation" and that I would very much like to be considered for the position. They must have liked my answer because shortly thereafter I was working for Pro Mujer, with specific responsibilities for cultivating its program in Mexico in addition to taking on the financial management functions.

I feel absolutely passionate about microfinance and Pro Mujer is a powerful organization. In establishing their Mexican program, I had several challenges ahead of me. The Mexican Federal Government had verbally agreed to fund the first million dollars to launch the program and the State Government of Hidalgo had committed to funding another million dollars. My responsibility was to formalize the funding agreement with the Mexican Government and to raise the third million-dollar component within the United States.

During a microfinance conference in Mexico, I had the good fortune to meet Geoff Davis who was starting a fund for microfinance organizations called Unitus. The fund was looking for a Mexican institution to invest in and we discussed a potential funding relationship. After about three months of negotiating, we came up with an agreement where Pro Mujer obtained a $400,000 grant for capacity building and a $1.5 million line of credit from Unitus. I feel very proud of having participated in launching such an incredible project in my country.

While initially it was difficult to make the decision to move from Goldman Sachs, one of the most profitable and respectable institutions in the world, to Pro Mujer, a small nonprofit organization with an entirely different host of challenges, I am incredibly proud of the accomplishments that we have made over the past three years. The two businesses represent completely different worlds, and I was forced to make financial sacrifices to work for something that I was passionate about. The opportunity for me to come to the United States to learn English at a young age was instrumental as it gave me the skills that led to these successes. My husband, parents, and five sisters have been behind me the whole way, and I don't think that I would have achieved what I have without their support.

DANIELLE CHANG

In 1998, while at Goldman Sachs as an equities associate, Danielle created a business plan for Simplycity, *a magazine that focused on the consumer woman's lifestyle. In 2002, after the magazine closed, she headed the U.S. office of Assouline, and then moved to the Bay Area to work with her family's business.*

> "I'm learning how to reconcile the fiercely independent, self-absorbed woman that I used to be with my new role as a mother and wife."

By the time I was 30, I had already held about 30 different jobs: bartender, professor of art history, art dealer, associate at Goldman Sachs, and editorial coordinator at *The New York Times*, to name just a few. I had also lived in New York, San Francisco, Hong Kong, and Paris. Compared with previous generations, women of my generation are blessed with more options than we know what to do with. We were also brought up to believe that we can—*and should*—"have it all." (Whatever that means!) Not surprisingly, as a result, we've jumped around a lot—not just in terms of what we do for a living, but also in terms of whom we date and where we live—in order to find our "voice" and to fulfill our dreams of "having it all." If there's a pot of gold at the end of the rainbow, mine is the generation that feels entitled to it.

In 1999, while at Goldman and with the support of a group of Goldman partners who became my first investors, I took a big professional risk and followed my passion to launch a new magazine called *Simplycity*. The idea was to create a new lifestyle magazine for urban-minded, professional women seeking to lead more balanced lives. We had a good publishing run of two years, where we steadily grew our circulation to over 200,000 both domestically and internationally, attracted prestige advertisers from Cartier to Evian, and carved out a good little niche for ourselves in the competitive magazine publishing industry. In the process, I learned a lot—about how to manage people (and how to fire your good friend), how to raise money (and how to tell the same investors later on that you've spent all their money) and, of course, about how to publish a magazine and run a small business.

I also realized that part of being an entrepreneur is knowing how to turn obstacles into opportunities. Just months after our first issue hit the newsstands, Time Warner launched what became our biggest competitor, *Real Simple*, another magazine that went after the same affluent, "culturally creative" consumer we targeted. Rather than fighting Time Warner with money that we didn't have, we aligned ourselves with them. In the end, the millions that Time Warner had spent to create a new "simplicity" category in women's magazines made it easier for us to convince partners—be it a top national distributor or advertisers—of the validity and timeliness of our concept.

Even though we eventually stopped publishing in 2002 when both advertising dollars and investment capital dried up after September 11, the experience was an overwhelmingly positive one. Luckily, at the end of the day, the risk I took was acknowledged and rewarded. Both the magazine and my career were featured widely by news outlets such as *The New York Times*, *The Wall Street Journal*, and CNN. I was also named one of *Working Women*'s "20 under-30 entrepreneurs to watch" as well as one of *Folio*'s under-30 rising stars. So the experience actually helped to jumpstart my career. After *Simplycity*, I was recruited to run Assouline, a French media company, in a management capacity that I could have only dreamed about before.

Fast-forward two years. If you had asked me just a few years ago what my life would look like today, I probably would have painted a different picture. In the span of a year, I got married, had a baby and moved across the country. When I was pregnant with my first daughter Colette, we decided to move out to California temporarily to be near our families and to work in my family's business as it went through a critical transition. Just a few weeks ago, I gave birth to my second daughter Clarissa. The past couple of years have been centered on family: both working within my family business as well as starting a family of my own. I'm learning how to reconcile the fiercely independent, self-absorbed woman that I used to be with my new role as a mother and wife. On a more practical level, I'm grappling with how to best integrate motherhood into a busy professional life. Even though I started a magazine about "living in balance," I'm beginning to realize that the superhuman juggling skills required to maintain this balancing act are beyond me. But I do still believe that it is possible to "have it all"—just not necessarily all at the same time, all *of* the time. We are now in the process of moving our growing family of four back to New York, where I plan to continue my work in the media industry. Stay tuned!

CHRISTINE LEENDERTSEN

Christine started her business career at Goldman Sachs and is currently working at Merrill Lynch. Her love for travel and education have now steered her onto a different path. Christine is enrolled in a master's in counseling program at St. Mary's in Moraga, California, where she is eagerly awaiting the start of her new career as a school counselor.

> "It's been a challenge to retrain my brain, learning to become consciously competent, and accepting the fact that I'm not flawless—that I'm basically growing and learning my craft before I can transform it into an art."

I have two great passions, travel and education, and it is becoming clear to me how they are intertwined. My passion for travel started when I was in college at Santa Clara and joined the Semester at Sea program that was offered through the Institute for Shipboard Education at the University of Pittsburgh. During the 100 days we were on the ship, we traveled to 10 different countries—Japan, China, Taiwan, Malaysia, India, Egypt, Greece, Russia, Ukraine, and Morocco. We took courses related to the countries we were visiting, covering such subjects as women's roles, religion, art, politics, and cultural history. The travel and the opportunity to make lasting friendships made this a truly amazing adventure.

When I graduated from college, I was hired by Goldman Sachs to work in their San Francisco office. I learned so much during my time there; it was an awesome experience. After three years I realized I was ready to travel again. I went into my year-end review and said, "I would like to take a sabbatical and backpack around the world." My boss was extremely supportive and said, "You have one life—you've got to go for it. If you want to come back, we'll help you find a job when you get back. We'll just worry about it then." I backpacked my way around the world and traveled to 17 countries. This global adventure boosted my self-confidence and built on what my previous travels had taught me about humanity.

I returned to a great job, working with a former boss from Goldman in Internet software training. After that I worked with NASDAQ traders, and I also decided to earn my certificate to teach English as a second language so that I could go on another backpacking trip with the end goal of teaching English in another country. For a short period of time I taught English to people from the neighborhood in which I was staying in Cambodia. I started the trip by traveling throughout Southeast Asia, New Zealand, and Australia. When I returned, I decided I wanted to work for an organization that serves Southeast Asia in some way. I soon discovered Room to Read, an amazing organization that builds schools and helps educate children in Cambodia, Vietnam, Nepal, and India—and has also partnered with 85 Broads! I have had the opportunity to volunteer for Room to Read periodically between my work and school, and it has been very rewarding.

My interest in teaching continued to grow as I spoke more and more with a good friend who is currently a school counselor. Her job sounded fascinating—working with students every day, helping them solve their problems, get into college, and most importantly, meet the challenges of their daily lives. I recalled my mentor on the Semester at Sea program advising me that I might want to get a master's in counseling some day, which was also a great motivator. So I started looking at programs that offer school counseling master's degrees.

I found a wonderful program at St. Mary's, where I'm now going to school. I had no idea how much I would love my new career. People ask me, "How do you handle a 40-hour a week job at Merrill Lynch and take three classes per week at night?" And the answer is: "I love my classes, I love my school, and I know now deep down inside that this is the right path for me." I have found the career that I really want to pursue, and it shows every day at school. I go there and I'm engaged. I love doing my projects, and I just can't wait to get out there and do my counseling.

The last year of my program I have to complete 600 hours of supervised counseling. That takes about a full school year, going two to three days a week. I will do 400 hours in a high school and 200 hours in another placement such as a middle school or one whose students' ethnicity is different from mine. The perspective I have gained from traveling around the world will help me work with a culturally, economically, and religiously diverse student population. I don't want to force my point of view, but I want to help the students find their place in the world and know where they want to go. I want to help them gain the confidence and the motivation to go in their own direction and define success on their own terms.

My favorite quote, from *The Four Quartets* of T. S. Eliot, captures my passion for learning, travel, and coming home with a new way of seeing my life, my country, and our place in the world:

> "We shall not cease from exploration, and the end of all our exploring will be to arrive where we started and know the place for the first time."

II

ROCKETS

One of the dictionary definitions of *rocket* is something that "propels bright light high in the sky, blazing the way...." So we've come full circle again to young women who are trailblazers—the next generation of trailblazers whose trajectories will lead the way for women in the future. Some are continuing to blaze new trails for women in investment banking, finance, and other professional career paths. Others are creating different paths for more women to follow as entrepreneurs, philanthropists, parents, teachers, and global citizens. All of them are truly defining success on their own terms.

This is probably the greatest legacy of 85 Broads and the one I take the most pride in. Finding yourself, your own voice, and your own happiness is a collective, not an individual, act. Others have come before you and others will follow you. How you make your own choices and write your own story matters most, and means the most, when you share yourself and your talent with others. That's what 85 Broads is all about: *Incredible women connecting with each other. Helping each other. Inspiring each other.*

Being able to connect with the members of 85 Broads every single day has become one of the greatest gifts of my life. I get to look through the virtual "window" we have created to see all these amazing women and to learn about what they are doing and going to do with their potential and their passion. More than anything else our network conveys the message that *they matter.* If things are working out for them, there are thousands of women to celebrate with them and to encourage them to achieve even greater levels of success and happiness. If things aren't working out or if they feel disconnected or isolated, there are thousands of women to help them and bolster their confidence. That's what gives 85 Broads its passion and its presence. No one should think, even for a split second, that there isn't someone out there for them and that they aren't out there for someone else. That is what it means to be connected as a *community*.

One of 85 Broads' most thoughtful event speakers and strongest supporters has been former Goldman Sachs partner Mark Schwartz, who as chairman of Goldman Sachs Asia and a member of the Management Committee was always a highly visible champion for women. At our "What's Your Gift?" event, Mark spoke candidly about our responsibilities to our communities and to ourselves.

> "You're the role models and the mentors, right here in this room and in this network. Many of you are running businesses or building organizations, even if you've only just graduated from school, so your actions and behavior will have significant consequences. You can distinguish and differentiate yourselves in your strong sense of purpose and in the passion that you bring to everything you do. When you're down, pick yourselves up. Most people don't. That is the reason why many people fail. A lot of people get knocked down, but they lack the energy and the sheer willpower to get back up. And when you get back on your feet, pick up someone next to you. Boost those around you and show them you've got the strength, the character, and the determination to succeed. *That's called leadership....*
>
> "I am a great believer in community—you've got to be organized among yourselves. You have to make the effort to help one another. And you're going to have to be really creative, take a lot of risk, challenge the status quo and challenge your organizations. You're going to have to break a lot of china—and if you're organized, if you're helping one another, then taking this kind of risk will be far more effective and will produce far more long-lasting results."

Communities thrive when they foster a unique sense of identity and connectivity among their members. *All of their members.* What makes 85 Broads such a strong and dynamic community for me are the incredible voices and passions of younger women still in college or just beginning their careers, women from tremendously different backgrounds and cultures, with very different ways of expressing themselves and defining their futures. It's no accident that I and many others feel so confident and so connected around these young "rockets." I want for them what we are all looking for—to open the doors that allow you to look into yourself, find yourself, and find your own happiness. And then to look beyond yourself and help others do the same thing.

One of my favorite "tough love" expressions, based on my own experiences as a parent, is: "If you think it's still about *you*, it's *not*, so get over it." You can never let the connection be about "you." What *you* want. What *you* need. How *you* see it. The network is larger than you, than any one of us; that's why we have it. I try to think in terms of *we* and *our*—our success, our happiness, our passions. If we can be agents of change, igniting the success and passions of others, then we've really done something. That's what rockets do. They create new orbits for themselves so others can go even further.

I see so many women in their thirties, forties, fifties, and beyond who aren't connecting with other women outside of their own comfort zones. It's still about how *they* did it, or about the injustices that *they* had to endure. They can't really relate to younger women or women from different cultures because they can't see beyond themselves. The young women in the 85 Broads network thrive on the inspiration and passion they get and give to others, not on formulas or how-to's. That's why our concept of co-mentoring, of creating partnerships between women of different ages and backgrounds, has been so powerful. Believing in young women and seeing them do a phenomenal job or build a business or start a philanthropy when they are 19 or 23 or any age is pretty incredible.

One of the people who had a profound influence on my own life was a man by the name of Dan Crowley, former vice chairman of finance at McGraw-Hill. He was 30 years older than I was and a member of St. Andrew's, the oldest men's golf club in the United States —where I was working in the pro shop after graduating from college. I certainly wasn't a member of the club or part of his peer group. There was no reason for him to take an interest in me or my future. But he did. He took an interest in how I viewed the world, what I wanted to do, and helped me to hugely expand that view. Most of all, his interest in me gave me confidence. The confidence to accept his challenge to leave my job at the pro shop and go to work at McGraw-Hill as a research analyst, even though I didn't understand the language of business or the markets (a language I would eventually come to love);

the confidence to apply and be accepted to Columbia Business School (even though they shared with me at the time that I had the lowest board scores of any applicant in Columbia's history!); the confidence to start at Goldman Sachs as one of the first women in the Fixed Income Division (where I had no accounts, no relationships, and no experience); and the confidence to now, 30 years later, reach across generational and cultural lines to connect with other women and to share that confidence, just like he did with me. Dan was smart enough to let me find my own way. He viewed me as a "rocket" and showed me how far I could fly on my own.

The same holds true for 85 Broads today. The most astonishing thing I find is how exciting it is for me to connect with young women in our network who come from or live in virtually every area of the world. Connecting via the 85 Broads website and by email is a very powerful community builder. It connects women from all walks of life who I think of as rockets—brilliant, passionate, and inspiring. Many of our members have told me that I inspire them. If this is true, then it is because they inspire me. If anything truly great has ever happened to me in my life, this is it.

Imagine having over 10,000 best friends, confidants, and extraordinary women each with her own story to tell, her own passions to understand, her own wisdom to share. Whether your own network has 10, or 100, or 1,000, or 10,000, it doesn't matter. It doesn't have to be 85 Broads or anything like 85 Broads. Challenge yourself to be a master builder. An architect. Use the Internet and any other resource at your disposal. If we've learned anything from 85 Broads, it is that all women need to do is share their stories and be passionate about helping others share theirs. What we can do and become collectively is so much greater than any single, individual achievement. So start your own network. Tell your own story in your own voice, and then listen to the stories and voices of others. Use the power of the connection you've created to build caring and compassion and confidence among those in your network. And remember to always define success on your *own* terms.

ANALISA L. BALARES

A graduate of the Harvard Business School and Mount Holyoke College, Analisa is global marketing product manager for Windows Live Spaces, as well as founder and co-CEO of the Global Entrepreneurship Network (GEN) Worldwide, an international nonprofit organization dedicated to driving economic development by "unleashing the power of innovation and entrepreneurship in countries around the world." Before attending Harvard, Analisa was an analyst in technology investment banking at Goldman Sachs and also worked for 85 Broads.

"It is love that defines who I am and drives what I do."

Toward the end of my final-round interview at HBS, my interviewer said, "You have done and accomplished many things. What drives you? Why do you do what you do?"

Now I enjoy pondering existential and psychoanalytical questions, but at that very moment I hadn't arrived at a ready answer to this. So I thought aloud: "Well, I suppose it could be a number of things—wanting to have an impact, a desire to achieve, a passion for giving back ...."

I paused. These were the expected answers. While I felt they were true for me, I felt empty and slightly pretentious saying them. I wanted to reach into my soul for a *real answer*, something closer to a universal theory of my brief existence. I had thought about the *real answer* before, but thought it sounded too "fluffy." I was afraid being earnest might cost me. Then I thought: If giving her an honest answer would mean *not* getting into HBS, then maybe HBS wasn't the place for me. It became a test of the institution, as much as it was a test of myself.

So I said, "Love. Love is what drives me."

She looked slightly surprised, so I explained: From a very young age, being fiercely independent-minded and fascinated with everything from science to metaphysics, I embraced the notion that I am given one life to live, a finite amount of time on earth. Regardless of my external environment (or what other people said), I believed I had choices—choices over how I spend my time, choices over where I dedicate my life and my work. Over time, and across my journeys around the world, I found that I dedicated my life and my time *to those people, activities, and institutions that I LOVE.* I had little time for anything else.

In my life, it appears there are six areas of such great love, which define who I am and which drive what I do:

I love my family and friends. My parents are priceless gifts to me and my brother. They gave us unconditional love, unquestioning support, and enduring faith. They did this amidst numerous challenges. My mother quit high school to work so she could help send my aunt to college. She helped my grandmother earn a living, selling everything from banana leaves to rice cakes. People say I inherited many things from my mother: her spirit and tenacity, her strength, her love for life, her laughter and good humor, her kind and generous heart, and her faith in God and in the goodness of people. They also say I inherited many things from my father: his patience, his generosity, his intellect. Awarded First Honors throughout elementary school, my father dreamed of becoming an engineer, but he left school after fifth grade so he could help my grandmother run the family farm, then worked as a laborer so he could send his youngest sister to college.

My parents' heroic lives are a constant inspiration. My family has been like a deep well of strength as I journey around the world. I have also been blessed in these journeys to see my family grow. Friends and mentors who I have met along the way—from Pearson College, Mount Holyoke, HBS, Goldman, 85 Broads, and Microsoft—have become like family away from home.

I love building and solving problems by empowering people. I love to build projects, activities, organizations, and businesses that solve problems and fulfill needs as well as make the world a better place. Whether it's building an education and achievement program for underprivileged children in Manila, drafting a policy roadmap for creating sustainable economic growth for ecologically threatened developing countries, or now working on an Internet communications services platform that better connects people around the world—I love the process of building something that makes other peoples' lives better.

Empowerment is about leading one's life and owning one's happiness. It is also about seizing problems and proactively finding solutions, regardless of the obstacles. At 12, I was elected Junior Village Captain of my community, to "shadow" the real Village Captain for a week. Viewing pollution as our gravest problem, I brought together the village's children to clean our community's streets. At 16, I was chosen to perform our City Mayor's duties for a week as Youth Mayor of Manila City. The city's problems were complex, so I worked with Manila's Youth City Council Members to create and pass into law 18 executive orders dealing with education, pollution, prostitution, and crime. We couldn't have done this without empowered young people.

Building and accomplishing great things come from empowered people working together.

I love the challenge of winning competitions. I received my first gold medal when I was five. It was for being first in my class. I grew up competing in every imaginable contest—drawing/painting, mathematics, journalism, theater, science research, public speaking, and debate. Through all of this, I learned that the greatest joy and excitement didn't come primarily from accumulating medals or trophies, but from the journey of overcoming difficult challenges—from the process of throwing myself against a high standard and emerging better for it. Beyond the journey, the competitive challenge brings people closer together. I competed with *and* against people who remain some of my best friends to this day. One of the reasons I love what I do now is because my main charge is driving my product to win in a very competitive market. The other reason is having a great team committed to winning.

I love entrepreneurship. I love "the pursuit of opportunities regardless of resources controlled." The process is in itself a source of energy. Whether it is starting a nonprofit organization like GEN, designed to have a positive impact on the world, or whether it is growing a small startup group within a large organization and competing head-to-head against the market's goliaths (which is what I do now), I find the entrepreneurial process intensely exciting and adventurous.

I love innovation and creativity. I grew up adoring people like Leonardo Da Vinci, who married science, mathematics, and the arts to create some of the most powerful ideas and concepts in history. I entered a science high school, where my team's science projects consistently led us to represent the Philippines in international science fairs in Japan and Asia. I pursued economics and mathematics in college, determined to model the economics of innovation and technological change, and I then became a participant in the capital-raising process of technology companies while at Goldman Sachs. I joined Microsoft to work on Windows Live Spaces, Microsoft's blogging and social networking product, which is all about marketing innovation and creativity.

Outside of work, I spend time in many creative pursuits. I took time after graduating from HBS to finish a digital film-making program in New York, where I wrote, produced, directed, and edited a short film (a romantic comedy) and a documentary about entrepreneurship. The film-making process (from writing to directing to editing a film) is one that consumes me entirely. It draws from all of my senses and my intellect.

I love the many things that are larger than my own little life—the people of my country, the people of the world, and ideals like freedom and liberty. I have a deep love for people around the world, and an enduring faith that our present and future are determined by the good people of this earth. My best friends come from all over the world—Bulgaria, China, Ethiopia, Germany, Italy, Japan, Kazakhstan, the Philippines, Russia, South Africa, Tanzania. In many ways, they are among the smartest, most talented, most amazing people from their countries. It is through intimately knowing them, their lives, and their aspirations that the world has opened to me, that I am able to share in their joys and their pain, and that I am able to love people around the world as deeply as I do. My friends and I built GEN out of love for people and for our home countries—because we want to empower the people of this world to determine their destinies and to drive the growth and development of their countries through successful entrepreneurship.

Love starts from home. I was born in Barrio Liberty, a village in the central islands of the Philippines. It is a place of peaceful beauty, a place where rain falls sudden and swift, where clouds race over hills and fields. It is also a land of sunshine, its warmth carried by the humble, jovial and goodhearted people that live in the *nipa* houses of the barrio. How aptly the village is named. It has given me a love for freedom and a passion for liberty that I later came to share with many others. It has also gifted me with a love for my country, which would grow into a love for life and for the world we live in.

At the end of the day, love should not be a surprising answer. In reality, love is the muse that has driven the creation of the most outstanding works of art, science, and industry. Love has caused the fall and rise of nations, the dissolution and creation of religions. It defines the present and future of humankind. Like all people before me, it is love that defines who I am and drives what I do. Love, after all, conquers all.

SASHA GRINSHPUN

Sasha is a global soul. Her first great journey was with her family as they emigrated to America from the Ukraine. Since then she has received a BA from Yale and an MBA from Harvard Business School, lived in five countries, and learned four languages. Sasha is currently a real estate advisor, investor, and realtor. She lives with her husband and daughter in Austin, Texas.

> "Tell me, what is it you plan to do with your one wild and precious life?"
>
> From "The Summer Day" by Mary Oliver

> "During Carnival, in Brazil, a crowd was gathering ahead of me. The cause of the commotion? It was a couple in their seventies. Both were gray-haired and the man had a cane. But, I assure you, they were not your typical senior citizens. They were dancing with each other, dancing with the kids next to them, and occasionally dancing

by themselves. Their unconditional love for one another, their embrace of the moment, their warmth and openness to the motley crew around them—I was humbled. 'I'd like to make them proud—those two strangers, who survived so much together, dancing the whole time.'"

Sasha Grinshpun's response

Maintaining the balance of being open to new experiences while being able to carve out my own space is my primary imperative. My focus on this delicate equilibrium stems from three major periods in my life that have most defined my identity: my family's difficult emigration from the former Soviet Union to America, my eye-opening college years at Yale, and the following two years working and living in Brazil. These very distinct experiences trace my evolution from a shy, Ukrainian immigrant forcibly thrown into a new role as an American, into a confident businesswoman creating a new life on my own terms. Through these transformations I have gained a strong sense of identity and an ability to adapt to my ever-changing environment. In a world where the only constant is change, I thrive on letting my intellectual curiosity be stimulated by my surroundings. At the same time, my aim to create a positive impact in both my personal and professional life has prompted me to examine what it really means to look at the world through my own unique lens.

In coming to the United States as a little girl, the notion of identity entered my consciousness early. I had to navigate between my Ukrainian origins and my new life in America. Noticing my innate curiosity and high adaptability, my parents signaled that the fertile playground of opportunities in the United States were mine for the taking. They never said "no" to me. Instead, they allowed me to learn from my own mistakes and to act on my instincts and insatiable curiosity. My family lived a spartan lifestyle, stressing the importance of education and the doors it would open for me. This simultaneous focus on academic achievement and self-discovery led to another identity conflict I surmounted. This time the struggle took place during my college years at Yale, combining my immigrant's self-reliance with the desire to challenge my comfort zone.

After evaluating the option to attend college on a full ride, as my older sister did, I instead chose Yale for the challenging learning environment and the certainty of exposure to a diverse and exceptional student body. I knew that what I would devote to Yale would last me a lifetime. By attending Yale, I fulfilled my dream of being the first member in my family to go away to college.

My insistence on paying my own way has taught me to be accountable for my decisions and to make sacrifices for my dreams, as my parents did.

Even with the sacrifices I had to make to receive my Yale education, it was well worth it. What Yale offered me was the chance to break out of my shell. Prior to college, I had attended public schools where my academic and extracurricular achievements were lauded by teachers, but made me stick out like a head-of-the-class geek. In the Yale classroom, I went from a quiet observer to one of the most active speakers. Beyond that, Yale's dynamic drama scene encouraged the actress and director within me that I did not even know existed. During my first college summer, I decided to balance the cancer research I was doing with a writing-intensive sociology course. This led to another startling fact: In addition to crunching numbers and coding lab results, I could also write. I began questioning my pursuit of a career in medicine. I had geared my whole life to reach that goal. Despite lacking a genuine enthusiasm for the field, I pursued it because I was an affirmed success at science. I remember the exact moment when I decided to quit medicine; it was the most difficult choice I have ever made.

Taking stock of my ambitions and talents, I discovered my passion for business. The challenge of making rapid-fire business "diagnoses" for companies intrigued me. My "doctor skills" of attention to detail, analytical skills, and raw intuition were easily adaptable to business. My instinct for interpersonal integration, intellectual curiosity, and optimism about the future were all valued in business. In reaching my decision, I realized that there is no generic formula for success. I learned the importance of following my instinct and choosing my own path.

During my sophomore year, I turned a catastrophe into a personal transformation. I was stricken with mild paralysis after a head-on car collision. Reflecting on my life while recovering, I went on a difficult journey of introspection. During the next two years of painful physical therapy, I learned the importance of patience, perseverance, and discipline in the face of adversity. The accident shaped my self-identity and encouraged me to embrace the notion of *carpe diem*—seize the day!

Following the accident, I strove to lead a well-rounded life, not focusing solely on academics and future professional success. I scratched the would-haves, could-haves, and should-haves out of my vocabulary, living more on the edge and becoming active in community service. I learned how to scuba dive in the winter waters off Cape Cod, rappelled down a 200-foot waterfall in Costa Rica, and went skydiving in Italy. Through my volunteer efforts with orphans, gifted children, and the elderly, I began to give back to society through the life I have been so lucky to keep. In almost stealing my life, the accident in fact gave me back a richer, more fulfilling one.

After graduating from Yale in 1996, I went to work for Monitor Group in Brazil, helping them launch their São Paulo office and advising several multinational and local corporations in emerging markets. Living and working in Latin America marked another redefinition of home and identity. This time, I would actively begin to shape my environment. With three days' notice to start a new consulting project, I packed a work visa and Portuguese-English dictionary and entered a new world for the third time.

Having neither a support network, nor any knowledge of the language, I had to adapt quickly. I was the first non-Brazilian to join Monitor's São Paulo office, and my first assignment was to implement a national branding and recruiting strategy for it. I gambled my career on the successful growth of a nascent office in an economically volatile market. The challenges were daunting. The firm had zero brand recognition in Brazil and only two months remained in the recruiting season. Headquarters suggested a straight adaptation of the U.S. policy, but I quickly realized that the corporate mold had to be broken.

To better grasp the local market, I met with the Brazilian consultants during informal cultural exchange lunches. The discussions revealed that the U.S. candidate profile, which favored a liberal arts degree, high GPA, and enough extracurricular activities to implode a Palm Pilot, was incongruous with the local market. Brazilian consultants often graduated with engineering and business administration degrees, and top candidates are distinguished primarily by their internship experience. I discovered that Monitor could quickly differentiate itself by marketing the chance for locals to work on international assignments, a rare opportunity for Brazilian consultants. My insistence on getting local input allowed me to customize the corporate standard and achieve strong results. Of the 15 candidates given offers, all had accepted and were still with the firm a year later. This success sprang from challenging the status quo and integrating lessons from my peers.

The two years I spent in Brazil were a period of tremendous personal development. I did not just learn more "about myself," but rather "who I am." I realized that my move had more psychological underpinnings than I had thought. Like my parents, who, with their four-year-old daughter, emigrated from the Ukraine to the United States to start a new life, I too, 20 years later, with nothing but my dictionary, moved to a different country and began a new life. My travels did not end there, however.

After three years in Brazil, I went to the Middle East and worked in product design for IDEO, the premier innovation consultancy and also worked in economic development for a nonprofit founded by Michael Porter called Center for Middle East Competitive Strategy. Then I returned to the States to attend Harvard Business School, where I launched a campuswide job mentoring program, served as creative director for our class video, and conducted research on the use of innovative qualitative techniques in marketing and design. It was at HBS where I met my future husband and dance partner, Jose Fernandez.

I graduated from HBS in 2002 and, soon after, Jose and I moved to Austin, Texas, where I currently work for Southwest Strategies as a licensed real estate adviser on commercial, investment, and residential transactions. I feel fortunate to combine my passion for real estate, urban development, and entrepreneurship with my eclectic background in sales, strategy consulting, facilitation, and innovative product design. An additional benefit of the competitive, but flexible, career is the time it affords me to spend with my baby girl, Lia Montserrat—who, of course, loves to dance!

My life has been an improbable journey so far, and I have no doubt that more challenges and more rewards await as I continue to discover who I am in this world and what I can give back in gratitude for this one "wild and precious life."

UMBER AHMAD

Umber's family emigrated from Pakistan to the United States just before she was born, literally with "one foot in each country." She received her BS in biogenetics at MIT and her MBA from Wharton. She went on to work as an investment banker at Morgan Stanley and recently joined the Private Equity division of Goldman Sachs. Umber is committed to empowering women in underdeveloped countries around the world, and she currently is a member of the Junior Advisory Committee for Arzu, a venture launched by former Goldman Sachs partner and 85 Broads member Connie Duckworth.

> "Believe in yourself to a point beyond any self-doubt. If you have trust in what you can do, you will find a way. Persevere to a point that is realistic, while being open to new ideas and opportunities. Ultimately, you will be exposed to the things that you have always been looking for."

I grew up in northern Michigan in a town where there were only three families that weren't Caucasian. As children, you learn to see everyone through one looking glass. I couldn't appreciate how different I was until I left for college.

Being accepted into MIT at the age of 16 years was too good to be true. It was a sign to me that I had a responsibility, something I couldn't fully understand at the time. I couldn't exactly turn MIT down—they had a genetics program, which was rare, and exactly what I wanted to study. The academic experience there was unparalleled, although one of the most intense experiences of my life. Immediately upon our arrival, we were told that MIT's goal was to break us and remold us. Their strategy was to "make butter," by which they meant beating the hell out of us until the cream rose to the top. Failure, they told us, was not an option. It was great preparation for Wall Street—and for life.

After graduating, I did research in the area of corneal regeneration and decided to pursue my master's of public health. I knew I wanted to make a difference in society on a global level and decided it would be through business and the allocation of funds. After graduating from the University of Michigan with my master's degree, I became a health care consultant. I worked on restructuring the Los Angeles County Health System, a project that expanded health care to more than a million people. In Toronto and Vancouver, I worked with hospitals to find ways to use their limited health resources most efficiently. As I started to do a lot of postmerger integration among hospitals, I became frustrated with my mandates to reduce workforces and make changes that weren't thoughtful or reasonable. To me, financial allocation meant more than just making ends meet; instead it should be used to enhance value and to make the entire process better.

After working in consulting for nearly four years, I found myself most interested in the allocation of money and in the way markets functioned, so I decided to go to business school. At Wharton, I pursued a double major in both health care and finance. With increasing exposure to the investment banking world, I realized that being on the finance side of the business, rather than the operational side, allowed me to have much more of an impact on the strategic direction of companies. During my first year at Wharton, Morgan Stanley recruited me to come and work for them during the summer, where I was able to work on mergers and acquisitions, raise equity for companies, and structure debt deals. When they offered me a position in their associate class after I had graduated from business school, I accepted. Making the decision to return full time to Morgan Stanley was a long and arduous process. It was tough for me to abandon the health care industry, yet I wanted the deal-making exposure that financial institutions banking would offer. I recognized that I would be doing a job that few women do and wouldn't have any free time. I marketed myself to the banking firms, acknowledging that money does not know gender nor does it know race, insisting that I was able to perform. As a woman, I found this very empowering. As a woman, I knew I would have to make choices.

Female empowerment is something that I have been passionate about for years. To the young women of my small Michigan town, empowerment meant graduating from high school before having a child. To my fellow women of MIT, empowerment meant succeeding in an academic environment where there were 11 men for every 3 women. At Wharton, where I received my business degree, and in the banking industry, where I continued my career after school, empowerment meant being one of the very few women in a room full of men.

While conducting research for my masters of public health thesis on Ceausescu's antenatal policies in Romania, I read a study released by the World Health Organization indicating that educating adolescent girls was the *number one* way to reduce infant mortality and morbidity. Educating a young woman empowers her to earn her own money, prepares her to make choices, and exposes her to opportunities offered outside of her current environment. I realized then how important financial independence is to the well-being of women—and ultimately to the whole of society. As one of the subjects of the documentary film, *Risk Reward*, which focused on the lives and decisions of four women in financial services, I literally found myself becoming one of the poster children for financial independence in modern society. What I came to understand is that the ability to provide for yourself and make your own decisions, while important in our society, is absolutely critical in the developing world. I am now working on a film that will showcase women in countries like Pakistan and Uruguay who have achieved financial independence through the means of microfinance opportunities.

Microfinance is an excellent way to begin empowering women in underdeveloped communities by issuing them small loans. Based on the concept of social collateral, there is a strong sense of moral obligation that a woman feels to her community. For example, if I issue a loan to Zahra and Zahra repays the loan, she will then become a spokesperson for microlending. Zahra will then say to Noor that if she is able to repay the loan, then everyone else in the village will be able to get loans, but if she defaults, then everyone will suffer. Putting decision-making into the hands of women fundamentally changes how life can and will be led in that country.

As a result of meeting Connie Duckworth, the founder of Arzu, through 85 Broads, I have recently begun committing my own time and energy to this microfinance program in Afghanistan. Arzu means "hope" in Dari, the native language of Afghanistan. To me, this word means empowerment for women. The Arzu that I am involved in is a creative microfinance organization dedicated to revitalizing the Afghan economy by means of expanding their export rug market. Arzu draws from the popularity of selling the rugs in the States to return the profits to the rug weavers in Afghanistan. It is this stable income that facilitates a woman's financial and emotional independence, thereby enabling her to enjoy a degree of autonomy over her decision-making that she would otherwise not have known had she remained dependent on a caregiver for her livelihood.

My long-term aspirations are to use the skills that I have acquired here in the States to give back to Pakistan and other countries by reinvigorating their economies and empowering their women. Ideally, I would like to start a small investment bank or private equity fund that has lending capabilities dedicated to populations that are currently underserved.

I attribute all of my success in life to my family. One of the most difficult decisions that my parents made was to move to the United States from Pakistan. My father had been offered an incredible opportunity to become a professor and surgeon at Harvard Medical School. My parents recognized that uprooting themselves from their home and all they knew to be true to move to the United States would provide their daughters with opportunities that they otherwise would not know. I display my gratitude and appreciation to these pioneers through my determination to do the same thing—to expand boundaries and discover new opportunities for myself and others, whenever and wherever I possibly can.

AUDE THIBAUT

Aude graduated from the London School of Economics in 1998 with an MS in politics. She traveled to Russia and did political research, learned everything she could about the people and their culture, and took singing lessons with one of the masters of the Russian vocal tradition. While in Russia, she joined the Yukos Oil Company in Moscow as chief investor relations associate. In 2001, Aude moved to

*New York and worked in international investor relations at Gavin
Anderson & Co. She received her MBA from Columbia Business
School in 2003 and then joined the Equities Division of Goldman
Sachs in London. She left banking in 2004 to pursue her passion for
the arts and is currently working in development with The Royal
Opera House in London.*

> "I've found that reaching out to people, and appreciat-
> ing their differences, is a very sincere and very effective
> way to network."

When the Greek soccer team won the world championship last June, I
immediately sent an email saying "Nikisame" ("We won!") to all of my Greek
clients. I never thought it would prove to be such a strong relationship
builder. But appealing to one's national pride and taking interest in one's local
sports is extremely powerful. For me it became the beginning of many friendships. Being born in Belgium, a country with three national languages, made
me comfortable with other cultures and languages. From a young age, I had
a curiosity about different parts of the world. I've found that reaching out to
people, and appreciating their differences, is a very sincere and very effective
way to network.

I learned the power of networking through my experiences of moving to
Paris, London, Moscow, New York, and back to London over the past 12
years. One of the challenges when you move to a new place is meeting people and creating a new circle of friends. If you let yourself indulge in your
loneliness, no one is going to come and pull you out of it. When you arrive
in a new city, you need to accept every invitation and pick up on every lead
that comes your way. You almost have to cold-call on friends of friends.
Although calling people you don't know can be uncomfortable at first, it is
the very best way to meet people in a new place.

One of the greatest satisfactions that I had while living in Russia was
organizing a dinner party where over 40 people showed up, after I had
lived there for only one month! A high point of the party was that two
people who met there are now married and have a child. After living in
five different countries, I can safely say that throwing a party is one of the
best ways to meet new people. In fact, some of the people that I cold-called
and invited to my parties have become and remained my closest friends.

But I didn't move to Russia just to make new friends and have parties!.
Russia was a country that had long fascinated me. When I finished my mas-

ter's degree at the London School of Economics, Russia had just opened up to the West. I wanted to be among the first people to move to this formerly closed country and learn about its culture. Securing a position doing political research in Moscow was the next step in making my dream come true. It was an eye-opening experience for me, as I realized for the first time how my Western-centric perspective shaped the way that I saw the world. Living in Russia taught me to see and interpret everything—from people to news to fashion—in a whole new context.

I absorbed as much as I could while I was there, taking full advantage of living in one of the "culture capitals" of the world. My mother was a singer, so I had been exposed to the arts and music from an early age, and Russia has a great tradition of classical singing as well as some of the world's best voice coaches. I couldn't let this opportunity pass me by. I enrolled in opera lessons with one of the most renowned classical singing professors, and for four hours a week I learned to interpret the passions of the Normas, Toscas, and Traviatas.

During a time of great political and economic change in Russia, I was offered the opportunity to create an investor relations position at Yukos, one of the country's largest fully integrated oil and gas producers. This type of role was something completely new to Russian culture. At the time, Russia was in the midst of embracing colossal changes and Yukos was an exciting place to be as it was transforming itself from a Soviet ministry type of entity into a global oil powerhouse. My role was to speak with Western investors about Yukos. As I researched the areas of company structures, investor behavior, and corporate governance, my knowledge of international business soared. As one of the few Westerners in the company, I gained incredible insight into the inner workings of Russian businesspeople.

While in Russia, I also met my future husband, introduced to me by one of the friends I had made there. ("What goes around, comes around!") Our timing was a little off, however. He was just leaving for New York to attend business school. I had always thought of myself as a hard-core, independent woman who would never follow a man; this went against my most fundamental principles. However, love is stronger than the will, so I agreed to move to New York with him, but only if I could find a job before I left. Truthfully, there was another component. I had grown very comfortable in Russia and was aching for a new challenge. Besides, I wasn't sacrificing anything to move to New York; it is a wonderful place with lots of different opportunities.

After returning to New York to a new position in public relations, followed by an MBA at Columbia University and a new position with Goldman Sachs back in Europe, I found that music had taken on more and more importance in my life. So I decided to leave Goldman to explore the possibility of finding my dream job combining my fund-raising skills with my love of singing. I am now thrilled to be working in development at The Royal Opera House in London. In the long term, I know that I want to settle down and remain in Europe, but perhaps not just yet as I still dream of doing a stint in Shanghai—a city that is rapidly becoming a world financial and cultural center—the New York of the 21st century!

KATHY NICHOLSON

Although Kathy Nicholson was born in Kittery, Maine, she spent most of her childhood living in places like Guam, Okinawa, Switzerland, and Saudi Arabia thanks to her father's military career. While pursuing a bachelor of science degree in computer science at Santa Clara University, Kathy began her own military career through active involvement with the Reserve Officer Training Corps. After graduation, she worked as a communications officer for the U.S. Air Force for five years, then attended Stanford's Graduate School of Business and Center for East Asian Studies where she earned her MBA and MA in East Asian Studies through the dual-degree program. Kathy is currently an associate director at the Borders Group, Inc. Her passions include international travel, reading, skiing, spending time with family and friends, and scuba diving.

> "The three things that were most important in enabling me to accomplish what I have done so far are a desire to achieve, a strong sense of responsibility, and optimism. These three things combine to create a belief that when I want to do something, I am responsible for making it happen, and it can be done."

When my parents made their first trip to Stanford for my graduation ceremonies, I realized that all my hard work had been worth the effort. They nearly didn't come to my graduation as graduate school was almost like a foreign country in itself to them. They felt that they wouldn't know any of the other parents and that they would be very uncomfortable. When they arrived, I was so proud to show them around the campus and explain to them what my life had been like during the past few years. My mom wanted a picture of herself with my graduation cap, since she had never graduated from high school. She had left school at a young age and had overcome a lot of adversity growing up in Vietnam. As I pinned the cap on her head, I felt so grateful, happy, and proud that I was able to accomplish what my mom had envisioned for me, an education she had never had the chance to complete. And though I might have academic degrees, I always keep in mind that it is my parents from whom I have learned the most. I'm very proud of my parents and admire them for everything that they have done, their choices, and their sacrifices—especially when my dad left the Air Force and decided to take a position in Saudi Arabia—so that their children would have better educational opportunities. They are ethical, wonderful, hard-working people who taught me a lot about life, hard work, good manners, and persistence.

Today, I am managing the Human Resources Information Systems Department at Borders Group and am in a position that enables me to combine my background in information systems with my new business skills in a fulfilling career. I manage a group of people who are extremely passionate about the work that they do in applying technology to making other peoples' lives easier. Working for Borders fulfills my desire to contribute to my community in that books, music, and movies help bring people together regardless of background or culture. It is this connection between people, this building of bridges, which I am most passionate about.

I am also very passionate about my relationships with those closest to me. I have a small group of friends with whom I keep in touch and visit as frequently as possible. Within my family, I try very hard to be a dependable daughter and sister. One of my goals is to visit Vietnam with my family, to meet my mother's relatives and get to know them. I would savor the opportunity to see where my mother grew up and to experience what her life in Vietnam was like.

Reflecting on where I am now, I am grateful for many things in my personal and professional life. I think of the people and the circumstances that made all of this possible. From my parents I've certainly learned about responsibility, perseverance, and having respect for others. On the professional side I learned a lot from my colleague and mentor, OT Solomon, whom I met when I was in active duty in Okinawa. OT took me under his wing and taught me how to let go of doing everything by myself and to trust others to get things accomplished. He taught me how to lead by example. And, he taught me how to accept and admit to my own mistakes and to learn from them. Every time I face a challenge, I think of the advice that OT would give.

The three things that were most important in enabling me to accomplish what I have done so far are a desire to achieve, a strong sense of responsibility, and optimism. I always feel there is more to be done, that even when much has been accomplished there is still so much more. I also believe that those who are fortunate to have opportunities also have a responsibility to contribute to society. Finally, I think that in order to persevere in one's efforts, one has to believe it can be done, despite what obstacles may arise. My optimism has ranged from naive to tempered, but as I continue to grow, my optimism remains a core part of who I am, always reminding me that "there must be a way." These three things combine to create a belief that when I want to do something, I am responsible for making it happen, and it can be done.

Michelle Kathryn Taylor

After a car accident left her briefly paralyzed during her freshman year at Rutgers, Michelle left school for a year to recover and then transferred to Howard University in Washington, D.C., where she took 21 credits a semester and went to summer school to "catch up" with her class and graduate in three years. After graduation, she headed to Wall Street to learn the municipal bond business. She then worked for Goldman Sachs for over three years on the global convertibles desk in New York before attending Columbia Business School. After receiving her MBA, she joined JP Morgan's debt capital markets group in London. To fulfill a lifelong goal, Michelle's next "bold" step was to move to Paris to learn a new language and begin working with the Paris Professional Women's Network. Michelle has recently joined Lehman Brothers as the head of European diversity recruiting in London. Her passions include world travel, sports, reading, and maintaining an open-minded attitude toward new cultures and experiences.

> "Our deepest fear is not that we are inadequate.
> Our deepest fear is that we are powerful beyond measure.
> It is our light, not our darkness, that most frightens us.
> We ask ourselves, who am I to be brilliant, gorgeous, talented, and fabulous?
> Actually, who are you not to be?"
>
> Marianne Williamson

I come from a long line of strong African-American women who were blazing trails for the rest of us. My mother was a Peace Corps volunteer in west Africa who took me to live with her in Niger when I was eight years old. My maternal grandmother was the treasurer and cofounder of a landscaping business while raising four children. My paternal grandmother went on, after the birth of my father and my aunt, to complete her high school, college, and postgraduate studies in the 1950s in Atlanta, Georgia. At the time of her death, she had done postgraduate work in theology at Harvard University and received several honorary PhDs. I can hardly imagine the challenges she faced as a young black woman and mother in a southern, racially charged environment. She went on to become the first vice president of a large international Baptist organization, traveling around the world to the various religious conferences. These women were such pillars of strength!

As her first granddaughter, I was often blessed to accompany my paternal grandmother on her travels. We went everywhere, including Asia. My grandmother is one of the most passionate advocates for education as the path to success in life, and I personally believe that the best education I ever received was seeing the world through her eyes. The more countries I saw, the bigger my dreams became. She taught me to believe that I could accomplish anything. If I ever had any doubts, Grandma would reassure me, "Of course you can do this; you are my granddaughter." Knowing yourself and remembering where you come from are also vital lessons taught to me by my parents.

I first became interested in finance while attending Howard University, and then I worked at Merrill Lynch, Chemical Bank and Goldman Sachs before deciding to apply to business school. I was accepted at Columbia, receiving a full tuition scholarship from the Robert Toigo Foundation. After my first year at Columbia, I interned during the summer at Merrill Lynch in Debt Capital Markets. The culture at Merrill was a lot different from what I was accustomed to at Goldman, and I soon realized that I probably should have gone back to my old boss at Goldman and asked him to sponsor me to move to another area. That's a lesson in the importance in building relationships. At the time I was so uncomfortable asking for things; I had even been afraid to ask for a day off when I moved. But I learned then and there that mustering up the courage to ask for the things that I wanted was going to be crucial going forward.

During business school, I continued to broaden my experience by traveling around the world, going from South Africa to Brazil to Turkey and beyond. During my second year, I organized a three-week study tour to South Africa with 21 of my fellow business school classmates. We visited investment banks in Johannesburg, the games parks in Kruger, vineyards outside of Cape Town, Robben Island where Mandela was imprisoned, and many other rich historical landmarks.

After graduating from Columbia in 1999, I joined JP Morgan, and after a short two-month training program I was immediately transferred to London. I loved Europe and didn't speak anything but English, so London as the financial capital of Europe seemed like an ideal spot for me to gain international work experience. Because I had always liked the marketing aspect of our business and was looking forward to combining my analytic skills with my desire to stay close to the markets, I joined the debt capital markets team as a generalist. As is typical, I worked long hours, including lots of weekends, and dealt with lots of difficult personalities, and soon longed for a break! While working those long hours I didn't get to see much of London, but I did manage to get enough time off during the holidays to travel to Australia, Thailand, Israel, and Egypt.

Ready for a change, I decided to take a leap across the Channel to Paris to learn French and get to know that culture. I have always been a risk-taker. As an ex–New Yorker living in Paris, I thought that I would adapt to the lifestyle without any problems. With an MBA and solid work experience on top of having traveled nearly the entire globe, I was confident that I would find the position I wanted. But I found myself frustrated about how difficult the business world there was. The culture is based around lifelong relationships that were difficult for me to tap into as a foreigner. I was fortunate to find a community of "ex-pats" to help ease my transition.

In an effort to engage myself in an even larger community, I began working for the European Professional Women's Network (EPWN). The network was started in 1996 by a group of "international superwomen"—INSEAD alums, entrepreneurs, women in the corporate world, and financiers who were looking for ways to connect with other professional women throughout Europe. With its classic and contemporary themes, the network broke the boundaries in a culture that is closed and risk averse. I was the 100th woman to join, and I remember feeling that I had finally found myself at home in Paris.

It was my "impression" that French women were initially hesitant to join us, due, it seems, to their misperceptions regarding networking. Time constraints and family priorities were, of course, another issue. But as the network quickly established itself as a rich resource of leadership, direction, and training, the membership started to grow. Joining the leadership team was both one of the most enriching things that I have ever done and at times a baptism by fire. I was immediately working on putting together a speaker series to rally enthusiasm among the members by educating them on financial issues relevant to their own personal financial matters. The series took place every six weeks, and I had the opportunity to meet and work with many amazing women in the investment management sector, as well as begin to understand the cultural subtleties of France. It was a great success and established EPWN as an organization that creates value for its members. Later, I created a club of women in the financial services industry as a way to further facilitate professional exchange.

Over the time that I was there, EPWN blossomed into a rich "cross-sectional training platform of professional women with an international outlook." EPWN has helped to turn the concept of networking from the perception of being tacky into à la mode! Our membership has expanded to well over 2,000, including women from all different socioeconomic levels, from all disciplines, and literally from all over the world. Some of the best and brightest women in Paris who were graduates of Les Grandes Écoles and top MBA programs joined EPWN and helped sponsor a study to understand issues facing women professionals in the top French companies. The study revealed that women indeed earn approximately 30 percent less than men in similar jobs and are financially penalized when returning to the workforce after taking maternity leave. Shortly after the results were released, we had a networking event where we had expected about 300 women to attend, and over 1,000 women showed up! From then on, our membership soared.

I recently made the decision to return to London to become the head of European diversity recruiting at Lehman Brothers, and I am thrilled to be working for a company that is committed to practicing good management. Senior management is behind this effort and has incorporated into the firm's strategy the commitment to make the employee base reflective of the diversity of their client base. The job will encompass the things that I am passionate about—recruiting the best people and promoting diversity while working in Europe's rich cultural environment. In addition, I am president of the EWPN in London.

Looking back on my life, I can see that during my twenties I was afraid to go after what I really wanted. I was almost a bit mousy. It is sad to me that when women are offered a job we are accustomed to immediately saying to ourselves, "I can't do that job," whereas men would never, ever say that. Women are really much more accomplished than they take credit for and must learn to believe in themselves and step up to take on the challenges. I encourage all women to be open to new cultures and things that may appear not to make any sense at first. We must believe in ourselves and take risks. Life is so much deeper than our initial judgment will ever let us see. We must be open to it all!

Patty Kao

In 1999, having just graduated from Berkeley, Patty joined the Public Finance Investment Banking Division of a Wall Street firm to gain some work experience before going to law school. A year later, she joined a start-up software company. Eventually deciding not to go to law school, Patty instead received her MBA from MIT's Sloan School of Business in 2004. She has since joined Lehman Brothers in capital markets trading.

> "My advice to others is to be confident and not to shy away from something simply because you may stand out. Make sure you understand the objectives of your organization or group and then find a way to make yourself valuable!"

Even though I never knew her, my grandmother, a single mother with five children who had to fend for herself, had a profound impact on me. She raised my mother to become a professional, independent, working mother, instilling the values of financial independence and self-reliance in my mother that filtered down to me. There was never any question whether I would have a career or not; the only thing left to circumstance was which path I would choose to follow.

While in high school I was on the debate team and had aspirations to go into the public sector. During college at Berkeley, I studied economics with the intention of eventually going to law school. Wanting to have at least some work experience before getting my degree, I did an internship in Washington, D.C., at the General Accounting Office (GAO) and then did another one at a bank in Hong Kong. My mother encouraged us to travel and see the world, so when I graduated, I took a job in New York doing public finance investment banking.

I didn't stay there for very long before I went to work for a software startup called Kiodex. I joined them because it was a great opportunity in 2000 to be part of developing a business platform, and the team was incredible. I wasn't unhappy in banking, but I was at the bottom of the pecking order in a fairly structured environment and realized that by moving to a smaller organization I would have the opportunity to make a greater, more immediate impact.

During my first year out of college, I spent a good amount of time studying for the LSATs. In the meantime, I was watching my boyfriend going through his first year of law school and decided that it just wasn't for me. I got laid off from the start-up in 2002, and given the state of the market, decided to go to business school. When I got my acceptance letter from Sloan I was thrilled. I was grateful to receive the opportunity to attend such an excellent school, known for its small class size and emphasis on entrepreneurship.

Phenomenal opportunities presented themselves to me right and left while I was at Sloan. Several of my classmates were from India, and I signed up to go on one of the trips that they had organized. One of our professors who specialized in entrepreneurship in developing countries teaches a class that culminates in an international project (different student groups go to different countries), which I immediately jumped on as well. I spent the month of January in Santiago, Chile. I also had a chance to apply my business school skills to several nonprofit organizations in the Boston area. While I had already chosen the direction of my career at that point, I thought it would be wise to keep myself open to as many opportunities that arose, and take advantage of those unique opportunities that would only be available then and there, in business school.

Women tend to shy away from Wall Street, and those who come to capital markets typically lean toward the sales side; however, I was interested in executing and making direct P&L [profit and loss] decisions as a trader. I like the fast-paced environment and the feeling that you never know what is going to happen in the markets that day. I also wanted a performance yardstick—instantaneous feedback on how I am doing. My advice to others is to be confident and not to shy away from something simply because you may stand out. Make sure you understand the objectives of your organization or group and then find a way to make yourself valuable. I always encourage women to seek out the nontraditional female roles on Wall Street.

Melissa Otto

Melissa is a "global investor" who, when making an assessment of a stock, often draws upon her experiences living in Peru, Japan, and the United Kingdom, as well as traveling to 35 countries around the globe. The opportunity to study economics with individuals from 40 other nations at Brandeis University's International Business School was an essential ingredient in taking her investing interest to the next level. She currently works as vice president of global consumer equities research at

DE Investment Research in Boston, serves as the Boston co-chair of 85
Broads, and was recently elected to the board of overseers at Brandeis to
help guide the business school's vision and ambitious phase of growth.

> "Stagnation is one of my worst fears. I seek opportuni-
> ties that force me to challenge myself and surpass my
> own internal thresholds, personally and professionally.
> Whether I am free-falling for a minute while skydiving
> or buying stock in an emerging market, I am always look-
> ing for ways to keep my edge and stay fresh."

After graduating from Ursinus College, I went to Piura, Peru, to work for
Fulbright and then moved to Japan where I worked for three years in consulting and research. I returned to the United States and enrolled in graduate school at Harvard University and Brandeis University. After I honed my
Japanese skills at Harvard, I worked as a summer associate at Goldman Sachs
in Tokyo, and returned with a new career interest. My training there and at
Brandeis provided the necessary stepping-stones for establishing and further-
ing my career in investing. It did take some courage to step out of my element and live in Japan, but knowing the language opened up opportunities
for me that changed my professional and personal life. Not only did I land
a great job, I also met my scientist husband, Dr. Kiichiro Yano, a 15th-gen-
eration son of sake brewery, Tama no ii, while hopping into an elevator!

I joined GE Asset Management's Tokyo office after graduation and
worked as an international equities analyst where I was responsible for covering over 50 international consumer stocks held in various portfolios, including my own, with a total of over $500 million in assets under coverage. I also
helped oversee the research issues of the entire Asia region for GE Asset Management and served on the board of the GE Women's Network.

While at GE, I managed a fund consisting of international large cap and
small cap consumer stocks. Running an international fund is an intense job.
I had to wear a lot of hats. Not only did I have to pick great stocks, manage
foreign currency risk, and identify which specific industries looked poised to
outperform, but I had to act on these insights in a timely fashion. Embracing the challenge, I learned front and center, through both successes and failures, what makes some investment ideas stars and others disasters. My fund
had positions in companies all over the world, requiring me to go to Asia,
Europe, and Africa to "kick the tires." I learn to expect the unexpected. Visiting a factory in India, I found myself quizzing management about capac-

ity and cash flow, while watching two children on an elephant cascade by, throwing colored powder into the air. Impressed with the company's management and their strategy, I took a position in my fund. The stock has more than tripled since that time. Trips like that led me to uncover investment ideas that were under the radar screen and to get in on them early.

After working in Japan for seven years, I can say with certainty that business with the Japanese requires patience and discipline. In Japan, every new venture, whether it is learning how to get from Narita airport into central Tokyo (which can take up to four hours!) or trying to buy a company, takes time and is a process with definite milestones. The Japanese take a long-term approach, and foreigners who want to be successful in Japan need to shift the way they think. This can be difficult for analysts and fund managers used to quarterly returns.

Because the perception of Japan, particularly in business, is that it is a male-dominated society, a lot of people ask me if being a woman was problematic. While the trend is changing and there are more Japanese women in the pipeline, 100 percent of the CEOs I met in Japan were men. However, despite the lack of women at senior levels, I never really felt that being a woman was a big issue. More importantly, I was a foreigner, someone who looks and acts in a manner different from a Japanese person. If anything, I believe that this difference has the greater significance. This is what made me want to learn as much as I could about the Japanese culture, its language, and its people. I believe it also made them want to learn more about me.

As my fluency in Japanese developed and my understanding of the cultural nuances sensitized, it became easier to get things done, to get involved, and to make friends. However, despite an understanding of Japanese language and culture, I was raised as an American and have also lived in Peru and the United Kingdom; therefore, my way of thinking, line of questioning, and general approach to life's everyday situations are unique. Japan is still a very group-oriented, consensus-driven culture. Their people tend to share the same way of thinking and doing things. A fresh perspective and a light-hearted approach go a long way whether you are a man or woman. Everyone loves a solution that has been delivered with the best interest of the team in mind. A good example is the importance of *nemawashi* in getting ideas accepted and executed. Its literal translation is "to dig around the root of a tree before transplanting it." *Nemawashi* is a common business term that means to gain buy-in for an idea by privately selling your ideas to all members of the group outside of a public forum. When the opportunity to articulate the idea appears in a large meeting, the original initiator of the idea can usually step forward and not worry about opposition. Everyone has already bought into it. I can still remember when I came up with the idea to have a GE/85 Broads joint event in Tokyo. The idea was "plugged" with about 25 people before it was thrown out in the open and, then, acted upon.

In the investment industry, it is easy to get caught up in the hoopla. In order to be successful and happy in the job, a person has to really enjoy the process, the nitty-gritty components of picking stocks and of mining through mounds of data. My favorite part of the process is meeting management and looking at the financial statements to figure out if these companies are really what they say they are. I love the process of finding an interesting investment and want to continue to focus on delivering terrific stock ideas to my clients. Long term, I would like to launch and manage a global fund. A strong reputation and a solid track record will be essential to making that goal come to fruition.

Stagnation is one of my worst fears. I seek opportunities that force me to challenge myself and surpass my own internal thresholds, personally and professionally. Whether I am free-falling for a minute while skydiving or buying stock in an emerging market, I am always looking for ways to keep my edge and stay fresh. I have spent a lot of time learning, taking in a tremendous amount of information, and now I want to get out there and take bigger risks, be a leader and a trendsetter. I want to look back and think that in addition to being professionally successful, I've done a lot of incredible things and had an impact on the way people think about the world.

Lindsay Tintenfass

Having been inspired by her parents and her experience at a Quaker high school, Lindsay has been engaged in work on race relations and multiculturalism since her freshman year at Princeton University. She graduates in 2006 from Princeton's Woodrow Wilson School of Public and International Policy, and in the summer of 2005 she joined a team of interns at 85 Broads/Milestone Capital Management to actively learn more about entrepreneurship, for-profit and nonprofit ventures, and all phases of business development.

> "True education destroys stereotypes, breaks down racism, and the real ills of society disappear. Education can unite people."

Spending my sophomore summer in Washington, D.C., working at a nonprofit public policy office, I learned that achieving a social mission is possible, but that it takes a whole lot more than a big heart to get the job done. In order to reach the most people in need on the most profound level, a nonprofit should be run as a business so that its limited resources are used most effectively. Therefore, I decided to dedicate my junior summer to "business," but I had no idea where to begin or what that would entail. And would being part of the business world mean that I would have to put my dedication to a social mission on the back burner?

I happened to receive an email about 85 Broads, a network that included undergraduate women interested in business and which was linked to Goldman Sachs—the company I had heard the most about since I arrived at Princeton. Perfect. With nothing to lose, I signed on, created a profile, and wondered how this group could help me figure out where I was going next.

Almost magically, Janet Hanson emailed me that she had read my profile and wanted to have a dinner with me and other Princeton women who would be interested in discussing opportunities for women in business. I compiled a list of prospects and within a month a bunch of girls were sitting down with Janet and her husband Jeff at an Italian restaurant near the Princeton campus—being inspired, united, and informed. Janet spoke about her commitment to the progress of women and helping them to define success on their own terms. She also mentioned how women in our generation want to be intellectually challenged, want to integrate their lives and their careers, and don't want to be 40 years old having a heart attack at their desk. That's when it hit me. She knew my story all too well even though we had just met.

Three years earlier, I was filling out my application to Princeton, brainstorming what I would write in response to the question: "What moment changed your life the most?" It was a moment of exquisite irony. I sat there laughing with my mom and dad about what there was to say because my life was so perfect! I lived with a perfect family, in their perfectly happy home. My parents' marriage was so strong that they even owned and ran a law firm together, touting they were "partners in law and partners in love." They never missed my soccer or lacrosse games, they were at every awards ceremony, and everything was perfect. Within months, out of nowhere, all of this would change.

A week after receiving my cherished early decision acceptance letter from Princeton, my family flew down to the British Virgin Islands for a sailing vacation. My father and I were snorkeling together over a reef off the coast of an island called Anegada when he suddenly had a massive heart attack. He was only 47 with no prior health complications. By the time I swam my father ashore, he was without a pulse or any sign of life. At that moment, I was in complete and utter shock, but my mom pulled my sisters and me aside and told us, "Your lives are changed, but your lives are not ruined. We will move forward from this, and we are going to accomplish anything you girls want to accomplish....We will make that happen, we have to do it for Dad." My mom was so strong. Somehow, she knew exactly what to say to calm and reassure my sisters and me.

In some ways, many things changed for me when I lost my father, but at the same time many things remained untouched. I still was able to attend Princeton and experience all the amazing things it has to offer, and I'm still doing everything I ever dreamed of. Yet my perspective on life and my vision for the future have been greatly revised. Experiencing the loss of a parent at a young age gave me an unbelievable, insatiable passion for life and learning and doing, because I realized you never know how long you're going to be here. It also taught me that there must be a work-life balance because without a healthy lifestyle—defined as working a job that you are passionate about, but one that still allows you to exercise, to care for your body, and care for your mind—you may not live to experience all the greatness around you. And Janet knew that as she had seen dear colleagues die young just like my father had.

After the amazing dinner with Janet, I knew she and her network would be able to provide me with advice regarding jobs where learning about business and creating social good were not mutually exclusive. Having attended Friends' Central, a private Quaker school in Philadelphia that emphasizes tolerance, embraces diversity, and promotes community service, I became a devout believer in giving back and taking a stand for what you believe in. I experienced firsthand the power of education to break down stereotypes and combat racism while fostering collaborative learning. Friends' Central is a diverse institution, socioeconomically and racially, where the Quaker philosophy of "There is that of God in everyone" sets the tone.

When I entered Princeton University, I was surrounded by some of the brightest people in the country, and we were told that we were going to be the future leaders. However, I felt the racial relations on campus were disappointing. After spending much of my freshman year learning that the "real world" was not like my Quaker school, I wondered how I, just one person, could do anything to fix the situation around me. In the spring, I took a class

with Cornel West and felt that he was able to create in the Princeton classroom a dynamic similar to what I had found in my Quaker school. In a class
of 300 students, I never thought I would get the chance to actually meet with
Cornel West and express to him how much I admired what he was doing.
But that summer I was working for *Philadelphia Magazine*, and I got press
tickets for a speech he gave at the Bar Association. It was an amazing speech,
and I approached him afterwards to introduce myself and thank him. He
asked me what I thought about Princeton, and I told him about my disappointment with the racial dynamic. Without a hesitation, he asked me what
I was going to do about it.

We decided to start "multicultural hangouts" on campus to foster better
intercultural relations at Princeton. The aim of our group is to have people
sit down together, talk about various issues, and to find all the commonali-
ties and begin to really understand each other—because you can never really
tackle the big issues like race in America unless you have some common background with people as a foundation of understanding. "The Gathering," as
we call it, has been one of the most rewarding experiences for me at Princeton, and it has taught me that what really makes me tick is to work with people like Cornel West and my peers on changing the status quo. This was
something I wanted to embrace, not only during my summer internship in
Washington, but throughout my life.

Just like Professor West, I was certain that Janet could provide me with
some sort of guidance, because she not only wants to impart advice on the
younger generation, she also wants to learn from us. Sure enough Janet had
the answer: work for her at 85 Broads/Milestone Capital Management to learn
about business, entrepreneurship, nonprofits, a women's network, and most
importantly, myself. While I received many confused looks and warnings
from my peers when I told them I was not working for one of the big
"i-banks" this summer, what I believe, and these past few weeks have confirmed for me, is that there is no risk in investing in yourself and going with
your passion. Working with the intellectual firepower of Janet, the 85
Broads/Milestone team, and the rest of the summer interns has been an
unparalleled experience where I have been involved in creating and running
a business at all stages *and* a business I believe in with all my heart.

While I am not sure what my next step postgraduation will be, I will look
to the women of 85 Broads to guide me on my way, help me when I falter,
and allow me to share with them my experiences.

BHAKTI MIRCHANDANI

Bhakti recently completed the joint MBA/MPA program at Harvard Business School and the Kennedy School of Government. After graduation, she heads first to Unitus's capital markets group and then to Lehman Brothers' Wealth and Asset Management Division. Bhakti previously worked in Salomon Smith Barney's Equity Research and Sales and Trading Divisions, as well as Women's World Banking's Global Network for Banking Innovation. She has founded three organizations: the Global Microentrepreneurship Awards, the Graduate Student MADVC (Microfinance and Development Venture Capital network), and the Harvard College Social Enterprise Club. She holds a BA in chemistry from Harvard College.

> "My passion is all about empowering communities and eradicating poverty.... Together, we can continue, as Mohandas Gandhi says, to 'become the change that we seek in the world.' This is only the beginning."

Growing up with parents and grandparents whose dedication to helping others is at the very core of their being, there was never a question of *if* I would do something to help people in need, it was just a question of *how* I would make that happen. At Harvard College, I discovered Harvard Business School's Social Enterprise Club, and with a few friends, founded a similar club for undergrads. Through this organization, I became aware of initiatives that helped underserved communities, both domestically and abroad, by providing the self-employed poor with access to business development and financial services. It gradually became clear to me that my path to helping the world would at least begin by helping small-scale entrepreneurs in such communities.

The Global Microentrepreneurship Awards were born when my former boss, Christina Barrineau, of the United Nations Capital Development Fund microfinance unit, requested that I coordinate microentrepreneurs to literally ring in the UN's International Year of Microcredit through opening ceremonies at stock exchanges worldwide. By way of background, the UN's International Year of Microcredit seeks to mobilize governments, businesses, nonprofits, and the media to increase the access of the economically active poor to microcredit. Accordingly, I led a worldwide network of students and professionals to organize opening ceremonies at 15 stock exchanges, including London, Nairobi, Zurich, Maputo, Madrid, Karachi, Mumbai, and the Dominican Republic. This stock market coordination was vital for two reasons: (1) to illustrate the importance of liberalizing financial systems and (2) to symbolize microentrepreneurs as dynamic economic contributors. We hoped that such symbolism would encourage the private sector in general and multinational corporations in particular to drive interest and innovation in "the fortune at the bottom of the pyramid."

We were also cognizant that the images of microentrepreneurs opening stock exchanges around the world would dramatically increase the media momentum gathering behind microfinance. But it took a conversation with microfinance expert Michael Chu to make me realize that a stock market coordination that did not illustrate anything substantive about microfinance or microentrepreneurship would be like having an advertisement at the Super Bowl without having a product. Aware of the power of harnessing the media, I recruited my friend and sectionmate Deirdre Cooper to create a product for the stock market opening. Together, and with the help of Christina Barrineau, we founded the Global Microentrepreneurship Awards—business competitions for the self-employed poor in a wide range of countries—to be linked to the stock exchange coordination.

Faced with a project of a much larger scope, I recruited two more classmates and friends, Mei Chee and Mike Kerlin, to create a core team of four. We established a network of 75 students, faculty, and alumni from universities worldwide to organize the Global Microentrepreneurship Awards. The student-faculty network recruited prominent leaders from each of the nine participating countries to judge the micro businesses and select the winners. Each country's prize categories were a function of its political, economic, and social context and goals. By first encouraging innovation in sectors that a country aspires to develop, or highlighting the accomplishments of microentrepreneurs in that space, the GMA was a vehicle for progress. In turn, this was intended to encourage microentrepreneurs in those countries to pursue higher value-added businesses that generate more sustainable profits. By highlighting effective business models to microentrepreneurs, the GMA could proliferate the best practices among all these entrepreneurs. To secure buy-in from and harness the accomplishments of existing microfinance networks and institutions, the GMA solicited input from them to finalize contest prize categories and criteria for evaluation.

Award competitions took place in Afghanistan, Cambodia, the Dominican Republic, Indonesia, Mexico, Mozambique, Pakistan, Rwanda, and New York City between October 28 and November 24, 2004. These nine competitions celebrated the entrepreneurial spirit of microbusiness owners by recognizing the recipients' innovation and perseverance under the most challenging conditions. Prizes ranged from cash to capital to livestock!

The student organizing team and winning entrepreneurs from New York City participated in an opening ceremony at the NASDAQ on November 18, thereby illustrating the parallels between entrepreneurs whose companies' IPOs were on the NASDAQ and the self-employed poor.

The winners are inspiring. Just one example is Fatimata Lonfo, New York City's Microentrepreneur-of-the-Year, who fled Côte d'Ivoire in October 2001 to give her children a better life. Now the proud owner of Windyla's Boutique and Hair Braiding Salon in Staten Island, Fatimata supports herself and her family; her oldest child started college last fall.

We plan to expand the Global Microentrepreneurship Awards over the next five years and have negotiated a three-way partnership on behalf of the founding student team with the UNCDF and Citigroup to grow the competition from 9 to 32 countries. The ultimate goal is for the awards to be truly global, and to act as a bridge between first world entrepreneurs, entrepreneurial financiers, and third world microentrepreneurs. Expanding the scale and scope of the Global Microentrepreneurship Awards will bolster their impact as a fuel for the engine of economic development. Tangible facets of this impact include (1) winning investors and donors to microfinance, (2) creating the next generation of microfinance networks, and (3) spreading the gospel of microfinance to the self-employed poor who have not yet heard its call.

Last year, due to heavy Ministry of Finance involvement in the Rwanda Microentrepreneurship Awards, I was able to travel to Kigali to meet with local government, business, and nonprofit leaders to ensure sufficient alignment to fund the competition in 2004 and to include Rwanda in the list for 2005. The poor have so many unmet needs—access to markets, financial services, infrastructure, clean water and heath care—that it is critical that the money devoted to microfinance be spent effectively. My most vivid memory from the trip to Rwanda was learning first-hand how microfinance helped them rebuild their families and communities after the genocide. The GMA finalists there were a combination of orphan children, demobilized soldiers, and conflict widows.

At the November 2004 gala at UN Headquarters in New York City for the launch of the International Year of Microcredit, Nane Annan, wife of UN Secretary General Kofi Annan, presented our extraordinarily committed team of student volunteers with an award in recognition of the founding and accomplishments of the Global Microentrepreneurship Awards. Seven hundred heads of state and business, nonprofit, and student leaders were in attendance. I was greatly encouraged by this demonstration of the depth and breadth of global support for microentrepreneurship and microfinance. However, I was most inspired by how the GMA winner from Indonesia, who was flown in for the event, provides jobs and training for low-income handicapped individuals in her community, despite being poor herself.

My passion is all about empowering communities and eradicating poverty. According to C. K. Prahalad, those who earn less than $2 per day generate $13 trillion in annual consumer demand. This market is overpriced and underserved. This means vast unmet demand and substantial profit potential. My goal is to promote the feasibility of doing well while doing good among financial and other business leaders and innovators. Together, we can continue, as Mohandas Gandhi says, to "become the change that we seek in the world." This is only the beginning.

CASSINDY CHAO

Cassindy graduated from Wellesley College in 1990 and went on to work at Bear Stearns as an analyst in corporate finance and then at JP Morgan as an associate in equity research. She joined Goldman Sachs in 1994 and became executive director of Asian investment research in 1997. She also was Group Managing Director of Asia Pulp and Paper Trading USA and President of Linden Trading. Today she is the CFO and co-founder of MicroAssembly Technologies. She lives in California with her husband and two young children.

> "And at this point, ironically, I've fit in, but in a different way—my parents joke that I make a lousy Chinese daughter but a pretty excellent son. Sigh. That's just fine with me—it's still progress."

Growing up in a Chinese family in Los Angeles, I did not fit in as the ideal Asian daughter or the ideal American girl. I felt like I was the odd gal out. Even today, "good Asian girls" must meet these expectations: they are good students, they are obedient to parents (and certainly don't talk back), and they marry nice Asian boys. Honestly, I wanted to be the ideal daughter and make my parents proud, but I just could not do it. I grew way too independent for my parents' taste, and much too outspoken. That meant that I was always in trouble with them. Plus, there were other rules—American rules.

I pushed to find my own path. While my parents argued for me to attend a local and affordable university in California, I wanted something different. I wanted to explore college on the East Coast. I started college on an Army ROTC scholarship, wearing purple-tinted glasses, determined to tame my unruly mane of hair while I perfected my marksmanship skills. I argued with my parents who wanted me to study chemistry and not art. Willing to try to fulfill their expectations, I took a stab at several science and mathematics courses, to great disappointment. I talked my way into an unlikely compromise with economics and Chinese studies. My grades wavered and my GPA was perhaps less distinguished than many expected as I explored a range of curricular, volunteer, and internship opportunities.

I chose a career in finance, since, at the time, it seemed fairly well-paying and I could travel. My first job was in a trading house investment bank. I was the only woman and the only minority in my pledge class. Investment banking was an eye-opener into a man's world. The positive note was that being Asian, everyone assumed that I was "good at numbers." However, being my own woman in a male-dominated environment, I certainly didn't fit in and encountered all sorts of troublemakers there. Men tickled my earlobes, grabbed my ankles. One time, I grabbed a stapler in frustration and bashed an aggressive colleague with it to make his inappropriate behavior stop. One boss even asked (well, actually ordered) me to babysit. Another told me that I should forget about a career in finance, that I just did not have it. But to prove them wrong, I just worked harder and perfected the art of not listening to demeaning critics. I plowed ahead to new opportunities, eventually landing a position with Goldman Sachs.

My days at Goldman Sachs in Hong Kong really launched me into a very different world—a world of opportunity for strong women. I met many wonderful, loud, talkative, argumentative, wildly brilliant women. Finally, people like me. I no longer felt that I needed to "mend my ways." I felt more like the Helen Reddy song, "I am woman, hear me roar." Being surrounded by women like me, and being respected in my job, I found my voice. I was encouraged to run with my ideas and make them become reality. I won an analyst award from Reuters Asia, and I chaired the first Communacopia Asia conference. After that conference, the chairman of Goldman called to congratulate me. I was on cloud nine.

Then life changed suddenly, and for personal reasons I had to leave Goldman Sachs and Asia. My mom was diagnosed with late-stage ovarian cancer, so I returned to the United States to be with her. Feeling confident in my business skills, and drawing on my strengths, I co-founded a small technology company with two friends. The company provides R&D for military and communications applications, and I am proud that today our company is profitable. Additionally, I lead a group of companies in the United States, and I head business development and management for an Asian consumer products company. Marketing Asian products in the U.S. heartland, where people don't really meet a lot of Asians, is really eye-opening. I am continually being referred to as "you people," which is rather disappointing. My internal voice says, "Just because I have Asian heritage means that I am not American enough? I was American enough to be in the ROTC and prepare to defend our country."

Even though my work life has changed, and my work is more self-directed since my days at Goldman Sachs, my plate is full in new ways. I have two young children (my daughter is three and a half and my son is seven months), and I want to spend as much time as I can with my mom who has already outlived the predictions of top oncologists. I'm learning how to integrate work with the needs of my family. Through the 85 Broads network, I am still able to retain the best part of working: interacting with amazing, warm, bright women, as I reach a different stage in my career and life. I have learned a lot from the women in my life. In fact, three of my former female colleagues at Goldman are my daughter's godmothers. I chose Goldman Sachs women because I would be so proud if my daughter and my son grew up to share their spirit.

MARY HARMON

Mary has worked in the investment industry for eight years, beginning in the Cayman Islands. From there, she moved to Goldman Sachs in New York to work with the Asset Management and the Private Wealth Management groups. She recently completed the full-time MBA program at UCLA's Anderson School of Business with a certificate in advanced international management. Mary is now working for the Trium Group, a boutique strategy execution firm in San Francisco.

"Building bridges is my passion. I have a vision of becoming an international bridge, an intermediary, connecting individuals between cultures, helping them to understand each other's business goals, problems, values, and industries. I am helping executives and organizations to better understand how leadership and culture influence strategy and how they can make a positive impact in the environment within their organizations. This work has such a great impact on so many people, not only inside the organization, but also in the environments in which these organizations operate. I am passionate about developing myself as a professional and as a leader."

After working in international funds management in the Caymans and then in Costa Rica, where I lived with a wonderful family and immersed myself in the language and culture, I moved to New York to join Goldman Sachs ("GS") Asset Management with their offshore mutual funds team. Some of the best interviews that I have had in my entire career were those that I experienced at GS; I immediately connected with the people there. It felt like the perfect transition as I knew that I could some day apply my love for Spanish to serve GS's emerging markets business in multiple ways. I thought private wealth management might be a good match for my skills and interests. My role in asset management involved dealing with fund vendors and clients from all over the world, while reporting into the London office. I was able to develop my skill set with top-notch managers and mentors, while continuing to be a "cultural bridge" within GS and with its offshore fund vendors.

About a year and a half later, my role in offshore funds would be transitioned to London, and my wonderful manager and mentor at the time, John Perlowski ("JP"), really worked with me to make sure that I would make the right decision. I wanted to stay in the United States after all of my international transition, and JP introduced me to a lot of individuals around the firm. I was asked to join a new division of the private wealth management group at GS. I saw an opportunity to build more bridges, between individual families and GS, as well as across international borders. We had a few Argentine relationships on the platform that I hoped would fall under my responsibility. I saw myself as a bridge to clients in better understanding their investments and the operations behind their complicated investment portfolios. It was a tough role, as the business within GS was in major transition. I met three wonderful mentors during this time: Linda Daines, Maire O'Neill, and Sally Pope Davis. I learned so much from them in terms of seeking to be the best that I could be in business, as well as managing my work and myself as a professional woman. I also learned from my clients and the choices that they made in their lives and portfolios. But at the same time, I started feeling that something was missing in my life.

After September 11, I started to feel a loss of direction. At work, I saw my role becoming very operations-focused, with less and less influence on the client relationship. I was no longer directly an intermediary to individuals overseas and I wondered where my life was going.

Suddenly I felt depressed and almost like I was falling apart. I was 29, single, and felt that life had little meaning. I cried on the subway every day on my way to work. I remember my mother asking me, "When was the last time you were in your bliss?" I went back to my dream, the dream of becoming some type of trusted adviser, bridge, or educated intermediary. I remembered my passion for watching people's faces light up when I helped them understand something complex and important. I remembered the way that the light fell in Costa Rica and the laughter of my host family when they came home from a hard day of work. I wanted to figure out how everything I had on my platform—my banking experience, my Spanish, my relationship management skills—could somehow be applied to reaching people like my host family. I decided to pursue my MBA at UCLA's Anderson School of Business in order to find that passion again.

Anderson has a special certificate program called advanced international management. Through this program, you can tailor your full-time MBA studies to a focus on management within specific regions and cultures of the world. I began my Anderson experience early by attending a summer quarter at ESAN in Lima, Peru, and then a year later did a term at the IESE School of International Management in Barcelona, Spain. In Lima, I lived with another very wonderful and warm host family while attending the business school. In Spain, I learned a great deal about cross-cultural management in business. I cherished my experiences, feeling even more certain that I would continue to focus my post-MBA career on opportunities to work across international borders, acting as a bridge across diverse cultures that needed to understand each other in some way.

In Peru, I found microfinance. To me, microfinance was my opportunity to create the bridge linking the portfolio of "Mr. or Ms. Jones" at an investment bank with very small businesses in developing countries. Microfinance takes the power of entrepreneurship to developing countries as a way to eradicate poverty and empower individuals. I spent my summer MBA internship during 2003 working at a for-profit microfinance company called Prisma. The company uses a commercialized model of microfinance to provide loans and other financial services to small businesses in Central America, using a stable capital flow as an incentive to investors. I helped the company to structure marketing documents to speak to potential investor clients like those that I worked with at GS. It was an extremely rewarding summer.

I served throughout the two years of the MBA program as a teaching associate with Anderson faculty for the Johnson & Johnson Head Start Program, which provides management training and strategy consulting services to the directors of Head Start. This experience helped me to see the opportunities to be the "bridge" that I wanted to be in a consulting capacity. I loved the issues of business strategy and looked for ways to combine my international interests and this new focus.

Now at Trium in San Francisco, I have been given that opportunity. I am working with individuals at the senior management level to understand issues that are important to them and to their organizations. As they are at multinational firms, I am still enjoying the experience of being a bridge across international cultures. While I am not working directly with developing countries on a day-to-day basis, I know that I will return to this, as I become a more experienced executive who can best give back what I've learned. I plan to continue to volunteer in the San Francisco community, looking for opportunities to assist members of the Spanish-speaking community in this city as they face their many challenges to survive and succeed in the United States.

It's been a long road of great travels, and from it I have come to really believe in my drive, in my dreams, and in myself. As Woody Allen once said, "90 percent of life is just showing up." I feel that I have done so, and I will continue to do so, in order to achieve my dream of giving back all that I have been given in this wonderful life of adventures!

JILL AMANN DILOSA

Jill grew up in New Orleans and earned a scholarship to attend Tulane University, where she graduated with honors and earned a joint BA/MBA in sociology and finance through a five-year combined degree program. As an MBA student, Jill interned with both Morgan Stanley and Goldman Sachs in Manhattan, and after graduating joined a consumer sector–focused hedge fund in New York City as a portfolio analyst. Managing approximately $150 million of the fund's assets, she oversaw all investments in the restaurant, food, beverage, gaming, lodging, and leisure industries. In 2005, she was honored with the Rising Tide Award, which is presented annually to a young graduate of Tulane who has excelled professionally in the field of

finance and also has served as a positive role model for the school's
students. Jill was the first woman to receive this award.

"To whom much has been given, much will be expected."
(Luke 12:48)

There are two numbers that I will never forget: 15 and 27. Fifteen is how old I was when I moved out of my parents' house. Twenty-seven is how old I was when I retired. This story is about the generous friends and mentors whose wisdom and encouragement helped me find my way between those two numbers.

I think that one of my greatest accomplishments was finishing high school. When I left home at 15, all of a sudden things like rent, utilities, and grocery bills added up. I wanted to drop out of school and work full time, but my grandfather kept telling me, "Being intelligent and being knowledgeable are two different things; you're intelligent, Jill, but if you don't study, you won't know anything." My grandfather was right. Even though working part time instead of full time meant that I could afford only my rent and utilities and not my groceries (I dropped from a size ten to a size two), I still knew that I was fortunate to have teachers like Diego "Gonz" Gonzalez, Lee Kansas, and Frank Magnuson at Ben Franklin High School, who encouraged me to stay in school and who never accepted anything other than my best. Sometimes that meant tough lessons like giving me an "F" on a term paper because I turned it in late, as Gonz did, or tutoring me in Algebra I (a freshman course) during my senior year because I had skipped too many classes to master the basic concepts, as Mrs. Kansas arranged for Mr. Magnuson to do. These special teachers taught me essential skills in life such as critical thinking, reasoning, and writing.

After graduating from high school I enrolled at Tulane, where I had the privilege to encounter a team of strong women advisers in the sociology department. April Brayfield, Beth Rubin, and Laura Sanchez awakened my sociological imagination. I studied concepts like "the glass ceiling," "the feminization of poverty," and "social capital." I learned to use demographics to understand market trends. With a heavy dose of statistics courses, I discovered how to organize and interpret data to make informed decisions. I also learned to think in terms of probabilities and risk versus reward, which was instrumental to my success as an investor. I still maintain that my sociology degree was more useful than my finance degree when it came to picking winning stocks.

While at Tulane, I spent my spare time reading books by Robert Kiyosaki, Suze Orman, and Thomas Stanley, who explain how concepts like the time value of money and compounding interest can help one achieve financial freedom. At that time, I believed that it would cost around $50,000 annually to live a modest lifestyle in New Orleans. I reasoned that if I could save a million dollars and earn at least 5 percent a year on it, then I would have sufficient financial independence to spend my time as I chose. Financial independence became the first of my three biggest goals in life; the other two are starting and running a business, and endowing a foundation to help with the emotional, spiritual, and educational development of girls and young women.

The counsel of Jill Rovaris, the director of the Educational Resource Center at Tulane, was invaluable in getting me started on goal one. She helped me to stop feeling sorry for myself, to move beyond my frustration with what I saw as my less than perfect family, and to focus on what was going right rather than wrong in my life. By enrolling in a math class during summer school and allowing it to be my singular focus, I learned to overcome my fear of numbers and earned my first "A" in the subject. As I gained confidence in my math skills, Jill encouraged me to pursue my interest in business. When my age became an issue regarding managing money, her advice was: "Don't let others turn your greatest asset into your greatest liability." She was right. I would soon realize that a funny thing about stocks is that they don't know how old you are!

I started my MBA program during what should have been my senior year of college. On the first day of business school I met Peter Ricchiuti, the Director of the Burkenroad Reports, an equity research program unique to Tulane where students write and publish investment reports that include financial models about "stocks under rocks"—which is what he called micro and small cap companies headquartered in the deep South. Peter's passion for investing was contagious, and he was instrumental in steering me toward a career in asset management. We traveled together to visit companies and to meet with senior management teams to learn about their businesses and strategies. Eventually I figured out that I wanted to do something like the Burkenroad Reports for a living.

My first step was landing a coveted summer internship at Morgan Stanley in private wealth management. I was one of two women in a class of 20 MBA students, and I was about 10 years younger than everyone else. I spent the first week practically hyperventilating at my desk, as it seemed that everyone around me was speaking Greek and I wasn't quite sure how I had gotten my job. I went to visit John Osbon, who was then directing the summer internship program, and asked him what he expected of me. He looked at me very seriously and said, "We didn't make a mistake when we hired you, Jill, so (1) relax, (2) be yourself, and (3) do your job." I wrote his words on a Post-It note and stuck it on my computer monitor. Every time I started to freak out about being in over my head, I read it and calmed down. I survived Morgan Stanley, and the next summer I was hired by Goldman Sachs in the Investment Management Division.

The best thing about my summer internship at Goldman Sachs was that Janet Hanson had founded 85 Broads, and as an employee I was eligible to join. I'll never forget the name of the first 85 Broads event—What's Your Destiny?—because I believe that my destiny was to work at Goldman Sachs just so I could join 85 Broads. At the event, woman after woman spoke candidly and sincerely about having a successful career, a family about whom they cared deeply, financial independence, and happiness. All of my life I had believed that it was possible to have these things simultaneously, but everyone had told me that it was impossible, and I didn't have any role models with which to prove them wrong. For the first time, I met women who were, in a sense, living a dream of mine and who proved the naysayers wrong. I wanted to join their ranks.

When it was time to look for a full-time job, I sought one thing above all else: unlimited upside. Investing is one of the only careers where it is possible to objectively prove your value to a company and be paid for it; I didn't want a constraint on my earnings power or subjective compensation. If saving a million dollars by the time that I was 30 was in the realm of possibility, I believed that I could make it happen. With the assistance of two people, Kevin Richardson, founder and principal of Prides Capital in Boston and Jeff Tannenbaum, founder and principal of Fir Tree Partners in New York, I was able to find a position with a young, growing hedge fund where I was afforded the prospect of unlimited upside.

Wall Street can often be inhospitable to women, and it wasn't unusual to find myself as the only woman in a room of 10, 20, even 50 men. I felt that my childhood years spent as the only girl playing on a boys' club soccer team prepared me for situations where occasionally members of the opposite sex resented my presence. But I was lucky to encounter dozens of men, many at a very senior level, including not only Bob Merritt, the former CFO of Outback Steakhouse, Jim Lawrence, the CFO of General Mills, and Glenn Schaeffer, the former CFO of Mandalay Resorts but also many other sell-side and buy-side analysts, as well as executives at the companies that I covered, who, as teachers, mentors, and colleagues, generously reached out and helped me succeed. I am indebted to them and to women who consistently helped other women in business and whose efforts directly benefited me. Caroline Levy, the beverage analyst at UBS, and Alice Elliot, CEO of Elliot Associates, always made a special effort to be inclusive of me and other women rather than exclusive. I appreciated not only their friendship but also the example they set for others. Through the assistance of these and many other friends, mentors, and colleagues, I was able to earn profits in every industry that I covered and exceed my financial goals three years earlier than I had hoped. At age 27, I decided to retire in order to focus on my health and well-being and to pursue my other two goals.

I have been the beneficiary of so much giving that I couldn't imagine having been more blessed. I have also had the honor of being a part of others' great visions through not only the Burkenroad Reports, but also Summerbridge (now called Breakthrough Collaborative) and Student Sponsor Partners (SSP). Through Summerbridge, I taught social studies classes to rising eighth graders at Wake Summerbridge in Raleigh, North Carolina, where I encountered bright, energetic children committed to improving their lives through better education. I now participate as a sponsor through SSP, a program that provides students who are underperforming at New York City public schools (and are at risk for becoming part of the 70 to 80 percent of students who do not graduate in four years) with an opportunity to attend a private high school.

I believe one of the most important ways that I can help others is not only through volunteering with a known organization or by providing financial support, but also by sharing advice and encouragement as so many people have done with me. While often time-consuming, some of the most rewarding giving that I do comes from motivational speaking and providing career guidance. I speak at schools like Tulane about topics such as "Finding Your Dream Job on Wall Street," and seeing the progress of the students with whom I work keeps me dedicated to this type of giving. Lately, I have been spending time with some members of "Broad2Be" in the 85 Broads network, helping to educate them about mutual funds and hedge funds, IRAs, compounding interest, picking stocks, writing résumés, and choosing careers. Comments like those of one woman, who wrote to tell me that she planned to invest her summer earnings through a newly opened IRA instead of in her checking account, allow me to know that my time spent is worthwhile. My favorite remark thus far from a Broad2Be came from an economics major who said, "I learned more from you in one afternoon than in any of my economics courses in college!" I've often wondered why financial literacy isn't taught at more educational institutions at the high school and undergraduate level. This field could be one area of focus for my foundation's efforts. I am absolutely passionate about encouraging others to become self-confident and financially independent.

I am grateful to my friends, my parents, my brother, and late grandparents for the ways in which each of them has touched my life and helped me live my dreams. As a final thought, I'd like to share the advice of a dear friend and mentor, Jerry Brassfield, who as an entrepreneur has already achieved extraordinary success in his life. He urged me not "to make the mistake of *not* dreaming big enough." Countless people told me that I would never meet my goals. Jerry believed that I would exceed them and then have to set new, even more ambitious ones. I encourage you to avoid naysayers and energy drainers. Find your Jerry Brassfield. Believe in yourself. Take risks. Compete. Define success on your own terms. Don't expect others to work for your dreams if you're not willing to work for them yourself. And remember, as the love of my life always tells me, "The only thing that really matters is how you touch the lives of the people around you."